AF560115

BUSINESS PROCESS TRANSFORMATION

BUSINESS PROCESS TRANSFORMATION

DR. MAMTA VYAS
M.A. (Eco.) M.B.A., Ph.D.
Professor
Sri Aurobindo Institute of Management & Science
Indore

REGAL PUBLICATIONS
New Delhi - 110 027

BUSINESS PROCESS TRANSFORMATION

ISBN 978-81-8484-305-7

© 2014 MAMTA VYAS

All rights reserved with the Publisher, including the right to translate or to reproduce this book or parts thereof except for brief quotations in critical articles or reviews.

Typeset by
RAHUL COMPOSERS
New Highway Apartments, Lakshmi Niwas
760, Pocket-D, Lok Nayak Puram, New Delhi - 110 041

Printed in India at
MAYUR ENTERPRISES
WZ Plot No. 3, Gujjar Market, Tihar Village, New Delhi - 110 018

Published by
REGAL PUBLICATIONS
F-159, Rajouri Garden, New Delhi - 110 027
Phone : 45546396, 25435369
E-mail : regalbookspub@yahoo.com, regaldeepbooks@yahoo.com

This book is dedicated

to my father

Late Dr. Shyam Sunder Vyas

&

my Professors

Contents

Preface

This book aims at clearly bringing forth concept of business process transformation for human resource students of MBA in different universities.

The change process which is inevitable in any company of today and resistence to change that invariably goes hand in glove with any change process have been thoroughly discussed.

There is elaboration on creating and preparing a dedicated workforce towards meeting the objectives. The whole book is dedicated to planning the change and emergence of TQM & sigma and its impacts on human resource have been discussed.

Experience proves that a business process transformation can yield more than a tenfold improvement in performance provided the HR process redesign is really carried out. It is essentially a clean-slate approach, which can, however, be frustrating if it does not work well. Therefore, understanding the implementation TQM methodology is necessary and this book is a humble effort in this direction.

I do not claim exclusive credit for the book. Most of the material has been collected from professional journals, periodicals, review articles, book discussion, personal communication, website and similar sources. However, every creation of mind requires refinement at every stage.

The author would welcome suggestions for the improvement of the book.

Dr. MAMTA VYAS

Acknowledgements

I acknowledge with all sincerity and gratefulness, all human resource management Gurus and writers, who directly and indirectly helped me in writing this book.

I express my sincere thanks to my parents, professors, colleagues and Directors to write this book, and my gratitude to Dr. R.D. Pathak, Dr. O.S. Gupta, Dr. Deepak Kaul, Dr. P.N. Mishra, Dr. P.K. Gupta, Dr. Rajeev Gupta and other Faculties of IMS, Indore.

I am also thankful to Sri Aurobindo Institute of Management and Science, Group Director Dr. Sudhakar Bharti and Dr. K. Santaram for their blessings, cooperation and guidance.

Dr. MAMTA VYAS

Chapter 1

Creativity and Innovation

WHAT IS CREATIVITY ?

A simple definition of creativity in the context of the workplace is given above.

Another more general definition is: "Creativity is the thinking associated with Ideas, Imagination, Inspiration, Intuition and Ingenuity." Creativity can be expressed through virtually any form of human behavior and everyone has a range of creative abilities. Two of the characteristics that separate highly creative people from the less creative are risk-taking and tenacity.

In this context 'risk-taking' describes the impulse to find and try original ideas, to go beyond one's familiar boundaries of knowledge and explore new possibilities rather than staying in the relative security of what we already know. The risk is that the ideas will be deemed impractical, inappropriate, crazy, etc. In the world of the workplace where not making mistakes is one of the desiderata for career progression this risk can be a significant one. Many ideas will be unworkable but finding the one good one or maybe more accurately the one that's time is right makes it all worthwhile both to the individual and the group and changes things in a positive way.

In the workshop we brainstormed the concept of creativity and then sought to experience the sense of 'Ambiguity' that arises when we go beyond immediate associate thinking by extending the definition of creativity.

WHAT IS INNOVATION ?

The words creativity and innovation are often used in the same sentence and they are also often randomly inter-changed as if they had the same meaning. There is some overlap in these definitions in that innovation can describe the process of coming up with new ideas but more often innovation refers to what happens after someone has been inspired with a creative idea. A working definition of innovation is given above. Innovation is more concerned with making creative ideas a reality. This begins with communication of the idea and ends with organized teams in various roles working together to bring the idea as efficiently and as quickly as possible to fruition.

Introduction of Innovation

Innovation is the development of new customers value through solutions that meet new needs, inarticulate needs, or old customer and market needs in new ways. This is accomplished through different or more effective products, processes, services, technologies, or ideas that are readily available to markets, governments, and society. Innovation differs from invention in that innovation refers to the use of a better and, as a result, novel idea or method, whereas invention refers more directly to the creation of the idea or method itself. Innovation differs from improvement in that innovation refers to the notion of doing something different (Lat. innovare: "to change") rather than doing the same thing better

The word innovation derives from the Latin word *innovates*, which is the noun form of *innovare* "to renew or change," stemming from *in*—"into" + *novus*—"new". Diffusion of innovation research was first started in 1903 by seminal researcher Gabriel Trade, who first plotted the S-shaped diffusion curve. Trade (1903) defined the innovation-decision process as a series of steps that includes: First knowledge :

1. Forming an attitude
2. A decision to adopt or reject
3. Implementation and use
4. Confirmation of the decision

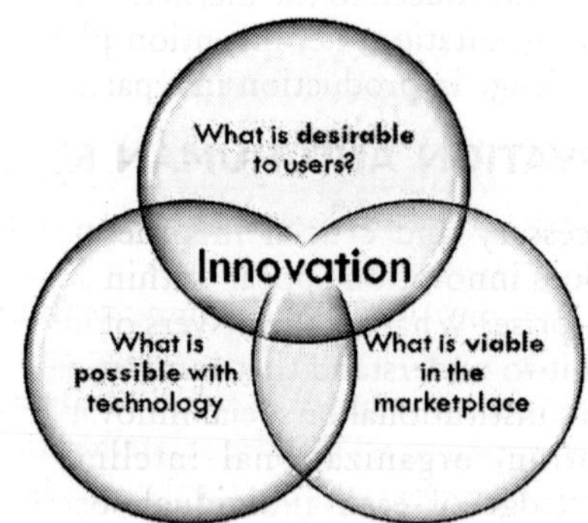

Figure 1.1 : Importance of Innovation

Innovation is inherently a highly cross-functional activity that, when it works well, creates a constructive tension between competing objectives of development cost, product value, performance, quality, and time to market. Product development touches every part of the company. Functions like strategic planning, sales, operations, customer support, purchasing, and finance are just as important to successful innovation as R&D and engineering. How well these very different functions work together in large measure determines how effective a company will be at developing successful products and services.

It is common to look to an organization's structure to suggest the relative roles and authorities of these functions.

Structure is often the first thing companies seek to change when they search for better organizational performance. The Booz Allen study found that over half of all companies had restructured their innovation organizations within the prior two years. Our experience indicates that there is no one right structure for a given innovation organization. Different structures work successfully under different circumstances. It also turns out that structure in itself is a poor predictor of how an organization will really behave. Independent of their organization structures, some companies seem to deftly mobilize their best capabilities to meet unexpected changes in the marketplace or competitive actions. Other companies seem immobilized by such challenges, unable to respond effectively. There are deeper factors at work. Factors that, to use a biological metaphor, are embedded in a company's Organizational DNA.

Invention *vs.* Innovation

Creativity is seeing what everyone sees and thinking what no one else has thought before. Invention is transforming these new thoughts into tangible ideas. Innovation is introducing these ideas to the end-user. Innovation is channeling creativity (managing its application, i.e. invention) so as to produce ideas/products that people can and wish to use (i.e. marketable). For an invention, the focus is on novelty and this is a key criterion for patenting. In other words, it must be new to its field all over the world. Innovation on the other hand does not have to be new except in a specific situation. Thus, as long as a firm (for instance) is having something for the first time, it is innovative in their context irrespective of whether it is new to their industry, country or the world. Characteristically, an invention is anything that is novel and potentially practically applicable; an innovation is essentially novel, practically applicable and introduced to the market. Thus, innovation may be seen as equal to invention plus exploitation, i.e. invention plus commercialization and/or application of new knowledge in production in a particular environment.

INNOVATION AND HUMAN RESOURCE

Innovation is necessary and crucial in order to develop further and stay competitive. But how does innovation appear within a company? What is necessary to be an innovative enterprise? What are the drivers of innovation in an organization? First of all it is important to understand that innovation has different facets such as technical, organizational, institutional or social innovation. Having a closer look on organizational innovation, organizational intelligence is established by the accumulation of knowledge of each individual, because each member of the organization contributes their ideas and values. The organizational intelligence as said so far is depending on the group and therefore a "social outcome resulting from the activities of the collective accumulated wisdom". There are many organizational factors which influence creativity and innovation but four have major consequences: leadership behavior, measurement systems, organizational structures and organizational cultures. Employees are an important resource for innovation but under which circumstances innovation can be created? It is necessary that the people have the available resources in order to be creative and hence innovative. An implemented reward system within an organization could give an incentive for employees to be motivated while working because they want to reach a certain goal. Consequently, the positive attitude affects the creativity. Therefore, motivation systems within an organization could support the innovativeness of the entire company. In various companies, the organizational culture has a negative impact on innovation. This happens when the structures are rigid and too much emphasis is put on how things are done. There is a lack of freedom for employees meaning that they are restricted to try new ways of doing things. Companies can help nurture creativity by applying innovation processes providing the mental space for new ideas to take root. Therefore it is crucial that the company requires an open culture meaning to share extensively its knowledge with the entire enterprise. Companies need to measure progress which is an important part of continuous improvement cycle. The individual and the organizational dimension have the importance as key factors in influencing and determining creativity. With the help of reward systems, employees stay motivated which furthermore leads to more creative minds. When employees have the possibility to be creative, they can share their new developed ideas with the entire organization which leads to innovation. Innovation does not come by its own but rather is dependent on human beings taking initiatives and being creative. The combination of task motivation, creativity skills and expertise constitutes creativity which is the motor and driver of innovation. It is important to understand that innovation has an impact on the creativity but creativity of employees is a necessary factor in order to establish innovation. The staff of an organization should aid improving business performance by creating ideas resulting for example in better products, services or work processes. Employee behavior is strongly influenced by a couple of factors, the two most important are incentive and reward systems and the organizational culture.

Types of Innovation

Technical (technology) innovation—Technology innovation is the process through which new (or improved) technologies are developed and brought into widespread use. In the simplest formulation, innovation can be thought of as being composed of research, development, demonstration, and deployment, although it is abundantly clear that innovation is not a linear process—there are various interconnections and feedback loops between these stages, and often even the stages themselves cannot be trivially disaggregated. Innovation involves the involvement of a range of organizations and personnel (laboratories, firms, financing organizations, etc.), with different institutional arrangements underpinning the development and deployment of different kinds of technologies; contextual factors such as government policies also significantly shape the innovation process. In the energy area, technology innovation has helped expand energy supplies through improved exploration and recovery techniques, increased efficiency of energy conversion and end-use, improved availability and quality of energy services, and reduced environmental impacts of energy extraction, conversion, and use. Most energy innovation is driven by the marketplace, although given the public goods nature of energy services (and reducing their environmental impacts), governments invest significantly in energy research and development programs as well as demonstration and early deployment of selected energy technologies. Still, most investments in energy innovation are targeted towards technologies with clear commercial applications and financial returns, with only marginal investments (at least in relation to the need) towards energy innovation for helping provide modern energy services to the two billion poor people worldwide who don't have access to such services

Non-Technical Innovation

Non-technological innovation is an important element of firms' innovation activities that both supplement and complement technological innovation, i.e. the introduction of new products and new processes. Non-technological innovation is defined as the introduction of new organizational methods or the introduction of new marketing methods. We find that the determinants of a firm's propensity to introduce technological and non-technological innovations are very similar and that both types are closely related. There are only small effects of no technological innovation on a firm' profit margin, which contrasts the strong effects to be found from technological innovation. However, non-technological innovation spurs success with product and process innovation terms of sales with market novelties and cost reductions from new processes.

SOURCE OF INNOVATION

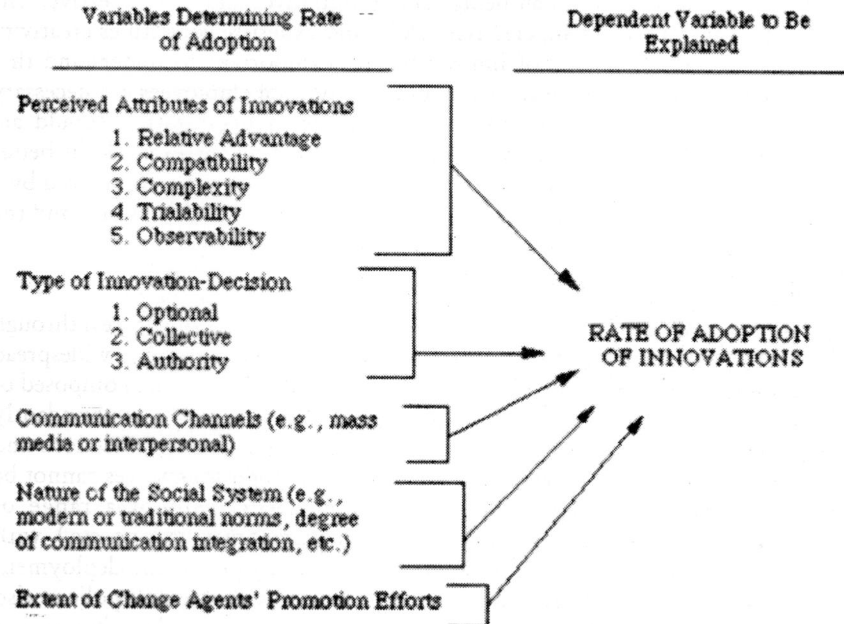

Figure 1.2 : Variables Determining the Rate of Adoption of Innovations

Source : Innovation.

7 Sources of Innovation (Peter Drucker)

Peter Drucker, one of the greatest management thinkers from the last century, defined in his book "Innovation and Entrepreneurship" (1986) 7 classes of "OPPORTUNITIES". He named these the "SOURCES OF INNOVATION", namely:

THE UNEXPECTED: An example of the unexpected is the development of Nutrasweet. A chemist developed a new chemical. Accidentally he got some of it in his mouth. To his surprise it tasted very sweet. This was the start of a development trajectory, that took many years before Nutrasweet was introduced by Searle into the market.

INCONGRUITIES: Incongruities or conflicts between opposing functions, requirements or values may be the start of an innovation. For example the request for a small car with still enough space on the inside seems to be incongruent. This however was solved in a new design as the Smart.

PROCESS NEEDS: An old proverb says that "necessity is the mother of invention". In the old days of the US many unskilled immigrants from Europe arrived. They were peasants that lacked in skills for the manufacturing of sophisticated artifacts such as guns. In those days one made every component of these guns by hand. To let them fit to each other and work properly required high skills in manufacturing. By making machines more precise and introducing standardization of the artifacts one could produce thousands of components individually. The machine or gun could be assembled using arbitrarily with ever component from the stores. The individual tasks could easily be learned by the immigrants, without years of training to become an overall master. In this way they could profit maximally from the existing economies of scale and learning curve.

INDUSTRY AND MARKET STRUCTURE: Industry markets and market structure may offer opportunity's for new types of services. Outsourcing of activities such as maintenance of the IT infrastructure is an example. Other examples are the merging of industry's such as for example the merging of the computer industry with consumer electronics or IT with business consulting services. The X box of Microsoft is just one example from many.

DEMOGRAPHICS: Demographics have long been a major source of innovation creating opportunities for new types of products and services. Life style drugs such as Viagra are just examples where the growing group of elderly people who feel themselves still very healthy and who would like to enjoy life longer can conquer the effects of biological aging.

CHANGES IN PERCEPTION: An example of changes in perception as source of innovation is the following. In older days health was seen as related to body mass, meaning fatter people were perceived as more healthy. In the last century this perception changed as a result of medical study's that revealed that overweight was a risk factor. Since that time many light products have come to the market. Many substitutes of sugar have been developed such as Nutrasweet. Also substitutes of fat have been developed although these have not been successfully introduced into the market yet.

NEW KNOWLEDGE: Last but not least new knowledge has produced many opportunities for new products. The emergence of micro-electronics and new programming methods and tools, biotechnology, nano-technology etc. have been the main motors of innovation and progress over the last decades. This will probably continue for the coming decades

INNOVATION—PARADIGM

Open innovation is a term promoted by Henry Chesbrough, a professor and executive director at the Center for Open Innovation at the University of California, Berkeley, in his book Open Innovation: The new imperative for creating and profiting from technology, though the idea and discussion about some consequences (especially the interfere cooperation in R&D) date back at least to the 60s. The concept is related to user innovation, cumulative innovation, know-how trading, mass innovation and distributed innovation.

> "Open innovation is a paradigm that assumes that firms can and should use external ideas as well as internal ideas, and internal and external paths to market, as the firms look to advance their technology"] or "Innovating with partners by sharing risk and sharing reward." The boundaries between a firm and its environment have become more permeable; innovations can easily transfer inward and outward. The central idea behind open innovation is that in a world of widely distributed knowledge, companies cannot afford to rely entirely on their own research, but should instead buy or license processes or inventions (i.e. patents) from other companies. In addition, internal inventions not being used in a firm's business should be taken outside the company (e.g. through licensing, joint ventures or spin-offs).

Closed *versus* Open Innovation

The paradigm of closed innovation says that successful innovation requires control. A company should control (the generating of) their own ideas, as well as production, marketing, distribution, servicing, financing, and supporting. The main cause behind this idea is that, in the beginning of the twentieth century, universities and government were not involved in the commercial application of science. Some companies therefore decided to do it all on their own. They created their own research and development departments to be able to control the whole new product development (NPD) cycle inside the company. There just was not the time to wait for the scientific community to become more involved in the practical application of science. There also was not enough time to wait for other companies to start producing some of the components that were required in their final product. These companies became relatively self-sufficient 'castles', with little communication directed outwards to other companies or universities.

Throughout the years several factors emerged that paved the way for open innovation paradigms:

- The increasing availability and mobility of skilled workers
- The growth of the venture capital market
- External options for ideas sitting on the shelf
- The increasing capability of external suppliers

These four factors have resulted in a new market of knowledge. Knowledge is not anymore proprietary to the company. It resides in employees, suppliers, customers, competitors and universities. If companies do not use the knowledge they have inside, someone else will. Innovation can be generated either by means of closed innovation or by open innovation paradigms. There is an ongoing debate on which paradigm will dominate in the future.

Theories of Innovation

1. Incremental vs. Radical Innovation

It is difficult to assess who pioneered the Incremental-Radical dichotomy, partly because the concept was used by many authors, often with a different terminology but expressing the same meaning. Abernathy differentiated incremental from radical innovation already in 1978 while Porter in 1986 illustrated a similar concept called continuous and discontinuous technological changes. We also had authors defining Incremental *vs.* Breakthrough innovations (Tushman and Anderson) and Conservative *vs.* Radical innovations (Abernathy and Clark).

There are two dimensions that we can use to separate an incremental from a radical innovation:

- The first is an internal dimension, based on the knowledge and resources involved. An incremental innovation will build upon existing knowledge and resources within a certain company, meaning it will be competence-enhancing. A radical innovation, on the other hand, will require completely new knowledge and/or resources and will be, therefore, competence-destroying.
- The second dimension, the external one, differentiates the innovation based on the technological changes and on the impact upon the market competitiveness. An incremental innovation will involve modest technological changes and the existing products on the market will remain

competitive. A radical innovation will instead involve large technological advancements, rendering the existing products non-competitive and obsolete.

Under this framework it is clear that incumbents will be in a better position if the innovation is incremental since they can use existing knowledge and resources to leverage the whole process. New entrants, on the contrary, will have a large advantage if the innovation is radical because they will not need to change their knowledge background.

Furthermore incumbents might have a hard time facing radical innovation both because they operate under a "managerial mindset" constraint and because strategically they have less of an incentive to invest in the innovation if it will cannibalize their existing products. Kodak illustrates this quite well. The company dominated the photography market over many years, and through out this extended period all the incremental innovations solidified its leadership. As soon as the market experienced a radical innovation, the entrance of the digital technology, Kodak struggled to defend its turf against the new entrants. The new technology required different knowledge, resources and mindsets.

Overall we can say that the Incremental-Radical dichotomy helped to explain some innovation patterns, and there was favorable evidence for the model within most mature industries. Over the last decades, however, the model lost some reliability as the pace of change accelerated in most sectors. There were cases where new entrants managed to displace incumbents with incremental innovations and other cases where incumbents kept their leadership exploiting a radical innovation. Consider the computer industry for instance, IBM was able to maintain its dominant position when there was a shift from vacuum tubes to integrated circuits, a radical innovation

2. Schumpeter—Theory of Innovation

The first part will be dedicated to the Austrian economist Joseph Schumpeter, a pioneer when we talk about innovation management. Around the 1930s Schumpeter started studying how the capitalist system was affected by market innovations. In his book "Capitalism, Socialism and Democracy" he described a process where "the opening up of new markets, foreign or domestic, and the organizational development [...] illustrate the same process of industrial mutation, that incessantly revolutionizes the economic structure from within, incessantly destroying the old one, incessantly creating a new one". He called this process "creative destruction".

After analyzing the capitalist model Schumpeter tried to understand what companies would be in a better position to innovate. He developed a theory where a company's ability to innovate was mainly connected to its size. Initially he defended that small companies should be in a better position due to their flexibility while large companies might get trapped in bureaucratic structures.

Some years later, however, he changed his view, stating that larger corporations with some degree of monopolistic power could have an advantage to develop innovations. Compared to smaller firms such large corporations have better resources and more market power. Unfortunately the innovation theory was only a marginal part of Schumpeter's work, it was derived from his analysis of the different economic and social systems. The theory therefore has no empirical foundation at all, there is no strong evidence to support a relationship between the size of a company and its ability to innovate.

One important insight arising from Schumpeter ideas, though, is that innovation can be seen as "creative destruction" waves that restructure the whole market in favor of those who grasp discontinuities faster. In his own words "the problem that is usually visualized is how capitalism administers existing structures, whereas the relevant problem is how it creates and destroy them

3. *The S-Curve Framework*

The S-Curve emerged as a mathematical model and was afterwards applied to a variety of fields including physics, biology and economics. It describes for example the development of the embryo, the diffusion of viruses, the utility gained by people as the number of consumption choices increases, and so on.

In the innovation management field the S-Curve illustrates the introduction, growth and maturation of innovations as well as the technological cycles that most industries experience. In the early stages large amounts of money, effort and other resources are expended on the new technology but small performance improvements are observed. Then, as the knowledge about the technology accumulates, progress becomes more rapid. As soon as major technical obstacles are overcome and the innovation reaches a certain adoption level an exponential growth will take place. During this phase relatively small increments of effort and resources will result in large performance gains. Finally, as the technology starts to approach its physical limit, further pushing the performance becomes increasingly difficult, as the figure below shows.

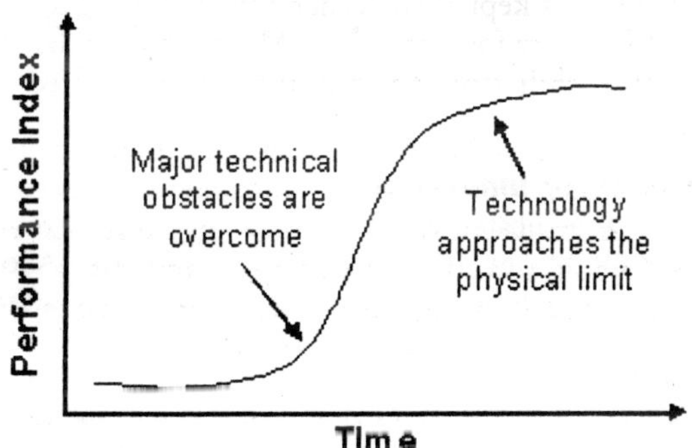

Consider the supercomputer industry, where the traditional architecture involved single microprocessors. In the early stages of this technology a huge amount of money was spent in research and development, and it required several years to produce the first commercial prototype. Once the technology reached a certain level of development the know-how and expertise behind supercomputers started to spread, boosting dramatically the speed at which those systems evolved. After some time, however, microprocessors started to yield lower and lower performance gains for a given time/effort span, suggesting that the technology was close to its physical limit (based on the ability to squeeze transistors in the silicon wafer). In order to solve the problem supercomputer producers adopted a new architecture composed of many microprocessors working in parallel. This innovation created a new S-curve, shifted to the right of the original one, with a higher performance limit (based instead on the capacity to co-ordinate the work of the single processors).

Usually the S-curve is represented as the variation of performance in function of the time/effort. Probably that is the most used metric because it is also the easiest to

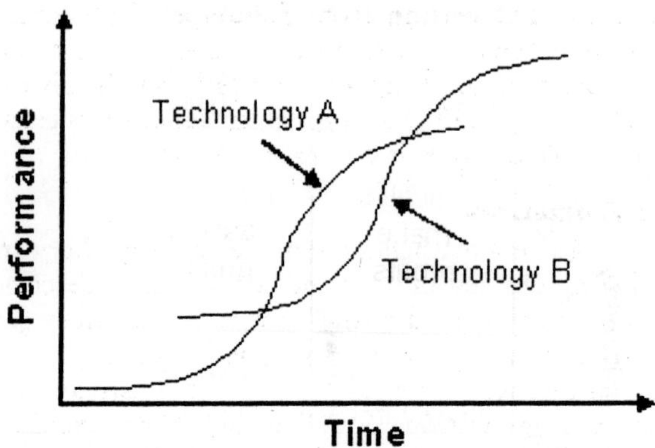

collect data for. This fact does not imply, however, that performance is more accurate than the other possible metrics, for instance the number of inventions, the level of the overall research, or the profitability associated with the innovation.

One must be careful with the fact that different performance parameters tend to be used over different phases of the innovation, as a result the outcomes may get mixed together, or one parameter will end up influencing the outcome of another. Civil aircraft provides a good example, on early stages of the industry fuel burn was a negligible parameter, and all the emphasis was on the speed aircrafts could achieve and if they would thus be able to get off the ground safely. Over the time, with the improvement of the aircrafts almost everyone was able to reach the minimum speed and to take off, which made fuel burn the main parameter for assessing performance of civil aircrafts.

Overall we can say that the S-Curve is a robust yet flexible framework to analyze the introduction, growth and maturation of innovations and to understand the technological cycles. The model also has plenty of empirical evidence, it was exhaustively studied within many industries including semiconductors, telecommunications, hard drives, photocopiers, jet engines and so on.

4. The Teece Model

David Teece clarified that two factors—imitability and complementary assetswill have a strong influence in *determining* who will ultimately profit from an innovation. Imitability refers to how easily competitors can copy or duplicate the technology or process underpinning the innovation. There are many examples of barriers a company could use to protect itself from imitation, including intellectual property rights, complex internal routines or tacit knowledge.

Consider the case of RC Cola, it was the first firm to introduce a diet cola on the market, but since it could not protect itself from imitation soon Pepsi and Coca-Cola jumped in, and using their complementary assets (distribution channels, brand name, etc.) they appropriated all the profits of the segment. Complementary assets, therefore, are equally important. They include any activity that gravitates around the core innovation such as distribution channels, reputation, marketing capabilities, strategic alliances, customer relationships, licensing agreements, among others.

Analyzing the two dimensions we conclude that if imitability is high and complementary assets are freely available or unimportant it will be difficult to make money out of the innovation (exceptions can be made at the very short-run). If instead complementary assets are tightly held and important and imitability is once

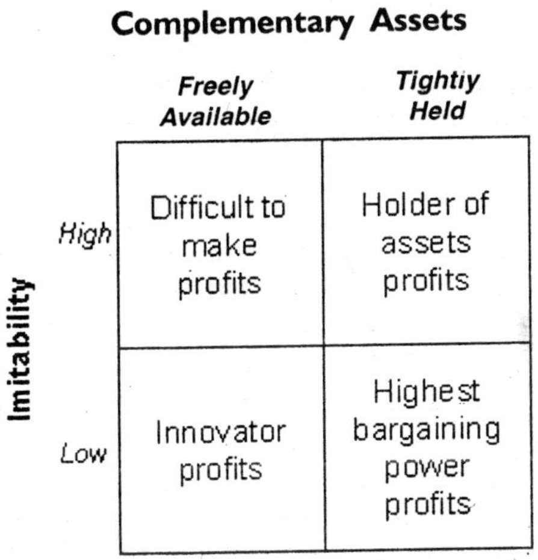

Complementary Assets

Imitability	*Freely Available*	*Tightly Held*
High	Difficult to make profits	Holder of assets profits
Low	Innovator profits	Highest bargaining power profits

again high, the holder of such assets will be the one profiting on the innovation, indecently of who developed it like in the diet cola case. If imitability is low the innovator will find himself in a much better position. When complementary assets are not controlled by other economic actors he will be able to collect most of the profits being generated. When, on the other hand, complementary assets are important and tightly held negotiation will take place, profits will be shared in proportion to bargaining power of the parts involved.

The Teece model can be used not only to predict who will profit from an innovation but also to understand what company will have higher incentives to invest in certain innovations. The threat of imitation and the importance of complementary assets had already being used under other frameworks, but usually they were employed individually or were used to dissect the overall market structure (i.e. Porter's Five Forces) and not the innovation dynamics. The major flaw one can find in the this theory is the lack of empirical evidence, which results from the difficulty to isolate the imitability and the complementarily effects from other factors.

5. The Abernathy—Utterback Model

Fluid Phase—the first phase they called fluid phase, where technological and market uncertainties prevail, a great deal of changes take place contemporaneously and outcomes may vary significantly. It is almost a large experimentation game in the market place. The manufacturing process relies on high-skilled labor and general purpose equipment, there is almost no process innovation and the many, small firms competing will base their advantage on differentiated product features. Competition will not be as fierce as in later phases because companies have no clear idea on potential applications for the innovation, nor on what direction the market might grow. There is low bargaining power from suppliers since no specialized materials are used in the production. The major threats come from the old technology itself and from the entrance of new entrants if the innovation was radical and competence-destroying.

In this phase a company can follow two strategies. Firstly, it can try outmaneuver the competitors and establish its product as the "dominant design" (explained in the next phase). This strategy will involve agreements with distributors and marketing investments to affect customers' perceptions. Alternatively the company can try to take control of complementary assets and wait for the appearance of the dominate design; then once the standard becomes clear it will try to secure most of the profits basing its competitive advantage on the distribution channels, supplier contracts, complementary technologies, value-added services, and others.

Variable	*Fluid Phase*
Innovation	Product changes/radical innovations
Product	Many different designs, customization
Competitors	Many small firms, no direct competition
Organization	Entrepreneurial, organic structure
Threats	Old technology, new entrants
Process	Flexible and inefficient

Transitional Phase—as producers start to learn more about the technology application and about customer's needs some standardization will emerge. Usually by this time the acceptance of the innovation starts to increase and the market starts growing, signals that we are entering into what the authors called the transitional phase. The convergence pattern in this phase will lead to the appearance of a "dominant design", which is a product deigns whose main components and underlying core characteristics do not vary from one model to another, it often comes out as a new product syntethised from individual innovations introduced independently in previous product variations. In Utterback words "the dominant design product has features that competitors and innovators must adhere if they hope to command significant market share following" (Utterback, J.M.—Mastering the Dynamics of Innovation, Harvard Business School, 1994).

Winning the battle for the dominant design is desirable because it will enable the firm to collect monopoly rents (given imitability is not so high or Intelectual Property Rights can be applied). Even is the standard is "open" the developer can build complementary products or enhanced versions faster, possibly establishing a new standard in the future. Microsoft managed to establish Windows as the dominant design for graphical operating systems also thanks to its previous dominant position with the MS-DOS operating system. The threat of new entrants on the transitional phase is linked to the technology involved in the innovation, if it is proprietary incumbents are favoured. Firms in this phase will use strategies to consolidate their product positioning and start increasing production capacity and process innovation in order to face the next phase, the specif phase.

Variable	*Transitional Phase*
Innovation	Major process changes, architectural innovations
Product	Less differentiation due to mass production
Competitors	Many, but declining after the emergence of a dominant design
Organization	More formal structure with task groups
Threats	Imitators and successful product breakthroughs
Process	More rigid, changes occur in large steps

Specific Phase—after the appearance of the dominant design competition will shift from differentiation to product performance and costs. Companies now have a clear picture of market segments and will therefore concentrate on serving specific customers. Manufacturing will use highly specialized equipment and employing high-skilled labour become less important since there is a commoditization taking place, which in turn means that bargaining power of both suppliers and customers will increase.

Competition becomes more intense and the market moves towards an oligopoly. As a consequence incumbents are able to secure their position through supplier relations, distributtion channels and other complementary assets that will create entry barriers to new entrants.

Variable	*Specific Phase*
Innovation	Incremental innovations, improvements in quality
Product	Heavy standardization in product designs
Competitors	Few, classic oligopoly
Organization	Traditional hierarchical organization
Threats	New technologies and firms bringing disrupting innovations
Process	Efficient, capital intensive and rigid

Summing up, the Abernathy-Utterback is one of the most complete and solid models we have covered so far. The analysis they carried was very broad, ranging from technological impact upon products and processes to market dynamics and competition to organizational structure and strategic decisions within companies.

6. Disruptive Innovation Theory

A disruptive innovation is an innovation that helps create a new market and value network, and eventually goes on to disrupt an existing market and value network (over a few years or decades), displacing an earlier technology. The term is used in business and technology literature to describe innovations that improve a product or service in ways that the market does not expect, typically first by designing for a different set of consumers in the new market and later by lowering prices in the existing market

Christensen defines a disruptive innovation as a product or service designed for a new set of customers.

"Generally, disruptive innovations were technologically straightforward, consisting of off-the-shelf components put together in a product architecture that was often simpler than prior approaches. They offered less of what customers in established markets wanted and so could rarely be initially employed there. They offered a different package of attributes valued only in emerging markets remote from, and unimportant to, the mainstream."

Christensen argues that disruptive innovations can hurt successful, well managed companies that are responsive to their customers and have excellent research and development. These companies tend to ignore the markets most susceptible to disruptive innovations, because the markets have very tight profit margins and are too small to provide a good growth rate to an established (sizable) firm. Thus disruptive technology provides an example of when the common business-world advice to "focus on the customer" ("stay close to the customer", "listen to the customer") can sometimes be strategically counterproductive.

How Low-end Disruption Occurs Over-time

Christensen distinguishes between "low-end disruption" which targets customers who do not need the full performance valued by customers at the high end of the market and "new-market disruption" which targets customers who have needs that were previously unsaved by existing incumbents. "Low-end disruption" occurs when the rate at which products improve exceeds the rate at which customers can

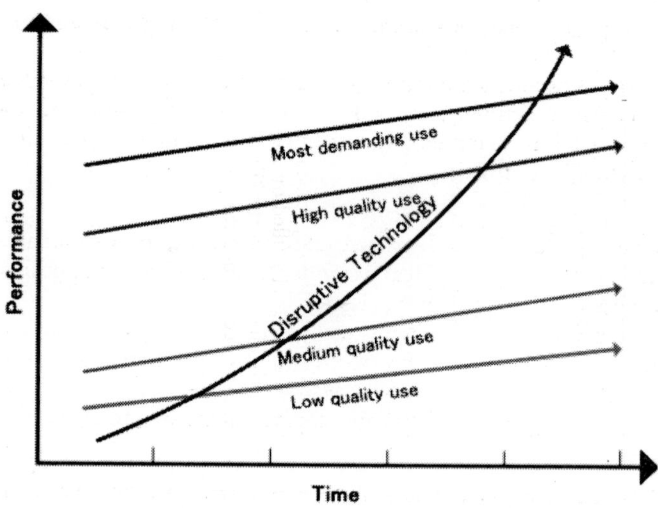

adopt the new performance. Therefore, at some point the performance of the product overshoots the needs of certain customer segments. At this point, a disruptive technology may enter the market and provide a product which has lower performance than the incumbent but which exceeds the requirements of certain segments, thereby gaining a foothold in the market.

In low-end disruption, the disruptor is focused initially on serving the least profitable customer, who is happy with a good enough product. This type of customer is not willing to pay premium for enhancements in product functionality. Once the disruptor has gained a foothold in this customer segment, it seeks to improve its profit margin. To get higher profit margins, the disruptor needs to enter the segment where the customer is willing to pay a little more for higher quality. To ensure this quality in its product, the disruptor needs to innovate. The incumbent will not do much to retain its share in a not so profitable segment, and will move up-market and focus on its more attractive customers. After a number of such encounters, the incumbent is squeezed into smaller markets than it was previously serving. And then finally the disruptive technology meets the demands of the most profitable segment and drives the established company out of the market.

"New market disruption" occurs when a product fits a new or emerging market segment that is not being served by existing incumbents in the industry.

(Examples of Disruptive Innovations see pages 15-18)

7. *First Mover Advantage Revisited*

If you want to win you need to be the first, right? The first mover advantage theory states that the first company entering a certain market will gain massive market share and, thanks to the competitive advantages developed, it will also be able to defend its leadership position from new entrants. The reasoning behind it is quite intuitive, it goes along way with conventional wisdom and, if that was not enough, the principle has also been proposed by academics and managers around the world. Andrew Groove, Intel's ex-CEO, defended that "the first mover and only the first mover, the company that acts while others dither, has a true opportunity to gain time over its competitors; and time advantage, in this business, is the surest way to gain market share".

Examples of Disruptive Innovations

Innovation	Disrupted market	Notes
(1)	(2)	(3)
8 inch floppy disk drive 5.25 inch floppy disk drive 3.5 inch floppy disk drive Bernoulli drive and Zip drive	14 inch floppy disk drive 8 inch floppy disk drive 5.25 inch floppy disk drive 3.5 inch floppy disk drive	The floppy disk drive market has had unusually large changes in market share over the past fifty years. According to Clayton M. Christensen's research, the cause of this instability was a repeating pattern of disruptive innovations. For example, in 1981, the old 8 inch drives (used in mini computers) were "vastly superior" to the new 5.25 inch drives (used in desktop computers). However, 8 inch drives were not affordable for the new desktop machines. The simple 5.25 inch drive, assembled from technologically inferior "off-the-shelf" components, was an "innovation" only in the sense that it was new. However, as this market grew and the drives improved, the companies that manufactured them eventually triumphed while many of the existing manufacturers of eight inch drives fell behind.
CDs and USB flash drives	Bernoulli drive and Zip drive	
Downloadable Digital media	CDs, DVDs	In the 1990s, the music industry phased out the single, leaving consumers with no means to purchase individual songs. This market was initially filled by illegal peer-to-peer file sharing technologies, and then by online retailers such as the iTunes Store and Amazon.com. This low end disruption eventually undermined the sales of physical, high-cost CDs.
Cloud computing	USB flash drives	While downloadable Digital media displaced CDs and DVDs as a medium for entertainment media, cloud computing displaces the need for local physical media to store digital data in general.
Hydraulic excavators	Cable-operated excavators	Hydraulic excavators were clearly innovative at the time of introduction but they gain widespread use only decades after. However, cable-operated excavators are still used in some cases, mainly for large excavations.
Mini steel mills	Vertically integrated steel mills	By using mostly locally available scrap and power sources these mills can be cost effective even though not large.
Minicomputers	Mainframes	Minicomputers were originally presented as an inexpensive alternative to mainframes and mainframe manufacturers did not consider them a serious threat in their market.

(Contd.)

(*Contd.*)

(1)	(2)	(3)
Personal computers	Minicomputers, Workstations. Word processors, Lisp machines	Eventually, the market for minicomputers became much larger than the market for mainframes. Similarly, the market for main frames and mini-computers was seriously disrupted by personal computers. Although they were not at all competitive at the time of their introduction in the 1970s, by the mid-1980s they had improved exponentially and could compete directly with the more expensive machines.
Desktop publishing	Traditional publishing	Early desktop-publishing systems could not match high-end professional systems in either features or quality. Nevertheless, they lowered the cost of entry to the publishing business, and economies of scale eventually enabled them to match, and then surpass, the functionality of the older dedicated publishing systems.
Computer printers	Offset Printing	Offset printing has a high overhead cost, but very low unit cost compared to computer printers, and superior quality. But as printers, especially laser printers, have improved in speed and quality, they have become increasingly useful for creating documents in limited issues.
Digital photography	Chemical photography	Early digital cameras suffered from low picture quality and resolution and long shutter lag. Quality and resolution are no longer major issues and shutter lag is much less than it used to be. The convenience of small memory cards and portable hard drives that hold hundreds or thousands of pictures, as well as the lack of the need to develop these pictures, also helped. Digital cameras have a high power consumption (but several lightweight battery packs can provide enough power for thousands of pictures). Cameras for classic photography are stand-alone devices. In the same manner, high-resolution digital video recording has replaced film stock, except for high-budget motion pictures.
High speed CMOS	Photographic film video sensors	When first introduced, high speed CMOS sensors were less sensitive, had lower resolution, and cameras based on them had less duration (record time). The advantage of rapid setup time, editing in the camera, and nearly-instantaneous review quickly eliminated 16 mm high speed film systems. CMOS-based cameras also require less power (single phase 110 VAC and a few amps for CMOS, vs. 240 V single- or three-phase at 20-50 A for film cameras). Continuing advances have overtaken 35 mm film and are challenging 70 mm film applications.

Steamboats	Sailing ships	The first steamships were deployed on inland waters where sailing ships were less effective, instead of on the higher profit margin seagoing routes. Hence steamships originally only competed in traditional shipping lines' "worst" markets.
Telephones	Telegraphy	When Western Union infamously declined to purchase Alexander Graham Bells telephone patents for $100,000, their highest-profit market was long-distance telegraphy. Telephones were only useful for very local calls. Short-distance telegraphy barely existed as a market segment, which explains Western Union's decision.
Automobiles	Rail transport	At the beginning of the 20th century, rail (including streetcars) was the fastest and most cost-efficient means of land transportation for goods and passengers in industrialized countries. The first cars, buses and trucks were used for local transportation in suburban areas, where they often replaced streetcars and industrial tracks. As highways expanded, medium- and later long-distance transports were relocated to road traffic, and some railways closed down. As rail traffic has a lower ton-kilometer cost, but a higher investment and operating cost than road traffic, rail is still preferred for large-scale bulk cargo (such as minerals). Since rail has always been faster than contemporary road vehicles, it is viable for passengers in populated regions like Western Europe, south and east Asia and the Northeast Corridor. When urban density increases, rail systems often become more attractive and make a comeback.
Private jet	Supersonic transport	The Concorde aircraft has so far been the only supersonic airliner in extensive commercial traffic. However, it catered to a small customer segment, which could later afford small private sub-sonic jets. The loss of speed was compensated by flexibility and a more direct routing (i.e. no need to go through a hub). Supersonic flight is also banned above inhabited land, due to sonic booms. The Concorde service was withdrawn in 2003.
Plastic	Metal, wood, glass etc.	Bakelite and other early plastics had very limited use—their main advantages were electric insulation and low cost. New forms had advantages such as transparency, elasticity and combustibility. In the early 21st century, plastics can be used for nearly all household items previously made of metal, wood and glass.
Light-emitting diodes	Light bulbs	A LED is significantly smaller and less power-consuming than a light bulb. The first optical LEDs were weak, and only useful as indicator lights. Later models could be used for indoor lighting, and future ones will probably be strong enough to serve as street lights. Incandescent light bulbs are being phased out in many countries.

(Contd.)

(Contd.)

(1)	(2)	(3)
Digital synthesizer	Electronic organ and piano	Synthesizers were initially low-cost, low-weight alternatives to electronic organs and acoustic pianos. Today's synthesizers feature many automated functions and have replaced them for home and hobby users.
Mobile Telephony	Mobile Discount Operators	Mobile Discount/No Frills Operators (MDOs aka. MVNOs) first focused on a low-distribution-cost-through-internet sales model. In later times, innovations like low-priced mobile-internet tariffs were brought to market. This tripped the development of a new discount category in the market which was later entered by the large discount retail chains with own branded offerings leveraging their distribution power in the lower tier of the market.
LCD	CRT	The first liquid crystal displays (LCD) were monochromatic and had low resolution. They were used in watches and other handheld devices, but during the early 2000s these (and other planar technologies) largely replaced the dominant cathode ray tube (CRT) technology for computer displays and television sets, although CRT technologies have improved with advances like true-flat panels and digital controls only recently.
Digital calculator	Mechanical calculator	Facet AB used to dominate the European market for calculators, but did not adapt digital technology, and failed to compete with digital competitors.
GPS navigation device	Navigational map	The old navigational system using maps, needed knowledge of the use and possession of a sextant, a clock and an astronomical almanac known as an ephemeris. A clear sky was paramount for the calculating of an exact position. GPS can show the exact position, either on a projected map or in degrees N/S/E/W (low end models), in any weather.
Ultrasound	Radiography (X-ray imaging)	Ultrasound technology is disruptive relative to X-ray imaging. Ultrasound was a new-market disruption. None of the X-ray companies participated in ultrasound until they acquired major ultrasound equipment companies.

There is a lot of theoretical evidence supporting the model, but does this evidence emerge empirically as well? Not quite. Consider the markets for safety razors, disposable diapers, photographic film, laser printers, game consoles, VCRs, energy drinks, personal computers, internet browsers, operating systems, search engines, online bookstores, online auctions, VoIP services, and the list goes on. In each and every one of these markets the leader position is held by a company that entered after someone was already commercializing their products.

The question then becomes: why, despite the lack of empirical evidence, people still embrace the idea that being the first to enter a market is extremely important? There are three main reasons: the industrial age environment, natural monopolies and the bias towards winners.

Industrial age environment: until the 1980s the pace of change in some industries was much slower. Being the first to enter a market characterized by stability and predictable incremental changes could actually yield significant advantages. Under the information age, however, discontinuities and market innovations are in the face of the day. Success, as a consequence, comes no longer from being the first to market but from evolving rapidly the product to become the dominant design. JVC's VHS recording technology came to the market almost two years after Sony's Betamax. Nonetheless by licensing out the technology to other producers, creating alliances with content creators and adapting the features to address the needs of customers and rental stores JVC managed to establish the VHS as the standard for video recording, driving Betamax out of the market.

Natural Monopolies: some markets present predominant capital costs and infrastructure constraints, meaning that the first mover can actually build a strong competitive position by merely entering the market before other players. This is the case of oil and gas distribution, water services and electricity. Natural monopolies as the ones mentioned, however, represent exceptions in most countries. In our modern economy being able to understand customers, manage innovation and adapt quickly to market discontinuities are much more important then merely entering a market first. The most evident example is internet. Google was not the first search engine. Amazon was not the first online bookstore. Ebay was not the first online auction site. All these companies were focused in understanding their customers, innovating and adapting their strategies to reflect market changes, that is what granted them such strong leadership position.

Bias towards winners: over the long term there is a natural tendency to forget failures and to over celebrate successes. It is not surprising, therefore, that people wrongly associate long term market leaders with the first to enter a certain segment. Consider the case of laser printers. In 1971 Xerox developed the first working model in its Palo Alto Research Center. IBM on the other hand was the first company to commercialize it in 1976.. HP entered the market almost 10 years later. HP, however, evolved the product rapidly to suit mass market requirements and managed to become the clear winner. HP has sold more than 100 million units, no wonder people think it was the first company to commercialize laser printers. Even important people get confused. In the mid 1990s, during a visit to HP facilities in Idaho, an ex-president of the US congratulated HP engineers for "inventing the laser printer and maintaining the United States technological leadership".

So, if being the first to enter a market is not important, what is then? Some of you might have already guessed. More important than entering the market first is to enter the market before a dominant design emerges and then understand better the customer needs, innovate and evolve your product or service to become the dominant design. Contrary to what most people think King Gillette was not the first to market safety razors. They were invented in 1880 by the Kampfe brothers, and a decade before King Gillette opened his company there were already commercial safety razors being sold. Gillette, however, evolved the product rapidly both by improving the design and by creating a business model where the profits would be made with the disposable blades. Neatly crafted business strategy, good understanding of customer needs and marketing enabled Gillette to dominate the safety razor market for such a long period, not being the first to enter the market.

Creativity and Innovation in the Workplace

There was a time when the concept of creativity was only associated with writers, painters, musicians and similar people in artistic professions. But with the ever-increasing necessity of cultivating a unique brand personality, the need for creative thinking has transitioned from the arts into everyday business. In addition, the act of producing a product that distinguishes itself from competitors in a marketplace where differences are often hard to come by demands a high degree of creativity both in innovation and marketing.

As a result, it's now become commonplace for companies—both large and small—to adopt policies that foster creativity and thereby promote innovation.

But what is meant by creativity? And how can it be harnessed effectively?

Creativity

How to Set-up a Creative Work Space to Foster Innovation

Establishing a creative environment takes more than just turning your employees loose and giving them free reign in the hope they'll hit on something valuable. As with any other system, the process of creativity requires the proper framework to operate effectively, which also enables management to evaluate the profitability of the results.

Popular approaches to fostering innovation through creativity include:

Create a stimulating environment. Offices that include stimulating objects such as journals, art, games and other items—some of which may not even be directly related to your business—serve as sources of inspiration. In addition, structuring the work area by removing physical barriers between people will improve communication and promote creative interaction.

Reward efforts through positive psychological reinforcement. Encourage your employees to take risks, rewarding them for creative ideas and not penalizing them when they fail. In doing so, you'll enable people to more readily take on assignments that stretch their potential (and that of your organization), discussing in advance any foreseeable risks and creating the necessary contingency plan. Encourage employees at all levels to contribute suggestions for improving current business operations.

Foster different points of view through outside perspectives. Innovation can often spring from a review of how your customers view and use your products and services. Soliciting their opinions can provide valuable insight into potential areas for improvement as well as areas where you're succeeding (essential knowledge for positioning against competitors). Other perspectives might include: vendors, speakers from other industries or consumers using a competitor's products or services.

Process of Creation and Management of Innovation Teams

Strategic Contents

1. Definition, accompaniment, management, direction and control of an innovation team in their process of identifying and managing innovating projects in different areas of an organization.

Strategic Methodology

1. Selection of persons with an orientation towards innovation.
2. Creation and formalization of an innovation team.
3. Regular meetings of the innovation team under the direction and management of Stravalue International, oriented towards development of innovating projects in different areas.

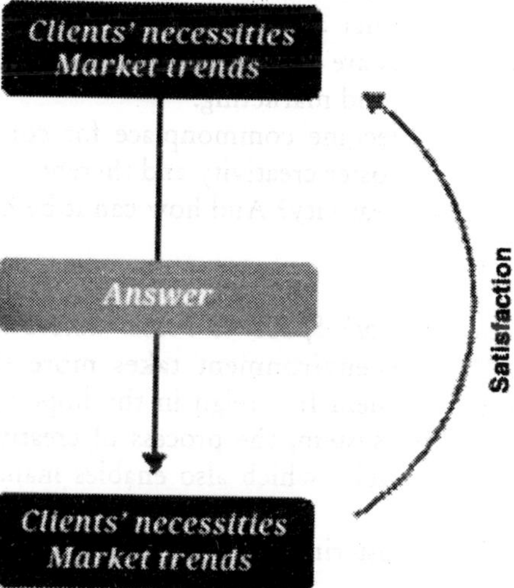

Figure 1.3 : process of creation and management of innovation teams

THE NATURE OF CHANGE

The adoption of new ideas and techniques does not occur naturally but results from hard work, trial and error. It is important to recognize this fact and to make an effort to develop information that is concise, readable and to the point and to make sure the information reaches people who can use it. A broad spectrum of skills is needed to lead to effective management of innovation and change. There is no magic formula for success—no such formulas exist.

Multiple channels of communication should be used to promote the adoption of an innovation. Never expect one report, one presentation, one telephone call or one conference to accomplish everything. Successful programs need to be carefully conceived and carried out. Human contacts are critical ingredients, and need to be used along with good written and visual materials. These materials are useless without an understanding of the needs, limitations and problems of the user.

Change agents can bring innovation for the user by examining their preconceived notions about the way things should be done. Personnel have to be receptive to change themselves, they have to be able to evaluate new ideas objectively and see their users—not as they have been—but as they might be.

Resistance to Change

The adoption of innovations involves altering human behavior, and the acceptance of change. There is a natural resistance to change for several reasons.

People Resist Change

- When the reason for the change is unclear. Ambiguity—whether it is about costs, equipment, jobs—can trigger negative reactions among users.
- When the proposed users have not been consulted about the change, and it is offered to them as an accomplished fact. People like to know what's going on, especially if their jobs may be affected. Informed workers tend to have higher levels of job satisfaction than uninformed workers.
- When the change threatens to modify established patterns of working relationships between people.
- When communication about the change—timetables, personnel, monies, etc.—has not been sufficient.
- When the benefits and rewards for making the change are not seen as adequate for the trouble involved.
- When the change threatens jobs, power or status in an organization.

(An unwilling user can always make an idea fail, no matter how good it is.)
Decision makers will be more responsive to change:

- If the information presented coincides with their current values, beliefs, and attitudes:
- If they perceive that the change will benefit them more than it will cost them:
- If the innovation requires marginal rather than major changes in their views or lives:
- If they have a demonstrated need for the innovation: and
- If the innovation is introduced gradually so that people can adjust to the resulting change.

IMPLEMENTATION BY UNITED STATES

Example of Change Worksheet

A way to understand resistance to change is to use the following worksheet. This should be filled out separately by people in an organization, then discussed. What are the consensus reasons why people in your organization resist change?

The following factors affect how an individual or an organization reacts to change. Pick the five you think are most important. When you have chosen the top five, then rank these on a scale of 1 (most important) to 5. Think of examples to back up your opinions.

Personal Factors

______ Age
______ Sex
______ Education
______ Marital status

_____ Experience
_____ Time in the same job
_____ Occupation
_____ Other (Explain) ____
____

Job Related Factors

_____ Number of Subordinates
_____ Breadth of Activity
_____ Degree of Autonomy
_____ Amount of Job Security
_____ Availability of Slack Time
_____ Prestige of Position
_____ Variety of Work
_____ Other (Explain) ____
____

Organizational Factors

_____ Size
_____ Structure (Degree of Centralization)
_____ Autonomy from Outside Political Pressure
_____ Funding/Budget
_____ Recognition
_____ Reward System
_____ Age of the Organization
_____ Prestige
_____ Other (Explain) ____
____

1. ______________________________ (Most Important)
2. ______________________________
3. ______________________________
4. ______________________________
5. ______________________________

DISCLAIMER NOTICE

This information is disseminated under the sponsorship of the United States Department of Transportation, Federal Transit Administration, in the interest of information exchange. The United States Government assumes no liability for the contents or use thereof. The United States Government does not endorse products or manufacturers. Trade or manufacturers' names appear herein solely because they are considered essential to the contents of these reports.

Managing Resistance to Innovate

Despite the potential positive outcomes, **innovation is nearly always resisted.** A degree of resistance is normal since change is:

- Disruptive, and
- Stressful.

Kotter and Schlesinger identified four key reasons why change is resisted:
Parochial self interest
Individuals are concerned with the implications for themselves
Misunderstanding
Communications problems
Inadequate information
Low tolerance of change
Sense of insecurity
Different assessment of the situation
Disagreement over the need for change
Disagreement over the advantages and disadvantages

Management trying to implement change will often come across other people in the business responding with phrases such as:

- "My needs are already being met"
- "We don't need to do this"
- "This sounds like bad news"
- "The risks outweigh the benefits"
- "What does this mean for me?"

Of course, a degree of skepticism can be healthy especially where there are weaknesses in the proposed changes. However, resistance will also impede the achievement of business objectives.

Some common reasons why change is resisted include:

Parochial self-interest	Individuals are concerned with the implications for themselves; their view is often biased by their perception of a particular situation
Habit	Habit provides both comfort and security Habits are often well-established and difficult to change
Misunderstanding	Communications problems Inadequate information
Low tolerance of change	Sense of insecurity
Different assessment of the situation	Disagreement over the need for change Disagreement over the advantages and disadvantages
Economic implications	Employees are likely to resist change which is perceived as affecting their pay or other rewards. Established patterns of working and reward create a vested interest in maintaining the *status quo*
Fear of the unknown	Proposed changes which confront people tend to generate fear and anxiety Introducing new technology or working practices creates uncertainty

We have touched earlier on personal barriers to change—there are also several organizational barriers to change, including:

- Structural inertia
- Existing power structures
- Resistance from work groups
- Failure of previous change initiatives

Change is also resisted because of the poor way in which change is managed! For example, a failure by management responsible for the change to:

- Explain the need for change
- Provide information
- Consult, negotiate and offer support and training
- Involve people in the process
- Build trust and sense of security
- Build employee relations

As a result of change resistance and poorly managed change projects, many of them ultimately fail to achieve their objectives. Amongst the reasons commonly associated with failed change programmers are:

- Employees do not understand the purpose or even the need for change
- Lack of planning and preparation
- Poor communication
- Employees lack the necessary skills and/or there is insufficient training and development offered
- Lack of necessary resources
- Inadequate/inappropriate rewards

At the heart of resistance is our *fear of loss*. Resistance is a result of this fear, an expression of how people feel about the change effort at hand. When things change, people begin to worry about what they might lose, including above four.

- Job
- Income
- Position/Status
- Reputation
- Turf
- Influence
- Responsibility
- Expertise
- Certainty/Security
- Autonomy/Control/Freedom of Choice
- Effectiveness
- Routines/Familiar Procedures
- Relationships/Mentors/Group Membership
- Meaning
- Future/Dreams/Plans
- Identity

This list is not comprehensive; we can all think of more losses that we face.

Any Change Stirs Up Resistance

As we move the workshop into the first "lecturette", we are surrounded by personal expressions and experiences of resistance. The participants already understand the nature of resistance and its destructive powers. Our challenge, as stated in the objectives, is to reframe this energy and help the participants turn the inevitable process of change and the resulting resistance into a productive organizational experience.

Yes, *any* change stirs up resistance. Examples are everywhere:

- People trained in problem-solving and/or statistical tools who do not use them;
- People saying yes when asked to complete a task and then not doing it or avoiding it;
- A "team" that resists confronting a particular member's not "getting with the program";
- Supervisors who continue to control processes and people and can't seem to let go;
- Management postponing training or cutting back on "key" programs;
- People saying "this will never work" or "it works already, so why do we have to change it"or "the company's making money, why do we have to change?" or "if it ain't broke, don't fix it", and so on; and
- Our reluctance to speak with someone who we are afraid of or who appears to oppose us.

It is normal to experience resistance whenever there is innovate . Understanding that there will be resistance to innovate will help you anticipate resistance, identify its sources and reasons, and modify your efforts to manage the issues of change to ensure the success of your innovate efforts.

Resistance is actually healthy. Try not to react against it defensively. It is good for you because it makes you check your assumptions and it forces you to clarify what you are doing. You must always probe the objections to find the real reason for resistance. Many times, it comes down to personal fear.

As the leader, you must take the time to understand resistance and you may have to come at it from several different angles before it is conquered. You must understand what your employees are feeling, as well as thinking.

Ways to reduce resistance to innovate :

1. Involve interested parties in the planning of innovation by asking them for suggestions and incorporating their ideas.
2. Clearly define the need for the innovate by communicating the strategic decision personally and in written form.
3. Address the "people needs" of those involved. Disrupt only what needs to be changed. Help people retain friendships, comfortable settings and group norms wherever possible.
4. Design flexibility into change by phasing it in wherever possible. This will allow people to complete current efforts and assimilate new behaviors along the way. Allow employees to redefine their roles during the course of implementing change.
5. Be open and honest.

6. Do not leave openings for people to return to the status quo. If you and your organization are not ready to commit yourselves to the change, don't announce the strategy.
7. Focus continually on the positive aspects of the change. Be specific where you can.
8. Deliver training programs that develop basic skills as opposed to processes such as: conducting meetings, communication, team-building, self-esteem, and coaching.

Basic Model Components for Creation Process for Problem-solving

Here's the model at the second level of recursion:

SEVEN STAGES OF THE CREATIVE PROCESS

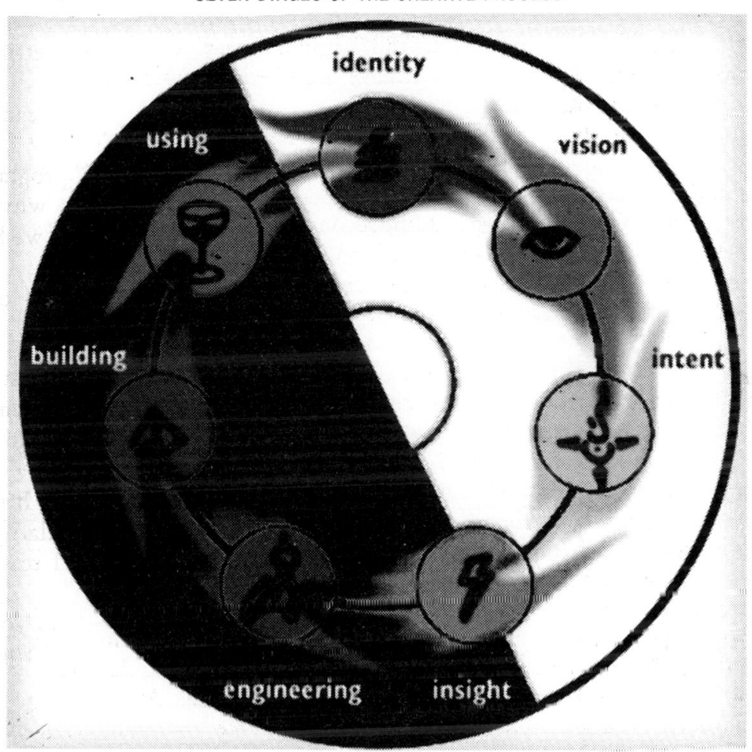

COPYRIGHT 1982 MG TAYLOR CORPORATION

Figure 1.4 : Showing the creation process

The most striking feature is the bipartite division that separates the Using stage from the Identity stage and cuts the insight stage in half. The model "starts" with the Identity stage and the purpose of the first half is creating the problem. The second half has the job of solving the problem which the first half created, thereby producing a new Condition in the Using stage, out of which the first half will again have to create a new problem. Well, after all, it's a cycle—no beginning and no end, with one stage feeding the next.

The first half of the process is individual and the last half collective. This is so because until an idea has a physical manifestation, it cannot be perceived in a useful collective manner. Ideas have no value merely as ideas; they must be expressed in specific form. Likewise, manifestations have no value unless they can be translated into ideas to be transported, improved and evolved. In the mid 80's one iteration of the Creative Process model had the following phrase forming a circle around its periphery: "A model is a representation of reality is a manifestation of a model is a representation of reality is a manifestation..."

Consider the process of writing a song, for example. Until the tracks are laid down in the studio, the musicians, songwriters and lyricists have different ideas [Vision], regardless of how they have struggled [Intent] to communicate them to one another. But once the song begins to materialize digitally [Insight], the process becomes necessarily collective and the fields of visions collapse into the various takes [Engineering], one of which will be packaged [Building] for distribution and consumption [Using]. This doesn't necessarily mean that the artists are satisfied with the fidelity of the finished product to the original vision. Constraints of ability, budget, timelines, and other factors will have modified the vision and the finished product may be quite different.

This doesn't imply that the first half excludes collaboration, for quite the opposite is the case. Collaboration is a necessary component of every stage of the model. So is independent work.

It has already been mentioned that the second half of the creative process creates a new Condition for the first half to act upon. The term "Condition" is key to understanding the significance of what we mean when we say "creating the problem." Many of us equate conditions with problems. The United States has a "problem" with students meeting educational testing standards, or a problem with drug abuse. Companies have cash flow "problems" or a problem with low sales or low productivity. But these are not problems; they are conditions. Nor are they symptoms of problems. This is more than just semantics, and in a sense it embodies much of the philosophy of MG Taylor Corporation. Stafford Beer, the organizational cyberneticist coined the phrase, "the purpose of a system is what it does." Low educational testing results are therefore a product of some system, whose purpose (by virtue of the way it's assembled and the interactions between its components) includes such results. It's hard for us to grasp this because we bristle at the use of the word "purpose" with unpalatable conditions. After all, it seems a harsh accusation of the hard working teachers, parents and administrators in the education system. But it is no such thing. It's not an accusation at all. It's an invitation to discover how the system generates the result that seems so undesirable. An invitation for understanding. If we cannot discern how the result is created, we shall never hope to support the evolution of the system into a different channel, and our interventions may cause more harm than good or perpetuate a system that ought not to be supported.

The whole purpose of the first half of the creative process is to investigate, discover and discern the operating mechanics, cybernetic connections, and principles of self-organization of the existing system. Then—maybe—we can act upon the system with intelligence. Or at least envision a new system that produces different conditions more in line with our vision.

We generally lack the patience to do this, however. We label the condition as a problem, automatically designating individuals in the system as the cause, thus alienating them from effective collaboration, and then begin hacking away at it and grafting new sub-systems onto it. We call these sub-systems solutions, even though they are only new subsystems. Meanwhile, war has erupted between the guardians of the system and the interventionists. The best possible outcome of such a zero-sum game is that each side thwarts the efforts of the other (a draw is the overall best outcome of a zero-sum game). All along, the system continues to churn out its conditions because we have failed to work together to understand how it does what it does (not "why" it does what it does).

We call this problem-solving.

There must be a different way...

Identity

Explore, discover and understand how the system produces the conditions. Even if you think you know how it's done, think again. Use techniques of collaborative, creative design to see the system from different vantage points. Break out of common assumptions and past practices (you can always go back to them if you need to). Build a working model of the current system that replicates the conditions you see. It probably won't be right but it will lend some needed insight. Creativity is the elimination of options. So generate some optional ways of seeing the system and its components. Work until you can see the truth in everyone's viewpoint. This means building models of these viewpoints. Then, maybe you can assemble components of the viewpoints together to get a more robust map of the system and conditions than you could by clinging only to your own opinions.

Vision

How do you see the system working in the future? Be careful not to merely derive a list of anti-conditions. Instead, build working simulations of how the new system will operate. Add new system components and delete others. Ask yourself to describe the difference between the existing system and the new system in terms of operational properties, components, cybernetics and self-organization. What is it about the new system that will allow it to produce different conditions? Describe parameters of autocatalytic closure for the new system to emerge. Whatever you do, don't write some nonsense vision statement. Get in the mud and do the work of building the vision, don't just talk about it in flowery terms.

Visions need to address the new system at all of the vantage points, from philosophy to task.

Frequently we have to shatter cherished beliefs during the visioning stage. Otherwise we're wasting time that would be better spent (although in vain) tweaking the system according to our current beliefs. We forget that our belief structures are mapped into the system as well as our perception of the system. They are integral to creating the conditions we're trying to change. Fortunately, we emerge stronger from these encounters with our personal philosophy, weeding out dogma and adding vibrancies and wisdom to our intercourse with the world.

Intent

Are you excited yet? Do you have the juice to live in the vision and do the work to bring as much of it it back to the present each day as you can? How long can you live with the ambiguity and paradox of working in two different worlds? Can you assume the mantle and the risks of the prophet and advocate? Intent is the well of energy that you'll return to over and over while you're working to bring your vision to the present. The greater the distance on the fitness landscape between the old and new system, the greater the challenge and the more energy you'll need to succeed.

Insight

At this stage, there's only one stumbling block: your vision is full of holes. You will have figured this out by now. Sometimes when working on simple problems, the vision really will contain a clear definition of the problem, and the answer, but usually there are lots of unknowns and gaps in understanding. The problem—the **PROBLEM**—is how to conceive of, invent, allow for the emergence of, or create the sub-systems and ecosystems that will fill the gaps in the vision—that will rework the vision to make it more powerful. The problem is not how to fix the conditions. The problem is how to imagine, design and allow for the evolution of new components of the system (or new systems) that will help the system create different (and hopefully more healthy) conditions. There's no other problem you can solve. You can't fix the conditions.

Imagine a group of people in a room. There's a thermostat on the wall connected to a heating system which is operating, but the heating vents in the room have been closed. It's getting cold in the room and the thermometer indicates that the temperature has fallen to 45°F (apologies to our European friends). The temperature in the room is the condition. One member of the group comes up with a response. He breaks the thermometer, pours in more mercury, and then reseals it. Now the gauge shows 72°F. Has he addressed the problem? No, he's messed with the gauge, and it's still cold in the room. Another member of the group begins hunting through the heating system, checking its various components and how they work together—troubleshooting the system—and discovers the blocked vents, which she opens, allowing the warm air to circulate through the room. The condition now has truly changed but only through an applied understanding of how the system works, and in this instance, changing the state of one component of the system. Of course now the faulty thermometer reads 99°F!

Problems with human enterprises are much trickier, being organic and not mechanical.

Engineering

Think of Engineering as a laboratory where various components of the vision, and perhaps different visions themselves are fully designed and tested. It's a breeding ground for new variations as they vie to see which is more fit (not necessarily "better" but more resilient in the current environment). The term Engineering can be misleading if you imagine one or several individuals running carefully controlled experiments. Instead it's more like a confusing market place filled with vendors, hawkers and customers buying and selling their stuff to each other. At least that's the metaphor to use when the problem to be solved is organizational in nature.

Simpler problems may actually be solved in controlled environments, particularly those that involve the design of physical materials, goods or services.

Engineering challenges involve cycles of rapid design, testing, and failure in order to ferret out the more resilient designs. Due to this type of cycling, a pendulum effect is set-up between the Intent and Building stages. At each engineering failure, the designers must retreat to the Intent well to gather more resolve, push through for the next Insight, and test it in Engineering until an idea survives well enough to proliferate on its own. If this pendulum effect is full of friction, it can generate enough heat to damage the process, or cause enough energy to bleed away to grind the process to a standstill.

Building

Nothing can be engineered without being built. This stage works hand in glove with the previous one. This applies in particular to organizations and enterprise-wide environments. While companies can run pilot tests to limit risk, remember that the people participating in the pilot—investors, producers and customers—are all real and committed and at risk.

If the problem is an organizational one, this stage really refers to assembling complexity. Very few human endeavors are actually built like a machine. Instead, ecosystems of ideas manifest themselves and self-organize into an autocatalytic whole, meaning that each idea creates niches to be filled by other ideas, and occupies niches created by them in turn. We can play a part in this assembly as designers and builders, but a major portion of the process is beyond the individual or collective control of anyone.

Using

At this stage, the idea has been manifested, and the system is now producing new conditions. All of the people in the enterprise, whether they are investors, producers or customers, are users and participate in the system. They can now truly evaluate whether the new conditions are better than the old conditions. Of course, in the process of using, they all develop attachments and dependencies on the system as it is. The cycle begins over again with Identity.

A sense of control that we were looking for in the Building stage can be found instead in this stage, as the new system will work to maintain its own homeostasis—its unique identity and viability—across a broad range of environmental conditions. So, for example, our current government and educational systems are extremely resilient in their ability to resist fundamental change that may threaten what they are. This is good (and bad)! It's good because without this ability, systems would never be stable for long enough to be of value. It's bad, clearly because it's what makes them so hard to change.

Releasing Creativity

Releasing Your Unlimited Creativity is a powerful technology of creativity. It is based on a unique interdisciplinary understanding of our creative ability and creative power and our inherent and unlimited creativity.

The Releasing Your Unlimited Creativity understanding and material provides a new paradigm about the nature of a human being and what lies in each heart. Analogous to the paradigm change that revolutionized physics at the beginning of the Twentieth Century and subsequently the world as we know it, the Releasing Your Unlimited Creativity provides a similar such paradigm as to the nature of man. Its application has released phenomenal creative insights and passion in individuals who have used and embraced the concepts.

The impact of the creativity released much parallels that reflected in the traditional story of Sham and Rumi where a cleric is transformed into a phenomenal poet of the heart. In many ways when properly applied within a space of unconditional love, the Releasing Your Unlimited Creativity understanding and material is capable of becoming the Shams to the creative spirit which lies in each heart. Here unconditional love being to give what is needed to nurture, sustain and allow for the growth and free enfoldment of the creative spirit with no expectations of return. It is not to give what mind wants to give or thinks should be given but to give what is needed. Key to giving this unconditional love and not give what mind wants to give is to learn how to use our intuitive guidance and to navigate from the heart.

Releasing Your Unlimited Creativity addresses two separate but related aspects of our creativity. Each is reflective of an aspect of the interdisciplinary nature of the understanding. In addressing each separately, a bridge can be built to provide a way to readily move between these two aspects if we so desire to do so.

One aspects addresses freeing what is best described as our creative spirit from a cage of our own making to access our unlimited creativity through a gentle phoenix process For some, this provides the door way to ultimate mystical experience individuals seek. The aspect is more realty to the mystical and spiritual aspects of our creativity. The full discussion as to exactly what this aspect is about is found in the topic, "What is Releasing Your Unlimited Creativity—an April 2008 Update." Studying this aspect about our inner creative ability and creative powerand is most related to finding inner satisfaction, the love of one's life, a soul mate, a beloved or the Beloved and the like.

The other aspect addressed is about managing and controlling energy. It is to learn how to consciously use our inherent and unlimited creativity to direct the energy which gives rise to creating any experiences we have including experiences as discussed in the April 2008 Update. This aspect of Releasing Your Unlimited Creativity is about creating what we desire to experience in, and with, our life, whether it be a spiritual, mental, emotion or physical experience. Studying this aspect is about our outer creative ability and creative power and most related to finding success in the external world.

Working these two aspects together provides the path to claiming our birthright as a creative being and to create a life worth living. Releasing Your Unlimited Creativity builds on the relationship our creative spirit has with our body to access the inner and outer creative ability and creative power necessary for a creative endeavor.

When many talk about creativity, creative ability, creative power or accessing creative power they think of creativity and creative power as having creative ideas which can solve the problems they face. Many see creativity as something we do or someplace we go to get an original or creative idea. Many see acting externally in the world to manifest the idea we have as creativity. Many do not see what needs to occur inside to create the space for the creative idea to arise and many do not see how learning about how the physical world works is necessary to accessing the creative power to act to manifest the desired creation. The Releasing Your Unlimited Creativity material lead us to the bridge point of the inner and the outer to help understand both our inner creative power and the outer creative power.

Areas of Applicability

Releasing Your Unlimited Creativity is applicable to any or all aspects of life - spiritual, mental, emotional, physical, private, professional, social, individually and/ or collectively within a group or organization. It spans the spectrum from simply finding creative solutions or innovative ideas to respond to any set of conditions we face to recreating our life or creating an alternative way to live our life. It has been used to create health,. inner satisfaction, and a variety of other objectives.

The Primary Issue—A doubly locked cage of one's own making

The fundamental understanding of the Releasing Your Unlimited Creativity material is that we are creative beings and we will always create. We cannot not create. The life we live is a creation. As any true creation, our life is something original and not seen or previously experienced by anyone before us or anyone who comes after us.

The problem we face in creativity is quite simple. The mind which created the problem it wishes to solve is not the mind that will solve the problem. Yet the creativity that mind seeks, which will provide the desired solution for whatever we wish to create, is held captive in a cage created by mind. In fact it is in a doubly locked cage.

To access the necessary depth and breadth of our creative ability and creative power for a given situation we will need two separate keys. Both keys are ultimately controlled by our mind and our belief structure and the resulting perspective we hold. That is, the keys are controlled by how and what we think and believe and why we think and believe the way we do. Hence a significant portion of the journey to release the necessary creativity is about learning to unlock the cage which mind itself has created. To access these keys, we begin by having to change our perspective. In particular, we need to adopt a creativity perspective and hold our creativity sacred.

The Main Reason for Releasing our Unlimited Creativity

The main reason for exploring the depth and breadth of our creativity to release our unlimited creativity is not about creativity as most understand creativity. It is not about getting creative ideas, creative solutions, creating things, or feeling good, although that will happen as a by product and is available through the Releasing Your Unlimited Creativity technology as an objective if that is what we wish to experience. Rather it is about accessing our inherent creativity and our creative ability and creative power at the deepest levels of being to create our experiences and the reality we experience.

Accessing are releasing our unlimited creativity is about accessing a different level of being. It is not about gaining power, money, influence and the like although that could be a by-product. In facing an issue where we need a creative solution, we have a choice. We can choose to face whatever obstacle exist to access the creativity we need to solve a particular problem. Or, we can go about reconstituting our creative ability and creative power to have available whatever we need when we need it.

It is much like the old proverb, "Give an individual a fish, they eat for a day—teach them how to fish, they eat for a life time." If we access the creativity we need to solve a particular problem is like getting a fish. Every time we have a problem we need to go the figure out how to solve it. Or, we can learn how to fish. That is, we reconstitute our creative ability and creative power. In that moment, our life becomes suddenly different. We no longer face problems where we lack creative solutions. Rather, we know what needs to be done in anyone moment. It is only a question if we want to do the work that we know needs to be done. We know how to do what needs to be done because we already have the creative answer we need. The creativity we need is always present. We do not have to look for it. It is as though we always have the answer to what needs to be done.

Accessing our unlimited creativity is about having the answer we need when we need it. In this awareness, the problems of life go away. Life is not necessary any easier. There are still things we need to face. But we now have choices and about knowing what we need to do to implement those choices. The only question is whether or not we wish to do the work to get what we choose. Fear, anxiety and the like dissipate for there is an awareness.

When we access our unlimited creativity, we know what we need to do when we need to do it. We know what serves us and the direction we need to go in life to create a life worth living. We know the truth of our being—+ and live that truth. There is a knowing about life. There is a certainty about life. The issue of fear no longer exists as something to be avoided. There is an awareness in the fear that we know how to address what gives rise to the fear and still move forward.

Living the truth of our being and the truth of our unlimited creativity is about living an alternative way. We no longer put ourselves in a box or a cage of our own making. It is about an internal knowing that all is fine exactly the way it is no matter what is happening. But it is to know what needs to be done to create an alternative way to what is occurring. A way that better serves us. It is to know an alterative way exists not out of judgment that what is occurring is wrong or bad or we are running from pain, fear and the like. Rather is about knowing an alternative way for we are the creators of our experiences and we do get to choose what we experience.

To access and live this alternative way there needs to be an understanding. An understanding about the cage of our own making in which we put our creative spirit and how we create that cage. It is an understanding about our mind, the judgments of our mind and the nature of right and wrong, pain and the gift that lies in pain, fear and the like. It is an understanding about an awareness which lies within the feelings of the body. We need to know we have an inner knowing and an inner awareness. We need to have a conscious experience of our inner knowing and learn to access it and use it in our life. We need the experience or experiences in life to have this all come together so we know the truth of it for ourselves. The Releasing Your Unlimited Creativity material is designed to assist us in gaining this understanding and provide some methods to become a conscious creator of the experiences we have to live this alternative way.

The Approach

Even when applied to a specific problem or issue, the Releasing Your Unlimited Creativity Approach keeps faith with the proverb, "Give an individual a fish, they eat for a day—teach them how to fish, and they eat for a lifetime." The approach does not only focus on helping an individual obtain a specific desire. It seeks to use the immediate desire we have as an example and as the occasion to learn how to release a sufficient portion of our creative spirit whenever it is needed. It does so in a way that we can consciously access the necessary creative ability and creative power to create whatever we desire. The Releasing Your Unlimited Creativity approach assists becoming creatively self-sufficient and creatively self-empowered. It assists and directs toward developing the ability to create the ability we need to create what we desire.

A question often asked is, "How is, or why is, the Releasing your unlimited creativity and understanding of creativity, our inherent creative ability and creative power, and the nature of Creation different than existing philosophical, esoteric, religious, spiritual, psychological, scientific, secular and similar related views of Creation and creativity?" The answer to this question is addressed in the topic, "How is, and/or why is, the Releasing Your Unlimited Creativity understanding of creativity different than others."

Each of us will, of course, have to decided if the Releasing Your Unlimited Creativity approach is for us and meets our creative needs.

Using this Material

There are a variety of applications to which the Releasing Your Unlimited Creativity understanding can be applied and a variety of ways in which it can be used. In general, there are five primary areas of use depending on what we desire to create. In order of frequency of use they are:

Free and obtain the necessary energy and a pathway to create what we desire
Create an alternative way to live life
Recreate our life
Explore the depth and breadth of our unlimited creativity
Recreate our life based on what we find in our exploration of our unlimited creativity

The material accessible through this site has been designed to be used in one of two complementary ways. One way is to follow the path as expressed in the sequential hyperlinks as applicable and noted at the bottom of each page. The second way is to explore this material our own way.

Truth in Labeling—An "up front" full Disclosure

There is an old saying. "An individual learns from their mistakes. A wise individual learns from the mistakes of others. A fool never learns." The Releasing Your Unlimited Creativity approach looks to help us become wise in our creative endeavors no matter what they may be and learn from the experience, and sometimes the mistakes, of others.

Modern society encourages truth in all labeling and/or "up-front" full disclosure on all products. It is encouraged so that the user can be aware of any hazards or side-effects to any products that are used and/or prevent false advertising. It is to help ensure the user is not deceived or advantage taken of their lack of understanding or lack of appropriate information.

Relative to our creative endeavors and/or pursuing the release of the depth and breadth of our unlimited creativity, there are several topics that fall under truth in labeling and/or up-front, full disclosure considerations. In these considerations, we can learn from the experiences and/or mistakes of others who have gone before us. exploring the world of creativity. Truth in labeling issues are found in the topic "Why truth in labeling and full disclosure."

Truth in Labeling—Disclaimer

The Releasing Your Unlimited Creativity technology can be used, and has been used, for health related issues. The Releasing Your Unlimited Creativity website, "Creating Health" provides some of the key lessons learned in creating health. However, no claim is made about the effectiveness of this technology in managing and/or dealing with your health issues The Releasing Your Unlimited Creativity is based on a different perspective than that found in the healing professions. It is based on a creativity perspective on health and the focus is quite different than a healing perspective.

The Releasing Your Unlimited Creativity technology is for our creative endeavors and creative needs. Most importantly it is for what we are willing to take direct responsibility for creating. So, as a creative tool, it can become a powerful ally for us if our creative endeavor is to create health.

However, because of the "physics" of the creation process and how we create the experiences we do, even if your creative endeavor is to create health, the Releasing Your Unlimited Creativity technology should not be used as a substitute for, or in lieu of, any traditional and/or non-traditional healing modalities, counseling or therapy for our health needs. It can be used in conjunction with such healing practices and arts if we are willing to take responsibility for our health. That is, take responsibility for what we have, or are, creating in, and with, our life, including our health, or lack of it, whether or not we understand how we are creating it.

Measures for Realizing the Creativity

Techniques and Tools

Many of the techniques and tools for creating an effective solution to a problem are described in creativity techniques and problem solving.

Creative-problem-solving techniques can be categorized as follows:

- Creativity techniques designed to shift a person's mental state into one that fosters creativity. These techniques are described in creativity techniques. One such popular technique is to take a break and relax or sleep after intensively trying to think of a solution.
- Creativity techniques designed to reframe the problem. For example, reconsidering one's goals by asking "What am I really trying to accomplish?" can lead to useful insights.
- Creativity techniques designed to increase the quantity of fresh ideas. This approach is based on the belief that a larger number of ideas increases the chances that one of them has value. Some of these techniques involve randomly selecting an idea (such as choosing a word from a list), thinking about similarities with the undesired situation, and hopefully inspiring a related idea that leads to a solution. Such techniques are described in creativity techniques.
- Creative-problem-solving techniques designed to efficiently lead to a fresh perspective that causes a solution to become obvious. This category is especially useful for solving especially challenging problems. Some of these techniques involve identifying independent dimensions that differentiate (or separate) closely associated concepts. Such techniques can overcome the mind's instinctive tendency to use "oversimplified

associative thinking" in which two related concepts are so closely associated that their differences, and independence from one another, are overlooked.

The following formalized methods and processes combine various creativity and creative-problem-solving techniques:

- TRIZ, which is also known as Theory of Inventive Problem Solving (TIPS), was developed by Genrich Altshuller and his colleagues based on examining more than 200,000 patents. This method is designed to foster the creation and development of patentable inventions, but is also useful for creating non-product solutions.

Mind mapping is a creativity technique that both reframes the situation and fosters creativity.

Brainstorming is a group activity designed to increase the quantity of fresh ideas. Getting other people involved can help increase knowledge and understanding of the problem and help participants reframe the problem. However, brainstorming seldom yields major innovations.

- Edward de Bono has published numerous books that promote an approach to creative problem solving and creative thinking called lateral thinking.
- Gerald Nadler, Professor of Industrial Engineering, University of Wisconsin, and later USC, spent over fifty years researching creative problem-solving, first producing a methodology called IDEALS, originally published in an Engineering text called Work Design, and later refining these ideas into a general set of techniques and methods called SQA/BT (Smart Questions Approach, and Breakthrough Thinking). The techniques have been generalized from the principles thus discovered into a general purpose innovative process for application in any problem domain. The process provides a very high level template of steps for disciplining both the context under which the creative process is fostered, including a highly structured analysis of the purposes for solving the problem as well as leading the innovative phase backwards from an idealized solution (thus the original name IDEALS) to a feasible one.

A frequent approach to teaching creative problem solving is to teach critical thinking in addition to creative thinking, but the effectiveness of this approach is not proven. As an alternative to separating critical and creative thinking, some creative-problem-solving techniques focus on either reducing an idea's disadvantages or extracting a flawed idea's significant advantages and incorporating those advantages into a different idea.

Creative-problem-solving tools typically consist of software or manipulatable objects (such as cards) that facilitate specific creative-problem-solving techniques

THE SIX MYTHS OF CREATIVITY

A new study will change how you generate ideas and decide who's really creative in your company.

Creativity

These days, there's hardly a mission statement that doesn't herald it, or a CEO who doesn't laud it. And yet despite all of the attention that business creativity has won over the past few years, maddeningly little is known about day-to-day innovation in the workplace. Where do breakthrough ideas come from? What kind of work environment allows them to flourish? What can leaders do to sustain the stimulants to creativity—and breakthrough the barriers?

Teresa Amabile has been grappling with those questions for nearly 30 years. Amabile, who heads the Entrepreneurial Management Unit at Harvard Business School and is the only tenured professor at a top B-school to devote her entire research program to the study of creativity, is one of the country's foremost explorers of business innovation.

Eight years ago, Amabile took her research to a daring new level. Working with a team of PhDs, graduate students, and managers from various companies, she collected nearly 12,000 daily journal entries from 238 people working on creative projects in seven companies in the consumer products, high-tech, and chemical industries. She didn't tell the study participants that she was focusing on creativity. She simply asked them, in a daily email, about their work and their work environment as they experienced it that day. She then coded the emails for creativity by looking for moments when people struggled with a problem or came up with a new idea.

"The diary study was designed to look at creativity in the wild," she says. "We wanted to crawl inside people's heads and understand the features of their work environment as well as the experiences and thought processes that lead to creative breakthroughs."

Amabile and her team are still combing through the results. But this groundbreaking study is already overturning some long-held beliefs about innovation in the workplace. In an interview with *Fast Company*, she busted six cherished myths about creativity. (If you want to quash creativity in your organization, just continue to embrace them.) Here they are:

1. Creativity Comes from Creative Types

When I give talks to managers, I often start by asking, Where in your organization do you most want creativity? Typically, they'll say R&D, marketing, and advertising. When I ask, Where do you *not* want creativity? someone will inevitably answer, "accounting." That always gets a laugh because of the negative connotations of creative accounting. But there's this common perception among managers that some people are creative, and most aren't. That's just not true. As a leader, you don't want to ghettoize creativity; you want everyone in your organization producing novel and useful ideas, including your financial people. Over the past couple of decades, there have been innovations in financial accounting that are extremely profound and entirely ethical, such as activity-based costing.

The fact is, almost all of the research in this field shows that anyone with normal intelligence is capable of doing some degree of creative work. Creativity depends on a number of things: experience, including knowledge and technical skills; talent; an ability to think in new ways; and the capacity to push through uncreative dry spells. Intrinsic motivation—people who are turned on by their work often work creatively—is especially critical. Over the past five years, organizations have paid more attention to creativity and innovation than at any other time in my career. But I believe most people aren't anywhere near to realizing their creative potential, in part because they're laboring in environments that impede intrinsic motivation. The anecdotal evidence suggests many companies still have a long way to go to remove the barriers to creativity.

2. *Money is a Creativity Motivator*

The experimental research that has been done on creativity suggests that money isn't everything. In the diary study, we asked people, "To what extent were you motivated by rewards today?" Quite often they'd say that the question isn't relevant—that they don't think about pay on a day-to-day basis. And the handful of people who were spending a lot of time wondering about their bonuses were doing very little creative thinking.

Bonuses and pay-for-performance plans can even be problematic when people believe that every move they make is going to affect their compensation. In those situations, people tend to get risk averse. Of course, people need to feel that they're being compensated fairly. But our research shows that people put far more value on a work environment where creativity is supported, valued, and recognized. People want the opportunity to deeply engage in their work and make real progress. So it's critical for leaders to match people to projects not only on the basis of their experience but also in terms of where their interests lie. People are most creative when they care about their work and they're stretching their skills. If the challenge is far beyond their skill level, they tend to get frustrated; if it's far below their skill level, they tend to get bored. Leaders need to strike the right balance.

3. *Time Pressure Fuels Creativity*

In our diary study, people often thought they were most creative when they were working under severe deadline pressure. But the 12,000 aggregate days that we studied showed just the opposite: People were the least creative when they were fighting the clock. In fact, we found a kind of time-pressure hangover—when people were working under great pressure, their creativity went down not only on that day but the next two days as well. Time pressure stifles creativity because people can't deeply engage with the problem. Creativity requires an incubation period; people need time to soak in a problem and let the ideas bubble up.

In fact, it's not so much the deadline that's the problem; it's the distractions that rob people of the time to make that creative breakthrough. People can certainly be creative when they're under the gun, but only when they're able to focus on the work. They must be protected from distractions, and they must know that the work is important and that everyone is committed to it. In too many organizations, people don't understand the reason for the urgency, other than the fact that somebody somewhere needs it done today.

4. *Fear Forces Breakthroughs*

There's this widespread notion that fear and sadness somehow spur creativity. There's even some psychological literature suggesting that the incidence of depression is higher in creative writers and artists—the de-pressed geniuses who are incredibly original in their thinking. But we don't see it in the population that we studied.

We coded all 12,000 journal entries for the degree of fear, anxiety, sadness, anger, joy, and love that people were experiencing on a given day. And we found that creativity is positively associated with joy and love and negatively associated with anger, fear, and anxiety. The entries show that people are happiest when they come up with a creative idea, but they're more likely to have a breakthrough if they were happy the day before. There's a kind of virtuous cycle. When people are excited about their work, there's a better chance that they'll make a cognitive association that incubates overnight and shows up as a creative idea the next day. One day's happiness often predicts the next day's creativity.

5. Competition Beats Collaboration

There's a widespread belief, particularly in the finance and high-tech industries, that internal competition fosters innovation. In our surveys, we found that creativity takes a hit when people in a work group compete instead of collaborate. The most creative teams are those that have the confidence to share and debate ideas. But when people compete for recognition, they stop sharing information. And that's destructive because nobody in an organization has all of the information required to put all the pieces of the puzzle together.

6. A Streamlined Organization is a Creative Organization

Maybe it's only the public-relations departments that believe downsizing and restructuring actually foster creativity. Unfortunately, I've seen too many examples of this kind of spin. One of my favorites is a 1994 letter to shareholders from a major U.S. software company: "A downsizing such as this one is always difficult for employees, but out of tough times can come strength, creativity, and teamwork."

Of course, the opposite is true: Creativity suffers greatly during a downsizing. But it's even worse than many of us realized. We studied a 6,000-person division in a global electronics company during the entire course of a 25% downsizing, which took an incredibly agonizing 18 months. Every single one of the stimulants to creativity in the work environment went down significantly. Anticipation of the downsizing was even worse than the downsizing itself—people's fear of the unknown led them to basically disengage from the work. More troubling was the fact that even five months after the downsizing, creativity was still down significantly.

Unfortunately, downsizing will remain a fact of life, which means that leaders need to focus on the things that get hit. Communication and collaboration decline significantly. So too does people's sense of freedom and autonomy. Leaders will have to work hard and fast to stabilize the work environment so ideas can flourish.

Taken together, these operating principles for fostering creativity in the workplace might lead you to think that I'm advocating a soft management style. Not true. I'm pushing for a smart management style. My 30 years of research and these 12,000 journal entries suggest that when people are doing work that they love and they're allowed to deeply engage in it—and when the work itself is valued and recognized—then creativity will flourish. Even in tough times.

According to most dictionaries, creativity is the ability to create. However, creativity cannot be defined. It is more than just a definition. It is an idea, a process, a thought, a state of mind. One cannot learn to be creative because creativity is innate and unique to each individual. Creativity can, however, be tapped into or released by discovery.

Creativity is sometimes hindered. This could be because the artist lacks self-confidence or self-esteem. It could also be because their creativity has not yet been discovered or acknowledged. Some people need encouragement to help release their creativity. There are quite a few ways to release it.

One way to release creativity would be to look for muses and inspiration. Looking at the world and admiring the differences in people and places helps. Creativity can be drawn from their beauty.

Creativity can also be discovered through the senses. A person can touch, taste, smell, hear, and see hundreds of different objects. Aromas from foods, textures of blankets, and sight of unusual objects can all give inspiration.

Many people are too concerned with how things should look. The focus should be on how it actually looks in the raw, to the human eye. Colors and shapes can be distorted by the mere fact that people want others to see it for what it is. It's more difficult for someone to let go of all that and just let their creativity flow, unhindered.

Another way to get the creativity flowing is to research what other artists have done or are currently doing. Their cultures and biographies alone can be an inspiration. Examining their works can help some appreciate artistic expression. New techniques can even be drawn from their works. Although some people are inspired in this way, the creativity still lies within them.

Some people are even inspired by everyday events. It's as easy as reading the newspaper or watching the news. Some can take other people's situations and describe how it makes them feel. That is a way to release creativity. Controversial issues, such as war or abortion can inspire writings, like poems. They can be used to express death, loss, tragedy, or devastation. General topics such as religion or politics can branch-off into many directions, sending creativity into overdrive.

Creativity is not always expressed by painting, drawings, or writings. It is most often expressed by one's actions. Romance, for example, is a form of creativity. Love and emotion are inspired by one person for another. Taking something inside and then putting it back out into the world as another thing is the very core of creativity. Knowing and loving someone so much that there is a need to express it is a very natural form of creativity.

Another form of creativity is talking. Some people are more blessed in this area than in more obvious ones, such as painting or drawing. They paint a "word picture". Speeches can flow with new ideas and thoughts. It can encompass all of one's being and transform it into either simple or complicated words.

One thing to remember is that creativity doesn't equal success. It equals expression. So, if at first the goal that is aimed for is not achieved, there is no need for worry or frustration. Creativity is not about reaching a goal or being a perfectionist. It's about being, feeling, and taking all that is inside and letting it out in one way or another.

Inspiration is vital to creativity. Even if it's only a slight feeling or thought that inspires. Creativity can be released each time attempts are made to use the body as an outlet. Remember that creativity is not an art form, but that it forms art.

THEORIES OF CREATIVITY

What makes some people more creative than others? Is it because they are raised in creativity-enhancing environments where they are encouraged to express their creativity by parents who themselves are creative? Then again, are creative people simply born that way? Is creativity part of their genetic makeup, inscribed in their DNA code, and, therefore, as inherent as eye color and shape of one's nose? In other words, is creativity the result of nurture or nature? Both? Or is creativity the result of something else entirely?

These are questions that psychologists and psychiatrists have been pondering and trying to answer for years, and through extensive studies, they have developed five major theories, each of attempts to explain the creative personality.

1. The Psychoanalytical Theory of Creativity

The main proponents of this theory include Freud, Jung, Kris, Rank, Adler, and Hammer; and the general argument is that people become creative in reaction to difficult circumstances or repressed emotions. For example, as Freud maintained, people repress memories of traumatic episodes or events, and the emotions related to these events are released through creative outlets.

The theory also argues the following:

- People are able to demonstrate creativity when they link the personal unconscious with the collective conscious.
- Regression precedes creativity.
- Feelings of inferiority contribute to creativity.

Arguably, however, other theorists maintain that the psychoanalytic theory lacks credence because it fails to take into consideration that people are both biological and social beings.

2. The Mental Illness Theory of Creativity

The proponents of this theory include Briggs, Eisenman, Goodwin, Jamison, Richards, and Martindale; and the major tenet is that some type of mental illness is actually necessary in order for people to be creative, even if that illness is exceptionally mild.

Studies have shown that the mental disorders most frequently associated with increased creativity are bipolar and manic-depressive syndromes, where sufferers undergo extreme mood swings that perhaps contribute to enhanced creative expression.

Of course, it's interesting to note that many other theorists argue that mental illness actually interferes with and even prevents creativity and while, granted, some highly creative individuals do suffer from some form of mental disorder, the majority of highly creative individuals do not suffer from any form of mental disorder at all.

3. Eysenck's Theory of Psychoticism

The main proponent of this theory was the late Hans Eysenck, who argued that highly creative individuals possessed a quality termed "psychoticism"—a disposition for psychotic tendencies. Eysenck also maintained that these psychotic tendencies were the foundation for creative personalities, and he developed a word-association test to measure a person's psychoticism, with results correlated to form a continuum, ranging from psychotic through average and from conventional to highly social to altruistic.

Other theorists, however, for example, Rothenburg, disagreed with Eysenck and argued that his theory relied too heavily upon the results of the test he himself developed and, more seriously, that Eysenck had designed the test specifically to support his theory, which invalidated the results.

4. The Addiction Theory of Creativity

The main proponents of this theory are Lapp, Collins, Izzo, Norlander, Gustafson, and Wallas; and its major tenet is that addiction, for example, to drugs and/or alcohol, contributes to and even causes creativity.

This theory, however, is not largely supported by the mainstream research community, but instead by independent researchers, as well as by some creative personalities who themselves suffer from addiction problems. In fact, Lapp, Collins, and Izzo conducted a placebo study with 114 male volunteers, giving half tonic water and half vodka, and found that the amount of alcohol consumed did not increase a person's creativity. (Dacey & Lennon, 1998)

On the other hand, it is interesting to note that the members of the study who simply *thought* they were intoxicated were the most creative of the entire group; and, in brief, although theorists have found there is often a correlation between addictive behavior and creativity, studies have not supported the argument that addiction either causes or contributes to creativity. (Dacey & Lennon, 1998)

5. The Humanistic Theory of Creativity

The main supporters of this theory include Maslow, Rogers, and Fromm, though the theory is based mainly upon *Maslow's Hierarchy of Needs,* a theory he developed, which maintains that humans have six basic needs that must be met in order for them to thrive and reach maximum potential.

People's lower needs, however, must be met in order for them to progress to the next highest level, and only upon reaching the uppermost level, self-actualization, where needs are related to purpose and identify, are they at last free enough and comfortable enough to express themselves creatively.

The supporters of this theory argue that environment is unimportant because even the most difficult of environments cannot hinder creativity if someone possesses the ability to self-actualize and, thus, obtain the highest level, where he or she can choose to be creative. In other words, people decide for themselves whether or not they will be creative.

It's interesting to note that the Humanistic Theory is the one theory with which few people find fault, perhaps because it makes perfect sense that a person cannot concentrate upon creative endeavors unless his or her most basic and primal needs have first been met. (Harman & Rheingold, 1994)

In conclusion, debate over what exactly makes one person more creative than another continues and most likely will continue for years to come because while there are many plausible hypotheses, there are yet no definitive answers and possibly never will be to explain the enigma known as the creative personality.

The Creative Environment

Innovation & Creativity in Organizations Introduction: Innovation is the spark that makes good companies great. It's not just invention but also a style of corporate behavior comfortable with new ideas and risk. Companies that know how to innovate don't necessarily throw money into R.& D. Instead they cultivate a new style of corporate behavior that is comfortable with new ideas, change, risk and even failure, according to "Americas most Admired Companies," fortune, March 3, 1997. Joseph V. Anderson has defined creativity as "nothing more than going beyond the current boundaries, whether those are boundaries of technology, knowledge, current practices, social norms, or beliefs. Creativity is nothing more than seeing and acting on new relationships thereby bringing them to life. While there are many definitions of innovation, it is defined here very simply: using creativity to add value. Value can be economic, social, psychological, or aesthetic. Creativity is not a personality trait available to only a few. Research has shown everyone has some creativity, but it has been stifled by Freud's thinking that artistry and creativity are associated with mental illness and the scientific emphasis on materialism and analytical thinking.

There are 120 different, special, and measurable aspects of creative thinking which particularly distinguish humans from other species. These wide-ranging creative faculties have been, and continue to be, critical to mankind's ability to adapt to changing situations, environments, and systems. Extensive studies of creative thinking have firmly established that individuals exhibiting higher than average scores in creative thinking also exhibit higher than average scores in areas of mental emotional health course of instruction is applied imagination produce significant gains in personality traits such as confidence, self-reliance, persuasiveness, initiative, and persuasiveness, initiative, and leadership. The challenge is to create an environment that will bring out the creativity of everyone and make those who have demonstrated creativity even more creative. The social can most definitely affect intrinsic motivation. A study has identified six factors of environmental stimulants to creativity (freedom, positive challenge, supervisory encouragement, work group supports, organizational encouragement and sufficient resources) and two environmental obstacles to creativity (organizational roadblocks and excessive workload pressure). A creative environment requires more than providing intrinsic rewards. It requires rethinking organizational designs. We have made organizations fit Newtonian mechanical models by putting responsibilities into functions and people into roles with boundaries and a secure sense of control. The Newtonian model of the world is characterized by reductionism, determinism, predictability, equilibrium, and control. The new model challenges us to accept that organizations are fluid, chaotic, and subject to unseen fields of energy, present concepts of leadership must change. Gone is the heretical model with the person at the top controlling everyone by holding all information? No one person possesses all of the knowledge or skills to control a fluid, rapidly evolving system. Leading gives way to facilitating relationships in a system where knowledge and skill are networked.

Leadership in the new organization consists of facilitating shared values. This facilitatorship must take place in an environment that has relationships that freely share ownership, information, and ideas. Facilitation and sharing are basic to creative problem-solving. Creative problem-solving is needed to transform an organization into a continuously innovative one. The steps to integrate creativity into a decisive decision involves many steps. Listed in order of development:

1. Vision
2. Goals
3. Situation analysis
4. Macro
5. Micro
6. Opportunities, problems, causes
7. Alternative—Solutions
8. Resources required
9. Evaluation of alternatives
10. Selection
11. Action plan
12. Implementation
13. Measure results

Taking innovation one-step further the Osborn-Parnes model stresses four critical rules that must apply to each stage: Withholding judgment, freewheeling, generating a quantity of ideas, and hitchhiking on the ideas of other.

Judging more than any other event will shut down idea generation. Judging is a psychological threat. Unfortunately, our culture has taught us that large doses of judgment are perquisites for extrinsic rewards. Hitchhiking creates ideas that combine the best ideas of everyone on the team. It can also help during implementation if all members see a piece of their idea in the final solution. Creating an environment that is tolerant of mistakes is difficult. It must be made clear that mistakes are acceptable if they are based on solid thinking, enhance learning of what will not work, and are caught early before damage is severe. There must be support for the people who were on the team of the project that failed. The Kirton Adapter-Innovator (KAI) inventory measures preferred styles for problem-solving. The adaptor prefers to be creative within the present system. The innovator wants to create new definitions of the problem and new systems. Thus, both types are creative, but their styles are different. Adapters include bank managers, accountants, production managers, and programmers. Innovators include persons in marketing, finance, and fashion buyers. Thomas Edison had all the characteristics of a risk taker innovator. He was a divergent thinker, making observations about the natural world. He was not afraid of failure. The lessons learned in one of his failures led to success in another project. In addition to the light bulb, his 1,093 patents included familiar ones such as the microphone & batteries.

Creative leadership must facilitate positive relationships in organizations to produce profitable growth through innovation. We now know that creativity is not a personality trait that is available for geniuses. Everyone has unique knowledge and experiences that can be tapped, given the proper environment. This environment must be free flowing and non-judging to take people through the mental block they learned in early childhood. These blocks are associated with the risk of being wrong. The motivation for innovating comes largely from the joy of doing something that has never been done before. It is like going on an expedition and risking everything to be the first person to climb a mountain or sail around the world. It taps the same drive that exists within a composer or an artist who wishes to create something forever. What seems to stop the flow of creativity and innovations within organizations? We've all experienced meetings where we've asked our staffs for their thoughts and ideas. We needed their creativity, innovation, and insight to resolve problems or to take advantage of opportunities. Their response or lack thereof, was very discouraging. We ask ourselves why does this happen? Many factors come into play. Fear. This discourages idea sharing. No one likes to look stupid in front of peers. Ideas are very personal. Presenting an idea in public puts the ideas creator in a glaring spotlight. When we were young, we became conditioned. The humiliation we experienced when we gave the "wrong" answer to the teacher's question in front of all of our classmates. The fear of public humiliation is enough to keep the most innovative person quiet.

Self-assessment. Before we will ever state an idea out long, we play it over and over in our heads. We look for different ways to discredit our own ideas, and weeventually discard the thought. Too often, we believe we have nothing of merit to provide because we didn't work directly within an issue or in a specific area. We tend to keep our thought to ourselves if they pertain to areas we are unfamiliar with. Not my problem. You stay in your turf and I'll stay in mine. If you want other people to stay out of your business, then you had better stay out of theirs. On one hand, the silence could be an issue of reciprocating turf protection. Then again, it could simply be motivated by slightly tilted dedication to common courtesy. If the problem isn't directly with the scope of our assigned duties and responsibilities, we might hold back. When the hope that our colleagues will do the same down the road when something comes up in our area. The remedies to these situations are really quite simple. The first thing you and your managers must do is to keep solicit ting ideas. Never stop asking what your staff are thinking, what opportunities they see that you and others might have missed. Give them a safe environment for sharing. No boundaries. All ideas are good ideas. It's simply a matter of some ideas being more doable then others. It's extremely important to your staff's development to be continually challenged by what they do. Boredom and routine kill creative thinking and problem-solving. The mind, like other muscles, needs to be exercised regularly. The work we once did with our hands is done increasingly in our heads. The United States is transitioning into an idea economy where innovation is replacing industrialization, and creativity is the key to selling products and services eventually discard the thought. Too often, we believe we have nothing of merit to provide because we didn't work directly within an issue or in a specific area. We tend to keep our thought to ourselves if they pertain to areas we are unfamiliar with. Not my problem. You stay in your turf and I'll stay in mine. If you want other people to stay out of your business, then you had better stay out of theirs. On one hand, the silence could be an issue of reciprocating turf protection. Then again, it could simply be motivated by slightly tilted dedication to common courtesy. If the problem isn't directly with the scope of our assigned duties and responsibilities, we might hold back. When the hope that our colleagues will do the same down the road when something comes up in our area. The remedies to these situations are really quite simple. The first thing you and your managers must do is to keep solicit ting ideas. Never stop asking what your staff are thinking, what opportunities they see that you and others might have missed. Give them a safe environment for sharing. No boundaries. All ideas are good ideas. It's simply a matter of some ideas being more doable then others. It's extremely important to your staff's development to be continually challenged by what they do. Boredom and routine kill creative thinking and problem solving. The mind, like other muscles, needs to be exercised regularly. The work we once did with our hands is done increasingly in our heads. The United States is transitioning into an idea economy where innovation is replacing industrialization, and creativity is the key to selling products and services.

Employees with a creative side are leading the way into the idea economy. About 38 million workers, roughly 30 percent of the work force are employed in creative professions, and the numbers keep growing. Today, highly skilled workers see themselves as artists who need space to think and create. Heavy-handed management just gets in the way of the creative process. To manage the creative enterprise is as much as art as science. Creative people are driven by exciting work more than by a paycheck, and they need to express themselves through their work. A mind set foreign to many employers. To manage creative people, feedback is important because creative employees are more emotionally involved with their work. The brainstorming and planning process is the desirable process for a creative mind. A manager should articulate the vision and goals to the creative employee and then let him go and create. It is important not to over manage. Creative people are not the best time managers. Time management is not their strong suit. Therefore a manager must set perimeters from the beginning of the project. A manager should also be flexible with scheduling because creativity and innovative employees need to get away from the four walls to come up with new ideas. They need time to go somewhere they can get inspired and be creative, because that is what they are being paid for. On a larger perspective, for a nation, to be healthy and creative it must have the ability to renew itself constantly. This applies to companies, organizations and governments.

Innovation is risky not just for the individual but especially for large companies. Studies show that the probability of economic success from innovation is between 20% and 30%. It takes guts to live with risk, get creative and innovate! As a 20% to 30% success rate, it becomes necessary to improve the chances of success. Leadership is of course the first key to success. Successful innovation requires a clear vision defined by the leadership of the organization as well as the creation of an environment where this vision can be shared by colleagues. This combination of vision and environment is called strategic context. Organizations rely on it to harness their creativity. Without a clear strategic context, creativity may blossom, but it will be misplaced. Strategic context gives purpose and direction, benchmarks and role models. It shows the way ahead. The second key to success is to learn how to manage risk. This means that senior and junior players in an organization act as innovators and entrepreneurs, and that they can inspire others to do the same. Taking risks is not just about jumping in foolishly, but assessing in a cool and rational way what the risks are and preparing for them. Innovation inevitably starts with creativity. Many of us have some creativity and it is the organizations role to provide an environment where we dare to be creative. Innovation is essentially an "enterprise of enterprise": it is a risky effort that must be borne by the whole organization. In order to implement innovation the whole organization has to take ownership of it.

Once innovation is in place then comes implementation. Edison once said that success is 2% inspiration and 98% perspiration. The best ideas can get lost in beau racy as well as in weighty details. This way, under situations of high uncertainty, project management is so vital. Managing the unknowable requires astute knowledge management, as well as being flexible and so on. Time is also a valuable resource and, to be innovative, speed in implementation must move along in a timely manner without compromising quality. A last key to insure success is marketing. In a competitive world where complete originality and genius are rare, good marketing is the innovators most important key to insure success.

Case Study: Home Depot—Motivating their workforce "The greatness of our company is the sum of the actions of our people," said Annettee Verschuren, President of the Home Depot. Every retailer knows that motivated and passionate store level employees are the key to ensuring customer satisfaction and financial success. Home Depot has to be considered one of retailing's great companies because of the financial success the company has achieved. Verschuren said that when she became president of the Home Depot in 1996 there were only 19 stores doing approximately $1 billion in annual sales. Now annual sales are approximately $ 4 billion.

Home Depot's success has mirrored its success in the United States. In 1997, Home Depot's total sales were $24.2 billion and by the end of last year, they had increased to $53.6 billion. Verschuren said that to get there will require the addition of $40,000 new employees each year, all of which also have to be highly motivated and passionate about the business. "You have to make your full team business partners with you. They are your competitive advantage", Verschuren said. "Take care of your people and they will take care of your company. Verschuren highlighted six areas that are essential for ensuring a culture of performance. There has to be an emotional appeal so that the employers feel good about the company. "Verschuren adds that many of our most successful hires are customers that have fallen in love with the company. There also must be a high level of trust in the products and services that are being sold. Management must have vision and leadership and the workplace environment has to be favorable. Home Depot offers part-time employees health care benefits and a bonus program. They work very hard to ensure that each store is a positive workplace environment. Recommendations & Analysis: As a CEO of a large organization, I strive continually to insure an environment that instills psychological safety for my staff.

Present in my view, is the reality that without fresh new ideas on a continual basis, innovation and growth are thwarted. My company cannot afford to hit a stagnate growth cycle. To provide the right environment a leader must be perceived as trustworthy. A leader's job is to work very hard to capture the trust and respect of his followers and staff. If a staff member feels intimidated and/or fearful they will just perform there job. Worse yet, they will not enjoy the job that they are performing. This is unacceptable to me as a CEO. The working environment must and should be a whole, balanced life perspective. As the organization that I lead adopts a balanced life perspective and philosophy, we embrace the attitude that the employee has needs and interests outside of the work force. With this in mind, the organization has a more relaxed attitude integrating a more flexible work schedule. As the employees work schedule is more conducive to their lifestyle, they can feel more relaxed and cared for as a whole. With the interest of the employer evident as a strong support mechanism the employee is free to be free from the constraints of legalism as well as fear, thereby, releasing the creative and innovative resources that innovators possess. My analysis consists of observing various organizations that have a very structured work environment. My observation lends me the freedom to assess that most of those systems are archaic and outdated. The baby boomers of the past are reaching retirement age and their work style is outdated.

The style for our current workforce is obviously teamwork, stressing cooperative brainstorming. The idea is that as a "whole" the group will produce better thinking and solve problems more rapidly with overall agreement and buy-in. The concept that I referred to earlier as piggybacking is very similar to this team approach. One idea generates to another and then another. Some in the field of leadership call this synergy. Solutions, new concepts as well as incredible innovative ideas come shining through as the group processes ideas back and forth. I believe whole-heartedly that the workforce other than a compliance agency should adopt this new and very successful way of operating. To further my point is to analysis the current level of employees that work from within their homes. This is a very cost effective way for employers to operate their operations. The new technology allows for accountability with each employee even though they are working from their home office. The virtual network interacts with all employees as they are tapped into the company's network. Each can share information and with e-mails exchange ideas without every having to have a face-to-face. My idea is that without the face-to-face employees are more comfortable to release some of their precious and very profitable ideas. Ten years ago, the technology was not in place to provide this type of working environment. How wonderful it is to have advanced to this point. Virtually, global companies exist without having bricks and mortar buildings, but have blossomed into multi-million dollar organizations.

Times are ever changing and change is inevitable. To not see and catch this wave as a CEO of an organization would be very sad for the organization that they lead.

Yes, it does mean letting go of some control but what the CEO obtains in doing so is more innovation, creativity, profitability and a happier workforce. Not a bad exchange if the company can weather the change

Environmental Stimulants to Creativity

1. Freedom in deciding what to do or how to accomplish the task
2. A good manager, enthusiastic, good communications skills, protects team from distractions and interference, matches tasks to skills and interests, sets a clear direction without micromanaging
3. Access to necessary resources - facilities, equipment, information, funds, people
4. Encouragement, enthusiasm for new ideas, atmosphere free of threatening evaluation
5. Organizational characteristics such as a formal mechanism for considering new ideas, climate marked by cooperation and collaboration across levels and divisions, atmosphere where innovation is prized and failure is not fatal
6. Recognition for creative work in the form of feedback, recognition and reward
7. Time to think creatively, explore different characteristics
8. Challenge, a sense of having interesting and important work to do, internalized by employees as personal challenges
9. Pressure arising from competition with other units, or a desire to do something important

There is also a list of environmental obstacles to creativity, although these are mostly the opposites of the stimulants, with a slightly different order. For example, the organizational characteristics are #5 for stimulants but #1 for obstacles. Intriguing, but I don't know what to make of the difference in order.

These nine characteristics agree well, I think, with the six characteristics in *Corporate Creativity.*

On the basis of this list, Amabile and co-workers developed a questionnaire for assessing workplace creativity called KEYS.

Amabile's in his book in Chapter 8 also has a summary of general social influences of creativity, by one of the best-known creativity researchers, Dean Keith Simonton. Simonton studied famous or eminent creative artists from previous ages. (Fame and eminence, as Amabile notes, may not be the best indicators of creativity, but may be sufficient for Simonton's study.) He carried out exhaustive analyses of each subject's activity, for example rating the unusualness of a composer's themes or motifs by cataloging each pair of successive notes, and then statistically finding out how often that pair was used for all of the composers. Similarly, for each creator that he studied, the output for each five-year period of the creator's life was calculated. Simonton did several such studies, for example ten classical composers, 127 generations of European creators, 12,761 important discoveries, 301 people rated as geniuses in a sample produced by Cox, etc. Many of these samples were the subject of individual studies by Simonton. In his own 1978 summary of this work, Simonton listed his main conclusions. These conclusions are summarized here, on the basis of Amabile's presentations:

- Social reinforcements such as honors, prizes and awards have no effect on creativity.
- Having contemporary creative competitors decreases the number of themes a composer produces.
- Discursive creativity (science, philosophy, literature and music) increases with the availability of more role models from the previous two generations, but decreases with the number of contemporary role models.
- The father's professional status has no effect on the fame of a creative genius
- Creativity in general increases with the amount of political fragmentation in the immediate past
- Political instability and was can have negative effects on creativity, but this will be positive if the disturbances are far away
- Poetry is produced at a younger age than prose
- The number of themes produced by a composer in each five year period increases with age, but then decreases after a certain point, although not to the lower levels of the younger years (inverted backwards J function)
- Famousness or eminence increases with increasing age, then decreases all the way after a certain period (inverted U function)
- Eminence or famousness for creators increases with the amount of formal education, then peaks and decreases after a certain point (inverted U function)
- The amount of versatility shown by a creator increases with the amount of formal education, with no decreases seen.
- Later creativity increases with the amount of childhood creativity (preciousness) shown
- The number of themes produced by a composer decreases in the presence of physical illness
- Biographical stress, such as the death of a spouse or close relative, does not affect the number of works produced by a composer, but does increase the originality of musical themes

Brainstorming and Creativity

Is your organization having problems coming up with ideas for activities? Try brainstorming creative ideas as individuals, as a group, or both. There are many different ways to brainstorm. Give the members a general idea of what is being brainstormed. Pull a word randomly out of the dictionary and use that word as a basis for ideas. No matter how you do it, your organization can be left with a lot of great ideas at the end of a brainstorming session. Just remember to follow a few important rules:

There should be one person who facilitates the brainstorming session to make sure that everyone participates and keeps focused.

Ideas must not be criticized or evaluated during the session.

Expand on other people's ideas.

Have fun with the ideas you come up with.

Keep a record of all of the ideas from the brainstorming session. These will help you with the evaluation process.

Creativity is not a gift; it is a state of being. Everyone has creative potential. Pull in the creative members of your organization and delegate the jobs requiring creativity to them. While they are doing these jobs, however, have them work with the not-so-creative members so they can be creative too. You can find great ideas on how to run meetings, prepare agendas, plan and promote activities, etc.

Creative thinking requires tools such as the brainstorm and the affinity diagram. Brainstorming is simply listing all ideas put forth by a group in response to a given problem or question. In 1939, a team led by advertising executive Alex Osborn coined the term "brainstorm". According to Osborn, "Brainstorm means using the brain to storm a creative problem and to do so "in commando fashion, each stormer audaciously attacking the same objective." Creativity is encouraged by not allowing ideas to be evaluated or discussed until everyone has run dry. Any and all ideas are considered legitimate and often the most far-fetched are the most fertile. Structured brainstorming produces numerous creative ideas about any given "central question". Done right, it taps the human brain's capacity for lateral thinking and free association.

Brainstorms help answer specific questions such as:

What opportunities face us this year?
What factors are constraining performance in Department X?
What could be causing problem Y?
What can we do to solve problem Z?
However, a brainstorm cannot help you positively identify causes of problems, rank ideas in a meaningful order, select important ideas, or check solutions.

To conduct a successful brainstorm:

Make sure everyone understands and is satisfied with the central question before you open up for ideas.
You may want to give everyone a few seconds to jot down a few ideas before getting started.
Begin by going around the table or room, giving everyone a chance to voice their ideas or pass. After a few rounds, open the floor.
More ideas are better. Encourage radical ideas and piggybacking.
Suspend judgment of all ideas.
Record exactly what is said. Clarify only after everyone is out of ideas.
Don't stop until ideas become sparse. Allow for late-coming ideas.
Eliminate duplicates and ideas that aren't relevant to the topic.

A brainstorm starts with a clear question, and ends with a raw list of ideas. That's what it does well - give you a raw list of ideas. Some will be good, and some won't. But, if you try to analyze ideas in the brainstorming session, you will ruin the session. Wait. Later, you can analyze the results of a brainstorm with other quality improvement tools. In particular, affinity diagramming is designed to sort a raw list, using "gut feel" to begin to categorize the raw ideas. It is most often the next step beyond brainstorming.

CREATIVE ORGANIZATION

Stop thinking of the creative spirit as a gift from God. You can get some down here on earth by following the four Ps.

A 2010 study of 1,500 chief executives conducted by IBM's (IBM) Institute for Business Value identified creativity as the :

No. 1 leadership competency of the future: This paints a broad role for creativity in the business world in spurring economic growth. Creative solutions are needed for organizations to thrive, but how can business leaders deliberately increase creativity? Allow us to introduce the four Ps of Creativity, a holistic model for looking at creativity that leverages People, Products, Process, and Press to build creative competency, develop radically innovative solutions, and increase revenue.

Strategy No. 1 People: Form diverse teams adept at ideating, clarifying, developing, and implementing. The Greek philosopher Plato believed people were born creative, but prevailing scientific research today refutes this theory. We now understand the question is not, "Are you creative?" but "How are you creative?" You can determine someone's level of creativity by identifying preference for the critical creative problem-solving skills of ideation (thinking up ideas), clarification (asking questions), developing (building solutions), and implementing (getting things done). Each individual is naturally inclined to enjoy one or a combination of these creative problem-solving skills, but no one is proficient at all. While some believe "big idea" folks are the most important to creativity, this is a myth. Innovation isn't an individual sport, but rather a team effort. Take James Cameron's 2009 release of the ground-breaking movie Avatar. A roll through the credits shows the great number of people with preferences for ideation, clarification, developing, and implementing it took to create the most significant 3D release of its time. To boost organizational creativity, business leaders need to understand how individuals are creative and build cross-functional teams staffed with diverse thinking styles. When work activities are aligned with individuals' preferences, they can perform at their best.

Strategy No. 2 Process: Implement the right creative process. To create radically innovative products or services, organizations need the right creative process. One of the most widely accepted creative processes is the Osborne-Parnes Creative Problem Solving Process (CPS). Business leaders can draw on the CPS framework to build an approach that works for their organizations. And they can do so backed by the confidence of five decades of longitudinal research proving CPS is both valid and reliable in building creative thinking skills in a multitude of business, educational, government, service-oriented, product-oriented, for-profit, and not-for-profit environments worldwide.

Strategy No. 3 Products: Leverage customer insights to stimulate radical innovation. Products are the lifeblood of organizations. When thinking about creative products that can transform industries, organizations, and our personal lives, it is important to understand the perspective of consumers. Reinventing the customer relationship and customer intimacy are top-of-mind among business leaders worldwide. A simple formula for building mutual value-creating relationships with consumers leverages dialogue, data, and insights. Some opportune ways for business leaders to learn about consumers include: Observing and connecting with consumers in their natural environments to learn how they think, feel, and act Mapping consumer insights into the decision-making and buying process Listening and interacting with consumers through social media channels Leveraging the data learned about consumers from various channels to create dialogue Inviting consumers to co-create products, services, and offerings By implementing consumer-centric practices, business leaders can spur radical innovation, unleash consumer potential, and realize their far-reaching business strategies.

Strategy No. 4 Press (an industry term for "organizational climate"): Create a culture of creativity. Dr. Theresa Amabile, a creativity scholar who studies the effect of an organization's climate on creativity, developed a model for determining key dimensions that either promote or inhibit creativity in organizations. Her research identified six stimulants and two obstacles to creativity.

Six Stimulants That Promote Creativity in Organizations Organizational Encouragement.

Employee Encourage in Organization - An organizational culture that encourages creativity through the fair, constructive judgment of ideas, reward, and recognition for creative work, mechanisms for developing new ideas, an active flow of ideas, and a shared vision of what the organization is trying to do.

Supervisory Encouragement. A supervisor who serves as a good work model, sets goals appropriately, supports the work group, values individual contributions, and shows confidence in the work group.

Supportive Work Groups. A diversely skilled work group in which people communicate well, are open to new ideas, constructively challenge each other's work, trust and help each other, and feel committed to the work they are doing.

Freedom. Freedom in deciding what work to do or how to do it; a sense of control over one's work.

Sufficient Resources. Access to appropriate resources, including funds, materials, facilities, and information.

Challenging Work. A sense of having to work hard on challenging tasks and important projects.

Two Obstacles to Creativity in Organizations.

Organizational Impediments. An organizational culture that impedes creativity through internal political problems, harsh criticism of new ideas, destructive internal competition, avoidance of risk, and an overemphasis on the *status quo*.

Workload Pressure. Extreme time pressures, unrealistic expectations for productivity, and distractions from creative work. Given these findings, the best way to build a climate for creativity is to identify how your company stacks up against the six stimulants and two obstacles, then address areas of opportunity in order to affect the dimension positively and affect creativity deliberately. Scholars have identified creativity as a complex interdisciplinary construct influenced by a combination of personality (people), outputs (products), sequence of tasks (process), and environmental setting (press). Intentional creativity is achievable by understanding and mastering these four Ps. Using the framework above, business leaders can master creativity, launch radically innovative products, and ignite economic growth.

Why are some organizations consistently good at innovating and/or adapting while others seem to be blindsided by change? Is it because of their disciplined innovation process or the knowledge and skills of their people? Or is it their determination to build a culture where challenging assumptions is not only encouraged, but expected? Our IBM Creative Leadership Study found that leaders who embrace the dynamic tension between creative disruption and operational efficiency can create new models of extraordinary value.

What, specifically, enables leading-edge organizations to capitalize on the inherent complexity in today's environment and catalyze innovation within their business models, products and services? According to the IBM 2010 Global CEO Study, the ability to embody creative leadership is among the most important attributes for capitalizing on complexity. And of the 700 CHROs throughout the world interviewed for the 2010 IBM Global Chief Human Resource Officer Study, 69 percent told us they are not effective in developing future leaders. What's more, 78 percent of HR executives said they are not effective in fostering collaboration and knowledge sharing.

Our IBM Creative Leadership Study found that to succeed in an increasingly interconnected world, creative leaders avoid choosing between unacceptable alternatives. Instead, they use the power inherent in these dualities to invent new assumptions and create new models geared to an ever-changing world.

Creative leadership in action enables a wide range of product, process and business model innovations. Organizations will need to act upon three imperatives to accelerate the development of creative capital:

- **Uncover the key capabilities of the creative organization**—Empower the organization's ability to understand how the world behaves. Expose those individuals who see opportunities where others do not and map out what is found. Connect ideas and people in novel ways. Try many and various ideas. Inspire belief that action is possible. Maintain the discipline to get things done.
- **Unlock and catalyze the creative capabilities of leaders**—Create high-impact, experiential learning tied to real business challenges. Develop inspirational role models who demonstrate accomplishment and empowered leadership. Unleash small, diverse teams to pursue bold ideas in response to challenges. Create work structures and incentives aligned with intrinsic motivation. Promote a culture of inspiring vision built on authenticity and powered by trust.
- **Unleash and scale organizational creativity**—Share information for collective vision. Tap into global expertise networks. Expand management and communication style repertoires. Build *ad hoc* constituencies of those sharing common goals. Influence collective behavior through real-time analytics.

Training for Creativity and Innovation

Creativity and innovation are becoming increasingly important for the development of the 21st century knowledge society. They contribute to economic prosperity as well as to social and individual well-being and are essential factors for a more competitive and dynamic Europe.

Education is seen as central in fostering creative and innovative skills. Creativity and innovation have strong links with *knowledge* and *learning*. While intelligence does not seem to be a precondition for creativity, research shows the relevance of previous knowledge, both in terms of knowing how to be creative and of domain knowledge.

Furthermore, creativity is seen by many researchers as a form of knowledge creation and of construction of personal meaning: it is therefore an essential skill for enhancing the learning process. *Creative learning* can be seen as a form of learning that favors understanding over memorization. Hence, any learning that does not imply mere content acquisition entails a component of creativity.

Creative learning requires *innovative teaching*. Innovative teaching is both the practice of teaching for creativity and of applying innovation to teaching. Both aspects call for an educational culture which values creativity and sees it as an asset in the classroom. Teachers are key figures in constructing a creative climate, but they need support from both policymakers and institutions. In particular, curricula and assessment are key areas to be addressed in order to allow creativity in the classroom.

Curricula should undergo a skilful and thorough development, giving the same importance to every subject, taking creativity into consideration and defining it coherently throughout the curriculum, allowing freedom and time for discovery, and taking learners' interests into account. Assessment should also allow creativity to flourish by valuing it, both at micro, everyday level and at macro, exam level. The three functions of assessment (diagnostic, formative and summative) must contribute to the development of both knowledge acquisition and skills development for learning and creating.

Creativity and Innovation Training Objectives

- Learn to identify hidden creative strengths
- Understand and utilise the 'process' of creativity
- Find unexpected solutions to your challenges
- Blend Right and Left Brain Thinking
- Break a few Rules
- Learn to Think Laterally
- Move from Competent to Brilliant
- Move from Brilliant to Amazing

Creativity Training

Our creativity training and innovation programme works by asking people to deliberately break the normal rules of planning, behaviour, decision-making, just to mess up current patterns. By overturning the predictable, new possibilities will emerge, including the absurd, the inappropriate, even the dangerous.

However, out of a bit of irreverence and rule-breaking comes original and innovative thinking, even for those who absolutely are convinced they aren't creative.

Your company may need to have various individuals or teams sharpen their creative capabilities to keep pace with your aspirations. Like so many organisations right now, you may be undergoing big changes and your people have to rise to the creative challenge to stay on top.

It may be that you simply need to have some additional innovative tools to spark creative thinking and get people outside those proscribed 'boxes' even if those boxes have proved excellent in the past.

Learning Organization

Make Learning Matter: Become a Learning Organization
What's a Learning Organization?

Organizations with the best chance to succeed and thrive in the future are learning organizations. In his landmark book, *The Fifth Discipline: The Art and Practice of the Learning Organization (compare prices)*, Peter Senge defined the learning organization. He said they were "organizations where people continually expand their capacity to create the results they truly desire, where new and expansive patterns of thinking are nurtured, where collective aspiration is set free, and where people are continually learning how to learn together."

Senge frames our understanding of the learning organization with an ensemble of disciplines which he believes must converge to form a learning organization. I will briefly describe each of these dimensions so that we share a basic understanding of the components that create a learning organization.

My main focus, however, is to suggest some ways in which you can promote a learning organization environment in your organization. These ideas will help you get started; true transformation will be the focus of many articles over the next few years.

- **Systems Thinking:** The underlying structure and the interlinking components of each of our work systems, shape a great deal of the behavior of the individuals who work inside of the work system. Think about Dr. W. Edwards Deming's admonition. When something goes wrong, rather than seeking someone to blame, ask, what about the work system caused that individual to fail?
- **Personal Mastery:** States Senge, "Personal mastery is the discipline of continually clarifying and deepening our personal vision, of focusing our energies, of developing patience, and of seeing reality objectively." He offers that an organization's learning can only be as great as that of each of its individual members. Consequently, personal mastery and the desire for continuous learning integrated deeply in the belief system of each person is critical for competitive advantage in the future.
- **Mental Models:** These are the deeply held pictures each of us holds in our mind about how the world, work, our families, and so on work. Mental models influence our vision of how things happen at work, why things happen at work, and what we are able to do about them.
- **Building Shared Vision:** By shared vision, Senge is referring to a process in which the original vision for an organization, probably determined by the leader, is translated into shared pictures around which the rest of the organization finds meaning, direction, and reasons for existing.
- **Team Learning:** Senge finds that "teams, not individuals, are the fundamental learning unit in modern organizations." It is the dialogue among the members of the team which results in stretching the ability of the organization to grow and develop.

Begin with the Role of the Leaders

Begin with the behavior and contribution of your leaders. Your leaders make four critical contributions to the development of a learning organization.

- Leaders provide the initial vision about why your organization exists and where you are going.
- They communicate this vision. They clearly communicate their belief that continuous growth, learning, and improvement will ensure its accomplishment.
- They build consensus and ownership around this vision, and are influenced by the views of others in the organization.
- They model the actions they want to develop in others.

Their expectations are verbal, but most importantly, actions that others can see. Leaders who want a learning organization continually learn themselves. They read books and articles and share the content with the rest of the organization. They attend training sessions and conferences.

They foster an environment in which people are empowered to make decisions about their work. They make intelligent risk-taking the norm. They assure that all information people need to make good decisions is communicated. They promote an organizational environment that supports learning and personal mastery.

Create Your Learning Organization

To become a learning organization, everyone must contribute. Following are my ideas about how you can ensure the development of this environment at work. (They are in no particular order; the more you do, the better your results.)

One printing shop, with thirty employees, set aside two lunch hours per week to read and discuss the book, The Goal, as a group. The marketing staff of a software development company voted on a book to read. The department members took turns leading the discussion of various chapters at staff meetings. The leadership team in a student health center read, Leading Change, together. The group discussed concepts and chapters at their weekly leadership team meeting.

Attend training and conferences. A recent study by the American Society for Training and Development suggests that there is a direct "causative relationship between training and performance but doesn't prove it." (The ASTD Benchmarking service continues to gather data each year which may prove the relationship over time.) Create the expectation that anyone who attends training or a conference will make presentations to other staff about the most important learning they took away from the event.

Provide alternative sources for learning such as CDs and online learning.

Debrief every project and initiative. If you have developed a new product, designed an ad campaign, or purchased new equipment, to cite a few examples, don't just move on to the next activity. Bring together everyone in the organization who contributed to the success or failure of the initiative.

Debrief what went right, what went wrong, and what you will do differently in the future. Learn from each project, initiative, and activity. In the debriefing process, seek not to place blame; aim for shared understanding. In the process, create an environment in which people feel safe to share the truth about what really happened

Here are twelve more tips about how to become a learning organization.

Build individual development plans quarterly. These should list negotiated expectations for growth and learning over the quarter. These plans may include cross-training, skill stretching assignments, and representing the department at organization-wide meetings, as well as education.

Put each person directly into contact with customers. When each individual personally knows customer needs, she is enabled to make better decisions to satisfy the customer. Remember also, the internal customers. Anyone to whom you provide a product or a service is a customer.

- **Promote field trips to other organizations.** Even organizations in different industries can provide opportunities for learning. See and learn what others are doing about the challenges you experience in your organization. I have found non-competing companies surprisingly gracious about sharing information.
- **Meet regularly across departments,** or in a smaller organization, as a whole company. Even in a larger organization, bring the whole company together, at least quarterly. People have to understand the whole work system; otherwise they improve just their small part of the system. While these small improvements are important, they do not necessarily optimize the success of the entire system. This is an area in which every technological advancement makes meeting easier.

- **Use cross-functional teams** to solve problems, scout for new opportunities, and cross-fertilize units with new ideas.
- **Pay for education for all employees.** In fact, some forward thinking organizations have determined learning is so important, that they pay for any educational pursuit, not just those related exclusively to the individual's current job. The goal is to foster learning and they presume that any investments in learning translate into more effective work performance over time.
- **Coach improved performance from all members of the organization.** Work constantly to enable people to set and achieve their next goals. Spend time with people thinking about and planning their next objective.
- **Form study groups.** Internally, and even externally, these groups can focus on creating a learning organization or any other topic that interests you. Check Peter Senge's Fieldbook.com Website for more information about organizing these groups. There may be people, who are close to you geographically, seeking members or holding group meetings.

Take time to read, to think, to talk about new ideas and work. Create discussion areas, conference rooms, and break areas that foster people communicating.

Hold brainstorming (idea generation) sessions on specific topics. Bring "experts" in to help you. As an example, a technical writer can add value to a discussion about print presentation.

Foster an environment of collegiality. Recently, I attended a meeting led by a young manager. I watched the interaction for a few minutes as she provided direction and led a discussion. The most striking feature of the interaction was that she talked to the group as if they were all colleagues working on the same goal. She demonstrated no need to be more important than any member of the group.

Use your performance management system effectively. In addition to the development plan, mentioned above, provide 360 degree feedback from peers, reporting staff members, and the boss.

Learning Architecture

What is it?

A learning architecture is a design or framework for a system of developmental activities and interventions. Its purpose is to help organizations use learning and development as levers to accomplish their business goals. A learning architecture can inform the process of talent management and help with filling the leadership pipeline.

The architecture answers these questions:

Who is to be developed?—Any groups of individuals within an organization who are subject to developmental activities: senior leadership; mid-level managers, front-line managers, high potentials, others, or all of the above.

What do they need to know, do and believe differently?—Individual and organizational capabilities needed to attain the organization's objectives.

How will it be accomplished?—Programs, job rotations, coaching, stretch assignments, etc.

An up-to-date learning architecture helps eliminate redundancies and identify critical gaps in capabilities. It can optimize spending of time and money, and ensure that development is directly tied to business outcomes.

How can CEO Help?

The exact process for developing a new learning architecture or revising an existing one will vary depending on client needs, but six steps are typically involved.

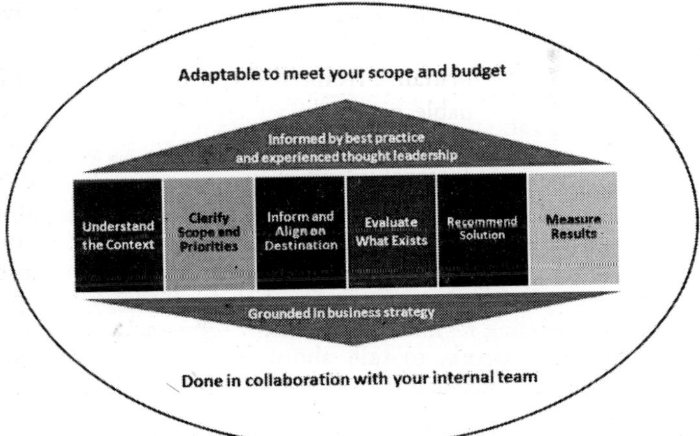

Figure 1.5 : Criteria for Understand the Architectures of Organization

Understand the Context—What business pressures does the organization face? What is its strategy? What organizational capabilities are needed to execute the strategy? What are its values?

Clarify Scope and Priorities—What are the guiding principles, mandate, scope, and team for this Learning Architecture project?

Inform and Align on Destination—What will learning architecture look like for this organization? What will each of us (client and Duke CE) bring to the table in a thought partnership to reach that destination? Are we aligned around the work to be done?

Evaluate What Exists—Which current offerings and approaches are strategic and important now? Which are focused on the desired destination? What is working and what isn't? What is right for this culture? What are the areas of leverage?

Recommend Solution—What needs to be changed? What needs to be added or bolstered? What needs to be cut or replaced? Craft a learning architecture and, as desired, a phased approach to implementing it.

Measure Result—What specific measures can gauge the impact of the recommendations once implemented? What business and behavioral changes are expected?

Creating a learning architecture can help develop the capabilities of internal learning and development teams. While Duke CE can do all the work, our preferred model is to create a project team where we work side-by-side in partnership with our clients so that once the initial architecture is created; internal staff know the process and can keep the architecture up-to-date as strategic priorities change. Thus, a one-time investment can have long lasting impact in creating a sustainable learning culture within your organization.

Creative Investment: Analysis

1. Innovation and Risk

Competitive pressures generate heterogeneous forms of innovation. Is it possible to evaluate unconventional projects? The term innovation is heavily associated with products and technologies. These may be evaluated in terms of patents and econometrics, but intellectual processes and organisational transformations are more elusive. Successful solutions to problems in the fields of science and technology often come from different disciplines (Lakhani *et al.*, *The Value of Openness*, 2007), while artistic creativity can stimulate shifts in traditional patterns of analytical thinking. How do we measure these aspects of innovation in the Arts and Humanities?

How can public organisations foster creativity without risking investment in areas that may not produce immediate outputs? The open-endedness of creative innovation poses a challenge to traditional modes of evaluation, since an element of risk is inherent in creative processes and innovative research. While the risk associated with open-ended innovation has gained acceptance in the economic world, there is little tolerance for risk in the Arts and Humanities, where it is often written out of funding proposals and replaced by specified goals and cost-effective outputs. A tension exists between public funding regimes and practices of research that call for 'open innovation' or long-term prospects.

Questions to be posed include:

- Are existing metrics adequate for assessing innovation?
- How can we assess the impact of knowledge transfer processes on the innovation economy?
- How far do instrumental ideas about knowledge apply to humanities research and practice-based innovation?
- Does an emphasis on goals and outputs constrain innovative practice?
- Can innovation in the Arts and Humanities be assessed in terms of economic impact? What are its transferable benefits?
- What is the cultural value and meaning of creative innovation?

2. Creativity and Innovation in Groups

Innovation is increasingly linked to collaborative research despite a traditional emphasis on the solitary researcher or lone creative artist. What are the tensions between innovation and creativity in individual research or creative practice and collaborative work? The second workshop will explore the relation between the production of knowledge and creative innovation in groups, drawing on specific expertise in group psychology and intellectual property alongside case studies of collaborative practice in the Arts and Humanities, making comparisons with science and technology collaborations.

As researchers are required to make their research accessible to disparate communities, broadening dissemination and deepening public engagement, the collaborative group becomes increasingly focal. Often overlooked in the promotion of collaborative and interdisciplinary groups are factors required for groups to work creatively within institutions. Despite the value placed on collaboration by research councils, there is little systematic implementation or understanding of collaborative models. The workshop will explore and identify factors that promote or impede collaborative research by groups in academic institutions and practice-based research.

Questions to be posed include:

- What are the demonstrable benefits of collaboration for creative innovation and how might these be identified?

- What specific problems and/or creative processes are associated with working in groups?
- How do current legislative practices governing accreditation and attribution of ideas (e.g. copyright law) impact on collaborative research and the wider innovative economy?
- How can collaborative work best be fostered in the Arts and Humanities, and what are its benefits for the innovation economy?

3. *Interdisciplinary and Innovation*

Creativity and innovation are now recognized as valuable currency in the highly competitive global market, while the tension between the two is a key factor in economic studies of 'open innovation'. If innovation can be distinguished from creativity by greater connectivity to the market and by its orientation towards social demands, what are the ideal conditions for the successful implementation of creative ideas? Is it possible to produce such conditions and translate them into institutional forms in the context of Arts and Humanities research? What are the respective benefits and risks of this undertaking?

Creative Investment: Arts and Humanities Research and the 'Innovation Economy' will explore these issues in order to address the question: how do we evidence and assess innovation? A series of three workshops will bring together participants from the Arts, Humanities and Social Sciences, along with policy experts and representatives of the creative industries, to investigate the potential contribution of Arts and Humanities research to the 'innovation economy'. Drawing on case studies from academic and practice-based arts research, each workshop will focus on examples of creative and innovative interactions between and across disciplines. Workshops will focus on the following core issues and questions: (1) the notion of evaluation and risk with respect to innovative processes; (2) the role of collaborative groups in relation to knowledge production, group psychology, and intellectual property; and (3) the relation between interdisciplinary, innovation and institutional transformation.

The aim of the workshops is to bring together researchers from different Arts and Humanities disciplines in dialogue with policy experts and practitioners from the creative industries to explore innovation within the Arts and Humanities domain, with particular reference to evaluation and risk, collaboration and innovation, and interdisciplinary and institutional change. The outcome will be the development of conceptual frameworks and policies that identify and optimize the contribution of Arts and Humanities research to the innovation economy.

The main objectives of the Workshops are:

- To advance knowledge and understanding of creative innovation within the Arts and Humanities domain and define values and risks associated with it;
- To assess the potential value of the Arts and Humanities for the innovation economy;
- To make evident the heterogeneous forms taken by innovation, drawing on case studies and practice-based Arts and Humanities research;
- To identify innovative modes of knowledge production and suggest institutional strategies to support and advance innovation in the Arts and Humanities domain.

Chapter 2

Team Building

With good team-building skills, you can unite employees around a common goal and generate greater productivity. Without them, you limit yourself and the staff to the effort each individual can make alone.

Team building is an ongoing process that helps a work group evolve into a cohesive unit. The team members not only share expectations for accomplishing group tasks, but trust and support one another and respect one another's individual differences. Your role as a team builder is to lead your team toward cohesiveness and productivity. A team takes on a life of its own and you have to regularly nurture and maintain it, just as you do for individual employees.

WHAT IS TEAM BUILDING?

Team building is a process where a team, with facilitator assistance:

- Builds awareness of factors that influence team performance
- Learns to examine performance with respect to those factors
- Takes action to improve effectiveness
- Sets common goals, makes decisions, resolves differences, and solves common problems

Team building supports and encourages risk taking, creativity, understanding, and trust—in ways that promote the teams mission while addressing individual needs.

OBJECTIVES

Through experience, TCA has identified several primary objectives of team-building efforts to:

- Create a realistic vision of improved effectiveness
- Develop teams that will address current business problems or expand World Class capabilities.
- Teach participants capabilities and skills
- Train internal resources to lead team meetings, instruct other teams, and coordinate the team-building processes
- Establish and document plans for the team-building process

APPROACH

Step-by-step approach to achieve team building objectives:

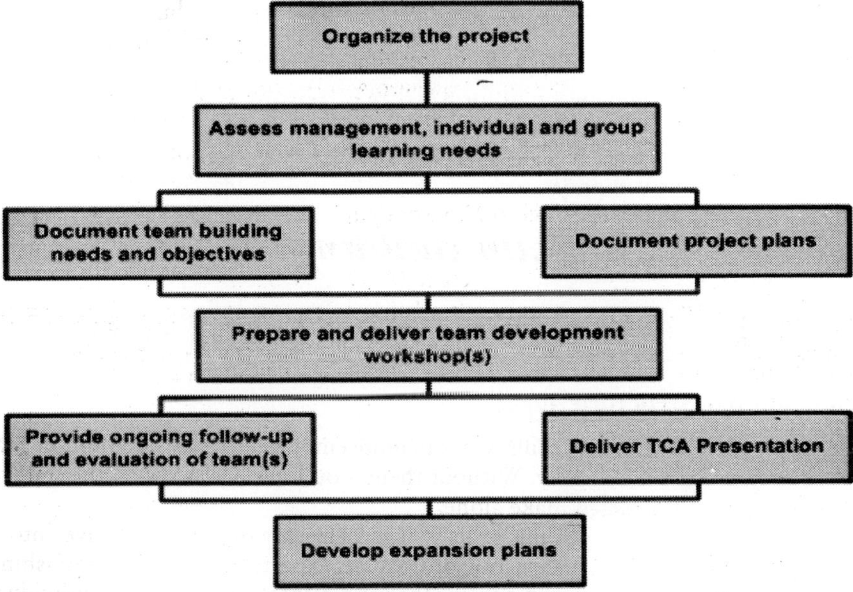

Figure 2.1 : Showing Step-by-Step Approach to Achieve Team Building Objectives

TEAM BUILDING CONSULTANT CONTRIBUTIONS

We support the execution of these steps by:

- Assessing each team's needs, concerns, issues, goals, and opportunities
- Structuring and documenting pilot implementation projects that address significant business problems
- Clarifying a shared vision, missions, roles, and guidelines teams
- Preparing and delivering team development workshops and team working skills training
- Maintaining the focus of the pilot teams on assigned project objectives
- Action planning for enhanced team effectiveness and long-term results
- Providing follow-on team training, support, guidance, and assessment
- Developing in-house resources for ongoing work

BENEFITS

An investment in assistance with your team building will yield many benefits: Team Building Consultant.

- You will overcome the inertia or organizational procrastination that can delay indefinitely the move to World Class technologies
- We will help you identify the best possible starting point in the form of carefully selected pilot projects
- Your management team will understand and apply team building concepts and principles

- Participants will have a greater understanding of their value as individuals and as team members, as well as the significant role each has in supporting growth, creativity, productivity, and quality
- You will be spared the frustration and expense of team-building programs that make people feel good, but produce too few lasting improvements or results
- Pilot team members will form a core of grass-roots experts to encourage and support expansion
- Your in-house coordinator will be capable of leading and project management support
- Expansion of your team-building program will be based on a clear vision of the role that team-building can play in addressing vital business needs and opportunities

Teams, not individuals, are the fundamental learning unit in modern organizations. Unless the team can learn, the organization cannot learn.

Organizational Structure Types

Following are the types of organizational structures that can be observed in the modern business organizations.

Bureaucratic Structures

Bureaucratic structures maintain strict hierarchies when it comes to people management. There are three types of bureaucratic structures:

1. Pre-bureaucratic Structures

This type of organizations lacks the standards. Usually this type of structures can be observed in small scale, start-up companies. Usually the structure is centralized and there is only one key decision-maker.

The communication is done in one-on-one conversations. This type of structures is quite helpful for small organizations due to the fact that the founder has the full control over all the decisions and operations.

2. Bureaucratic Structures

These structures have a certain degree of standardization. When the organizations grow complex and large, bureaucratic structures are required for management. These structures are quite suitable for tall organizations.

3. Post-bureaucratic Structures

The organizations that follow post-bureaucratic structures still inherit the strict hierarchies, but open to more modern ideas and methodologies. They follow techniques such as total quality management (TQM), culture management, etc.

Functional Structure

The organization is divided into segments based on the functions when managing. This allows the organization to enhance the efficiencies of these functional groups. As an example, take a software company.

Software engineers will only staff the entire software development department. This way, management of this functional group becomes easy and effective.

Functional structures appear to be successful in large organization that produces high volumes of products at low costs. The low cost can be achieved by such companies due to the efficiencies within functional groups.

In addition to such advantages, there can be disadvantage from an organizational perspective if the communication between the functional groups is not effective. In this case, organization may find it difficult to achieve some organizational objectives at the end.

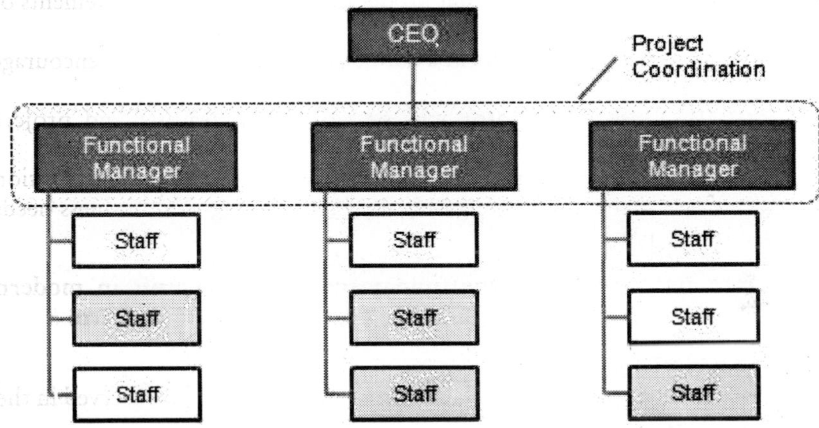

Divisional Structure

These types of organizations divide the functional areas of the organization to divisions. Each division is quipped with its own resources in order to function independently. There can be many bases to define divisions.

Divisions can be defined based on the geographical basis, products/services basis, or any other measurement.

As an example, take a company such as General Electrics. It can have microwave division, turbine division, etc., and these divisions have their own marketing teams, finance teams, etc. In that sense, each division can be considered as a micro-company with the main organization.

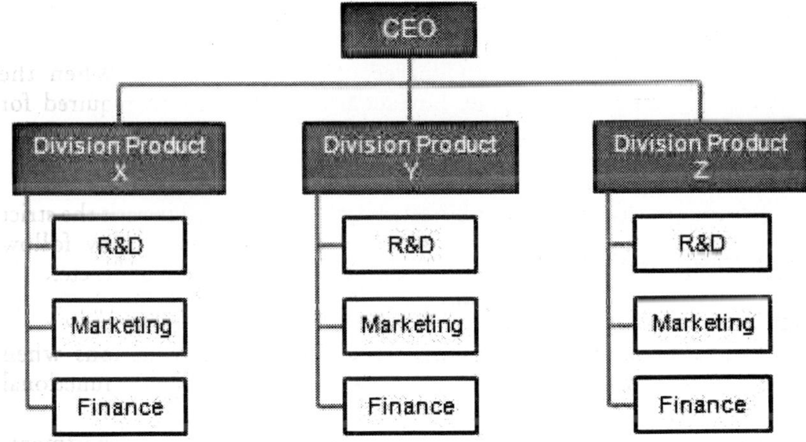

Matrix Structure

When it comes to matrix structure, the organization places the employees based on the function and the product.

The matrix structure gives the best of the both worlds of functional and divisional structures.

In this type of an organization, the company uses teams to complete tasks. The teams are formed based on the functions they belong to (ex: software engineers) and product they involved in (ex: Project A).

This way, there are many teams in this organization such as software engineers of project A, software engineers of project B, QA engineers of project A, etc.

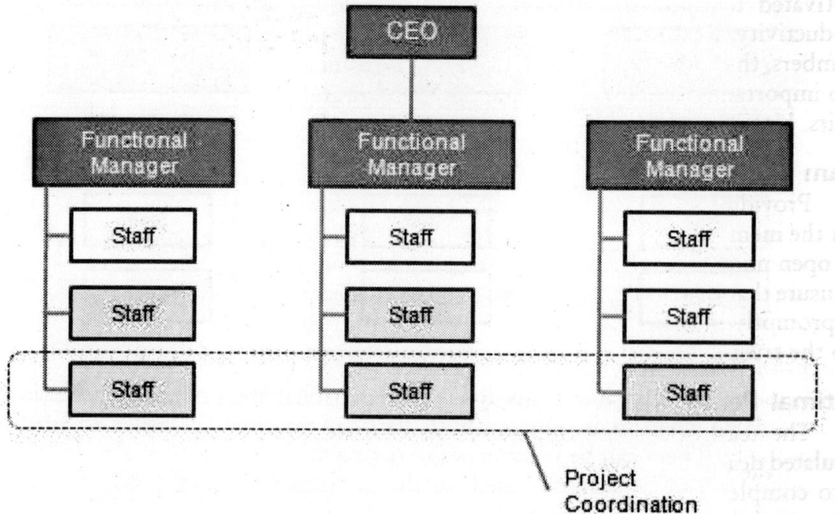

Every organization needs a structure in order to operate systematically. The organizational structures can be used by any organization if the structure fits into the nature and the maturity of the organization.

In most cases, organizations evolve through structures when they progress through and enhance their processes and manpower. One company may start as a pre-bureaucratic company and may evolve up to a matrix organization.

Effective Team Building Skills

As a leader, you need to know that team building doesn't happen on its own. You will get a group of people, but you need to put in some efforts to carve that group into a perfect team, which can yield good results. This can be done through various team building activities such as trust building exercises and outdoor team building games.

Coordination within the Team

When it comes to team building, one of the most important aspects of a successful team is coordination between the team members. Only when information will seep through each layer of the organization, various fractions of the team will know what the other fractions expect from them. Ideas and suggestions communicated during team meetings have to be properly scrutinized and implemented if feasible.

Efficiency and Competence Levels

As the leader of the team, the individual must be well versed with the efficiency of the team members and thrive to increase it with time. The competency levels of the team members does reflect on the final achievements of the team as a whole. Therefore, it's important that the team leader ensures that every person in the team gives his or her best. This is, in fact, one of the most important skills that the leaders to inculcate in their team.

Distribution of Power and Responsibility

Each member of the team should be given equal freedom. They should be motivated to come up with new ideas, methods, skills, etc. to enhance team productivity. Encouraging such behavior will fine-tune the participation by all team members, thus improving the efficiency of the team as a whole. At the same time, it's also important that all the team members are aware about their responsibilities and limits. Untoward behavior, if any, should be promptly brought under check.

Team Bonding

Providing team members with a flexible work environment can help in ensuring that the members give their best performance. The flexibility aspect can be defined as the open mindedness and trust between the members of the team. Leaders can work to ensure that there is proper bonding within the team, and personal differences if any are promptly resolved. Trust doesn't just refer to trust within the team members, but also the trust of the organization leadership on the team.

Optimal Performance

The team as a whole should be accountable for the results as well as the stipulated deadlines. Instead of coaxing team members to give their best performance or to complete the specified targets, the leader should ideally make the members understand the importance of giving their best performance, achieving their targets, teamwork, etc. Once the team understands this, they will indeed work as a single unit which will indirectly show in the performance of the organization. Optimal performance is in fact the best measure of proper team functioning.

Ideally team building workshops feature various games and activities which can provide members of the team a work friendly environment—and bring out the best in them. All these efforts are undertaken only to ensure optimal performance from available resources.

Conflict in Organizations

The workplace is a site of immense social interaction. Layered onto relationships that may be formal, informal, collegial or even friendship-based are hierarchical structures of reporting relationships, supervision and authority. Human relationships go hand in hand with the carrying out of work processes. Clearly, some form of conflict is likely to emerge in the operation of such complex structures. Workplace conflict takes many shapes and forms. It can be as overt as a strike by workers over an issue of concern or as covert as an individual, dissatisfied with his or her lot expressing anger or frustration as increased absenteeism, lower productivity or sabotage. Alternatively, an interpersonal dispute between two colleagues can manifest itself through refusal to work together, hostility or bullying. Conflict in the workplace is as much about dissention over management authority as it is about individual interaction. Resolving these conflicts, whilst being a responsibility of supervisors and managers, often involves HR managers.

Guiding Principles
Team building can lead to:

Good communications with participants as team members and individuals
Increased department productivity and creativity
Team members motivated to achieve goals
A climate of cooperation and collaborative problem-solving
Higher levels of job satisfaction and commitment
Higher levels of trust and support
Diverse co-workers working well together
Clear work objectives
Better operating policies and procedures
Other Resources
Organization Development Specialists in Development & Training

Steps to Building an Effective Team

The first rule of team building is an obvious one: to lead a team effectively, you must first establish your leadership with each team member. Remember that the most effective team leaders build their relationships of trust and loyalty, rather than fear or the power of their positions.

Consider each employee's ideas as valuable. Remember that there is no such thing as a stupid idea.

Be aware of employees' unspoken feelings. Set an example to team members by being open with employees and sensitive to their moods and feelings.

Act as a harmonizing influence. Look for chances to mediate and resolve minor disputes; point continually toward the team's higher goals.

Be clear when communicating. Be careful to clarify directives.

Encourage trust and cooperation among employees on your team. Remember that the relationships team members establish among themselves are every bit as important as those you establish with them. As the team begins to take shape, pay close attention to the ways in which team members work together and take steps to improve communication, cooperation, trust, and respect in those relationships.

Encourage team members to share information. Emphasize the importance of each team member's contribution and demonstrate how all of their jobs operate together to move the entire team closer to its goal.

Delegate problem-solving tasks to the team. Let the team work on creative solutions together.

Facilitate communication. Remember that communication is the single most important factor in successful teamwork. Facilitating communication does not mean holding meetings all the time. Instead it means setting an example by remaining open to suggestions and concerns, by asking questions and offering help, and by doing everything you can to avoid confusion in your own communication.

Establish team values and goals; evaluate team performance. Be sure to talk with members about **the progress they are making toward established goals so that employees get a sense both of their success and of the challenges** that lie ahead. Address teamwork in performance standards. Discuss with your team:

What do we really care about in performing our job?
What does the word success mean to this team?
What actions can we take to live up to our stated values?

Make sure that you have a clear idea of what you need to accomplish; that you know what your standards for success are going to be; that you have established clear time frames; and that team members understand their responsibilities.

Use consensus. Set objectives, solve problems, and plan for action. While it takes much longer to establish consensus, this method ultimately provides better decisions and greater productivity because it secures every employee's commitment to all phases of the work.

Set ground rules for the team. These are the norms that you and the team establish to ensure efficiency and success. They can be simple directives (Team members are to be punctual for meetings) or general guidelines (every team member has the right to offer ideas and suggestions), but you should make sure that the team creates these ground rules by consensus and commits to them, both as a group and as individuals.

Establish a method for arriving at a consensus. You may want to conduct open debate about the pros and cons of proposals, or establish research committees to investigate issues and deliver reports.

Encourage listening and brainstorming. As supervisor, your first priority in creating consensus is to stimulate debate. Remember that employees are often afraid to disagree with one another and that this fear can lead your team to make mediocre decisions. When you encourage debate you inspire creativity and that's how you'll spur your team on to better results.

Establish the parameters of consensus-building sessions. Be sensitive to the frustration that can mount when the team is not achieving consensus. At the outset of your meeting, establish time limits, and work with the team to achieve consensus within those parameters. Watch out for false consensus; if an agreement is struck too quickly, be careful to probe individual team members to discover their real feelings about the proposed solution.

Symptoms that Signal a Need for Team Building

- Decreased productivity
- Conflicts or hostility among staff members
- Confusion about assignments, missed signals, and unclear relationships
- Decisions misunderstood or not carried through properly
- Apathy and lack of involvement
- Lack of initiation, imagination, innovation; routine actions taken for solving complex problems
- Complaints of discrimination or favoritism
- Ineffective staff meetings, low participation, minimally effective decisions
- Negative reactions to the manager
- Complaints about quality of service

Organization Design

The demands on the human resources function have never been greater. Since 1970, the world's 50 biggest companies have tripled in size, and the number of consumer products introduced each year has increased 16-fold (Useem & Useem, 2005). Many firms have expanded internationally, and even those that have not face new competition from abroad as their products and services rapidly commoditize.

As businesses become more complex, so must the HR organizations that support them. The design of the HR department must parallel the many dimensions of the business. If there are multiple products, customers, geographies, or service lines, then HR needs to support them all. As a result, today's HR organizations face many of the same dilemmas as the businesses they work with, such as how to:

1. Build strong functional/product expertise while aligning around customer segments
2. Design in flexibility without adding cost

Work Redesign

Work design describes how jobs, tasks, and roles are structured, enacted, and modified, as well as the impact of these structures, enactments, and modifications on individual, group, and organizational outcomes. An example of a traditional work design issue concerns the low level of autonomy that machine operators have over their work methods and task timing. A more contemporary example concerns the high levels of interdependence and time pressure experienced by software designers who collaborate with, and receive feedback from, customers, suppliers, and co-workers. In each case, the work can be redesigned, by the organization or in some cases by employees themselves, to alter the structure and content of the work, with the goal of improving outcomes such as employee motivation, performance, and well-being.

The decision to execute the concept of work redesign is challenging. It must involve top management who are visionary, persuasive, and consistent. The need for work redesign may be initiated by financial challenges, often a reduced budget. Other reasons include:

- Strategic planning demonstrates the need for a change
- Leadership sees problems and challenges coming
- Customers report a need for change
- Regulatory changes require a review
- Leadership wants to be a distinguished competitor

Prior to initiating work redesign, it is very important to be clear about why the organization is promoting a concept or solution called "work redesign". As a leader or HR professional supporting initiating this sort of change, you need to be prepared to address the questions identified below.

- What is the driving purpose of the redesign? In particular consider scope and impact.
- What is the desired result or outcome? In particular examine potential financial savings, efficiency or improvement to employee well-being.
- How will we engage individuals and teams within the process of review?

In a change there are four dimensions at work:

- **People**—The characteristics, attributes and skills of the people working in the environment, PEOPLE make an organization and need to be our number one priority
- **Systems/Process**—The structure, equipment, methods and technologies used to get the work done
- **Results**—How we know and let others know that we are successful?
- **Culture**—How we relate with one another, customers and do our work together?

This comprehensive model examines the current and future state, and lays the foundation to enable ongoing systematic improvement.

Procedure

1. Identify a Change Management Team with Leader

An Organizational Effectiveness (OE) consultant will partner with leadership and HR to facilitate group meetings and develop a contract for the change. Other experts may be brought to the team as needed.

Make sure those engaged in the work team are on the team and that a clear outcome is identified. This team will also make recommendations related to communication needs and operational considerations as the change moves forward.

2. Conduct "As Is" Systems Assessment

- Look at current organizational structure. Look at acquired and accumulated roles and resources. Is accountability and authority clear? Do staff trust one another and work well together? What is the readiness of the group to take on the effort? How is conflict resolved in the current environment?
- Examine other benchmarks, when necessary.
- Unit collects data to support need for change.

Possible consultant activities:

Leader group assessment

- Objectives and measures of success
- Review organizational chart and current staffing model=what are the major tasks and priorities? How even are the workloads? Are there peak times? Are the job descriptions current? Are the classifications appropriate?
- What things are not getting done?
- Where are there redundancies?
- Are there conflict or performance issues?

Employee interviews or focus groups

- What are your major priorities
- How long do major tasks or projects take? What are the smaller tasks that are built in?
- What are the barriers to efficiency?
- What doesn't get done as timely as you'd like?

Benchmarking

- They do it, have them pick who should do it
- Have them develop the questions, what information is important?

3. Create an infrastructure to sustain the change

Use this time to step back and look for new solutions.

- Prepare organizational chart for the future
- Consider span of control for managers
- Review key functions: services, culture, etc.
- Review key processes: identify new workflow or business changes, are work processes continuously improved?

- Review system: Are methods and procedures carefully defined? Determine measures of success or desirable outcomes.

4. ***Complete Talent Pool Assessment with Key Leaders***
   - Take into consideration
   - Current effectiveness of potential individual leaders
   - Levels of role complexity
   - Potential for future roles in organization
   - Impact analysis related to diversity
   - Are leaders appropriately skilled and knowledgeable? Are they fully committed? Commitment is demonstrated by "walking the talk", modeling the behavior change that has been articulated.
   - Have broader leadership discussions to explore questions—Is anyone left out?
   - Do we have gaps and need to hire in order to improve performance, or do we need to engage in performance management?
   - Are we being fair to individual choices and career paths?

5. ***Support New Organizational Model***
   - Identify growth and maintenance pieces.
   - Do policies and practice support new organizational model?
   - Redefine job descriptions and evaluations as needed.
   - Redefine performance metrics.
   - Develop reward and recognition programs to sustain and encourage the change.

6. ***Implement New Organizational Model and Communicate Often***
   - Offer rationale and opportunity for ongoing feedback from internal staff and customers.
   - Provide support for remaining and exiting personnel if needed.
   - Provide support for manager, emphasize leadership accountability to process.

7. ***Manage Change of New Organization***
   - Acknowledge staff participation and contributions to change effort.
   - Modify and communicate frequently, recommend some form of follow-up with group at 3 and 6 months, and one year.
   - Review and evaluate original performance metrics frequently the first year of implementation with the leader.

WORK REDESIGN OPTIONS

- When you do the same job day-in and day-out, it can become mundane or boring. It may seem like you show up to work, go through the motions and come back the next day to do it all over again. Sometimes it's not the type of work that needs a makeover but the tasks, responsibilities and roles that do. **Job redesign** looks specifically at ways to expand an employee's job by redesigning certain aspects relating to the scope and depth of what it is that an employee does and is responsible for at the organization. In doing so, the manager essentially prevents an employee from losing motivation and interest in their work. There are three ways a manager can redesign an employee's job: job enrichment, job enlargement and job rotation.

Job Rotation

- o The periodic shifting of a worker from one task to another.
- o The strengths of job rotation are that it reduces boredom and increases motivation through diversifying the employee's activities.
    - **Job rotation** is the final job redesign strategy that assigns workers to an alternate job on a temporary basis. Job rotation is useful and motivating in several ways. First, it provides employees with something new to learn and do beyond what their normal job does. Second, it provides employees with a broader perspective on how the organization operates as a whole. Third, it increases the employee's understanding of what his or her co-workers do, which leads to a higher degree of respect for what others do. Finally, it offers an employee the chance to gain additional skills, which increases their value to the organization. Essentially, job rotation is great at adding variety and encouraging respect among peers, while sparking new interest in the organization.

      For example, Jane and Bob both work at a furniture store. Jane in customer service and Bob is in delivery. To help motivate Jane and Bob, as well as expose them to the dependence their individual jobs have on each other, their managers decide to have Jane switch jobs with Bob for the week. After just a few hours, the two quickly realize that the other person's job is not as easy as they used to think it was. They learn about the tasks and responsibilities the other person has to account for in their jobs. This newfound knowledge creates a new interest and enthusiasm for both Jane and Bob.

Job Enlargement

- o The horizontal expansion of jobs.
- o Job enlargement attacks the lack of diversity in overspecialized jobs, but does little to instill challenge or meaningfulness to a worker's activities.
    - **Job enlargement** is a job redesign strategy that increases only the tasks of a particular job. While job enlargement is limited in that it does not provide the additional responsibilities or authority that job enrichment does, it is useful in reducing some of the monotony associated with doing the same thing day-in and day-out. The belief is that once boredom is reduced, motivation to perform at higher levels of productivity increases.

      For example, Jeff works as a trash man for the city. His boss might switch the routes that Jeff has to cover or may ask him to pick up the recycling routes in addition to his routine trash routes. Even though Jeff is not given an extra authority or challenge by taking these additional routes, it does provide Jeff with new tasks that can lessen the repetitiveness of his usual trash route

Job Enrichment

- o The vertical expansion of jobs.
- o An enriched job organizes tasks so as to allow the worker to do a complete

activity, increases the employee's freedom and independence, increases responsibility, and provides feedback

- **Job enrichment** provides an employee with more tasks to do as a part of their job, as well as the responsibility and authority needed to complete those additional tasks. What works particularly well to increase motivation is when job enrichment includes additional tasks that match the skills, knowledge and abilities the employee already has. For example, let's say Molly works as a receptionist at a beauty salon. Her duties typically include answering the phone, setting up appointments, greeting customers and completing payment transactions after the client is finished with their stylist. However, there are times when Molly is left with nothing to do but stare out into the parking lot. Molly often complains that she is bored and has even told some of her fellow employees that she is considering looking for a new job that is more challenging.

Alternative Work Schedule Options

All departments have formal or informal policies on alternative work schedules. An overview of time-off and leave information is also available in your *MIHR Information* account.

Due to the nature of work being performed, some options are not available to all employees. In addition, changes to work schedule requires supervisor and Appointing Authority approval.

- **Modified Work Schedules.** Modified schedules allow employees' flexibility in when they start and stop work, and even what days they report. The schedule is regularly maintained permanently or for an extended period of time. For example, during the summer, an employee might report for work at 6:00 a.m. and leave at 2:30 p.m. with a half hour for lunch.
- **Flexible Work Schedules.** Allow employees to vary their start and stop time through the week. The schedule varies from week-to-week to accommodate both employee and the employer needs.
- **Compressed Work Weeks.** The most common compressed work-week is a four-day, 10-hour schedule (a 4/40 plan). Operational needs may make this option more practical during certain times of the year than at other times. The schedule does not have to provide a 3-day weekend.

The following are existing programs that allow employees to work fewer than 40 hours per week.

- **Voluntary Work Schedule Adjustment Program (VWSAP).** This is a mutually agreed upon arrangement that allows an employee to voluntarily take unpaid time-off for a portion of the year (Plan C) or change to a part-time schedule (Plan A) to meet personal needs. Benefits are maintained during the reduced schedule. Banked Leave Time (BLT) hours must be exhausted prior to use of unpaid Plan A or Plan C hours. Employees must complete a *Voluntary Work Schedule Adjustment Agreement* form when requesting Plan A or C leave.
- **Permanent-Intermittent or Part-Time Work.** For some employees with on-going family obligations, a permanent part-time schedule may be

desirable. Collective bargaining agreements vary regarding benefit eligibility and state contribution for insurances.

- **Job Sharing.** This allows two employees to do the work of one full-time employee by sharing hours, responsibilities, etc. There are challenges associated with job sharing, and it requires cooperation and good communication between the employees and with the supervisor to maintain job efficiency and effectiveness. Collective bargaining agreements vary regarding maintenance of benefits and state contribution for insurances.

TEAM Conflict Styles and Their Consequences

Conflict is often best understood by examining the consequences of various behaviors at moments in time. These behaviors are usefully categorized according to conflict styles. Each style is a way to meet one's needs in a dispute but may impact other people in different ways.

- **Competing** is a style in which one's own needs are advocated over the needs of others. It relies on an aggressive style of communication, low regard for future relationships, and the exercise of coercive power. Those using a competitive style tend to seek control over a discussion, in both substance and ground rules. They fear that loss of such control will result in solutions that fail to meet their needs. Competing tends to result in responses that increase the level of threat.
- **Accommodating**, also known as smoothing, is the opposite of competing. Persons using this style yield their needs to those of others, trying to be diplomatic. They tend to allow the needs of the group to overwhelm their own, which may not ever be stated, as preserving the relationship is seen as most important.
- **Avoiding** is a common response to the negative perception of conflict. "Perhaps if we don't bring it up, it will blow over," we say to ourselves. But, generally, all that happens is that feelings get pent up, views go unexpressed, and the conflict festers until it becomes too big to ignore. Like a cancer that may well have been cured if treated early, the conflict grows and spreads until it kills the relationship. Because needs and concerns go unexpressed, people are often confused, wondering what went wrong in a relationship.
- **Compromising** is an approach to conflict in which people gain and give in a series of tradeoffs. While satisfactory, compromise is generally not satisfying. We each remain shaped by our individual perceptions of our needs and don't necessarily understand the other side very well. We often retain a lack of trust and avoid risk-taking involved in more collaborative behaviors.
- **Collaborating** is the pooling of individual needs and goals toward a common goal. Often called "win-win problem-solving," collaboration requires assertive communication and cooperation in order to achieve a better solution than either individual could have achieved alone. It offers the chance for consensus, the integration of needs, and the potential to exceed the "budget of possibilities" that previously limited our views of the conflict. It brings new time, energy, and ideas to resolve the dispute meaningfully.

The Role of Perceptions in Conflict in the Team

As noted in our basic definition of conflict, we define conflict as a disagreement through which the parties involved perceive a threat to their needs, interests or concerns. One key element of this definition is the idea that each party may have a different perception of any given situation. We can anticipate having such differences due to a number of factors that create "perceptual filters" that influence our responses to the situation:

- Culture, race, and ethnicity: Our varying cultural backgrounds influence us to hold certain beliefs about the social structure of our world, as well as the role of conflict in that experience. We may have learned to value substantive, procedural and psychological needs differently as a result, thus influencing our willingness to engage in various modes of negotiation and efforts to manage the conflict
- **Gender and sexuality**: Men and women often perceive situations somewhat differently, based on both their experiences in the world (which relates to power and privilege, as do race and ethnicity) and socialization patterns that reinforce the importance of relationships vs. task, substance *vs.* process, immediacy vs. long-term outcomes. As a result, men and women will often approach conflictive situations with differing mindsets about the desired outcomes from the situation, as well as the set of possible solutions that may exist.
- **Knowledge (general and situational)**: Parties respond to given conflicts on the basis of the knowledge they may have about the issue at hand. This includes situation-specific knowledge (i.e., "Do I understand what is going on here?") and general knowledge (i.e., "Have I experienced this type of situation before?" or "Have I studied about similar situations before?"). Such information can influence the person's willingness to engage in efforts to manage the conflict, either reinforcing confidence to deal with the dilemma or undermining one's willingness to flexibly consider alternatives.
- **Impressions of the Messenger**: If the person sharing the message—the messenger—is perceived to be a threat (powerful, scary, unknown, etc.), this can influence our responses to the overall situation being experienced. For example, if a big scary-looking guy is approaching me rapidly, yelling "Get out of the way!" I may respond differently than if a diminutive, calm person would express the same message to me. As well, if I knew either one of them previously, I might respond differently based upon that prior sense of their credibility: I am more inclined to listen with respect to someone I view as credible than if the message comes from someone who lacks credibility and integrity in my mind.
- **Previous experiences**: Some of us have had profound, significant life experiences that continue to influence our perceptions of current situations. These experiences may have left us fearful, lacking trust, and reluctant to take risks. On the other hand, previous experiences may have left us confident, willing to take chances and experience the unknown. Either way, we must acknowledge the role of previous experiences as elements of our perceptual filter in the current dilemma.

The Cost and Value of Conflict

Conflict has both upsides and downsides for a workplace. Workplace conflict, improperly managed, can have a tremendous cost on the health of any workplace. This has an effect on a company's performance. Conflict wastes the time of managers, human resources professionals, labour representatives and employees themselves. It effects the quality of decisions that are made because people in conflict are less likely to share vital information and more likely to get into power struggles. Poorly managed conflict can result in the loss of valuable employees and the expense of hiring and retraining new ones. It can lead to costly restructuring and even sabotage, theft and property damage. In addition, poorly managed conflict effects the health of workplace participants causing increased stress levels, and increased usage of sick leave and disability claims. In the end, conflict can lead to compromised job satisfaction, poor motivation and lack of engagement among employees, and thus low human performance.

While conflict can come at great cost to any workplace, it can also have tremendous benefits when managed properly. Conflict can be used as a catalyst for healthy competition in workplaces that rely upon competition to promote excellence. Conflict can bring underlying workplace issues into the open so that they can be resolved. Conflict can promote a better understanding of differences. When brought to the surface it can dissipate anger and raise awareness of other peoples' needs. It can also be used as a way of placing focus upon common goals. It can lead to increased team spirit. Properly managed conflict fosters healthy dialogue and can motivate people to raise issues and discuss new ideas. Conflict challenges existing inadequacies in the workplace and can lead to a reassessment of workplace structures. Thus while poorly managed conflict is destructive, properly managed conflict can lead to workplace renewal.

Workplace Conflict Management System

Every workplace has a conflict management system. In a non-union workplace the system generally consists of managerial decision-making, organizational and government regulation, peer negotiation, and the exercise of the exit options—resignation or dismissal. Unionized workplaces rely primarily upon the grievance procedure to manage conflict. Many modern workplaces use a variety of other options to supplement their system (see image below).

CONFLICT MANAGEMENT SYSTEM OPTIONS

Interest-Based Options	Rights-Based Options	Communication-Based Options	Power-Based Options
Interest-Based Negotiation Peer Mediation	Peer Review Panel Investigation	Information Exchange Facility Open Door Policy	Workplace Regulation Managerial Decision Making
Managerial Mediation	Arbitration	Personality and Group Dynamics Testing Instruments	Resignation/ Dismissal
External Mediation	Mediation-Arbitration	Training and Education	
Training and Education	Training and Education	Ombuds	
Ombuds Conflict Coaching	Ombuds Grievance Procedure		
Open Door Policy Workplace Partnering	Early Neutral Evaluation Courts		
360 Reviews			

In Workplaces That Work, we have determined 21 measures of a conflict management system. These measures are categorized into 4 quotients: Justice, Efficiency, Engagement, and Resource as seen below.

The Justice Quotient gauges how well the system performs from a procedural justice perspective. It considers: access to the system, applicability of the system to all workplace conflicts, independence of the system from manipulation, how well protected and supported employees are when they use the system, how fair the procedures are, how adequate the enforcement mechanisms are, and how well it protects participants' legal rights.

The Efficiency Quotient measures the smooth operation of the system. It considers how well the system uses interest-based, rights-based and power-based options, how well it supports self-help alternatives, how expensive the system is, how flexible it is, how timely the processes are, and how well the system educates participants.

The Engagement Quotient measures the level of participant involvement and buy-in to the system. Without engagement, the system will largely remain unused and participants will craft their own remedies. Engagement measures the extent to which the system encourages positive, voluntary participation in the system.

The Resource Quotient measures commitment to the system through investments in resources needed from development through to implementation. A system cannot be Just or Efficient without adequate resources. Proper investment shows the company is serious about conflict management thus increasing participant buy-in. The Resource Quotient measures the adequacy of human, financial and facilities resources devoted to the system, and the processes in place to enhance continuous improvement of the system.

MEASURES OF A CONFLICT MANAGEMENT SYSTEM			
JUSTICE QUOTIENT	EFFICIENCY QUOTIENT	ENGAGEMENT QUOTIENT	RESOURCE QUOTIENT
Access Applicability Independence Protection Support Procedures Enforcement Legal	Interests Alternatives Self-Help Cost Flexibility Education Timeliness	Buy-In Involvement	Human Facilities Financial Improvement

How does a unionized workplace compare to a non-union workplace?

In Workplaces That Work, we have analyzed traditional non-union and union workplaces using the diagnostic tool described above. Without modifications, neither type of workplace fares well in this analysis. The non-union workplace has primary deficiencies in the Justice and Engagement Quotients. Too much unmodified employer power may lead to abuse of authority. It also marginalizes opportunities for fair and protected workplace participant feedback. This results in reduced engagement among workplace participants in the system.

The unionized workplace, without modification, also leaves much to be desired. Although the Justice Quotient is strong, the Engagement and Efficiency Quotients are often weak. It is difficult to engage an employer in a system that does not meet its interest in flexibility. In fact the most significant problem with an unmodified unionized workplace is the lack of flexibility inherent in the structure. The structure is built to house an adversarial rights-based system of conflict management.

The benefits of a unionized work environment are:

- A relatively well developed system for conflict management.
- Employee access to union resources and protections.
- The ability to share the cost between employees and the employer.

The challenges of the unionized work environment are:

- The adversarial nature of the process.
- Suspicion over alternative methods of resolving disputes.
- Lack of flexibility in a traditional union-management relationship.

Professionals Unions are Good Conflict Management Partners

Ironically, those factors cited in support of the notion that unions and professionals are incompatible are actually the very reason why professional unions can make superlative conflict management partners. Professional unions are not generally as dogmatic in nature—tending more toward a problem-solving approach to conflict management. Thus it is easier to engage professional unions in creative modifications to the traditional grievance procedure.

Professionals are generally more open to options that provide flexibility for the employer and thus increase employer buy-in. Problem-solving teams, internal review panels, and mediation diversion are prominent features in many professional union collective agreements. Professionals are often more engaged in their workplace structure and governance than traditional union staff. And they are generally more concerned with the employer's interest in seeing the company flourish. All of these proclivities make professionals good candidates for workplace partnership.

Therefore, unionization is an opportunity for professionals to give positive and constructive feedback to their employer. Unionization allows a collective effort to ensure consistent, flexible and fair conflict management in the workplace. It can be a powerful vehicle for professionals to enhance their careers, improve their voice in the company's operation and promote the company's effectiveness. Rather than stifle professionalism, unions can enhance the professional experience by allowing professionals to make positive contributions to their company without fear of reprisal. In short, professionals and unions do mix.

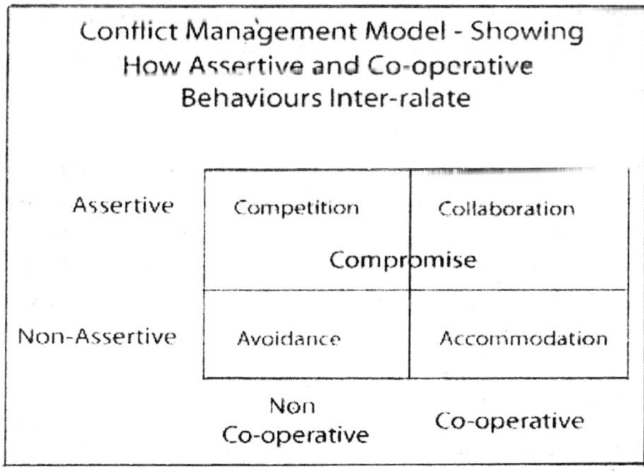

In any situation involving more than one person, conflict can arise. The causes of conflict range from philosophical differences and divergent goals to power imbalances. Unmanaged or poorly managed conflicts generate a breakdown in trust and lost productivity. For small businesses, where success often hinges on the cohesion of a few people, loss of trust and productivity can signal the death of the business. With a basic understanding of the five conflict management strategies, small business owners can better deal with conflicts before they escalate beyond repair.

Accommodating

The accommodating strategy essentially entails giving the opposing side what it wants. The use of accommodation often occurs when one of the parties wishes to keep the peace or perceives the issue as minor. For example, a business that requires formal dress may institute a "casual Friday" policy as a low-stakes means of keeping the peace with the rank and file. Employees who use accommodation as a primary conflict management strategy, however, may keep track and develop resentment.

Avoiding

The avoidance strategy seeks to put off conflict indefinitely. By delaying or ignoring the conflict, the avoider hopes the problem resolves itself without a confrontation. Those who actively avoid conflict frequently have low esteem or hold a position of low power. In some circumstances, avoiding can serve as a profitable conflict management strategy, such as after the dismissal of a popular but unproductive employee. The hiring of a more productive replacement for the position soothes much of the conflict.

Collaborating

Collaboration works by integrating ideas set out by multiple people. The object is to find a creative solution acceptable to everyone. Collaboration, though useful, calls for a significant time commitment not appropriate to all conflicts. For example, a business owner should work collaboratively with the manager to establish policies, but collaborative decision-making regarding office supplies wastes time better spent on other activities.

Compromising

The compromising strategy typically calls for both sides of a conflict to give up elements of their position in order to establish an acceptable, if not agreeable, solution. This strategy prevails most often in conflicts where the parties hold approximately equivalent power. Business owners frequently employ compromise during contract negotiations with other businesses when each party stands to lose something valuable, such as a customer or necessary service.

Competing

Competition operates as a zero-sum game, in which one side wins and other loses. Highly assertive personalities often fall back on competition as a conflict management strategy. The competitive strategy works best in a limited number of conflicts, such as emergency situations. In general, business owners benefit from holding the competitive strategy in reserve for crisis situations and decisions that generate ill-will, such as pay cuts or layoffs.

Skills for Strategic Human Resource Management

- The Skills Needed for Strategic Human Resource Management for managing disruption in the organization.

Strategic human resource management refers to the well-rounded approach to business and human capital management that HR leaders use to ensure their organizations are successful. Based on the principle that human capital—a phrase used to describe employees' collective talents, expertise and qualifications—is an organization's most valuable commodity, strategic human resources leaders need to have certain skills to formulate strategy useful for HR functional and tactical processes.

Critical Thinking Skills and Disruption Management

Human resources strategic leaders are entrusted with information, data and projections pertaining to the workforce as well as the entire organization. Consequently, business ethics, principles and discretion are essential skills and characteristics. Strategic management within the context of human resources means HR leaders must have the ability to use their discretion and always put the interests of the company first. Analytical and critical thinking skills are paramount regarding access to confidential information and data. HR leaders also must be cognizant of circumstances that cause inadvertent and unintentional disclosure of information that could disrupt a strategic plan.

1. Leadership Skills and Disruption Management

HR strategic management requires leadership skills, which are fundamental to consensus building, negotiation and day-to-day management of human resources functions. Consensus building—something almost all HR leaders face during their careers—is simpler with the appropriate leadership skills to support the HR expert's position. For example, delivering a passionate plea for additional human resources funding may be ineffective, unless the HR leader can illustrate to the organization's executive and finance officers the return on investment in HR functions and the resulting impact on the organization's bottom line. An HR practitioner with few leadership skills or capabilities would likely be unable to make such an argument for additional HR funding.

2. Communication Skills and Disruption Management

Communication skills comprise more than just the ability to produce well-constructed memos, reports and speeches. Effective HR strategic management depends on another component of communication—listening. Listening to the organization's human capital and observing employment trends and best practices that successful companies embrace are all part of the communication process. HR strategic leaders' attention to employee feedback enables better understanding of what employees need from their employer to develop a strategy that supports the organization's goals.

3. Business Management Skills and Disruption Management

Human resources leaders need to have more than simple knowledge of HR functions and employment and labor law. Strategic HR management involves a well-rounded approach to business and HR. Therefore, business acumen is something HR leaders can't be without. More and more corporations are hiring human resources leaders who know more about business than they do about human resources disciplines. The reason is because managing human capital from a strategic point of view requires a business foundation.

WORK FLOW ANALYSIS AND PRODUCTIVITY

How to Improve Productivity in any Organization Using Workflow Analysis

Workflow techniques are typically used in large organizations with repetitive tasks, clearly defined roles and interactions. However, simple workflow management techniques like the ones discussed here can help improve productivity and reduce skewed workloads in any type of organization.

Henry Ford ushered in the second industrial revolution (and affordable personal transportation) by using assembly lines and mass production techniques to produce cars.

Mass production led to the development of workflow techniques to improve productivity and quality. Work flow has since become integral to managing repetitive work situations and concepts like TQM (Total Quality Management), Six Sigma and BPR (Business Process Reengineering) are attempts to improve workflows.

A workflow is nothing but the way work flows in the organization. It is about defining where a particular job starts, who does what to it and where the output moves next, and further on till the output moves outside the boundaries of the organization. So, while workflows are typical in assembly lines, they also work well in situations including software development and call centers, where code or calls are routed to different departments based on a set of rules. Typically, the concept of workflow and optimizing the workflow are used in large organizations with clear cut job roles and is often automated using complex software. However, the basic principles of workflow management, along with some common sense can be used in almost any work situation in an organization of any size to improve planning, productivity and quality, and more importantly, to reduce skewed work loads.

Basic Elements of Workflow

For the purposes of our understanding, we will define the following seven elements of a workflow. Please note that these are not necessarily standard definitions, but are for our understanding.

Element—An element of workflow is that part of the process which is executed by a given person. An element could be "call next number in the list" or "paint the box red" or "check code block for errors" and so on.

Input—Whatever goes in, or is given to a person to do his job. This could be information, raw material, a function definition (for coding) code, an incoming call, a number to dial out to, etc.

Output—Whatever that person hands over to the next person in the sequence to continue the workflow. This could be modified code, comments on or about the code, finished or semi-finished goods, an ongoing call, etc.

Processing—Processing is the work done on the element by the person with whom it is at the moment. For example, processing could be dialing the number, or writing the code module or handing over the call to a supervisor and so on.

Conditions—Conditions are what determines where the work moves next in the workflow sequence. In the simplest of workflows, there are no conditions and work simply moves forward to the next person in the flow. However, most workflows are not like that and usually there are conditions that determine where it moves to next. These are typically based on approval, behavior or response. For example, "if code is okay, send it to the next stage, else send it back for reworking", or "if solution works, close call, else escalate to tier II support" or "if measurements within tolerance, stamp 'pass', else stamp 'failed'."

Time—The amount of time required to execute the element. Time could be in any unit—minutes, hours, days and so on—depending on the type of job. Cycle time is the time required to complete the entire workflow and is the sum of the time required for all elements of the workflow. Here we should note that the actual execution time may be longer than the cycle time, if any of the elements take longer than scheduled or if at any point, the workflow is reversed, for say, correcting errors.

Choke point—A choke point is a point (person) where work piles up because of very high work loads, leading to delays. This can be because of under staffing or because work keeps coming back to the same person again and again (typically for verification). Choke points tend to delay the process beyond planned cycle time and throw things out of schedule.

A Simple Workflow

A simple workflow is linear, that is the next person in sequence to handle the job is always the same and there are no changes to this based on conditions. It is represented by a series of arrows pointing to the right, with each arrow representing an element.

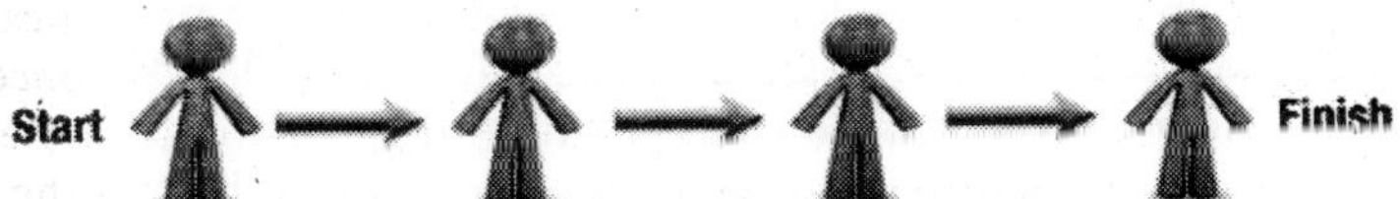

Let us for the sake of an example consider a file moving from one department to another. This file could be electronic or otherwise and could pertain to say the purchase of a new plant and machinery. Within each department, the file would need to be processed by different people. In your case, this may be an incoming call or a piece of code or a part of a machine. Our objective is to increase the productivity and to even out the work load on the people concerned.

How to Increase Productivity?

We increase the productivity by reducing the total cycle time. From the perspective of workflows, we can improve productivity by smoothing the workflow itself or by reducing processing time. Smoothing is done by reducing the number of elements and by identifying and removing choke points. Processing time can be reduced by decreasing the time spent on each element and the number of reworks; that is the number of times when the workflow is reversed to correct errors or to attain defined specifications. Of these, we will focus more on the first set—of how to smoothen the workflow.

There is another important factor that contributes to low productivity and higher processing time, particularly in unstructured office-like situations and that is defining and accepting competence.

Calculating Cycle Time

With the definitions out of the way, lets move on to the real task of improving the productivity. We start by mapping the actual workflow. That is, we create a diagram of the process as it moves actually forward at your place. On this diagram, note the conditions for forward or backward movement and the time taken by each.

Chances are that you will end up with a highly complex diagram for what you thought was a simple sequence of elements. If you do not, you have a miracle at hand. If you do, you now know the source of many of your problems.

Now add up the number of elements and the time taken by them individually. And that brings us to the first question: Are you spending more time than you have at hand for completing the full job? We have not reached the stage of whether you are spending more time than you should. The question at this stage is whether there is enough time at hand to complete the job as it currently exists? In a recent example that I was involved in, there were 14 elements in a particular job (not counting reworkings) that had to be completed in a cycle time of 12 days. The minimum time requirement for each task in this case was estimated to be at least one day. So, you had 12 days to complete a job that was designed to take at least 14! Obviously, there was no way the job could be completed on time, and people were working extra hours and weekends, without really being aware where the basic problem was!

Reducing Cycle Time

If the cycle time is longer than what you can afford to give it or what you think it actually should be, then you absolutely need to reduce cycle time. This can be done using one or more of four methods:

Reduce repetition—You will often find in unplanned workflows that some elements tend to be repeated with different people doing the same or similar things. For example are there too many QC stages? Can they be consolidated into one?

Eliminate unnecessary elements—In any workflow, particularly in unplanned and unmanaged ones, elements tend to get added over time. Typically this happens with approval tasks getting introduced in between. If that has happened in your case, it is time to take a really hard look at each one of them and eliminate all that can be removed.

Reduce time for individual elements—Take a hard look at each of the remaining elements and see whether they are taking more time than they should. Is there any way the time spent on individual elements be reduced? Maybe assigning more resources to elements that require them could do the trick.

Run elements in parallel—Unmanaged workflows have another bad tendency—to become completely sequential. That is, each element waits for all others before it to complete. Perhaps more than one element can run parallel, saving on time.

Workflows and Choke Points

The next big issue to resolve is that of choke points. Choke points easily develop in workflows when there is too much of loading on one individual or team. Another easy way in which choke points develop is when the work keeps coming back to the same person/team for checking multiple times. This could be like when code keeps coming back to the same QC team after every stage, or more likely, there is some senior person in the office who wants to check the work after every stage or in the case of multiple elements of work, wants to individually check every element himself or herself.

I recently came across an example where more than 30 percent of all elements of a workflow were with one person! The impact of this load on that person as well as on the rest of the team is imaginable!

Very clearly, such choke points have to be identified and eliminated from the workflow.

Defining Roles and Accepting Competence

Another area where unmanaged workflows go out of control is when there is no clear definition of the roles and there is no acceptance of competence. Let me explain this. Consider an office where a file is moving from one person to another. Now, if each person thinks that the person(s) before them was not competent enough, then they will start checking everything or even redoing everything from start. Sounds funny? Look around and you will be surprised at how many instances you can spot of this particular problem. Add some perfection seekers into the equation and the problem worsens by an order of magnitude.

The only way of handling this is to clearly define the role of each person/team in the flow and to have every one accept the competence of others. So, to take the example of a magazine like DARE being created, there is a team of writers, a team of copy editors, and a team of designers and so on. If the copy editors accept the competence of the writers on the subject being written about, then their role becomes limited to language and presentation. Else they will end up getting all worked up about (and working on) the content and the scope of their part in the workflow increases to consume more time and thus extend the cycle time. Similarly, if the competence of the designer is not accepted, everyone would end up thinking about the design rather than concentrating on their task.

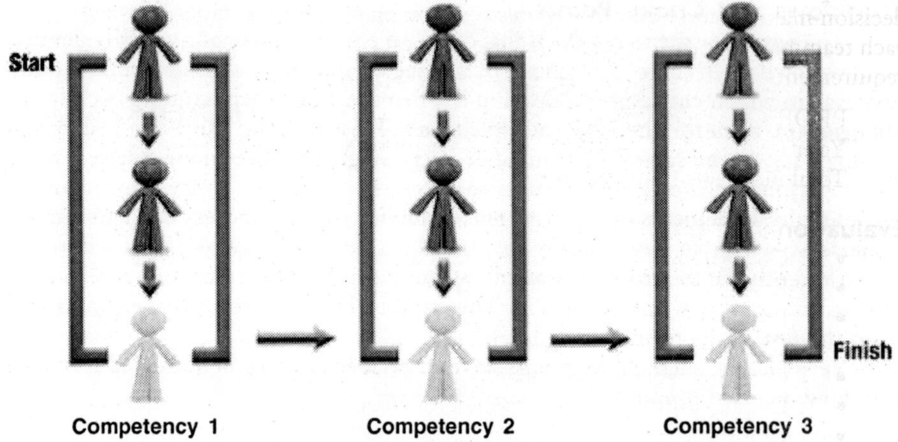

Okay, I can hear the questions. What if others are not competent? Who said the others are all incompetent and only you are competent? And even if that were true, wouldn't it be easier to spend some time in building up the competence rather than spending forever in catching up on delayed workloads?

Another way of increasing competence would be to create teams which would crosscheck each other's work on a given element rather than have everyone check everyone else's work.

And finally, aligning and optimizing the workflow is not a one time effort. Over time, changes creep into what has been set-up due to a variety of reasons. Changes in the business environment also would require re-optimization of the workflow. How frequently you need to re-look at your workflow would be a function of your business and the teams you have.

Team/Peer Performance Appraisal

Companies want one thing: the tools to hire the right people and keep them for longer. A company that bleeds talent has problems. On PAR (On Performance Appraisal Research) involves creating team appraisals to measure work performance from the moment new people start work. It means that with the right set of circumstances in a business, team members can assess the work they do and deal with any problems or issues as they arise, as a group. It involves dealing with problems as you go along, rather than leaving it up to the boss to fix. It means taking responsibility for your own development on a continuing basis, not leaving small tremors that then grow into earthquakes

The following team/peer appraisals will be used in part to determine appropriate project grades for each team member. Each team member **must individually** fill out a team/peer appraisal form.

Please divide 100 points among you and your teammates according to their level of participation in your team's project. If you feel all members have contributed equally, then assign each team member 25 points (assuming there are a total of four members). Please try to be fair to your teammates and objective about your own performance.

You may also comment **briefly** on each team member's performance. Your evaluation should use standard evaluation criteria, such as technical competence, effort, productivity, creativity, quality, dependability, communication, initiative, decision-making, and leadership. If desired, you may assign a number between 1-5 for each teammate, for each category (where 1 is best or "outstanding", 3 is ok or "meets requirements", and 5 is worst or "unsatisfactory").

PROJECT/TARGET TITLE: ____________ TEAM NUMBER _______
Your name: ________________ Team role: ____________________
Total number of points: ______________

Evaluation Attributes

- Competence: possesses or seeks required knowledge
- Effort: tries to accomplish assigned tasks
- Productivity: level of work generated
- Creativity: produces useful, innovative approaches and ideas
- Quality: demonstrates accuracy and thoroughness
- Dependability: follows through on responsibilities
- Communication: listens, expresses ideas/concepts clearly
- Initiative: seeks out new assignments
- Decision-making: sets objectives, evaluates alternatives
- Leadership: fosters good teamwork, solves team problems

General Comments

Teammate #1: ______________ Team role: ____________________
Total number of points: ______________

Evaluation Attributes

- Competence: possesses or seeks required knowledge
- Effort: tries to accomplish assigned tasks
- Productivity: level of work generated
- Creativity: produces useful, innovative approaches and ideas
- Quality: demonstrates accuracy and thoroughness
- Dependability: follows through on responsibilities
- Communication: listens, expresses ideas/concepts clearly
- Initiative: seeks out new assignments
- Decision Making: sets objectives, evaluates alternatives
- Leadership: fosters good teamwork, solves team problems

General Comments

Teammate #2: ________________ Team role: ________________
Total number of points: ______________

Evaluation Attributes

- Competence: possesses or seeks required knowledge
- Effort: tries to accomplish assigned tasks
- Productivity: level of work generated
- Creativity: produces useful, innovative approaches and ideas
- Quality: demonstrates accuracy and thoroughness
- Dependability: follows through on responsibilities

- Communication: listens, expresses ideas/concepts clearly
- Initiative: seeks out new assignments
- Decision-making: sets objectives, evaluates alternatives
- Leadership: fosters good teamwork, solves team problems

General Comments

Teammate #3: ____________________ Team role: ____________________

Total number of points: ______________

Evaluation Attributes

- Competence: possesses or seeks required knowledge
- Effort: tries to accomplish assigned tasks
- Productivity: level of work generated
- Creativity: produces useful, innovative approaches and ideas
- Quality: demonstrates accuracy and thoroughness
- Dependability: follows through on responsibilities
- Communication: listens, expresses ideas/concepts clearly
- Initiative: seeks out new assignments
- Decision Making: sets objectives, evaluates alternatives
- Leadership: fosters good teamwork, solves team problems

General Comments

Your signature ________________________________ Date: __________

Building and Leading High Performance Teams

When a sports team is working well together, it can feel like magic. We've all experienced it, either as a team member or as a fan. Fortunately, you do not have to be Michael Jordan or Mia Hamm to have the skills you need to build and lead high performing teams in your organization.

An important leadership competency for any size organization, the ability to build and lead high performing teams is especially critical in small-to-midsize businesses. Here, people must work closely together, wear many hats and work effectively across the organization to get tasks accomplished quickly enough to remain competitive.

In order to understand the competencies needed to build and lead high performance teams, it is helpful to first define a team. Here is a simple but effective description from *The Wisdom of Teams* (Harvard Business School Press, 1993.)

"A team is a small number of people with complementary skills who are committed to a common purpose, performance goals, and approach for which they hold themselves mutually accountable."

Using this definition, we can outline three important competencies for the effective team builder and leader.

- **Promoting understanding** of why a group of people need to be a team. The team needs to understand its shared goals and what each team member brings to the team that is relevant and crucial to its overall successes.
- **Ensuring the team has adequate knowledge** to accomplish its task. This includes information relevant to the team's goals and individual job competencies.

- **Facilitating effective interaction** in such a way as to ensure good problem-solving, decision-making and coordination of effort.

CHARACTERISTICS OF HIGHLY EFFECTIVE PERFORMANCE TEAMS

To better understand how these competencies create effective teams, let's examine some characteristics of highly effective teams.

An effective team understands the big picture. In an effective team, each team member understands the context of the team's work to the greatest degree possible. That includes understanding the relevance of his or her job and how it impacts the effectiveness of others and the overall team effort. Too often, people are asked to work on part of a task without being told how their role contributes to the desired end result, much less how their efforts are impacting the ability of others to do their work. Understanding the big picture promotes collaboration, increases commitment and improves quality.

An effective team has common goals. Effective teams have agreed-upon goals that are simple, measurable and clearly relevant to the team's task. Each goal includes key measurable metrics (that are available to everyone on the team), which can be used to determine the team effectiveness and improvement. Understanding and working toward these common goals as a unit is crucial to the team's effectiveness.

An effective team works collaboratively, as a unit. In an effective team you'll notice a penchant for collaboration and a keen awareness of interdependency. Collaboration and a solid sense of interdependency in a team will defuse blaming behavior and stimulate opportunities for learning and improvement. Without this sense of interdependency in responsibility and reward, blaming behaviors can occur which will quickly erode team effectiveness.

THE ROLES OF LEADER IN PERFORMANCE TEAM

In order to encourage this level of collaboration and interdependency, the team leader must provide the necessary support and structure for the team, starting with putting together the right people. Team members should be selected and their tasks assigned with their natural skills in mind. Not every person is capable of doing every job.

The team must also have the resources and training required to develop the skills needed to do their jobs. This includes cross-training. Cross-training gives team members a greater awareness of how their jobs are interdependent, increasing the team's flexibility and improving response time.

The quality of the team's response is highly dependent on the timeliness of the feedback received from the team's leader, other team members and customers. Receiving timely feedback is crucial to the effectiveness of the team. The effective team leader ensures that feedback reaches the entire team on its goals and metrics, as well as feedback to each individual team member. This feedback must be received in time to make adjustments and corrections. Often, feedback is received too late to have any practical value in the moment, and consequently, it feels like criticism. While it might be useful for future planning, it does not promote immediate corrections in performance.

Feedback is a form of constructive communication, another necessary tool in the effective team leader's tool chest. No matter how traditional or innovative the work design, consistent and constructive communication throughout the team is essential. The act of constructive communication can do more than anything else to improve quality and productivity. Timely and appropriately delivered feedback can make the difference between a team that hides mistakes and a team that sees mistakes as opportunities.

When a team views mistakes as opportunities for improving the team's process and results, it's a sign that the team leader has successfully created an environment that promotes problem-solving. People are problem-solvers by nature. When they are allowed to create their own solutions (rather than having expert solutions imposed upon them) team members are more proactive and engaged. Teams also have greater ownership of solutions they discover for themselves.

Creating an environment that promotes problem-solving is part of creating an effective team structure. Poor team structure can actually create negative, ineffective behaviors in individuals and impede communication. The responsibility for poor performance is usually a function of the team structure rather than individual incompetence; yet, it is individuals who are sent to human resources or training programs for fixing. If team members feel like they are pitted against one another to compete for rewards and recognition, they will withhold information that might be useful to the greater team. When a team has problems, the effective team leader will focus on the team's structure before focusing on individuals.

CASE STUDY

Donnelly Grand Haven Case

Donnelly is a family owned business that was founded in 1905 in Holland, Michigan. Donnelly has a long history as one of the most progressive companies in America in participative management. Workers, who are all salary, decide how fast to run the production line, when to shut it down, and the size of their own pay increases. Employees are organized into self-directed work teams and most operate with no managers. Job rotation is common. All plants are on a Scanlon Plan, which means employees share in the profitability of the plant and in good years have gotten a 10% or more bonus. Donnelly makes side view and rearview mirrors for automotive customers. Business has been volatile with the ups and downs of the market. Since the early 1990s, auto companies in the United States have been reducing the number of suppliers they have and giving larger shares of business to a small number of big suppliers. They have also been demanding price decreases each year, and have high demands for quality and delivery performance.

Their Grand Haven plant makes exterior mirrors, some painted and some unpainted, primarily for Honda. They built the plant to serve Honda in 1988 and business has been growing ever since. This was the first contract Donnelly received for painted mirrors and the large, multimillion dollar paint booth has always been a source of defects.

The overall process is simple. The plant purchases plastic resins, which are used to injection mold the housings for the mirror. These are either painted or sent directly to assembly. Many purchased parts are also sent to assembly and the housings plus purchased parts are all assembled, boxed, and shipped.

In 1995, because of too many shipped defects and too many late shipments, Honda threatened to pull their business, which would have shut Grand Haven down.

The plant had been experimenting with lean manufacturing methods for some years but made little progress. They decided they better get serious and quickly move the plant to lean manufacturing. The first line of attack would be to organize the long assembly lines into one-piece flow manufacturing cells by customer, as well as reduce the large inventory buffers between injection molding and the later operations, paint and assembly. To reduce inventory buffers they will need to reduce die changeover times from the current 2-3 hours to world class levels of under 10 minutes. Also, work needs to be done to improve the reliability of the paint process.

There were some concerns because this plant was a model of participative management and decisions are usually made slow and by consensus. There had been a past unionization drive a couple of years earlier because Grand haven wages were significantly lower than the Donnelly wages in Holland. Also, with the poor performance of the plant the Scanlon bonus was down sharply.

Sample Question

Assume it is 1995. Given what you know about change management and what you know about the company from the case, how would you recommend that the Donnelly managers approach this change? Use both theory from the class and evidence from the case.

Chapter 3

Total Quality Management

CONCEPT AND DEFINITIONS

Total Quality Management (TQM) is an approach that seeks to improve quality and performance which will meet or exceed customer expectations. This can be achieved by integrating all quality-related functions and processes throughout the company. TQM looks at the overall quality measures used by a company including managing quality design and development, quality control and maintenance, quality improvement, and quality assurance. TQM takes into account all quality measures taken at all levels and involving all company employees.

The term quality is used in a variety of ways. Sometimes
it refers to the grade of a product such as USDA or 'Grade A' eggs
it refers materials workmanship or special features such as waterproof or subtle aroma
it is relative to price i.e., cheap or expensive

There are many definition of Total Quality Management

"TQM is an encompassing dynamic process in an organization to promote never ending improvement in the effectiveness and efficiency of all elements".

—Parag Diwan

"TQM is a management philosophy ,embracing all activities through which the need of customer, the community and the objectives of the organization are satisfied in the most effective manners".

—Brockman

"Total Quality Management is the management approach of an organization, centered on quality on the participation of all its member and aiming at long-term success through customer satisfaction and benefits at all members of the organization and to society".

—ISO

"Total quality management is a process designed to focus on customer expectation, preventing problem building commitment to quality in the workforce and promoting open decision-making".

—Tohn Gilbert

Total Quality Management is based on three pillars.

—TQM

TQM views an organization as a collection of processes. It maintains that organizations must strive to continuously improve these processes by incorporating the knowledge and experiences of workers. The simple objective of TQM is "Do the right things, right the first time, every time". TQM is infinitely variable and adaptable. Although originally applied to manufacturing operations, and for a number of years only used in that area, TQM is now becoming recognized as a generic management tool, just as applicable in service and public sector organizations. There are a number of evolutionary strands, with different sectors creating their own versions from the common ancestor. TQM is the foundation for activities, hich include:

- Commitment by senior management and all employees
- Meeting customer requirements
- Reducing development cycle times
- Just In Time/Demand Flow Manufacturing
- Improvement teams
- Reducing product and service costs
- Systems to facilitate improvement
- Line Management ownership
- Employee involvement and empowerment
- Recognition and celebration
- Challenging quantified goals and benchmarking
- Focus on processes/improvement plans
- Specific incorporation in strategic planning

This shows that TQM must be practiced in all activities, by all personnel, in Manufacturing, Marketing, Engineering, R&D, Sales, Purchasing, HR, etc.

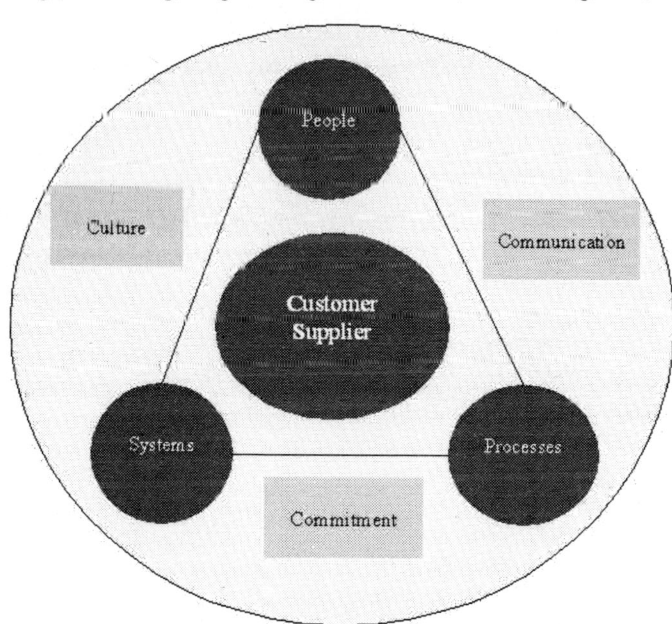

The core of TQM is the customer-supplier interfaces, both externally and internally, and at each interface lie a number of processes. This core must be surrounded by commitment to quality, communication of the quality message, and recognition of the need to change the culture of the organization to create total quality. These are the foundations of TQM, and they are supported by the key management functions of people, processes and systems in the organization.

Origins of TQM

The history of quality control is undoubtedly as old as industry itself. The concept of specialization of labor was introduced during the Industrial revolution. As a result, a worker no longer made the entire product, only in a portion—brought about a decline in workmanship. Because most products manufactured during that early period were not complicated, quality was not greatly affected. In fact, because productivity improved there was a decrease in cost, which resulted in lower customer expectations. As products became more complicated and jobs more specialized, it became necessary to inspects after manufacture.

Industrial revolution	Concept of specialization of labor decline workmanship complexity and less quality required inspection after production
1924	W.A. Shewart of Bell Telephone laboratories . Developed a stati stical chart for the control of product variables .Later in the same decade H.F. Dodge and H.G. Roming developed the area of acceptance sampling as a substitute for 100% inspection
1942	Recognition of the value of SCC (Statistical Control Chart)
1946	American Society for quality (ASQ) formed
1950	E. Deming and Joseph M. Juran made their valuable lectures and sharing on SCC to Japanese engineers and management's response to achieve quality. Joseph Juran made his first trip to Japan in 1954 and further emphasized management's responsibility to achieve Quality. He began his cost of quality approach, emphasizing accurate and complete identification and measurement of costs of quality.
1960	The concept of 'Zero-defects' gained favor. Philip Crosby, who was the champion of Zero-defects concept focused on employee's motivation and awareness. The first quality control circles were formed in Japan for the purpose of quality improvement. Simple Statistical Tech. were learned and applied by Japanese
1970-early1980	U.S. Managers were frequent troops to Japan to learn the Japanese miracles. A quality success began to occur in U.S. products and services
Middle1980s	concept of TQM were being publicized
The Late 1980s	The automotive industries began to emphasize statistical process control (SPC) The Malcom Baldrige National Quality Award and became the means to measure TQM.
	Genechi Taguchi introduced his concepts of 'Parameter and

	Tolerancedesign' as a valuable quality improvement tool
1990	Emphasis on quality control in the auto industries.
1996	Saturn Automobile ranked first in customer satisfaction. In addition, ISO-9000 became the model for a quality management system worldwide, ISO-14000 was approved as the world wide model for Environment Management system
	Quality assurance begins as a priority for engineers and managers.
1996-2000	Transmission to open economy, domestic and international competitions starts.
	TQM is the ultimatum for continuous improvement and sustainable growth
2001-07	High growth of economy—the new millennium brought about increased emphasis on worldwide quality and the Internet

Conceptual Developmet of TQM (In Indian Scenario)

Step—1	The year 1991 (economic liberalization) brought about a lot of changes in the Indian Economy and overall business environment in our country.
Step—2	Lots of Foreign MNCs started operations in India in the form of Joint ventures (JV) like—Hero Honda, Maruti Sujuki, etc.
Step—3	Professor Yasutosi Washio, has predicted that the quality of Indian man will overtake that of Japan in 2013
Step—4	Mahindra's Tractor unit is the first tractor unit in the world to win DEMNG Award
Step—5	Indian industries even small industries interested to evolve themselves sunder total quality management process by using the tools and techniques like TPM (Total Productive Maintenance) and other standards

The year 1991 brought about a lot of changes in the Indian economy and the overall business environment in the country. During the liberalization process, a lot of foreign multinational corporations (MNCs) started operations in India. Most of these operations were in the form of Joint Ventures (JVs) with domestic companies. It was not that all the JVs started during the period after 1991 only, Some JVs, such as Maruti-Suzuki, Hero Honda, TVS Suzuki, Escorts Yamaha, etc., had already started in the early and mid 1980s due to the decision of the Indian Government to allow the entry of MNCs in selective sectors of the industry. These MNCs could set-up JV switch Indian Companies only if the Indian company held a majority stake. This condition existed only in the 1980s. After 1991, the Government continued more rigorously with its liberalization programme, and we saw most of the earlier restrictions, such as the majority stake of the Indian JV partner, being withdrawn by the Government.

Finally, it is true that the effort on quality improvement will intensify only when it becomes an issue for survival and sustainability and that is dependent upon the intensity of fair competition in the market place. In this context, it is high time that the Indian companies follow business excellence model of survival and growth to face the threat of competition effectively.

The MNCs can now set-up 100% subsidiaries in India in most of the sectors of economy. This has brought about a lot of competition, especially from the point of view of the domestic industry. It has become a 'do' or 'die' situation for most of the domestic companies, which had bȩn operating, for a long period of time, in a seller's market of the license Raj. Most of the JVs formed during the 1980s and 1990s have ended with either the MNC taking full control of the venture, or the MNC exiting the JV to set-up its separate 100% owned subsidiary in direct competition with the JV. Joint ventures such as Kinetic Honda, Shriram Honda, TVS Suzuki, etc. are to name a few, JVs which ended up in this manner. Table 1 shows the evolution of TQM related activities in India and projection for the future given by Mehta (1999).

Principles of TQM

TQM can be defined as the management of initiatives and procedures that are aimed at achieving the delivery of quality products and services. A number of key principles can be identified in defining TQM, including:

- **Executive Management**–Top management should act as the main driver for TQM and create an environment that ensures its success.
- **Training**–Employees should receive regular training on the methods and concepts of quality.
- **Customer Focus**–Improvements in quality should improve customer satisfaction.
- **Decision-making**–Quality decisions should be made based on measurements.
- **Methodology and Tools**–Use of appropriate methodology and tools ensures that non-conformances are identified, measured and responded to consistently.
- **Continuous Improvement**–Companies should continuously work towards improving manufacturing and quality procedures.
- **Company Culture**–The culture of the company should aim at developing employees ability to work together to improve quality.
- **Employee Involvement**–Employees should be encouraged to be pro-active in identifying and addressing quality related problems.

The Cost of TQM

Many companies believe that the costs of the introduction of TQM are far greater than the benefits it will produce. However research across a number of industries has costs involved in doing nothing, i.e. the direct and indirect costs of quality problems, are far greater than the costs of implementing TQM.

The American quality expert, Phil Crosby, wrote that many companies chose to pay for the poor quality in what he referred to as the "Price of Non-conformance". The costs are identified in the Prevention, Appraisal, Failure (PAF) Model.

Prevention costs are associated with the design, implementation and maintenance of the TQM system. They are planned and incurred before actual operation, and can include:

- **Product Requirements**–The setting specifications for incoming materials, processes, finished products/services.

TABLE I

Changes in social and economic environment	Development in quality	Quality control (QC) tools	Quality assurance (QA) systems	Change of concepts in policy management
1947-82 India becomes independent Regulated economy slow rate of economic growth very low competition	QC in inspection stage (Identification of defectives)	Inspection	Regulation of inspection	
1983-94 Initial phase of deregulation of economy slow growth rate Imported kits merging domestic competition	Quality awareness growing Regulation of product audit Attempted use of QC circles	7 Tools of QC	QA systems Compliance with ISO9000 quality system requirement	To attach importance to measures or means in addition to target
1995-2000 Transition to open economy Adequate growth rate of economy Growing domestic competition Select international competition	QC in manufacturing stage (prevention of detectives)	Various statistical methods Design of experiments Failure mode effect analysis and fault tree analysis	Regulation of process control QC process chart, control chart, and check sheet Quality tables deploying required qualities	To attach importance to coordination to management of all the divisions in addition to that of each division
2001-07 Deregulation of economy High growth of economy Open competition	QC In design stage (making new products to satisfy new customer requirement	Multivariate analysis Weibull probability paper 7 management tools	Quality tables transforming required qualities to design qualities	To attach importance to mid-term and long-term policies in addition to those specified annually

- **Quality Planning**–Creation of plans for quality, reliability, operational, production and inspections.
- **Quality Assurance**–The creation and maintenance of the quality system.
- **Training**–The development, preparation and maintenance of processes.

Appraisal costs are associated with the vendors and customers evaluation of purchased materials and services to ensure they are within specification. They can include:

- **Verification**—Inspection of incoming material against agreed upon specifications.
- **Quality Audits**—Check that the quality system is functioning correctly.
- **Vendor Evaluation**—Assessment and approval of vendors.

Failure costs can be split into those resulting from internal and external failure. Internal failure costs occur when results fail to reach quality standards and are detected before they are shipped to the customer. These can include:

- **Waste**—Unnecessary work or holding stocks as a result of errors, poor organization or communication.
- **Scrap**—Defective product or material that cannot be repaired, used or sold.
- **Rework**—Correction of defective material or errors.
- **Failure Analysis**—This is required to establish the causes of internal product failure.

External failure costs occur when the products or services fail to reach quality standards, but are not detected until after the customer receives the item. These can include:

- **Repairs**—Servicing of returned products or at the customer site.
- **Warranty Claims**—Items are replaced or services re-performed under warranty.
- **Complaints**—All work and costs associated with dealing with customer's complaints.
- **Returns**—Transportation, investigation and handling of returned items.

Continuous Improvement and TQM

TQM is mainly concerned with continuous improvement in all work, from high level strategic planning and decision-making, to detailed execution of work elements on the shop floor. It stems from the belief that mistakes can be avoided and defects can be prevented. It leads to continuously improving results, in all aspects of work, as a result of continuously improving capabilities, people, processes, and technology and machine capabilities.

Continuous improvement must deal not only with improving results, but more importantly with improving capabilities to produce better results in the future. The five major areas of focus for capability improvement are demand generation, supply generation, technology, operations and people capability.

A central principle of TQM is that mistakes may be made by people, but most of them are caused, or at least permitted, by faulty systems and processes. This means that the root cause of such mistakes can be identified and eliminated, and repetition can be prevented by changing the process.

There are three major mechanisms of prevention:

1. Preventing mistakes (defects) from occurring (Mistake—proofing or Poka-Yoke).
2. Where mistakes can't be absolutely prevented, detecting them early to prevent them being passed down the value-added chain (Inspection at source or by the next operation).
3. Where mistakes recur, stopping production until the process can be corrected, to prevent the production of more defects. (Stop in time).

The basis for TQM implementation is the establishment of a quality management system which involves the organizational structure, responsibilities, procedures and processes. The most frequently used guidelines for quality management systems are the ISO 9000 international standards, which emphasize the establishment of a well-documented, standardized quality system. The role of the ISO 9000 standards within the TQM circle of continuous improvement is presented in the following figure.

→ Diagnostics → Planning and Implementation → Evaluation		
Quality Management	Quality Assurance	Quality Control
• Identification of what to improve • Selection of the approach to organizational innovation • (TQM, re-engineering, bench-marking, etc.)	• Standardization of key quality processes • Development and maintenance of the quality system • Documentation • Training ←ISO 9000→	• Measuring and monitoring • Inspection • Audits • Certification • Management Revision
← Feedback and adjustment ←		

Continuous improvement is a circular process that links the diagnostic, planning, implementation and evaluation phases. Within this circular process, the ISO 9000 standards are commonly applied in the implementation phase. An ISO 9000 quality system also requires the establishment of procedures that standardize the way an organization handles the diagnostic and evaluation phases. However, the ISO 9000 standards do not prescribe particular quality management techniques or quality-control methods. Because it is a generic organizational standard, ISO 9000 does not define quality or provide any specifications of products or processes. ISO 9000 certification only assures that the organization has in place a well-operated quality system that conforms to the ISO 9000 standards. Consequently, an organization may be certified but still manufacture poor-quality products

Elements of TQM

Total quality management can be summarized as a management system for a customer-focused organization that involves all employees in continual improvement. It uses strategy, data, and effective communications to integrate the quality discipline into the culture and activities of the organization.

- **Customer-focused.** The customer ultimately determines the level of quality. No matter what an organization does to foster quality improvement—training employees, integrating quality into the design process, upgrading computers or software, or buying new measuring tools—the customer determines whether the efforts were worthwhile.
- **Total employee involvement.** All employees participate in working toward common goals. Total employee commitment can only be obtained after fear has been driven from the workplace, when empowerment has occurred, and management has provided the proper environment. High-performance work systems integrate continuous improvement efforts with normal business operations. Self-managed work teams are one form of empowerment.

- **Process-centered.** A fundamental part of TQM is a focus on process thinking. A process is a series of steps that take inputs from suppliers (internal or external) and transforms them into outputs that are delivered to customers (again, either internal or external). The steps required to carry out the process are defined, and performance measures are continuously monitored in order to detect unexpected variation.
- **Integrated system.** Although an organization may consist of many different functional specialities often organized into vertically structured departments, it is the horizontal processes interconnecting these functions that are the focus of TQM.
  - Micro-processes add up to larger processes, and all processes aggregate into the business processes required for defining and implementing strategy. Everyone must understand the vision, mission, and guiding principles as well as the quality policies, objectives, and critical processes of the organization. Business performance must be monitored and communicated continuously.
  - An integrated business system may be modeled after the Baldrige National Quality Program criteria and/or incorporate the ISO 9000 standards. Every organization has a unique work culture, and it is virtually impossible to achieve excellence in its products and services unless a good quality culture has been fostered. Thus, an integrated system connects business improvement elements in an attempt to continually improve and exceed the expectations of customers, employees, and other stakeholders.
- **Strategic and systematic approach.** A critical part of the management of quality is the strategic and systematic approach to achieving an organization's vision, mission, and goals. This process, called strategic planning or strategic management, includes the formulation of a strategic plan that integrates quality as a core component.
- **Continual improvement.** A major thrust of TQM is continual process improvement. Continual improvement drives an organization to be both analytical and creative in finding ways to become more competitive and more effective at meeting stakeholder expectations.
- **Fact-based decision-making.** In order to know how well an organization is performing, data on performance measures are necessary. TQM requires that an organization continually collect and analyze data in order to improve decision-making accuracy, achieve consensus, and allow prediction based on past history.
- **Communications.** During times of organizational change, as well as part of day-to-day operation, effective communications plays a large part in maintaining morale and in motivating employees at all levels. Communications involve strategies, method, and timeliness.

These elements are considered so essential to TQM that many organizations define them, in some format, as a set of core values and principles on which the organization is to operate

A Model for Organization Excellence and TQM

The roots of Total Quality Management (TQM) go back to the teachings of Drucker, Juran, Deming, Ishikawa, Crosby, Feigenbaum and countless other people that have studied, practiced, and tried to refine the process of organizational management. TQM is a collection of principles, techniques, processes, and best practices that over time have been proven effective. Most all world-class organizations exhibit the majority of behaviors that are typically identified with TQM.

No two organizations have the same TQM implementation. There is no recipe for organization success, however, there are a number of great TQM models that organizations can use. These include the Deming Application Prize, the Malcolm Baldrige Criteria for Performance Excellence, the European Foundation for Quality Management, and the ISO quality management standards. Any organization that wants to improve its performance would be well served by selecting one of these models and conducting a self-assessment.

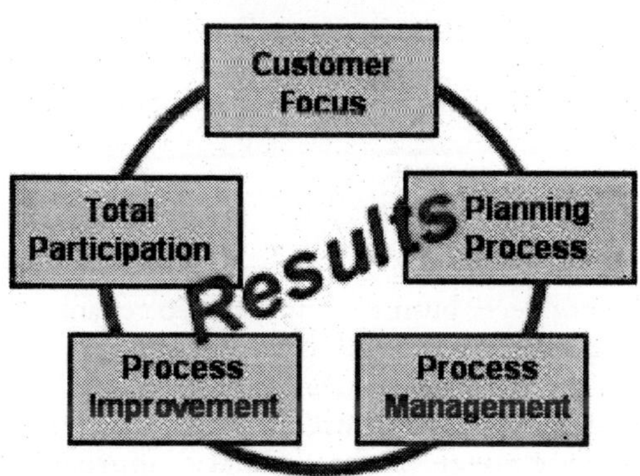

The simplest model of TQM is shown in this diagram. The model begins with understanding customer needs. TQM organizations have processes that continuously collect, analyze, and act on customer information. Activities are often extended to understanding competitor's customers. Developing an intimate understanding of customer needs allows TQM organizations to predict future customer behavior.

TQM organizations integrate customer knowledge with other information and use the planning process to orchestrate action throughout the organization to manage day to day activities and achieve future goals. Plans are reviewed at periodic intervals and adjusted as necessary. The planning process is the glue that holds together all TQM activity.

TQM organizations understand that customers will only be satisfied if they consistently receive products and services that meet their needs, are delivered when expected, and are priced for value. TQM organizations use the techniques of process management to develop cost-controlled processes that are stable and capable of meeting customer expectations.

TQM organizations also understand that exceptional performance today may be unacceptable performance in the future so they use the concepts of process improvement to achieve both breakthrough gains and incremental continuous improvement. Process improvement is even applied to the TQM system itself!

The final element of the TQM model is total participation. TQM organizations understand that all work is performed through people. This begins with leadership. In TQM organizations, top management takes personal responsibility for implementing, nurturing, and refining all TQM activities. They make sure people are properly trained, capable, and actively participate in achieving organizational success. Management and employees work together to create an empowered environment where people are valued

Total quality management is a philosophy that emphasises three principles for achieving high levels of process performance and quality. These principles are customer satisfaction, employee involvement, and continuous improvement in performance.

Customer Satisfaction

Customer satisfaction occurs when a customer's expectations regarding a service or product have been met or exceeded. Often, they use the general term quality to describe their level of satisfaction. To your average customer, quality can have many meanings:

- **Conformance to specifications**–Although customers evaluate the service or product they receive, it is the processes that produced the service or product that are really being judged. In this case, a process failure would be the process's inability to meet certain advertised or implied performance standards.
- **Value**–some customers will define quality through value, that is, how well the product or service serves it's intended purpose at a price they are willing to pay. How much value a product or service really has is dependent on the customer's expectations the purchase.
- **Fitness for use**–when assessing how well a service or product performs its intended purpose, the customer may consider the convenience of a service, the mechanical features of a product, or other aspects such as appearance, style, durability, reliability, craftsmanship, and serviceability.
- **Support**–to some customers, post sales support is just as important as the quality of the actual product or service itself. For example, if warranty claims are delayed or if a company's employees are not helpful when problems arise.
- Psychological impressions–people often evaluate the quality of a service or product on the basis of psychological impressions: atmosphere, image, or aesthetics. If you're providing a service in which there is close contact with the customer, your appearance and actions are especially important. In manufacturing, product quality is often judged on the basis of knowledge and personality of salespeople, as well as the product image presented in advertisements.

In general, a business's success depends on the accuracy of its perceptions of quality. In general, a business's success depends on the accuracy of its perceptions of consumer expectations and its ability to bridge the gap between those expectations and operating capabilities.

Employee Involvement

Another important element of TQM is employee involvement. This includes changing organizational culture and encouraging an atmosphere of teamwork: Cultural change–one of the main challenges in developing the proper culture for TQM is to get your employees to fully understand your customers. For example, employees that have little contact with external customers may have difficulty in seeing how their jobs contribute to the whole effort. Additionally, it should be noted that each employee also has at least one or more internal customers, that is, other employees who rely on their output within processes. Internal customers must first be satisfied in order to satisfy external customers.

- **Teams**—Employee involvement is a key tactic for improving processes and quality. One way to achieve employee involvement is by the use of teams, which are small groups of people who have a common purpose, set their own performance goals and approaches, and hold themselves for success.

Continuous improvement

Continuous improvement, based on a Japanese concept called kaizen, is the philosophy of continually seeking ways to improve processes. It involves identifying benchmarks of excellent practice and instilling a sense of employee ownership in the process

The focus of continuous improvement projects is to reduce waste.

The bases of continuous improvement philosophy are the beliefs that virtually any aspect of a process can be improved and that the people most closely associated with a process are in the best position to identify changes that should be made.

An approach in problem solving with continuous improvement in mind is the plan-do-study-act cycle, also known as the Deming Wheel. The cycle comprises the following steps:

Plan—the team selects a process that needs improvement. The team then documents the selected process, sets qualitative goals for improvement, and discusses various ways to achieve the goals. After assessing the benefits and costs of the alternatives, the team develops a plan with quantifiable measures for improvement.

Do—the team implements the plan and monitors progress. Data is collected continuously to measure the improvements in the process. Any changes in the process are documented and further revisions are made as needed.

Study—the team analyses the data collected during the 'do' step to find out how closely the results correspond to the goals set in the plan step. If major shortcomings exist, the team re-evaluates the plan or ceases the project.

Act—if the results are successful, the team documents the revised process so that it becomes the standard procedure for all who may use it. The team may then instruct other employees in the use of the revised process.

BUSINESS PHILOSOPHY AND TQM

Total Quality Management (TQM) is a business philosophy that seeks to encourage both individual and collective responsibility to quality at every stage of the production process from initial design and conception through to after sales service. Many businesses may not use the term TQM anymore but the philosophy is still very much part of most business thinking. It is seen as being a way in which a business can add value to its product and to gain competitive advantage over its rivals. The former may allow a business to charge a higher price for its product or service whilst the latter can be a key feature of its marketing programme. TQM requires a change in the way in which businesses operate. It implies a number of things if it is to work successfully:

- Management structures have to be more consultative and less hierarchical.
- Workers have to be empowered to be able to make decisions at all levels of the organization.
- Workers have to be trained and involved in the building of the philosophy.
- Communication links between workers and management and between the business and all aspects of the supply chain must be excellent.
- Commitment to TQM must be backed by action, which the customer can see, and experience.
- Commitment to the process must be led by the senior management of the business—paying 'lip service' will invariably end up in failure.

TQM can be addressed in a business in a number of ways. The most common are:

- A policy of **zero defects**—any problems in the production process are filtered out before they get anywhere near the customer.
- **Quality chains**—each stage of the production process is seen as being a link in the chain right down to the relationship between one worker in the process and another.
- **Quality circles**—meetings of those directly involved in the production process to discuss and solve problems and make improvements to the production process.
- **Statistical monitoring**—the use of data and statistics to monitor and evaluate production processes and quality.
- **Consumer feedback**—using market research and focus groups to identify consumer needs and experiences and to build these into the process.
- **Changing production methods**—many businesses, where appropriate, have looked at the layout of their production processes—it could be the move to open plan offices, the development of teams or the use of cell production to improve worker commitment to the philosophy.

TQM invariably involves some sort of cost. Re-organising the business in any of the ways above not only involves capital cost but also the cost of training staff. High quality change management is therefore an essential ingredient of the success of such strategies.

Costs can however be saved if the change is successful. The cost of replacing damaged or faulty goods can be high—if the business waits until the end of the process other resources will have been wasted. The improved communication between suppliers and the firm should help to reduce defective components.

Other benefits may involve the effect on customer loyalty and repeat purchases, as well as winning over customers from rivals. Image and reputation can take many years to win but only a short time to lose so the stakes for the business are high.

To prove that the business has rigorous quality standards, external certification by a respected body is seen as being important. Such external certification could be through the Investors in People programme—a recognized standard in the training and professional development of staff in a business—and through such bodies as the ISO.

Two certificates are particularly sought after—ISO 9000 and ISO 14000. The former is concerned with quality management in relation to customer requirements, customer satisfaction, adherence to regulations and the pursuit of continuous improvement. ISO 14000 is related to the impact of the firm's activities on the environment and the firm's attempts to improve its performance in this respect. Getting certification means that the company can send a message to companies throughout the world, which recognise this standard—currently, around 90 countries—of the quality that they can expect when dealing with the company. The standards for the ISO 9000 family deal with the following areas:

1. **Quality management systems**—establishing and monitoring the process whereby product and service quality are maintained.
2. **Management responsibility**—how the management establish, maintain, monitor and communicate their commitment to the standards.
3. **Resource management**—how the business provides the resources—both physical and human—to enable the standards to be met and maintained.
4. **Product realization requirements**—how businesses establish and monitor quality from concept to final product or service delivery.
5. **Measurement, analysis and improvement requirements**—how businesses use data to monitor their quality control and how this data is used to improve quality provision.

The terminology related to quality management could be regarded as being a bit 'nineties' but the philosophy is still one that drives many businesses as they seek to find ways in which, in an increasingly competitive global market, they can gain some form of competitive advantage or add value to their business

The TQM philosophy focuses on teamwork, increasing customer satisfaction, and lowering costs. Organizations implement TQM by encouraging managers and employees to collaborate across functions and departments, as well as with customers and suppliers, to identify areas for improvement, no matter how small. Teams of workers are trained and empowered to make decisions that help their organization achieve high standards of quality. Organizations shift responsibility for quality control from specialized departments to all employees. Thus, total quality management means a shift from a bureaucratic to a decentralized approach to control.

CONTRIBUTION OF TQM GURUS

Deming's Contributions

Deming was an American who worked in the 1930s with Walter A. Shewhart at Bell Telephone Company. Shewhart was a statistician who had the theory that product control could best be managed by statistics. He developed a statistical chart for the control of product variables. Deming developed a process, based on Shewhart's, using statistical control techniques that alerted managers of the need to intervene in the production process.

He then utilized these techniques during World War II while working on government war production. In 1947, Douglas MacArthur and the U.S. State Department sent Deming to Japan to help the war-devastated Japanese manufacturing plants. He introduced these "statistical process control" methods in a series of lectures on statistical methods to Japanese businessmen and engineers. The Japanese were an attentive audience and utilized Deming's ideas readily. They found him charming and considerate and listened to his ideas. His concept of employees working toward quality fit well into their personal ideas. His philosophy went beyond statistical quality control and encouraged building quality into the product at all stages.

The U.S. Department of Defense's Definition of Total Quality

Total Quality (TQ) consists of continuous improvement activities involving everyone in the organization Managers and workers a totally integrated effort toward improving performance at every level. This improved performance is directed toward satisfying such cross-functional goals as quality, cost, schedule, missing, need, and suitability. TQ integrates fundamental management techniques, existing improvement efforts, and technical tools under a disciplined approach focused on continued process improvement. The activities are ultimately focused on increasing customer/user satisfaction.

Deming developed the chain reaction: as quality improves, costs go down and productivity goes up; this leads to more jobs, greater market share, and long-term survival. He stressed worker pride and satisfaction and considered it management's job to improve the process, not the worker. Quality circles, a central Deming theme, are based on the importance of employees meeting regularly in groups to comprehensively discuss product quality. The GDP in Japan rose steadily from 1960s by more than 10 percent per year. By 1951 the Japanese had named their quality prize in his honor. Deming's book, Out of the Crisis, emphasized improving quality of the product as more important than short-term financial goals. He de-emphasized quantity, and emphasized quality. He believed that "statistical process control" was an invaluable instrument in the quest for quality. Deming developed fourteen points for management which can be summarized as:

Create a plan; publish the aims and purposes of the organization.
Learn and adopt the new philosophy of quality.
Understand the purpose of inspection; stop depending on inspection.
Stop awarding business based on price alone.
Improve the system constantly.
Institute training.
Teach and institute leadership.
Drive out fear, create trust, and create a climate for innovation.
Optimize the efforts of teams, groups and staff areas.
Eliminate exhortations, and targets for the work force; provide methods of achievement.
Eliminate numerical quotas for the work force.
Remove barriers that rob people of pride for workmanship.
Encourage education and self-improvement for everyone.
Make action to accomplish the transformation, make it everyone's job.

Besides the fourteen points, Deming is known for the Deming Cycle and the Seven Deadly Diseases. The Deming Cycle is illustrated in Figure 1. It involves five steps: consumer research and planning of the product (plan), producing the product (do), checking the product (check), marketing the product (act), and analyzing how the product is received (analyze.)

The Seven Deadly Diseases can be summarized as:

Lack of constancy of purpose to plan products and services.

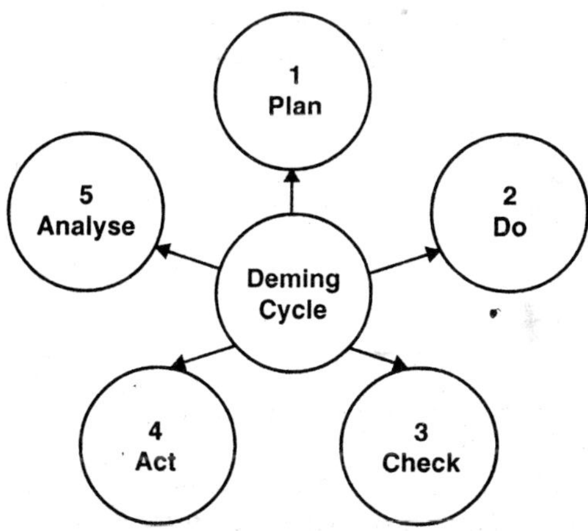

Figure 1 : The Deming Cycle

Emphasis on short-term profits.
Personal review systems for managers and management by objectives.
Job hopping by managers.
Using only visible data in decision-making.
Excessive medial costs.
Excessive costs of liability driven up by lawyers that work on contingency.

JURAN'S CONTRIBUTIONS

Joseph M. Juran, like Deming, went to Japan in 1954 and assisted the Japanese in their quest to achieve quality. Like Deming, Juran emphasized planning, organizing and controlling. However he emphasized customer satisfaction more than Deming did and focused on management and technical methods rather than worker satisfaction. Juran was a prolific author, publishing over a dozen books. His most influential book Quality Control Handbook (later called Juran's Quality Handbook) was published in 1951 and became a best seller.

By 1960 Japan was using quality control circles and simple statistical techniques learned and applied by Japanese workers. Juran developed basic steps that companies must take, however he believed there was a point of diminishing return, a point at which quality goes beyond the consumer needs. For example, if the consumer trades his car in after 50,000 miles, the car need only be built to perform trouble-free for 60,000 miles. Building a better car would drive up costs without delivering the expected product. This is called the Pareto Principle, or the Juran 80/20 rule: 80 percent of the trouble comes from 20 percent of the problems. The rule is named for Vilfredo Pareto, an economist, but it was Juran that applied the idea to management. It can be expressed as: "concentrate on the 'vital few' sources of problems; don't be distracted by less important problems." Juran's trilogy involves:

Quality planning (determine customer needs, develop product in response to needs).
Quality control (assess performance, compare performance with goals, act on differences between performance and goals).
Quality improvement (develop infrastructure, identify areas of improvement and implement projects, establish project team, provide teams with what they need).

Juran's ten steps to quality improvement are:
Build awareness of opportunities to improve.
Set goals.
Organize to reach goals.
Provide training.
Carry out projects to solve problems.
Report progress.
Give recognition.
Communicate results.
Keep score.

Maintain momentum by making annual improvement part of the systems and processes of the company.

The Union of Japanese Scientists and Engineers (JUSE) considered Juran's vision of top-to-bottom quality management even more important to their quality turnaround than Deming's insights. JUSE asked Juran if it could name its top-level award, a 'super-Deming award' after him, but he declined. This medal is called the Japan Quality Control Medal.

CROSBY'S CONTRIBUTIONS

Philip Crosby, author of Quality is Free, founded the Quality College in Winter Park, Florida. Crosby emphasized meeting customer requirements by focusing on prevention rather than correction. He claimed that poor quality costs about 20 percent of the revenue; a cost that could be avoided by using good quality practices. He pushed for zero defects. His "absolutes" are: (1) quality is defined as conformance to requirements, not goodness; (2) the system for achieving quality is prevention, not appraisal; (3) the performance standard is zero defects, not that's close enough; and (4) the measure of quality is the price of non-conformance, not indexes.

Crosby's method does not dwell on statistical process control and problem-solving techniques that the Deming method uses. He stated that quality is free because prevention will always be lower than the costs of detection, correction and failure. Like Deming, Crosby had fourteen points:

Manage commitment, that is, top level management must be convinced and committed and communicated to the entire company.
Quality improvement team composed of department heads, oversee improvements.
Quality measurements are established for every activity.
Cost of quality is estimated to identify areas of improvement.
Quality awareness is raised among all employees.
Corrective action is taken.
Zero defects is planned for.
Supervisor training in quality implementation.
Zero defects day is scheduled.
Goal setting for individuals.
Error causes are removed by having employees inform management of problems.
Recognition is given, but it is non-financial, to those who meet quality goals.
Quality councils meet regularly.
Do it all over again (i.e., repeat steps one through thirteen).

Looking at the history of quality management, we see several stages of development. The first was quality control, which involved setting up product specifications and then inspect the product fore for leaves the plant. The second state is quality assurance, which involved identifying the quality characteristics and procedures for quantitatively evaluating and controlling them. The next phase is the true total quality control, a term actually coined by Feingenbaum in 1983. At this stage the quality became a total organization effort. It effected production, profit, human interaction and customer satisfaction. The fourth stage is total quality management. In TQM the customer is the center and quality is an organization-wide effort.

QUALITY PRIZES

The top three quality prizes are the Deming Prize, the Baldrige Award and the European Quality Awards. Union of Japanese Scientists and Engineers have annually awarded the Deming Prize since 1951. For three decades it was the quality award and is still the most prestigious award. The Deming Prize is given to a person or group of people who have advanced the practice and furthered awareness of TQC. The Deming Application Prize goes only to companies based on successes attributable to implementing TQC. The second major quality prizes was established by Congress in 1987 (Public Law 100-107) and is called the Baldrige Award. The award set a national standard for quality and companies use the criteria as a management guide.

1931	**Walter A. Showhart of Bell Laboratories publishes Economic Control of Quality of Manufactured Products and introduces statistical quality control.**
1950	**W. Edwards Deming addressed Japanese scientists, engineers, and corporate executive on subject of quality.**
1951	**First Deming Prize awarded by the Union of Japanese Scientists and Engineers (JUSE).**
1952	**Joseph M. Juran publishes the Quality Control Handbook.**
1970	**Philip Crosby introduces the concept of zero defects.**
1978	**Crosby publishes Quality is Free.**
1980	**Ford Motor Company invites Deming to speak to executives.**
1981	**Bob Galvin, Motorola's chairman starts quality improvement, which leads to the six sigmas.**
1982	**Deming publishes Quality, Productivity and Competitive Position.**
1984	**Crosby publishes Quality without Tears: The Art of Hassle-Free Management.**
1987	**Congress creates the Malcolm Baldrige National Quality Award.**
1992	**First European Quality named, which is sponsored by the Foundation for Quality Management with support from the European Organization for Quality and the European Commission.**

Figure 2 : Chronology

Applicants must address seven specific categories: leadership, strategic planning, customer and market focus, information and analysis, human resource focus, process management, and business results. Winners are required to share their successful strategies. U.S. Department of Commerce's National Institute of Standards and Technology administer the Malcolm Baldrige National Quality Award. The third award is the awarded by The Foundation for Quality Management with support from the European Organization for Quality and the European Commission. It is called the European Quality Award and was first awarded in 1992.

QUALITY IN THE U.S.

The U.S. was slow to see the advantages of TQM, although the American Society for Quality Control (now known as American Society for Quality) was formed in 1946. Huge markets for American-made products after World War II kept American industries producing products with little change in manufacturing methods. It wasn't until the late 1970s that U.S. manufacturing came up against foreign competition and the trade deficit, and at that time it became obvious that Japanese companies were far ahead of U.S. companies in quality.

One of the first companies in the U.S. to grasp and utilize TQM was Motorola. In 1981 Bob Galvin, Motorola's chairman, called for an across-the-board improvement of 10:1 in five years. To accomplish this they needed a breakthrough technique. This breakthrough is detailed in the Six Sigma process:

Faith that the improvement target could be achieved.
Total customer satisfaction.
Powerful new tools, especially design of experiments.
Cycle-time reduction.
Designing for ease of manufacturing.
Manufacturing innovations.
True partnerships with key suppliers.
Training for all employees.

Within five years Motorola had achieved their goal. In 1988 they were awarded the Malcolm Baldridge National Quality Award for their impressive Six Sigma process. Keki R. Bhote nurtured the Six Sigma project for eleven years at Motorola and then went on to consult with other companies.

In the early 1980s when Donald Petersen was CEO of Ford, Ford executives were investigating the secret of the Japanese success. They discovered W. Edwards Deming's holistic blend of statistics and management. Deming's ideas came to Detroit. Ford was in serious trouble because of Japanese competition. Deming introduced the statistical methods needed to improve processes. These are the foundation of what became known as Six Sigma, a statistical measure that refers to 3.4 defects per million. Besides this scientific method of improving quality, Deming emphasized that all employees needed to work toward quality. He advocated teamwork and cross-department collaboration, close work with suppliers and employee training. Other companies that adopted the Deming quality methods were General Motors, Florida Power & Light, and Procter and Gamble.

Not all U.S. attempts at quality improvement have been successful. Frequently cited reasons for failure are poor leadership, team-mania (setting up teams before management or employee have been trained in team work), and lack of integration of quality efforts into the whole organization. Obstacles and barriers to success have been researched by Robert J. Masters. He lists eight common problems that lead to failure:

Lack of management commitment—Management must commit time and resources and clearly communicate the importance and goals to all personnel.

Inability to change the organizational culture—Change takes time and effort. In order for the culture to change, the employees need to want change and be willing to participate. This requires reasons that management must convey. The change will only occur if the employees trust the management. It cannot occur from a state of fear.

Improper planning—Planning must involve all parts of the organization and be communicated clearly to employees.

Lack of training—The most effective training comes from senior management. Informal training needs to occur on a continual basis.

Organizational structure problems and isolated individuals or departments—Multifunctional teams will help break down some of these barriers. Restructuring is another method.

Ineffective measurement and lack of data—Effective decisions require that the employees have access to the necessary data.

Inadequate attention to internal and external customers.

Inadequate empowerment, lack of teamwork—Teams require training. Their recommendations should be followed whenever possible. Individuals need to be empowered to make decisions.

IMPLEMENTING TQM

Although different authorities on total quality management emphasize different techniques and use different terminology, all share three common ideas: quality, teamwork and process improvement. Although many books have been written to guide U.S. companies through TQM, one of the major writers was Joseph Jablonski. In Implementing TQM, he identified three characteristics: (1) participative management; (2) continuous process improvement; and (3) utilization of teams.

Participative management is the opposite of the hierarchical management style of the early twentieth century businesses. It involves all employees in the management process and decision-making by having managers set policies and make key decisions based upon the advice and ideas of subordinates. This method provides management with more information from the front line and motivates the workers as they have some control of the decisions. Continuous process improvement is one of Deming's major ideas and involves small steps toward the ultimate goal. This involves patience on the part of management. Teamwork refers to cross-functional teams of workers that share in problem solving.

Jablonski went on to list six attributes necessary for success: (1) customer focus; (2) process focus; (3) prevention *versus* inspection; (4) employee empowerment and compensation; (5) fact-based decision-making; and (6) receptiveness to feedback.

U.S. companies have long relied upon company organization by functions. TQM emphasizes a decentralized structure to encourage leadership and creativity. The purpose of this change in structure is to change the behavior of the employees. This is a major change for most U.S. companies. However, successful companies have more functional integration and fewer layers of hierarchy.

QUALITY AND THE 1990S AND BEYOND

In the 1980s many U.S. companies implemented total quality management systems in order to be competitive in the global market place. Successes lead them to be interested in hiring managers and engineers with some TQM training. This prompted universities to start teaching quality methods. To help universities in this, the University Challenge program was developed by a group of companies that had implemented TQM successfully. Their goal was to encourage universities to commit to integrating TQM in their own operations and courses. Initially eight universities with both business and engineering schools were chosen. Milliken worked with North Carolina State University and Georgia Institute of Technology. IBM worked with Massachusetts Institute of Technology and Rochester Institute of Technology. Motorola worked with Purdue University. Procter & Gamble Company worked with University of Wisconsin at Madison and Tuskegee University. Xerox worked with Carnegie Mellon.

Another area of transformation by TQM since 1990 is in human resources. Numerous studies have indicated that human resource practices that improve the corporate culture lead to better profits. Therefore, many companies have extended TQM to the HR department. Yet another area of development of TQM in American firms is in the area of ethical philosophy and behavior of top management. Recent corporate scandals have increased interest from the public in corporate responsibility and accountability. Corporate responsibility is defined as how a company's operating practices affect its stakeholders, such as consumers, and the natural environment. This is new quality movement is being called total responsibility management. It involves responsible vision and values, leadership build on these values.

TQM has had a wide acceptance in the U.S., which has been growing since the 1970s. Quality management principles have had a remarkable influence on every sector of American business and are spreading to non-profit organizations and universities. It is essential that this trend continue for U.S. companies to be competitive in the global market and to meet consumer demands.

BENEFIT OF TQM ON HUMAN RESOURCES

An effective TQM program has numerous benefits. Financial benefits include lower costs, higher returns on sales and investment, and the ability to charge higher rather than competitive prices. Other benefits include improved access to global markets, higher customer retention levels, less time required to develop new innovations, and a reputation as a quality firm. Only a small number of companies use TQM because implementing an effective program involves much time, effort, money, and patience. However, firms with the necessary resources may gain major competitive advantages in their industries by implementing TQM.

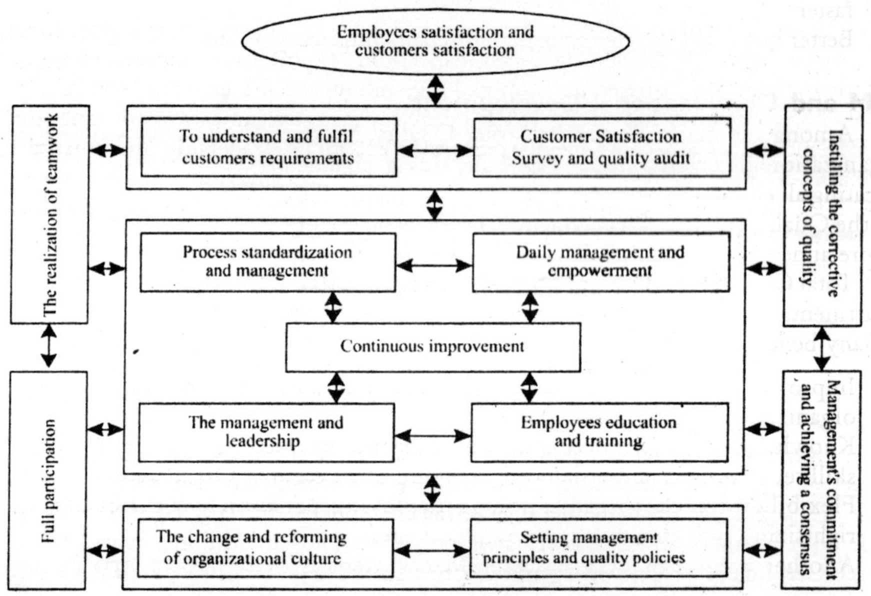

- Improving process efficiency brings about many benefits to the organizations in terms of costs and time.

The major benefits of TQM in terms of cost savings include:

- elimination of non-confirmation and repetitive work
- elimination of waste costs and reject products
- elimination of repairs and reworks
- reduced warranty and customer support costs
- process efficiency leading to improved profit per product or service
- fiscal discipline through elimination of unnecessary steps and wasteful expenditure

TQM frees up management time from redressing problems and directs management time and effort to:

- increase production
- extend the range of products
- improve existing products

TQM and Customer Satisfaction

A major long-term benefit of Total Quality Management relates to customer satisfaction. TQM aims at improving quality, and identifies the best measure of quality as matching customer expectations in terms of service, product, and experience. TQM interventions quantify problems and aim to achieve the best state defined in terms of such customer expectations.

Some examples of the application of Total Quality Management to improve customer satisfaction include:

Reduction of waiting time by changing the method of appointment scheduling or client handling

Making changes to the delivery process so that the product reaches the customer faster

Better quality products requiring no repairs improving customer loyalty

TQM and Organizational Development

Among the major benefits of Total Quality Management is improvement in Organizational Development. TQM heralds a change in the work culture by educating all employees on quality and making quality the concern of everybody, not just the Quality Control Department. The focus on quality leads to a proactive work culture aimed at preventing mistakes rather than correcting mistakes.

Total Quality Management's focus on teamwork leads to the formation of cross-departmental teams and cross-functional knowledge sharing. Such interventions lead to many benefits such as:

Improvement in communication skills of individual employees and overall organizational communication

Knowledge sharing, resulting in deepening and broadening of knowledge and skill-set of team members, and the making of a Learning Organization

Flexibility for the organization in deploying personnel, contributing to rightsizing, and ensuring cost competitiveness.

Another benefit of Total Quality Management is that TQM promotes the concept of internal customer/supplier satisfaction. For instance, the HR department considers employees as internal customers and processes their queries or requests within the specified time limit. The lab technician in a hospital processes the clinical tests required by the doctor, an internal customer in a timely and efficient manner, according to the laid down customer satisfaction norms.

TQM and Human Resources

A major application of benefits of Total Quality Management relate to Human Resource Management. Application of TQM in an organization brings about the following benefits to the Human Resources of an organization:

- TQM extends the ownership of the business process to each employee involved in the process by empowering them to rectify mistakes on the spot without supervisor review or action. This generates intrinsic motivation and creates an atmosphere of enthusiasm and satisfaction among the workforce.
- TQM's thrust on eliminating mistakes and improving productivity contributes to accomplishment of targets faster. The resultant free time allows employees to enhance their knowledge and apply their creativity to improve existing products and develop new products.
- TQM's thrust on quality leads to identifying skill-deficiencies in employees and providing training and other interventions to bridge such deficiencies. Cross-functional and cross-departmental teams allow employees to share their experience and solve issues jointly, leading to benefits such as broadening skill-sets, and improvement of existing skills.
- TQM's focus on eliminating mistakes and bringing about process efficiency heralds a direct approach such as counseling and other remedial actions to solve issues such as absenteeism.

The enhanced productivity brought about by TQM translates to better profits for the organization, and consequently better wages.

TQM AND QUALITY CONTROL

TQM is an Extension of Quality Control

TQM can be viewed as a logical extension of quality control. Quality was achieved by inspection initially—screening out defects before the customer noticed them. Quality control created the systematic approach to not only detecting, but also treating the quality problems. Quality assurance widened the responsibility to include functions other than direct operations. TQM obtained most of this but developed its own themes, which were distinctive. TQM is concerned with the following:

Meeting the needs and expectations of customers
Covering all parts of the organization
Including every person in the organization
Examining all costs which are related to quality
Getting things 'right first time', i.e. Designing in quality rather than inspecting it in Developing the systems and procedures which support quality and improvement
Developing a continuous process of improvement

This development of quality can be seen as an extending cube, expanding the boundaries, forcing the more outward approach, rather than the original inward looking inspection approach.

The Natural Expansion to Quality Management

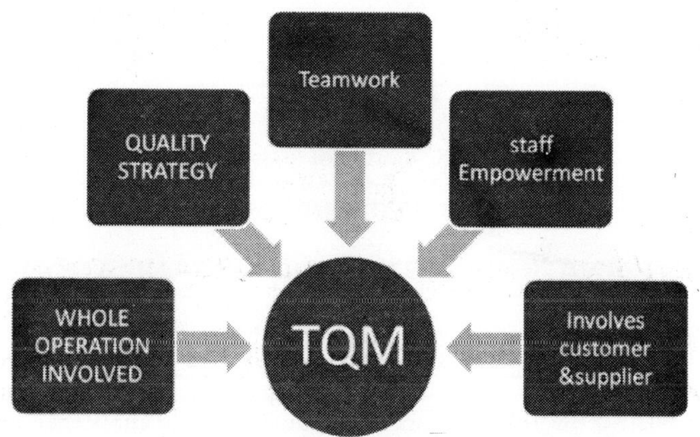

The Natural Expansion to Quality Management

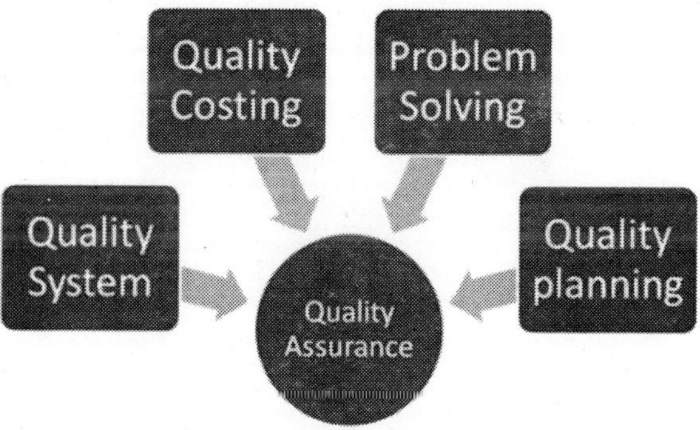

The Natural Expansion to Quality Management

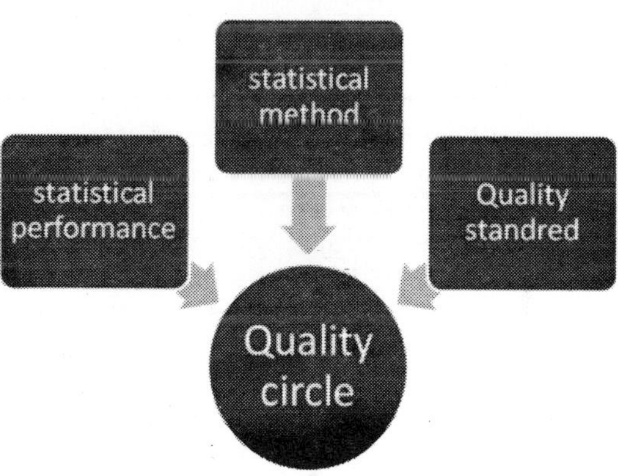

The Natural Expansion to Quality Management

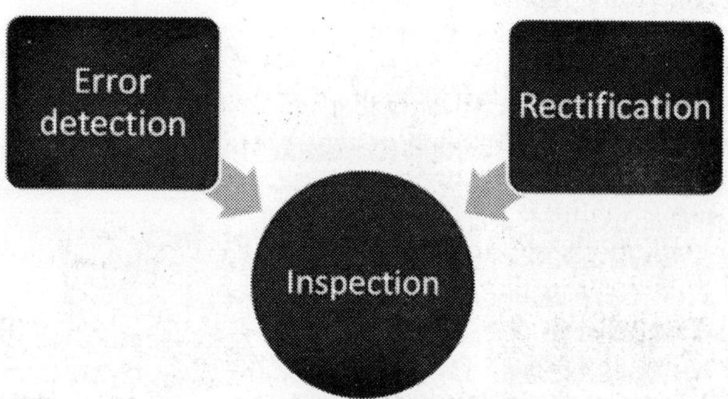

INTERNATIONAL STANDARD ORGANIZATION

A Brief History of ISO

Standards are important in international trade because incongruent standards can be barriers to trade, giving some organizations advantages in certain areas of the world. Standards provide clear identifiable references that are recognized internationally and encourage fair competition in free-market economies. Standards facilitate trade through enhanced product quality and reliability, greater interoperability and compatibility, greater ease of maintenance and reduced costs. ISO covers a wide variety of standards with the exception of electrical and electronic engineering standards covered by the International Electrotechnical Commission (IEC), telecommunication standards covered by the International Telegraph Union (ITU) and information technology covered by JTC 1 (a joint committee between ISO and IEC).

The organization which today is known as ISO began in 1926 as the International Federation of the National Standardizing Associations (ISA). This organization focused heavily on mechanical engineering. It was disbanded in 1942 during the second World War but was re-organized under the current name, ISO, in 1946.

Even the name of the organization is standardized. The name, "ISO" is not an acronym but was derived from the Greek word "isos" meaning "equal". (The relation to standards is that if two objects meet the same standard, they should be equal.) This name eliminates any confusion that could result from the translation of "International Organization For Standardization" into different languages which would lead to different acronyms.

ISO is a voluntary organization whose members are recognized standard authorities, each one representing one country. The bulk of the work of ISO is done by the 2700 technical committees, sub-committees and working groups. Each committee and sub-committee is headed by a Secretariat from one of the member organizations. The American National Standards Institute (ANSI) is the United States representative to ISO. The ANSI ASC Z-1/ASQ Standards Group coordinates the United States representation in the ISO Technical Committees 176 and 207 which are concerned with the ISO 9000 and ISO 14000 standards respectively.

The ISO Standardization Process

Each member body who has an interest in the work of a committee is entitled to be a member of that committee. Standards are reached by consensus with each member organization representing the interests of the vendors, manufacturers, consumers, professionals, and government of it's country.

Each standard goes through a six stage process before being published as an ISO standard. The first stage is the proposal stage in which a need for a standard is determined and members are identified who are willing to work on it. The standards then enters the preparatory stage where a working draft of the standard is developed. When the working draft is completed, it enters the committee stage and is sent out for comments until a consensus is reached. The output of this stage is the Draft Internation al Standard (DIS). The DIS then enters the enquiry stage where it is circulated among all member bodies and then voted upon. If a DIS does not receive 75% of the vote, it returns to lower stages and work on it continues. If it passes the enquiry stage, it becomes a Final Draft International Standard and enters the approval stage. During this stage it will again circulate through all member bodies for a final vote and again it must pass this stage with 75% of the vote. If the standard passes this stage, it enters the publication stage and is sent to the ISO Central Secretariat for publication.

Because certain technologies are changing so rapidly, ISO has instituted a Fast Track procedure that allows a standard which has been proven in the market to enter the approval process at the enquiry stage.

Overview ISO 9000

The ISO 9000 standards for quality assurance and quality management were published in 1987 by ISO Technical Committee 176. This series of standards had a dramatic impact due to their scope and rate of acceptance. This series of standards applies to all sizes and types of manufacturing and service companies and cover almost everything in a company's business functions with the main focus on processes, procedures and practices. As Hall states, "The focus was to do things right in the first place rather th an the retrospective, and more expensive, doctrine of inspection for faults after the event." (Hall, T.J. The Quality Systems Manual: the definitive guide to the ISO 9000 family and Tick It. John Wiley and Sons: Chicester, England,1995).

The history behind this series of standards can be traced to the USA during World War II. From the USA, the concept of quality assurance spread to Europe via NATO where it evolved into the Allied Quality Assurance Publication (AQAP). This series of documents discussed everything from production efficiency to selection of suppliers. The AQAP series were adopted by the UK Ministry of Defense for the British Armed Forces. This series had a trickle down effect as organizations began to require quality ass urance programs from their suppliers. The problem was that there was much diversity in the requirements for different organizations

The diversity issue was addressed by the British Standard BS 5750 which was based on the AQAP series and was introduced in 1979. The BS 5750 standard was considered so effective that it was adopted almost without change by ISO in 1987 as ISO 9000. The formation of the European Union and the perception that it was required in order to do business with Europe lead to the widespread acceptance of the ISO 9000 series.

The main documents in this series are:

ISO 9000—Guidelines for selection and use.

ISO 9002—Quality Systems Model for quality assurance in design, development, production and servicing.

ISO 9003—Quality Systems Model for quality assurance in final inspection and test.
ISO 10011—Guidelines for auditing quality systems.
ISO 10012—Quality assurance requirements for measuring equipment.
ISO 10013—Guidelines for developing quality manuals.

The main value of the 9000 series is that the analyses of processes required by the standard leads to improving or re-engineering of processes. The benefits to a company who follows the standard's practices are said to be new markets for their goods and services, increased cost-efficiency, improved employee morale and increased customer satisfaction

ISO 14000 Overview

Many believe that environmental protection movements originated in the 1960s. However, the sentiments of environmentalism can be seen in the conservation efforts that began in the late 1800s. The first environmental protection law in the United States was the Refuse Act of 1899. However, it was not until the 1960s that the environment became a political and consumer issue.

Increased environmental activism in the 1980s created a greater consumer awareness of the environmental issues. More and more environmental regulations were enacted and companies began to use their adherence to these regulations as marketing tools. The Rio Conference on the Environment in 1992 reflected increased global concerns about the environment and called for a world commitment to the protection of the environment. These concerns, coupled with the GATT negotiations in Uruguay in 1986 which called for the removal of non-tariff trade barriers, were the impetus behind ISO 14000.

ISO Technical Committee 207 is responsible for the ISO 14000 series of standards. Just as the ISO 9000 standards are based on the British BS 5750 standard of 1979, the ISO 14000 series are based on the British standard BS 7750 which was instituted in 1992. This standard also served as the basis for the European Union's Eco-Management and Audit Scheme (EMAS), a more stringent set of standards strongly influenced by the high environmental standards of German companies. EMAS differs from ISO 14000 in that it emphasizes public environmental reporting.

Many organizations had taken little interest in ISO 9000 when it was in development and were surprised by the overwhelming acceptance of ISO 9000. These organizations were wary of a new international standard in ISO 14000 and they took a more active inte rest in it's development. Subsequently, the standards of BS 7750 were softened in order to be acceptable by countries outside of Europe. In particular, US companies who can be subjected to expensive civil suits, were very hesitant to endorse a stringent set of environmental management standards. The fear is that violation of these standards could result in litigation. Some organizations, for example, fear that the extensive documentation required by the ISO 14000 series could be used against them in any legal action regarding violation of environmental regulations.

The actual environmental standards of ISO 14000 deal with how a company manages the environment inside it's facilities and the immediate outside environment. However, the standards also call for analysis of the entire life cycle of a product, from raw material to eventual disposal. These standards do not mandate a particular level of pollution or performance, but focus on awareness of the processes and procedures that can effect the environment. It should be noted that adherence to the ISO 14000 standa rds does not in anyway release a company from any national or local regulations regarding specific performance issues regarding the environment.

Some of the standards in the ISO 14000 series are:

ISO 14001—Specification of Environmental Management Systems
ISO 14004—Guideline Standard
ISO 14010 through ISO 14015—Environmental Auditing and Related Activities
ISO 14020 through ISO 14024—Environmental Labeling
ISO 14031 through ISO 14032—Environmental Performance Evaluation
ISO 14040 through ISO 14043—Life Cycle Assessment
ISO 14050—Terms and Definitions

Although the ISO 14000 standards are similar to the ISO 9000 standards, the nature of the environmental standards creates a need for people who are technical environment professionals in addition to those required to maintain the documentation necessary for certification.

REASONS FOR DEVELOPMENT OF ISO 14000

Several converging factors relating to the developing global marketplace led to the development of the ISO 14000 Series International Environmental Management Standards. As industrialization has spread to countries throughout the world, citizens and their governments have voiced their concerns about the effects of that industrialization on the environment. As a result of such concerns, the concept of sustainable development was developed. Its pursuit has been adopted as a goal by governments and business groups around the world.

Sustainable development was articulated as a goal and defined in 1987 by the World Commission on the Environment and Development (World Commission), a body established by the United Nations. In Our Common Future, the World Commission defined sustainable development as development which "meets the needs of the present without compromising the ability of future generations to meet their own needs."

For more than a decade, sustainable development has been at the center of discussion of environmental issues, especially with respect to the effects of increased trade on the environment. Sustainable development was the focus of discussion at the United Nations Conference on the Environment and Development held in Rio de Janeiro in 1992, and it was listed as one of ten goals in the Environmental Side Agreement to the North American Free Trade Agreement (NAFTA), which took effect on January 1, 1994. And in 1996, the ISO incorporated the attainment of sustainable development as a major goal in its new ISO 14000 Series International Environmental Management Standards.

Another impetus for ISO 14000 was the desire of businesses to self-regulate and minimize their exposure to government regulation. Such regulations can be burdensome. For example, in the United States, environmental regulations fill more than 20,000 pages of the Federal Register, and there are thousands of additional environmental regulations at the state and local levels.

A third impetus for the ISO 14000 Series Standards came from the United Nations Conference on the Environment and Development (UNCED), which was held in Rio de Janeiro in 1992 and attended by representatives of more than 100 nations. In response to documents issued by UNCED, the international business community adopted a "Business Charter for Sustainable Development." The document includes 16 proposals that set out basic elements for any environmental management system (EMS).

A fourth source of inspiration for development of the standards comes from environmental management programs proposed by groups of concerned citizens around the world. For example, in response to a major oil spill off the coast of Alaska by a ship called the Exxon Valdez, a group of environmentalists, investors, government agencies, and economists formed the Coalition for Environmentally Responsible Economies (CERES). The CERES group issued a set of principles that was first known as the Valdez Principles and was later renamed the CERES Principles. The CERES Principles give guidelines designed to lead to an international standard for EMS. CERES has been recognized as a direct impetus for the ISO 14000 series and similar programs.

A fifth impetus for the ISO 14000 series is the need for harmonization among various environmental management and auditing programs. Such harmonization is needed within the United States. For example, the EPA has designed several different environmental management programs, including the XL Program, the Star Track Programs, and the Environmental Leadership Program (ELP). ELP is a voluntary program in which a participating business creates its own EMS according to EPA guidelines. The incentive for participation is that the EPA may treat the company leniently in instances of non-compliance, and, upon certain conditions, the EPA refrains from conducting routine enforcement inspections at the company's facilities. Various state-level counterparts to the EPA have developed similar programs.

In addition, there are industry-specific environmental review programs such as the Chemical Manufacturers Associations (CMA's) Responsible Care program (also known as CARE). All members of the CMA are required to participate in the program, which sets out conformance standards in the areas of pollution prevention, emergency response, and employee health and safety protection and awareness.

Harmonization is also needed internationally. Companies must deal with EMSs originating in the various countries in which they operate. For example, in 1995 the British Standards Institute (BSI) became the national standards setting organization for the United Kingdom. In that same year it became the first national organization to implement a program recognizing independently verified EMSs. In 1995 the European Union (EU) implemented an Eco-Management and Audit Regulation (EMAR) program. EMAR includes the Eco-Management and Audit Scheme (EMAS), which took effect in 1995. It is a voluntary program through which a company may register a site as being in compliance with the system. The objectives of the program are to promote adherence to standards for environmental management and to inform the public about the environmental performance of companies.

Businesses are searching for a way to harmonize EPA standards, state standards, private industry standards (such as the CARE program), and requirements of other countries and trade organizations. They want to avoid the record keeping involved in compliance with multiple environmental systems and other management systems, such as quality control systems. In addition, they want to avoid dealing with conflicts between and among substantive provisions of such systems. Elimination of multiple sets of standards or, at least, harmonization of such standards became particularly important in the late 20th century in connection with the globalization of business. Today, large and small companies deal with the laws and regulations of multiple countries and must comply with the requirements of various trade organizations. It is an essential part of doing business as we move into the 21st century

ISO 14001 is known as a generic management system standard, meaning that it is relevant to any organization seeking to improve and manage resources more effectively. This includes:

single site to large multi-national companies
high risk companies to low risk service organizations
manufacturing, process and the service industries; including local governments
all industry sectors including public and private sectors
original equipment manufacturers and their suppliers.

All standards are periodically reviewed by ISO to ensure they still meet market requirements. The current version of ISO 14001—ISO 14001:2004 is under review as of April 2012.[5]

Basic Principles and Methodology

Plan—establish objectives and processes required

Prior to implementing ISO 14001, an initial review or gap analysis of the organization's processes and products is recommended, to assist in identifying all elements of the current operation and if possible future operations, that may interact with the environment, termed environmental aspects (Martin, 1998). Environmental aspects can include both direct, such as those used during manufacturing and indirect, such as raw materials (Martin, 1998). This review assists the organization in establishing their environmental objectives, goals and targets, which should ideally be measurable; helps with the development of control and management procedures and processes and serves to highlight any relevant legal requirements, which can then be built into the policy (Standards Australia/Standards New Zealand 2004).

Implement the Processes

During this stage the organization identifies the resources required and works out those members of the organization responsible for the EMS' implementation and control (Martin 1998). This includes documentation of all procedures and processes; including operational and documentation control, the establishment of emergency procedures and responses, and the education of employees, to ensure they can competently implement the necessary processes and record results (Standards Australia/Standards New Zealand 2004). Communication and participation across all levels of the organization, especially top management is a vital part of the implementation phase, with the effectiveness of the EMS being dependant on active involvement from all employees (Federal Facilities Council Report, 1999). Check—measure and monitor the processes and report results.

During the check stage, performance is monitored and periodically measured to ensure that the organization's environmental targets and objectives are being met (Martin, 1998). In addition, internal audits are regularly conducted to ascertain whether the EMS itself is being implemented properly and whether the processes and procedures are being adequately maintained and monitored (Standards Australia/ Standards New Zealand, 2004).

Act—take action to improve performance of EMS based on results.

After the checking stage, a regular planned management review is conducted to ensure that the objectives of the EMS are being met, the extent to which they are being met, that communications are being appropriately managed and to evaluate changing circumstances, such as legal requirements, in order to make recommendations for further improvement of the system (Standards Australia/

Standards New Zealand, 2004). These recommendations are then fed back into the planning stage to be implemented into the EMS moving forward.

Continual Improvement Process

The core requirement of a continual improvement process (CIP) is different from the one known from quality management systems. CIP in ISO 14001 has three dimensions (Gastl, 2009):

Expansion: More and more business areas get covered by the implemented EMS.
Enrichment: More and more activities, products, processes, emissions, resources etc. get managed by the implemented EMS.
Upgrading: An improvement of the structural and organizational framework of the EMS, as well as an accumulation of know-how in dealing with business-related environmental issues.

Overall, the CIP-concept expects the organization to gradually move away from merely operational environmental measures towards a strategic approach on how to deal with environmental challenges.

Benefits and Other Issues 9000/14000

The Benefits of ISO 14000 certification.

The benefits of acquiring ISO certification go beyond the satisfaction of doing a good deed. Adhering to the standard may result in better conformance to environmental regulations, greater marketability, better use of resources, higher quality goods and services, increased levels of safety, improved image and increased profits.

The environmental awareness and the documentation that are required by the ISO 14000 standards assist a company in conforming to environmental regulations. This means that a company, by diligently adhering to the standard, is less likely to violate environmental regulations and is always ready for inspection by a regulatory agency. In addition, the certification and documentation may aid a company in acquiring capital, in defending itself during environmental litigation and in receiving insurance or per mits.

A wider market for a company's goods and services may result from certification. Many corporations and governments will be looking for suppliers that are ISO 14000 certified in order to maintain their own certification and environment-friendly image. Al though the European Union claims that ISO 9000 certification is not required to do business in Europe, that was the message received by many non-European firms and lead to the amazing success of that standard. If ISO 14000 is similarly successful, the companies who are already ISO 14000 certified will have an advantage in global markets. Also, producers of consumer goods may find that many consumers not only try to purchase goods from environment-friendly companies, but will spend a little more if they feel they are helping the environment. In order to reap this benefit, a company must make their environmental efforts known through advertising and labeling.

The process analyses that go along with ISO 14000 certification may result in streamlining processes and more efficient use of resources and raw materials and subsequently reduce a company's costs. Finding ways to capture emissions or recycle the products may, in the long-run, reduce the amount of raw materials and utilities used. Reducing the amount of potentially dangerous substances in an end-product may result in less use of dangerous chemicals in a plant. This leads to a safer internal environment for employees and the possibility of reduced insurance premiums. Improved employee morale may result when employees feel that the workplace is safer and they are contributing to the environmental effort.

The Costs of ISO 14000 Certification

Critics of the ISO 9000 series complain that the certification was expensive and ISO 14000 will prove to be no less expensive. Additional costs occur due to the administrative costs, increased variable and fixed operating costs. A possible non-tangible c ost is the negative publicity that could occur if undesirable or hazardous situations are brought to light during the certification attempt.

Companies that have sought ISO 9000 certification have complained that the extensive documentation introduces more bureaucracy into a company. Some say that ISO 14000 will build on top of ISO 9000 registration, but others point out that the ISO 14000 documentation requirements will only compound the already burdensome task and that the extra administrative costs will reduce profit margin. ISO 14000 requires not only additional personnel to take care of the documentation, but requires knowledgeable personnel with expertise in the technical processes of an organization and the effect they have on the environment.

Investment in fixed capital may rise if a company must implement pollution reduction equipment. Other costs may rise if more environmentally friendly materials and processes lead to higher production costs. If a company passes the increase on to customers, it could result in reducing it's share of the market if competitors do not do the same.

A potential hazard of the certification process is the uncovering of potentially harmful current practices. If the analysis of the company reveals environmental risks, the ability of the company to attain capital, insurance and permits may be compromised.

Other Issues

It has been several years since ISO 9000 was published and in that time, some concerns have come to light regarding international quality standards. These have to do with the quality of process rather than product, multiple registration schemes, the cost *vs.* the benefits of certification, and the business of third party certification.

Implicit behind ISO 14000 and ISO 9000 is the assumption that a quality process will lead to quality products and a clean environment. However, both the ISO 9000 and the ISO 14000 standards focus on the management processes behind the product. There is no guarantee that a quality process will yield a quality product or a better environment. Additionally, despite the claims that these standards will help to reduce costs, there is no guarantee that certification in either or both will result in increased profits for a company.

The intent of an international standard is to avoid diverse and sometimes replicating standards. But the publication of international standards for quality assurance has not eliminated multiple standards. For example, the big three auto makers have imposed QS 9000 standards on their suppliers. QS 9000 standards use ISO 9000 as a starting point but require even more extensive documentation on a wider set of processes. Now along comes ISO 14000 which is stricter than ISO 9000 in not only it's documentation on requirements but the number of people with technical and regulatory skills that will be required to analyze and maintain certification. This is leading some to ask when this onslaught of standardization will end. Bob Garvey, a chairman and CEO of Bi Framingham Steel who has been through both ISO 9000 and QS 9000 has been quoted as saying "I don't wish [QS 9000] on anyone." And Beryl Spiers of Stelco Fasteners says that they are "getting fed up with the whole standards process" and won't consider ISO 1 4000 certification "unless our customer base says so." (Both in Mullin, Rick and Sissel, Kara "Merging business and environment." *Chemical Week*. Oct. 9, 1996, Vol. 158, No. 37, p. 52.)

The problem of multiple registration schemes is not limited to the United States. Antonio Silva Mendes, quality chief of the European Union Directorate-General III has also voiced concern over multiple registration schemes (Zuckerman, Amy "Stanching the flow of new quality standards." New Steel. Sept. 1996, Vol. 12, No. 9, p. 82). Despite this, there is already a movement underway for the development of international occupational health and safety standards on top of ISO 9000 and ISO 14000.

The whole question of third party certification does not sit well with many US companies. Some are complaining that third party assessment does not distinguish between barely meeting the standard and fully meeting or surpassing it. Others note that ISO 14000 certification does not currently reduce any customer or regulatory requirements. (However, the EPA is investigating how ISO 14000 standards can be linked to environmental regulations.) Then there is the question of who certifies the third party as assessment auditors. Standard certification has become a big business and some critics are now calling for standardization of the certification process.

Finally, many complain that the ISO standards do not reflect the variety of businesses in the world. For example, small businesses have difficult time dealing with the expense of certification and fear that they will not be able to compete internationally. On the other extreme, some multinational companies which are highly decentralized and diverse complain that the standards do not coincide with the realities of the ways these companies function. Under the ISO 9000 and ISO 14000 standards, multisite registration of subsidiaries is permitted only if there is a common management and central control of each site. This violates the autonomous and decentralized approach taken by many multinational companies.

The general consensus is that organizations are being cautious before jumping on the ISO 14000 bandwagon. Many already have environmental management systems in place and, after experience with ISO 9000 certification, are adopting a wait-and-see attitude towards ISO 14000.

PERSPECTIVES OF BUSINESS—ISO 14000 STANDARDS

The benefits and detriments of the ISO 14000 standards depend on the perspectives of the speaker. Therefore, this section looks at the ISO 14000 standards from the perspectives of business organizations, governments, and environmentalists.

Benefits to the Individual Business

ISO 14001 certification may bring various rewards to a company, most of which can ultimately provide a financial advantage to the company. Seven potential rewards are explored below, but this list could be expanded.

First, many firms are hoping that, in return for obtaining ISO 14001 certification (and the actions required to do so), regulatory agencies such as the EPA will give them more favorable treatment. For example, businesses are hoping for less stringent filing, or less monitoring, or even less severe sanctions for violations of environmental laws.

Many state regulatory agencies have suggested that the ISO 14001 certificate may be classified as a voluntary audit program that will, in turn, qualify a business for leniency in filing or monitoring requirements or even, less severe sanctions for violations of environmental regulations. In fact, some states have already acted to provide such leniency. For example, the Pennsylvania Department of Environmental Protection (PA DEP) grants regulatory relief to companies that conduct voluntary environmental compliance audits. If a company, local government body, or an individual completes an environmental compliance audit and discovers a problem, discloses the problem to the PA DEP, and takes action to correct the problem, the DEP will not take civil or criminal action. James M. Seif, secretary of the PA DEP stated, "Our policy is centered on one simple premise: You find it, you fix it, you tell us—no penalty." At least 14 other states have adopted legislation or policies to encourage voluntary environmental audit programs and to limit penalties associated with violations discovered in the process of those audits. Those states include Arkansas, Colorado, Idaho, Illinois, Indiana, Kansas, Kentucky, Minnesota, Mississippi, Oregon, Texas, Utah, Virginia, and Wyoming.

In a state that has not adopted legislation or policies to provide regulatory relief to businesses that implement an EMS, a business can at least benefit from an enhanced relationship with environmental regulatory agencies and regulated businesses. A cordial and cooperative relationship between the business and regulators can be valuable in many instances.

A second benefit to businesses that choose to become certified to ISO 14001 is that substantial numbers of citizens can be influenced in their buying decisions. Obtaining ISO 14000 certification is a way for companies to demonstrate their environmental stewardship and accountability to the public.

Third, ISO 14000 certification can attract investors to the business organization. A growing number of individual investors as well as investment managers and managers of mutual funds search for environmentally responsible businesses.

Fourth, the company may save money on insurance premiums. For example, some insurance companies give reduced rates on insurance to cover accidental pollution releases if the insured company has successfully implemented an EMS.

Fifth, actions taken in the process of implementing the EMS are likely to reduce the likelihood of toxic spills endangering employees and members of the community.

Sixth, financial institutions are sensitive to environmental risks and their impact on collateral. ISO 14001 may help a corporation obtain loans and protect it from allegations of investor fraud.

Seventh, by implementing an EMS, a company may realize internal cost savings as a result of waste reduction, use of fewer toxic chemicals, reduced energy use, and recycling.

COSTS AND DETERMINANTS TO THE INDIVIDUAL BUSINESS

A company's costs in becoming ISO 14001 certified depend on the scope of the EMS. For example, the EMS might be international, national, or limited to individual plants operated by the company. National and international systems can be very costly. With respect to a company operating in more than one legal jurisdiction (whether that means two states of the United States or two countries, such as the United States and Mexico), it will be necessary to assess the company's compliance with the laws of all national, state, and local jurisdictions involved.

Lawyers studying the ISO 14000 standards are discussing a number of legal issues related to use of environmental audit documents prepared as a part of the ISO 14001 certification process. There are serious questions as to whether a governmental regulatory agency can require disclosure of information discovered during a self-audit by a company. The use of a third-party auditor may weaken a company's argument that information is privileged. In view of the fact that some companies conducted environmental audits for various reasons prior to the creation of ISO 14001, this is not a new area of the law. It is still developing, however, and questions specific to ISO 14001 must be resolved. Taking one step to deal with such problems, the EPA has implemented an Interim Environmental Audit Policy that encourages business organizations to conduct environmental audits. It provides the potential for eliminating or reducing civil penalties and avoiding criminal prosecution when specified conditions are met. Similarly, various states have adopted some form of environmental audit privilege.

The ISO 14000 series has potential consequences with respect to international trade, also. ISO 14000 is designed to provide a series of universally accepted EMS practices and lead to consistency in environmental standards between and among trading partners. It has the potential to lead to two kinds of cultural changes: one of them would be within individual companies and the other would be a global change. First, within the corporation, the ISO 14000 Series can promote consideration of environmental issues throughout the company's operations. Managers of companies that have implemented ISO 9000 have learned to view their companies' operations through a "quality of management" lens. Similarly, it is hoped that implementation of ISO 14000 will lead to use of an "environmental quality" lens by businesses. Second, the ISO 14000 series has the potential to become part of a global culture as the public comes to view ISO 14001 certification as a benchmark connoting good environmental stewardship.

PERSPECTIVES OF GOVERNMENT ON THE ISO 14000 STANDARDS

Perspectives of Developing Countries

The perspectives of developing countries differ substantially from those of industrialized countries such as the United States and Britain for a variety of reasons. The ISO 14000 Series standards were developed by business representatives from industrialized countries. Developing countries from Latin America, Africa, and elsewhere had little input. As compared to developed countries, developing countries and their businesses suffer from limited financial resources, and they have less experience in environmental law enforcement. In many cases, control of industrial sources of pollution is seen as a "luxury" as compared to other more pressing needs of citizens. Their citizens' needs include food, basic housing, clothing, electricity, and clean drinking water.

Because their attentions have been on even more pressing matters, the governments of many developing countries have not developed and consistently enforced environmental legislation. Thus, there has been much discussion about whether the ISO 14000 series standards can be used as an alternative to environmental law in those countries. Some commentators even argue that it could be adopted as law. Some developing countries such as Mexico are reviewing the ISO 14000 series standards and considering incorporating their provisions within their own environmental laws and regulations. Zimbabwe has incorporated ISO 14001 into its national regulatory system. It is important to note, however, that Zimbabwe's plan is to use ISO 14001 in conjunction with its additional legislation and a "tuned up" monitoring system.

On the other hand, various commentators as well as the governments of some developing countries argue that the ISO 14000 environmental standards are functioning as nontariff barriers to trade. This assertion is based on the fact that costs of ISO 14000 registration are prohibitively high for poorly funded companies. Thus companies in developing countries, especially small to medium size companies, will suffer disproportionately if ISO 14000 standards become a "de facto" requirement of doing business with other nations.

Varying Approaches by Various Countries

Governments' approach to the standards varies widely from one industrialized country to another. Within the EU, efforts are under way to minimize such variance. The European Commission (EC) is the primary legislative body for the EU, and harmonization of standards is a primary missions of the EC. Various European governments provide backing to privately run standards organizations; some grant government charters to their standards organizations. Portugal's primary standards organization is part of its Ministry of Industry, and in Germany and Britain the government makes contracts to obtain standards services as a part of its efforts to serve the public.

Because the countries of the EU are, collectively, the United State's largest trading partner, its standards activities are important to U.S. businesses that trade with its members. U.S. companies doing business with Europe must design their products and ensure that their management practices conform to the requirements of the EU.

Perspectives of the U.S. Government

The perspectives of the U.S. government merit separate examination because of the dominant place the United States occupies in world commerce. But it is important to remember that U.S. perspectives are those of a wealthy, highly industrialized society with a highly developed regulatory law system.

Agencies of the U.S. government have been actively following the development of the ISO 14000 series standards and have provided input in various contexts. For example, the EPA, the Department of Defense, and the Department of Energy provide representatives to the U.S. Technical Advisory Group (U.S. TAG). The U.S. TAG, in turn, provides input to TC 207, the ISO technical committee responsible for the ISO 14000 series.

The United States has a highly developed regulatory system designed to protect the environment. The EPA, in conjunction with state-level counterparts, enforces a myriad of environmental protection statutes including, but not limited to, the Clean Air Act; the Clean Water Act; Comprehensive Environmental Response, Compensation, and Liability Act (Superfund); and the Toxic Substance Control Act. Thus, unlike a developing country, which may lack a comprehensive regulatory scheme in the area of environmental protection, the United States does not view the ISO 14000 series as a potential substitute for statutes and regulations. Nevertheless, implementation of an EMS by a company certified to ISO 14001 does have the potential to improve that company's rate of compliance with state and federal environmental law.

PERSPECTIVES OF ENVIRONMENTALISTS ON THE ISO 14000 STANDARDS

Environmentalists and their organizations were active in debate and discussion before the United States joined the NAFTA. As a consequence of their concerns the Environmental Side Agreement was added to NAFTA before the United States joined the agreement.

In contrast, environmentalists have not been outspoken with respect to the benefits and limitations of ISO 14000. Their quiet approach to ISO 14000 can be explained, however, by the differing nature of the two sets of documents. The ISO 14000 series standards are not laws. The standards were prepared by business representatives for use by businesses, and environmentalists were not parties in the drafting of the standards.

Yet, as consumers and investors, environmentalists can play an important part in the success (or lack of success) of ISO 14000. At a minimum, the ISO 14000 series will provide environmentalists with further information to enable them to choose to "do business" with environmentally responsible companies. They can choose to purchase the products and services of companies certified to ISO 14001, and they can invest in those companies by purchasing their stock offerings.

Certification to ISO 14001 standards by a business serves one of the purposes of community right-to-know (RTK) and worker right-to-know (RTK) laws. Community RTK and worker RTK laws provide citizens with some of the information they need in order to make decisions about their exposure to toxic chemicals. Similarly, knowledge of the fact that a company's facility is certified to ISO 14000 can provide citizens with useful information as they choose products and services and invest their savings.

THE STRENGTHS AND LIMITATIONS OF ISO 14000

What can the ISO 14000 Series Promote or Accomplish?

On a limited basis, certification to ISO 14001 can help reduce the workload of environmental inspectors. To the extent that businesses regulate themselves, government will not have to do as much work to identify violations of environmental law. In days of reduced budgets, the EPA may be able to allocate enforcement personnel and funds to investigation of companies that do not implement self-imposed EMSs.

ISO 14000 series standards require a participating company to review environmental statutes and regulations as it prepares its EMS and as it undergoes periodic review of its environmental practices under the EMS. Self-assessment is likely to increase compliance rates.

Further, the ISO 14000 series can provide a company with a systematic approach for implementing an EMS that will qualify it for participation in the EPA's Excellence in Leadership (ELF) program. Participation in the ELF program can result in leniency by the EPA toward a company that self-discovers violations of environmental law and makes timely efforts to comply with the law. In addition, participation in ELF will exempt the company from certain routine enforcement inspections.

STEPS TO ACHIEVE ISO 9000 REGISTRATION

Steps to Follow

These eight steps—along with their sub-steps—are based on what many major companies have followed to achieve their own ISO 9000 registration. These steps are also useful for companies simple seeking to conform to the ISO 900 standards, but not formally become certified.

These steps are a good guide for establishing a timeline, schedule, and potential costs for the process of becoming ISO 9000 certified.

1. Get top management commitment
   Top management considers ISO 9000 registration
   Quality steering committee meets to evaluate process
   Committee informs top management of ISO 9000 costs, schedule, etc.
   Top management commits to pursue ISO 9000 registration
2. Train personnel
   Hold basic quality and ISO 9000 training for all employees
   Select and train personnel to be internal auditors
3. Prepare Quality Policy Manual
   Study and understand ISO 9000 requirements as they apply to your company
   Write (or re-write) company Vision and Mission statements
   Write basic Quality Policy Manual outline
   Complete first draft of Quality Policy Manual
   Send copy of manual to customer desiring ISO 9000 compliance (if necessary)
4. Prepare Operating Procedures
   Define responsibilities, using Quality Manual as a guide
   Have those responsible for functions outline their procedures
   Interview managers and fine-tune procedures
   Compare Operating Procedures with Quality Manual for consistency
5. Hold internal audit
   Hold internal audit of ISO 9000 manual *vs.* ISO 9000 compliance
   Implement corrective action items from audit
6. Select registrar
   Research registrars and their cost
   Qualify possible registrars
   Select third party registrar
7. Go through registration process
   Apply for registration and audits
   Agree to audit process etc. with registrar
   Hold pre-assessment audit
   Take any needed corrective action
   Have ISO 9000 registration audit
   Take any needed corrective action
   Re-audit as needed
   Take any needed corrective action
8. Obtain ISO 9000 registration

This verifies that you operate your business in compliance to the ISO 9000 requirements.

ISO 9001 REGISTRATION : HOW MUCH DOES IT COST?

The cost of ISO 9001 Registration will vary depending on the size and complexity of your organization and on whether you already have some elements of a quality management system in place.

First, there are typically three options for an organization seeking registration:

- Create everything (Documentation, training, etc.) on your own by reading and interpreting the standard.
- Use documentation templates and training programs (like ours) to train your organization. .
- Hire an ISO consultant to complete the entire process with you.

The cost of ISO 9001 Registration will vary depending on the size and complexity of your organization and on whether you already have some elements of a quality management system in place.

ISO 9000/14000 Registration costs have 3 parts:

1. **Contracting a Registrar**—The registration audit is performed by a Registrar and the cost will depend on how big and how complex your organization is. They will charge you depending on how many audit days they spend at your organization. There will be travel costs if the Registrar is not local and there are administrative and accreditation fees as well. Contact a Registrar directly to obtain a quote for their services for your company, or use our estimated Registrar Costs.
2. **Internal Cost**—The time your employees will need to spend building and implementing the system. Our free Quick Start guide can help you estimate the time needed from employees throughout the project.
3. **Outside help**—This is either consultant fees or the purchasing of tools to help you with the project. You can save quite a bit of money if you do not use a consultant. Use our All-in-One Documentation and Training Package to simplify your job and save money.

IMPLEMENTATION COST

Estimated Costs of ISO 9000 Implementation for your Company: ILLUSTRATION

Select the chart from the selection below which best fits the characteristics of your company:

Click the $ *Employees*	*Existing Quality Management System*		
	None	*Basic*	*Good*
? 58	$	$	$
? 433	$	$	$
? 583	$	$	$
? 833	$	$	$
? 4333	$	$	$

1-25 Employees, no quality System in Place Yet

Estimated costs of doing the implementation in-house yourself using our All-in-One Documentation & Training Package, and by hiring a consultant.

	*Cost in **Dollars** for All-in-One Package or Consultant*	*Cost in terms of your company's employee **hours** spent*
All-in-One	$997	96*
	Consultant	$4800* 48*

*These are estimates.
Remember to add the cost of the Registration Audit to your total cost estimate.

1-25 Employees, basic quality system in place

Estimated costs of doing the implementation in-house yourself using our All-in-One Documentation & Training Package, and by hiring a consultant.

	*Cost in **Dollars** for All-in-One Package or Consultant*	*Cost in terms of your company's employee **hours** spent*
All-in-One	$997	72*
Consultant	$3600*	36*

*These are estimates.
Remember to add the cost of the Registration Audit to your total cost estimate.

1-25 Employees, good quality system in place

Estimated costs of doing the implementation in-house yourself using our All-in-One Documentation & Training Package, and by hiring a consultant.

	*Cost in **Dollars** for All-in-One Package or Consultant*	*Cost in terms of your company's employee **hours** spent*	
All-in-One	$997	38*	
	Consultant	$1,920*	19*

*These are estimates.
Remember to add the cost of the Registration Audit to your total cost estimate.

26-100 Employees, no quality system in place yet

Estimated costs of doing the implementation in-house yourself using our All-in-One Documentation & Training Package, and by hiring a consultant.

	*Cost in **Dollars** for All-in-One Package or Consultant*	*Cost in terms of your company's employee **hours** spent*
All-in-One	$997	288*
Consultant	$14,000*	144*

*These are estimates.
Remember to add the cost of the Registration Audit to your total cost estimate.

26-100 Employees, basic quality system in place

Estimated costs of doing the implementation in-house yourself using our All-in-One Documentation & Training Package, and by hiring a consultant.

	Cost in Dollars for All-in-One Package or Consultant	*Cost in terms of your company's employee hours spent*
All-in-One	$997	216*
Consultant	$10,500*	108*

*These are estimates.
Remember to add the cost of the Registration Audit to your total cost estimate.

26-100 Employees, good quality system in place

Estimated costs of doing the implementation in-house yourself using our All-in-One Documentation & Training Package, and by hiring a consultant.

	Cost in Dollars for All-in-One Package or Consultant	*Cost in terms of your company's employee hours spent*
All-in-One	$997	115*
Consultant	$5,600*	58*

*These are estimates.
Remember to add the cost of the Registration Audit to your total cost estimate.

101-250 Employees, no quality system in place yet

Estimated costs of doing the implementation in-house yourself using our All-in-One Documentation & Training Package, and by hiring a consultant.

	Cost in Dollars for All-in-One Package or Consultant	*Cost in terms of your company's employee hours spent*
All-in-One	$997	512*
Consultant	$25,000*	256*

*These are estimates.
Remember to add the cost of the Registration Audit to your total cost estimate.

101-250 Employees, basic quality system in place

Estimated costs of doing the implementation in-house yourself using our All-in-One Documentation & Training Package, and by hiring a consultant.

	Cost in Dollars for All-in-One Package or Consultant	*Cost in terms of your company's employee hours spent*
All-in-One	$997	384*
Consultant	$18,750*	192*

*These are estimates.
Remember to add the cost of the Registration Audit to your total cost estimate.

101-250 Employees, good quality system in place

Estimated costs of doing the implementation in-house yourself using our All-in-One Documentation & Training Package, and by hiring a consultant.

	*Cost in **Dollars** for All-in-One Package or Consultant*	*Cost in terms of your company's employee **hours** spent*
All-in-One	$997	205*
Consultant	$10,000*	102*

*These are estimates.
Remember to add the cost of the Registration Audit to your total cost estimate.

251-500 Employees, no quality system in place yet

Estimated costs of doing the implementation in-house yourself using our All-in-One Documentation & Training Package, and by hiring a consultant.

	*Cost in **Dollars** for All-in-One Package or Consultant*	*Cost in terms of your company's employee **hours** spent*
All-in-One	$997	960*
Consultant	$48,000*	480*

*These are estimates.
Remember to add the cost of the Registration Audit to your total cost estimate.

251-500 Employees, basic quality system in place

Estimated costs of doing the implementation in-house yourself using our All-in-One Documentation & Training Package, and by hiring a consultant.

	*Cost in **Dollars** for All-in-One Package or Consultant*	*Cost in terms of your company's employee **hours** spent*
All-in-One	$997	720*
Consultant	$36,000*	360*

*These are estimates.
Remember to add the cost of the Registration Audit to your total cost estimate.

251-500 Employees, good quality system in place

Estimated costs of doing the implementation in-house yourself using our All-in-One Documentation & Training Package, and by hiring a consultant.

	*Cost in **Dollars** for All-in-One Package or Consultant*	*Cost in terms of your company's employee **hours** spent*
All-in-One	$997	384*
Consultant	$19,200*	192*

*These are estimates.
Remember to add the cost of the Registration Audit to your total cost estimate.

501-1000 Employees, no quality system in place yet

Estimated costs of doing the implementation in-house yourself using our All-in-One Documentation & Training Package, and by hiring a consultant.

	Cost in Dollars for All-in-One Package or Consultant	*Cost in terms of your company's employee **hours** spent*
All-in-One	$997	1152*
Consultant	$57,000*	576*

*These are estimates.
Remember to add the cost of the Registration Audit to your total cost estimate.

501-1000 Employees, basic quality system in place

Estimated costs of doing the implementation in-house yourself using our All-in-One Documentation & Training Package, and by hiring a consultant.

	Cost in Dollars for All-in-One Package or Consultant	*Cost in terms of your company's employee **hours** spent*
All-in-One	$997	864*
Consultant	$42,750*	432*

*These are estimates.
Remember to add the cost of the Registration Audit to your total cost estimate.

501-1000 Employees, good quality system in place

Estimated costs of doing the implementation in-house yourself using our All-in-One Documentation & Training Package, and by hiring a consultant.

	Cost in Dollars for All-in-One Package or Consultant	*Cost in terms of your company's employee **hours** spent*
All-in-One	$997	461*
Consultant	$22,800*	230*

*These are estimates.

LIMITATIONS OF ISO 9000/14000

LIMITATIONS OF ISO 14000

A limitations of the ISO 14000 series is that participants are self-selecting. Because participation is voluntary, it covers only a limited segment of the business community.

A second major limitation of the ISO 14000 series is that it depends on self-enforcement. Thomas Ott, corporate manager for environment, safety, and industrial hygiene with Motorola Corporation, is the U.S. chairperson of the ISO's working group on environmental auditing. He observed, "Having a certificate doesn't mean you have a clean company.... The bad guys who pollute today will still do it, and they'll have a certificate." The successful implementation of an EMS within an individual company will depend substantially on the leadership of the managers of the company. The organization must show its commitment through its statement of policy in the EMS, articulation of goals, and communication of the policy and goals to its personnel. Further, the company must allocate adequate funds for implementation of its goals and for training of personnel.

A related limitation is that the quality of the environmental audit depends on the qualifications and integrity of the registrar who performs the audit. As increased numbers of companies seek certification to ISO 14001, increased numbers of auditors will be needed for initial audits and continuing, periodic audits. Certification of registrars depends on the accrediting body or bodies of individual countries. For example, in the United States, the American National Standards Institute operates as a partner with the U.S. Registrar Accreditation Board (RAB). RAB is a nonprofit organization that accredits ISO 9000 registrars, and many of those same registrars are beginning to provide ISO 14000 audit services. Even with the services of an accreditation board, a company must choose its auditors and other consultants carefully.

A fourth limitation is that certification to ISO 14000 series standards does not serve as a substitute for conformance to environmental management standards that have been adopted by other organizations. For example, the CMA's Responsible Care (RC) program is not as broad as ISO 14001; an organization meeting RC requirements must do more before it can also be certified to ISO 14001. Because membership in the CMA requires conformance with RC, a chemical company may not wish to undergo the number of audits (and costs) involved in conformance with RC and certification to ISO 14001.

The effects of ISO 14000 around the world will vary depending on the needs and perspectives of participating companies, their governments, and individual citizens. In developing countries, adoption of ISO 14000 is likely to lag because of limited resources of developing businesses and their governments. ISO 14000 may even act as a nontariff barrier to trade for those companies.

The perspectives of companies from developed, industrialized countries such as the United States and the members of the EU are different. Overall, the ISO 14000 series can provide a useful supplement to governmental environmental regulation in such countries. It will cause companies to engage in self-examination and self-correction of many environmental problems. That, in turn, may free government environmental enforcement personnel to concentrate on companies that are not in compliance with environmental law.

Even in industrialized countries with highly developed regulatory systems, however, ISO 14000's reach is limited. It is a voluntary program and, as such, can provide only a supplement to governmental environmental regulation. The effectiveness of ISO in promoting environmental stewardship within individual companies depends on the leadership of the company's managers and the creation of a corporate culture in which environmental management permeates the daily operations of the business in all areas. Further, a company must hire well-qualified consultants and registrars (auditors) as it formulates and implements its EMS. In the end, the success of the ISO 14000 series program depends on qualified, committed people and the allocation of sufficient resources to accomplish the goals identified in the company's EMS.

Limitation of ISO 9000—an organisation can be faced with:

- **Costs not fully quantified**—the costs of implementing a QMS often are known. What is usually not known is the continuing costs of having and maintaining a QMS, particularly as a basis for continuous improvement;
- **Not necessarily more efficient**—ISO 9000 does not address the question of efficiency. Most organisations actually seem to improve internal efficiency, but it is mostly through codifying current processes, not by re-examining the processes themselves in detail;
- **Limited flexibility**—a QMS written to achieve ISO 9000 with the

minimum of effect is likely to be inflexible in dealing with new or changed areas of business;

- **Bureaucracy**—a QMS developed without the user in mind will sit in shelves and gather dust. Similarly, people will ignore, or finds ways of avoiding, a QMS with excessive form-filling;
- **Internal focus**—developing a QMS is a mainly internal process, creating a QMS with an internal focus. The user or customer can feel ignored; and
- **Process, not content**—ISO 9000 itself does not guarantee the *content* (that is, inherent quality) of what is produced, merely that the *process* of producing it satisfies a standard and that the organisation follows its procedures.

Malcolm Baldrige National Quality Award

The Malcolm Baldrige National Quality Award recognizes U.S. organizations in the business, health care, education, and non-profit sectors for performance excellence. The Baldrige Award is the only formal recognition of the performance excellence of both public and private U.S. organizations given by the President of the United States. It is administered by the Baldrige Performance Excellence Program, which is based at and managed by the National Institute of Standards and Technology, an agency of the U.S. Department of Commerce. Up to 18 awards may be given annually across six eligibility categories—manufacturing, service, small business, education, health care, and non-profit. As of 2011, 90 organizations had received the award. The Baldrige National Quality Program and the associated award were established by the Malcolm Baldrige National Quality Improvement Act of 1987 (Public Law 100–107). The program and award were named for Malcolm Baldrige, who served as United States Secretary of Commerce during the Reagan administration, from 1981 until Baldrige's 1987 death in a rodeo accident. In 2010, the program's name was changed to the Baldrige Performance Excellence Program to reflect the evolution of the field of quality from a focus on product, service, and customer quality to a broader, strategic focus on overall organizational quality—called performance excellence. The award promotes awareness of performance excellence as an increasingly important element in competitiveness. It also promotes the sharing of successful performance strategies and the benefits derived from using these strategies. To receive a Baldrige Award, an organization must have a role-model organizational management system that ensures continuous improvement in delivering products and/or services, demonstrates efficient and effective operations, and provides a way of engaging and responding to customers and other stakeholders. The award is not given for specific products or services.

Criteria for Performance Excellence

The Baldrige Criteria for Performance Excellence serve two main purposes: (1) to identify Baldrige Award recipients that will serve as role models for other organizations, and (2) to help organizations assess their improvement efforts, diagnose their overall performance management system, and identify their strengths and opportunities for improvement. In addition, the Criteria help strengthen U.S. com improving organizational performance practices, capabilities, and results facilitating communication and sharing of information on best practices among U.S. organizations of all types serving as a tool for understanding and managing performance and for guiding planning and opportunities for learning.

The Baldrige Criteria for Performance Excellence provide organizations with an integrated approach to performance management that results in delivery of ever-improving value to customers and stakeholders, contributing to organizational sustainability improved organizational effectiveness and capabilities organizational and personal learning.

The following three sector-specific versions of the Criteria, which are revised every two years, are available for free from the Baldrige Program:

Criteria for Performance Excellence
Education Criteria for Performance Excellence
Health Care Criteria for Performance Excellence

Early History of the Baldrige Program

In the early and mid-1980s, many U.S. industry and government leaders saw that a renewed emphasis on quality was necessary for doing business in an ever-expanding and more competitive world market. But many U.S. businesses either did not believe quality mattered for them or did not know where to begin.

The Malcolm Baldrige National Quality Improvement Act of 1987, signed into law on August 20, 1987, was developed through the actions of the National Productivity Advisory Committee, chaired by Jack Grayson. The nonprofit research organization APQC, founded by Grayson, organized the first White House Conference on Productivity, spearheading the creation of the Malcolm Baldrige National Quality Award in 1987. The Baldrige Award was envisioned as a standard of excellence that would help U.S. organizations achieve world-class quality.

In the late summer and fall of 1987, Dr. Curt Reimann, the first director of the Malcolm Baldrige National Quality Program, and his staff at the National Institute of Standards and Technology (NIST) developed an award implementation framework, including an evaluation scheme, and advanced proposals for what is now the Baldrige Award.

In its first three years, the Baldrige Award was jointly administered by APQC and the American Society for Quality, which continues to assist in administering the award program under contract to NIST.

Program Impacts

According to Building on Baldrige: American Quality for the 21st Century by the private Council on Competitiveness, "More than any other program, the Baldrige Quality Award is responsible for making quality a national priority and disseminating best practices across the United States."

The Baldrige Program's net private benefits to the economy as a whole were conservatively estimated at $ 24.65 billion. When compared to the program's social costs of $ 119 million, the program's social benefit-to-cost ratio was 207-to-1.

In 2007, 2008, 2009, and 2010, Leadership Excellence magazine placed the Baldrige Program in the top 10 best government/military leadership programs in the United States based on seven criteria: vision/mission, involvement/participation, accountability/measurement, content/curriculum, presenters/presentations, take-home value/results for customers, and outreach of the programs and products.

Since the program's inception in 1987, more than 2 million copies of the business/nonprofit, education, and health care versions of the Criteria for Performance Excellence have been distributed to individuals and organizations in the United States and abroad. In 2010, more than 2.1 million copies of the Criteria were accessed or downloaded from the Baldrige Website.

Public-Private Partnership

The Baldrige Award is supported by a distinctive public-private partnership. The following organizations and entities play a key role:

The Foundation for the Malcolm Baldrige National Quality Award raises funds to permanently endow the award program.

The National Institute of Standards and Technology (NIST), an agency of the U.S. Department of Commerce, manages the Baldrige Program.

The American Society for Quality (ASQ) assists in administering the award program under contract to NIST.

The Board of Overseers advises the Department of Commerce on the Baldrige Program.

Members of the Board of Examiners—consisting of leading experts from U.S. businesses and education, health care, and nonprofit organizations—volunteer their time to evaluate award applications and prepare feedback reports for applicant organizations. Board members also share information about the program in their professional, trade, community, and state organizations. The Panel of Judges, part of the Board of Examiners, makes award recommendations to the director of NIST.

The network of state, regional, and local Baldrige-based award programs known as the Alliance for Performance Excellence provides potential award applicants and examiners, promotes the use of the Criteria, and disseminates information on the award process and concepts.

Award recipients share information on their successful performance and quality strategies with other U.S. organizations. List of Baldrige Award Recipients given in appendix Baldrige Award Recipients.

Criteria for Performance Excellence

http://www.quality.nist.gov/Criteria.htm. The Baldrige Criteria for Performance Excellence provide a systems perspective for understanding performance management. They reflect validated, leading-edge management practices against which an organization can measure itself. With their acceptance nationally and internationally as the model for performance excellence, the Criteria represent a common language for communication among organizations for sharing best practices. The Criteria are also the basis for the Malcolm Baldrige National Quality Award process. http://www.quality.nist.gov/Criteria.htm.

The Baldrige criteria form an excellent model of Total Quality Management (TQM). The criteria are divided into seven key categories:

Leadership
Strategic Planning
Customer Focus
Measurement, Analysis, and Knowledge Management
Workforce Focus
Process Management
Results

Each category is scored based on the approach used to address the category, how well it is deployed throughout the organization, the cycles of learning generated, and its level of integration within the organization. An excellent way to improve your TQM maturity is to use the criteria as a self-assessment and then compare your organization's methods and processes with winners of the Baldrige award. An integral part of the Baldrige process is for winners to share nonproprietary information from their applications so you have a ready-made benchmark for your organization's TQM maturity.

Winning the Baldrige Award is about as good as it gets with respect to being recognized as a world-class organization. Most states have quality award programs based on the Baldrige criteria. Participating in state programs can be an excellent first step toward winning the Baldrige award. Most state programs always include site visits so you not only will benefit from creating the application and the resulting self-assessment, but you will also get a third party assessment of your organization's quality maturity.

So how can TQE help?

TQE's core competence is in the areas of Hoshin Kanri, process management, and process improvement. By using TQE's products and training services your organization can begin to implement processes that address specific categories of the Baldrige Criteria for Performance Excellence.

Hoshin Kanri directly supports the Strategic Planning category of the criteria. Baldrige applicants are required to define their overall planning process and how they integrated critical factor information like customers, markets, suppliers, technology, and societal issues into their plan. Applicants are also required to describe how the organization's plan is deployed and tracked to assure success.

Any organization that has implemented the Hoshin Kanri planning process will have an easy time addressing the Baldrige Strategic Planning category. The biggest problem most non-Hoshin users have is that they do not have a systematic planning process. Hoshin Kanri provides the planning structure to assure plans are developed consistent with the category criteria. With a Hoshin plan in place, you will be able to clearly describe what your organization is trying to accomplish and the timetable for reaching its goals. You will be able to describe how your objectives address the challenges facing your organization's situation. You will be able to describe how plans are deployed throughout the organization and how resources are allocated to assure success. You will be able to show graphs of key performance measures and compare them with industry benchmarks. You will be able to describe how plans are reviewed and adjusted as required.

TQE can help your organization implement the Hoshin Kanri planning process. TQE's Hoshin Handbook describes the Hoshin Kanri process and provides step by step instructions. The handbook is also used as the text for the on-site workshop. It will help get you and your team up to speed quickly. To complete your Hoshin implementation, TQE provides both web-based and PC based software to help reduce the paperwork and provide structure for your planning process. The software will help make your Hoshin plan become the way you manage instead of a document collecting dust on the shelf. Implementing Hoshin Kanri can be a giant step toward winning the Baldrige award.

TQE's Process Management and Improvement workshops directly address the Baldrige category of Process Management. After completing the training and implementing the concepts you will be able to clearly describe how day-to-day operation of key processes ensures meeting key performance requirements. You will be able to show key performance measures/indicators and how they are used to control and improve processes. You will be able describe how processes are systematically improved and how the improvements are shared with others as appropriate.

To help organizations implement the concepts of process management and process improvement, TQE provides on-site training. The training teaches people how to use basic quality tools to manage and improve processes. Once the basic tools are mastered, people are able to determine if their processes are capable of meeting customer requirements. If processes are capable, people will know how to standardize the process to assure stable and capable performance. If processes are found to be not capable, then people will know how to use the PDCA model to begin improving the processes so that they will meet customer requirements. If you want to see if you are proficient with the basic quality tools, take this quiz and find out.

Understanding how to use basic quality tools allows people in the organization to take responsibility for the processes they manage. In general, the tools will allow anyone to understand and continuously improve about 80-90% of the processes they manage. For the 10-20% of processes that require more sophisticated tools, TQE also provides training in Design of Experiments. This class teaches engineers and other technical personnel the techniques used by TQM organizations to achieve breakthrough process improvement.

Deming Prize

The Union of Japanese Scientists and Engineers (JUSE) invited Dr. Deming to Japan in July 1950. He held a series of lectures and seminars during which he taught the basic principles of statistical quality control to executives, managers and engineers of Japanese industries. His teachings made a deep impression on the participants' minds and provided great impetus in implementing quality control in Japan.

In appreciation, JUSE (English), created a prize to commemorate Dr. Deming's contribution and friendship and to promote the continued development of quality control in Japan. The prize was established in 1950 and annual awards are still given each year.

The Deming Prize, especially the Deming Application Prize which is given to companies, has exerted an immeasurable influence directly or indirectly on the development of quality control and management in Japan.

Winners of The Deming Prize for Individuals

Given to individuals who have made outstanding contributions to the study of TQM or statistical methods used for TQM, or individuals who have made outstanding contributions in the dissemination of TQM. List of **DEMING PRIZE for individuals given in APPENDIX.**

Winners of the Deming Application Prize

Given to companies or divisions of companies that have achieved distinctive performance improvement through the application of TQM in a designated year. Deming application prize given in appendix.

Winners of the Quality Control Award for Operations Business Units

Given to operations business units of a company that have achieved distinctive performance improvement through the application of quality control/management in the pursuit of TQM in a designated year. Quality control Award given in appendix.

Winners of the Japan Quality Medal

The Japan Quality Medal was established to encourage Deming winners to continue practicing and upgrading TQM. The Medal is only awarded to those companies that demonstrate continuous improvement efforts toward quality and dependability of products according to guidelines established by the Deming Prize

Committee. List of winners of the JAPAN QUALITY MEDEL GIVEN IN APPEXIDE.

RAJIV GANDHI NATIONAL AWARD

Rajiv Gandhi National Quality Award was instituted by the Bureau of Indian Standards in 1991, with a view to encouraging Indian manufacturing and service organizations to strive for excellence and giving special recognition to those who are considered to be the leaders of quality movement in India. This award is intended to generate interest and involvement of Indian Industry in quality programmes, drive our products and services to higher levels of quality and equip our Industry to meet the challenges of domestic and International markets.

The award has been named after our Late Prime Minister Rajiv Gandhi, recognizing the new thrust he had given to the quality movement in India so that India could move into 21st Century with pride.

Rajiv Gandhi National Quality Award would help Indian Industry to improve quality by:

a) Encouraging Indian Industry to make significant improvements in quality for maximizing consumer satisfaction and for successfully facing competition in the global market as well;
b) Recognizing the achievements of those organizations which have improved the quality of their products and services and thereby set an example for others;
c) Establishing guidelines and criteria that can be used by industry in evaluating their own quality improvement efforts; and
d) Providing specific guidance to other organizations that wish to learn how to achieve excellence in quality, by making available detailed information on the 'Quality Management Approach' adopted by award winning organizations to change their culture and achieve eminence.

The award has been designed in line with similar awards in other developed countries, like Malcolm Baldrige National Quality Award in USA, Deming Prize in Japan and European Quality Award.

FREQUENCY

Rajiv Gandhi National Quality Award is an annual feature on the basis of financial year. The 2008 award will be considered for results achieved by the organization from 1 April 2007 to 31 March 2008.

BENEFITS TO THE APPLICANT ORGANIZATIONS

- It will enable the organization to assess its own level of commitment to quality. It will also indicate the extent to which this commitment is being deployed through every level of the organization and in all areas of activities.
- Further, after the process of self-assessment is completed, the organization will be in a position to analyze its strengths and weaknesses.

BENEFITS TO THE AWARD WINNERS

- Award winning organization(s) will be reckoned as champions of quality movement in India.

- Award winners can publicize their achievements on their printed and publicity material. However, if a unit of an organization is selected for the award, it will be permitted to publicize its achievements on the printed and publicity material of that unit only, and not that of entire corporate body.
- Awards will be presented in a glittering ceremony in presence of top ranking personalities from government, professional bodies, industry, and consumer associations.
- Award winners may have leverage in business on being recognized as the best.
- Financial incentives
  - Organizations winning the BEST OF ALL Award would be given cash award of Rs. 500,000.
  - Organizations winning the other awards would be given cash award of Rs. 100,000.
  - Organization receiving the commendation certificates would be given cash award of Rs. 50,000.

AWARDS AND COMMENDATION CERTIFICATES

There are five awards consisting of one for large scale manufacturing organizations, one for small scale manufacturing organizations, one for large scale service sector organizations, one for small scale service sector organizations and one for BEST OF ALL. In addition, there are eight commendation certificates each for large scale and small scale manufacturing organizations as per industrial sectors given below:

a) Bio-technology,
b) Chemical industry;
c) Electrical and electronic industry;
d) Food and drug industry;
e) Gems, jewellery and allied industry;
f) Metallurgical industry;
g) Textile industry; and
h) Engineering industry and others.

Further, there are six commendation certificates each for large scale and small scale service organizations in the following sectors:

a) Education,
b) Finance,
c) Health Care,
d) Information Technology,
e) Utilities, and
f) Others.

The number of awards/commendation certificates indicated above is maximum. In the event of non-availability of suitable applicants as per assessment criteria decided by the National Awards Committee (NAC), any of the above awards/ commendation certificates may not be given.

The BEST OF ALL award consists of a certificate and a plaque, gold plated silver salver of 25 cm diameter. The plaque will be inscribed with logo 'Q' in oval shape containing a line profile of late Rajiv Gandhi. It will also bear the inscriptions 'Rajiv Gandhi National Quality Award, 2008—BEST OF ALL' and the name of the winning organization. In addition, the winner will also be given financial incentive in the form of a cash award of Rs. 500,000.

The other awards will consist of a certificate and a plaque, silver salver of 20 cm diameter. The plaque will be inscribed with logo 'Q' in oval shape containing a line profile of late Rajiv Gandhi. It will also bear the inscriptions 'Rajiv Gandhi National Quality Award, 2008—Category' and the name of the winning organization. In addition, the winners will also be given financial incentive in the form of a cash award of Rs. 100,000 each.

The commendation certificate will consist of a certificate and a plaque, silver salver of 15 cm diameter. The plaque will be inscribed with logo 'Q' in oval shape containing a line profile of late Rajiv Gandhi. It will also bear the inscriptions 'Rajiv Gandhi National Quality Award, 2008—Commendation (Industrial Sector)' and the name of the winning organization. In addition, the recipients of commendation certificates will also be given financial incentive in the form of a cash award of Rs. 50,000 each.

ELIGIBILITY TO COMPETE FOR THE AWARD

An organization is eligible to compete for the award, if it satisfies all the following conditions:

a) Applicant organization is located in India,
b) Applicant organization has been in existence for at least three years as on last date of the application,
c) Applicant organization is situated at one place or a unit of an organization housed at one location,
d) Applicant organization has never been convicted by any court for deficiency in product or service and/or found guilty of financial irregularities by any regulatory authority or court. An undertaking to this effect will have to be submitted, and
e) Applicant organization is not manufacturing products, like tobacco and liquor, etc. which are injurious to health.

A Sub-unit which performs only support functions for the parent organization such as, sales, marketing, distribution, finance, human resources and health are not eligible. [A Sub-unit is a Unit or Division of a larger organization (Parent organization) which owns or has organizational and/or financial control of sub-unit]

Further, if an applicant organization has earlier received an award, it is not eligible to apply for an award for next three awards. However, this condition will not apply to those applicant organizations which have received commendation certificate.

FEE

Application Fee

For large scale organizations (manufacturing or service)	Rs. 5000
For small scale organizations (manufacturing or service)	Rs. 1500

The application fee includes the cost of preliminary screening of the application, and shall be payable along with the application form. In case application form , downloaded from BIS website, is used for applying for the award, an additional amount of Rs. 200 is required to be submitted along with the application fee.

Assessment Fee

The applicant organization, which after preliminary screening is selected for fact-finding and evaluation visits, will have to pay the assessment fee as under:

For large scale organizations (manufacturing or service) (two-days visit)	Rs. 40,000
For small scale organizations (manufacturing or service) (one-day visit)	Rs. 10,000

In addition to the above assessment fee, the applicant organizations will also have to bear to-and-fro travel and local hospitality expenses for evaluation committee members visiting their organizations.

Application fee and Assessment fee are non-refundable and shall be paid by Demand Draft in favour of Bureau of Indian Standards payable at New Delhi.

ASSESSMENT CRITERIA

The assessment for large scale organization will be made on the basis of nine parameters, namely, Leadership; Policies, Objectives and strategies; Human resource management; Resources; Processes; Customer focused results; Employees' satisfaction, Impact on environment and society; and Business results.

The assessment for small scale organization will be made on the basis of six parameters, namely, Leadership; Human resource management; Processes; Customer focused results; Impact on environment and society; and Business results.

Emphasis will be placed on quality achievement and quality improvement as demonstrated through the information provided by applicant organization.

ASSESSMENT PROCESS

All the applications received shall be screened as per the criteria laid down on the basis of information provided by the applicant organization. Applicants selected in preliminary screening will become eligible for fact-finding and evaluation visits. A team of experts appointed for this purpose would visit the applicant organization for on-the-spot study and evaluation.

APPLICATION FORMS

Interested organizations may obtain the application form in person against the payment of Rs. 200 by cash or Demand Draft in favour of 'Bureau of Indian Standards' payable at New Delhi, from Sales Counter, Bureau of Indian Standards (BIS), 9, Bahadur Shah Zafar Marg, New Delhi. Those interested in obtaining the same by post may send a Demand Draft of Rs. 250 in favour of 'Bureau of Indian Standards' payable at New Delhi, to 'The Director & Head (Management & Systems), Bureau of Indian Standards' at the above address, superscribing the envelope as 'Rajiv Gandhi National Quality Award 2008—Application Form Request'. The application form will be sent by Speed post/Courier/Registered Post.

EMPLOYEE INVOLVEMENT AND TQM

Employee involvement is a vital aspect of total quality management solutions, and also in the success of any business. The need to both grow and succeed in an increasingly competitive marketplace has seen the implementation of various quality initiatives in different companies and organizations. One of the important concepts of TQM is employee involvement. This is a relatively new method, which is a contrast to conventional management practices, wherein management takes all decisions and workers just follow them to accomplish their jobs. This top-down management style is slow and inflexible with little room for competition. Survival in today's time-starved, customer driven market requires rapid response times from manufacturers and other businesses to the ever-changing customer needs

Problem-solving and process improvements are crucial to the company's quality initiatives, and demonstrate proactive actions are being taken to prevent problems. **Total Quality Management (TQM)** is a continuous process that strives to increase customer satisfaction, lower costs, and minimize defects and variations in every process of the business. TQM involves a number of concepts like "Just-In-Time", quality circles, employee involvement, continuous process improvement, empowerment, and world-class quality. The basic philosophy of TQM is to involve every employee in the organization along with its suppliers and distributors to improve product quality and thus enhance customer satisfaction.

(a) Management and Worker Expectations

Many proponents of TQM claim that it "empowers" workers. Critics equate it with work intensification and stress. The study finds that neither picture is accurate. Managements in the organisations studied did not use the language of empowerment and had more pragmatic goals. One manager summed this up: "empowerment is not a word used at local level; we can and do involve people more but we need to have constraints".

Workers reported higher effort levels, but most liked the pace at which they worked. Those who were working harder and who were most subject to the measurement of their performance were also the most likely to favour quality programmes. These programmes seem to promote a narrowly focused but real sense of discipline and purpose, rather than being a means to make workers work harder, the report concludes.

(b) Conditions for Success

Acceptance of TQM was greatest where several conditions prevailed:

- A strong sense of job security was a key element in encouraging acceptance of quality initiatives.
- Training was important; it was not the overall amount which mattered, but the extent to which programmes were specifically linked to quality or teamwork.
- Cooperative relationships with employee representatives were an important element in easing the acceptance of TQM. All the case study firms were unionized, and it was found that firms which maintained working relationships with their unions were also the most likely to maintain their quality programmes effectively.
- Short-term pressures tended to undermine TQM initiatives. They were of two kinds: production pressures, which made it hard for quality activities to be maintained; and financial pressures, which could reduce the resources for and commitment to TQM.

EMPLOYEE EMPOWERMENT

In addition to employee involvement, **employee empowerment** is another management concept—the basic theme of which is to give employees the means for making important decisions, and making those decisions the "right" ones. When done right, the results are heightened productivity and a better quality of work life.

While the actual practice of employee empowerment varies across organizations, empowerment is based on the fundamental concepts of job enlargement and job enrichment. **Job enlargement** involves changing the scope of the job to include a greater portion of the horizontal process. **Job enrichment** involves increasing the depth of the job to include responsibilities that have traditionally been carried out at higher levels of the organization.

Benefits Employee Involvement and Empowerment

While both employee involvement and employee empowerment are each distinct practices and are usually mutually exclusive to one another, the benefits of each can be similar. The main benefits of employee involvement and empowerment are enhanced morale, more productivity, healthier co-worker relationships and creative thinking.

(1) Improved Morale

Involving employees in decisions and policy changes that directly affect their jobs while also empowering employees to be more autonomous, greatly improves company morale at large. When employees are treated as an asset and their input is given consideration, confidence increases among every team member, and the organization sees significant gains in different facets such as productivity and loyalty. Improved morale can also increase employee longevity with the company, as the longer an employee is associated with the company, the more experienced they become. This makes them mentors to new employees and therefore indispensable to managerial staff.

(2) Increased Productivity

Both quality management practices also translate into increased productivity. Employees with an investment in the best interest of the organization increase their role in the company, and foster a stronger work ethic. When employees are given independence and expected to be more self-sufficient, they eventually become more efficient as they learn to navigate their responsibilities with minimal interference and/or relying less on managerial staff for direction. This allows managerial staff more time to tend to their own responsibilities other than giving assignments to subordinates and decreases micromanagement, which minimizes productivity.

(3) Team Cohesion

Employee empowerment fosters better relationships between employees and with their managers, as employees that are given more independence tend to form better working relationships. Each sees the other as mutually benefiting from their working relationship. In addition, more self-governance in the workplace lessens dependence on managers and supervisors and redirects that reliance laterally to co-workers.

(4) Innovation

Employee empowerment cultivates innovation, as employees that have a stake in company growth and sustainability will offer more ideas and problem-solving solutions when obstacles arise. As the employee meets particular challenges or finds improvements in policies, procedures or products, it will foster growth and more critical and imaginative thinking. Employees can offer different perspectives than a manager, and be able to offer a creative solution not otherwise considered by staff.

ROLE OF LEADERSHIP IN TOTAL QUALITY MANAGEMENT

TQM principles and the importance of the leadership ethical dimension TQM is based on a set of principles, which determines the content of this management philosophy. These principles comprise the organization in its broader sense, in its formal and also its informal dimension. Therefore the nature and scope of these principles is different. Some of them are of a technical nature and can be described as tools or devices in management's hands because their implementation depends on management's willpower. Those principles are focused on efficiency improvement and are basically a matter of organizational design, formal organization (structure, work processes, monitoring systems and HR policies. However, there is a second set of principles which are of a socio-technical and behavioral nature, which deal with the social dimension that every organization has. Those principles are related not only with formal arrangements that could be framed in the formal organization, but also with the feelings and personal beliefs which belong to the informal organization scope (The full implementation of this group of principles depends not only on managerial will, but also on the members' "discretionary effort"). Apart from its different nature, the other distinctive characteristic of TQM management principles is that they are related with each other in a systemic and sequential way Leaning on these two main ideas—the principles' different nature and the sequential relation amongst them—two main groups of principles could be distinguished. The first group, labeled as primary or driver principles, would include those whose design and implementation depends on management willpower and purpose. These principles deal with the organization design (product and process conformance to design and standards, management by process, fact-based management, training and teamwork).

They shape the firm's framework that enables—

A manager who places his/her capacity to influence on the power derived from his/her hierarchical position, and on his/her technical knowledge, may successfully implement these principles, which are a necessary condition to implement quality systems with a broader scope. Nevertheless, as will be stated next, fair criteria and decision-making are needed during the process, and the ethical dimension is not absent from its implementation TQM demands a high degree of decentralization and this requires that all the members in the firm receive enough education and training. Employees must be enabled to get knowledge about quality concepts, and to incorporate skills (handling of quality tools and techniques) and attitudes (active listening, co-operation) to be able to apply standards and a philosophy of continuous improvement in which they can participate.

Basically this is Total Quality Management. The success of the company which managed to achieve the quality control is based on these key concepts:

- concern for the consumers
- continual improvement
- process control
- taking preventive actions
- leadership and team work

Clearly leadership is one of the important concepts of TQM. The principles and practices of Total Quality Management can be deferent between various industries and enterprises, but there is a universal agreement about the importance of leadership for its achievement. Good management is a precondition for the success of strategies and planes. Those enterprises that succeeded to achieve total quality control managed that because of the strong leadership.

The leader is the one that promotes the importance of quality in the organization, provides conditions for continuous education and training of employees, as well as maintaining constant contacts with the employees, consumers and suppliers. Primarily, the leader needs to be a strong instigator of the organization, provocateur of changes, by seating aggressive goals of constant improvement and by searching for opportunities for making a larger benefit he has to primarily have the needs and expectations of the costumers. Within the organization he has to be seen as a trainer, instead of a boss. The success of the organization depends of the abilities of the leader and the behavior of the top management. In that case, it is necessary:

- to create a convenient organizational culture and selection of appropriate policies for initiation and application of quality control in an organization;
- the quality control to be a part of the activities of employees and to be formulated into a promotional plan and promoted through the organization;
- to acquire the necessary education and proper information about the quality control and how to implement it;
- to provide a system for protection of quality;
- to check if the actions for implementation of the quality control correspond with the previously determined plans, and policies and if it's necessary to take corrective activities;
- to establish a control system of the individual functions if it is necessary to accomplish the control more thoroughly;
- all this instructions don't refer just to the managers; they also have to be understood, accepted and applied by the employees of all levels of the organization;
- In many cases the managers don't realize the real importance and nature of the relation between consumers and suppliers. This relation opens the possibility for establishing mutual trust and support. This is the key to success;
- Getting a certificate for quality achievement in an organization doesn't indicate the end of the process for achieving Total Quality Management. Often managers have the feeling that they achieved work quality by

getting the certificate, but, on the contrary the TQM is a process that needs to be maintained continuously; and
- The quality needs to be understood at the same way between managers and employees from every level in the organization, or the implementation of TQM program will be difficult.

Role of Leadership Practices and TQM

leader ship managerial practices	leadership Dimension	impact of Leadership on TQM
•ASSIGNATION OF TASK •Direct supervision and control •Endowment & allocation of resouces •formalized practical routiness and procedures •setting of objective & goal •Information decision system •Remuneration System •Evaluation system •Training •Recognition &reward system •others	•Non techical implemention •psychoEmotion •techical & Ethical	•Improving the interests of the costumers; • Improving the services and products; • Process improvement (systems, technologies) • Improvement of employees (training, education) • Improving the relations with the consumers; • Improving the relations with suppliers; • Improving the measurement system

Clearly leadership is one of the important concepts of TQM. The principles and practices of Total Quality Management can be deferent between various industries and enterprises, but there is a universal agreement about the importance of leadership for its achievement. Good management is a precondition for the success of strategies and planes. Those enterprises that succeeded to achieve total quality control managed that because of the strong leadership.

The success of the organization to achieve quality control depends on the ability and attitude of the top management. According to how it's designed, which fazes it covers and what the above model of leadership predicts the success by achieving the TQM program is expected.

Reasons for Failure of TQM

Oftentimes, despite the effort of the management, the implementation of Total Quality Management in an organization might fail. The reasons for failure are numerous, but generally the reasons are the following:

- The access for initiation and accomplishment of TQM has to be adjusted to the nature of every organization separately. Often the companies get instant solution from consultants for achieving this goal which is totally wrong.
- Many managers are impatient and don't understand the importance of the existence of long-term goals that additionally interfere the implementation of the process.

The organizational culture plays out a very important role in the transformation of an organization. The inability to change the organizational culture might lead the attempt for achievement of TQM to fail.

- The managers focused on the transformation, forget to understand how to transform themselves.
- The lack of discipline in the organization inhibits its transformation.
- The accomplishment of TQM requires dedication from the managers on the inner processes in the organization.

The biggest contradiction leys in the larger dedication on the inner, rather than the external processes, like maintaining continuous contacts with consumers, losing perspective of their perception, and losing their affection which is a big loss for every company.

CASE STUDY

A Ten Year Follow-up of a Quality Initiative

Many industries have embraced total quality to achieve a competitive edge in the international marketplace. What is not always understood in the beginning, however, is that implementing a total quality program introduces considerable and often drastic cultural change into the organization. It would be beneficial for any company considering such change to look at a few case studies to anticipate what might happen over time, and avoid unintended consequences.

Implementing cultural change within an organization is always challenging, but in the case of quality, it should be a win-win proposition. Unfortunately, outcomes are not always as anticipated. In this real case study, critical mistakes in communication at the planning stage, and failure to foresee potential problem areas almost blocked the change before it could be fully implemented and did reduce its' eventual effect. Process improvements, however, though modest by original intent, have been well worth the efforts. Lessons learned from this case should be helpful to others considering or planning a major cultural change. For this qualitative research all data were obtained through direct observation in the plant and through confidential conversations with both hourly (union) and salaried (management) personnel at regular intervals over the period of the study. Observations and conversations were recorded in writing after each visit was concluded. Full confidentiality was observed, and no individual was directly identified, nor was any data vetted by union or management. All descriptions are real, but locations and identities have been carefully obscured.

The Need for Change

A major manufacturer opened an assembly plant in a mid-western state in the late 1960s to produce automobiles. Business boomed and the plant ran seven days per week with two shifts of twelve hours each. By 1981, however, the automotive industry in the United States, and in that plant in particular, was struggling to survive. Business at the plant was down and operations were reduced to one shift with lack of orders still forcing weeks of temporary lay-offs.

By the early 1990's both local company management and United Auto Workers (UAW) officials realized that they needed to bring in a new product if they were to insure the future of the plant. Fortunately, the plant was the newest facility in the company's collection and there was room for expansion because they also owned the surrounding property. Therefore, the plant was selected when the decision was made to increase the production of a new line of vehicles.

With the expanded production facility, local company and UAW officials expressed interest in a less adversarial relationship. The company decided to explore a team concept; after all, the Japanese were having fabulous success with it.

When local company management approached union leadership, the union leaders realized that a cooperative relationship was also in their best interest; and necessary for the survival of the plant and the jobs that it provided. After much negotiation, and with much fanfare, the new operating agreement emphasizing total quality initiatives was born.

The team concept, as encompassed by the new operating agreement, allowed the work group more autonomy to make daily decisions dealing with meeting work group tasks. Rather than allowing the production supervisor to make all the manpower decisions, the team now had an equal vote in decision-making, and the supervisor began to function as a coordinator for the TQM case study 4 team, providing it with assistance in resolving issues. The team elected a team leader; and the team leader was responsible for determining operation coverage, defect containment within the zone, scheduled days off, and training.

Union leaders saw the new team initiative as a way for the hourly employees to have more power and input into production decisions. The company saw it as a way to force accountability down to hourly workers and pull them into a mutually beneficial relationship instead of an adversarial one, as had been the history. In short, the change should have been a win-win agreement.

A Case of Miscommunication

After the agreement was made, some job duty changes took place. The senior hourly employees from the old production division became the product specialists in the new division, managers from the old division filled the newly available senior manage positions, and for the most part, people hired from outside the company became the new frontline supervisors to help avoid any preconceptions associated with the previous method of management.

All product specialists and new supervisors were given extensive training on the team concept, and all new hourly employees were given extensive testing before being offered a job.

This process of screening was known as "best in class". After employees were hired, they were then given a additional 40 hours of training. It was assumed that these practices would insure the success of the new operating agreement, but one crucial element was overlooked: middle and upper management. They did not understand nor accept the new team concept. Most senior managers had spent their entire careers under the old regime and saw no incentive to accept the new system.

When the new supervisors started turning decisions over to the teams, they were belittled by their managers and dismissed as weak. The Product Specialists also had difficulty accepting the new method of operating and were often reluctant to make decisions.

Ultimately, most of the original product specialists returned to the traditional operating system already established in the older production division. The team leaders were members of the newly hired group, however, so the new system worked much more smoothly at the lower levels.

Eventually, the demand for production increased, and a new shift and crew were added.

Unfortunately, by the time the initial problems involving hiring, training, assigning and managing an entire new shift and crew had been resolved, annual manpower reductions were requested by corporate headquarters. Manpower reductions are losses in time authorization to build the product because of gains in operator efficiencies brought about by doing the same task repeatedly. That resulted in a reduction in the number of operations required to assemble the product, but not the number of employees at the facility. According to the new operating agreement, the teams were expected to take an active role in determining where work previously done at one work station would be moved, or combined with another operation. But, no hourly employees were to lose their jobs; once an operation was reduced, employees would be assigned to another position, or as extra manpower when others have days off.

The union hierarchy, however, decided that in spite of the agreement, that "no union brother would help eliminate the job of another". This effectively put a halt to the original intent of the new process. Frontline supervisors did not have the support of their managers and the union forbade their ranks to participate. These contradictions between the new operating agreement and UAW directives prevented the team leaders from being successful, and as soon as TQM case study 6 team leaders started to fulfill their requirements under the agreement, they were labeled "too company" and voted out. What had started out as a win-win situation was rapidly becoming a lose-lose situation.

Shortly after the turmoil caused by the annual manpower reductions had passed, the company introduced a new product line. Everyone had to be trained to build the new vehicles, but the new production managers, none of whom had training or experience in quality systems, the team concept or the new operating agreement, made the decision to eliminate the team trainers from each team as an additional manpower reduction. This change was made with the launch of the new product line, further eroding team autonomy. Now, each operator was skilled in his or her own job, but no others. The team leaders and supervisors had to go to the department manager to make a case for additional training, though this was usually disallowed.

Despite the problems, the launch was considered an enormous success and another shift and crew were added. Employee numbers rose from just under 2,000 to more than 6,000. In spite of the increase in the number of employees, the training system from the original launch was abandoned, and employees were given no training on the new operating agreement or in team concepts. Though not abandoned altogether, the teams were not functioning in the manner originally specified in the operating agreement.

What Went Wrong?

Ultimately, the change was not completely successful because upper management of both the company and union did not accept the change and communicate it to all levels of the organization. Detert (2000) believes that culture has to change for a change initiative to be successful. Another position expressed by Knights (1999) is that hierarchical power structures TQM case study 7 and capital accumulation impose on total quality management thereby restricting its effectiveness.

Several quality improvements were, however, retained and are now standard operating procedure.

- All team leaders are now sent to basic statistical process control training. Then they, along with the rest of the team, determine their customers' number one problem, and adopt it as their quality issue to solve. They chart the progress over time and present actions and results on a rotating basis at daily quality meetings, which the plant manager attends.

- Relevant external information such as J.D. Powers survey results affecting product quality is summarized in a brief, easy to read format and distributed to all levels of production for review in team meetings.
- When an issue is determined to be critical to quality, operators, the team leader and the supervisor audit the operation process daily to insure compliance.

According to Jusko (1999) part of the change initiative did stick because U.S. manufactures need to continuously improve performance to survive in the marketplace.

Though the worker empowerment emphasis of the original agreement has not been kept in its entirely, the motto of "doing it right the first time" has been maintained. This supports Crosby's belief that as quality improves, cost will decrease due to the elimination of rework and scrap (1999). According to Delery (1999), the plant is not alone in its partial adoption of quality management; this practice in common in American owned plants.

Though it is easy to focus on what went wrong and why, it is more productive to focus on lessons learned. The plant faced a lack of support and understanding from the top levels of TQM case study 8 the company management and union leadership. The only people who really accepted the changes were the new supervisors and the new hourly operators. To be successful, the changes should have been tied to total plant performance. Rather than focusing solely on volume of production, successful implementation should have been a factor in the overall year-end plant scorecard.

Leaderships' single, most obvious oversight was in not retraining mid-level managers in how to operate a business using the team concept. No one showed them how this concept worked, and they weren't held accountable for its success.

Detert (2000) noted that the organizational culture will either support or inhibit change implementation. The production forces, upper levels of management, and union leadership all had a different vision of what the system should look like. Unfortunately, no one brought them all together to form one unified vision.

Another problem arose when all of the trainers for the original operating agreement were employed by the state, not by the company. Once the training was complete, the trainers left, and no one was asked to evaluate what was learned, nor was there any follow-up to review implementation.

So what is the status of the quality initiative 10 years after the beginning of the new operating agreement? The team concept was not completely abandoned; the teams still have some autonomy and the company is trying to work through the teams to accomplish its objectives. The many limitations imposed by both the management and union leadership have, however, prevented the teams from operating as they originally intended.

Quality process improvements, though modest by original intent, have been effective. All team leaders receive basic statistical process control training, then return to work with their teams on quality issues and all issues determined to be critical to quality are audited daily.

External information on quality production is summarized in an easy to read format and reviewed in regular work group meetings, and a daily quality meeting is held which the plant manager attends.

Chapter 4

Basic HR Issues in Total Quality Management

The related areas include TQM pitfalls caused by people barriers, employee commitment, employee involvement, and people management. Derived from the relevant literature, this research is to discover a quality working climate that will explicate the conditions for an overall quality HR-TQM concept. This is the environment that this research assumes will enhance quality HRM activities to ensure performance excellence, which is also called the mediating factor. The testing and evaluating of the research framework are supported by data collected from questionnaire survey and case study interviews of Malaysian universities. Meanwhile, the self-assessment performance criteria from Malcolm Baldrige National Quality Awards were used to evaluate organizational performance. Our results largely support that there is a significant relationship between quality working climate and organizational performance

EMPLOYEE COMMITMENT IN QUALITY INITIATIVES

Employee commitment to organizational initiatives is always important, as they are the people who are going to perform the quality mission in daily operations. They are also the front-liners who are directly interacting with customers. Customers' evaluation and perception to determine whether they are satisfied with the service provided or not would be the main indicators of quality and excellent performance. Therefore, this section aims to present evidence from previous study on the significant impact of employee commitment to quality working environment. Most of the researches done in the selected literature are in a service-oriented context, including public and private organizations

SIX SIGMA

"Six Sigma is a useful management philosophy and problem-solving methodology but it is not a *comprehensive management system.*" (McAdam & Evans, 2004).

"A Six Sigma initiative is designed to change the culture in an organisation by the way of *breakthrough improvement in all aspects of the business.*" (Breyfogle III *et. al.*, 2001)

"Six Sigma is a programme that combines the most effective statistical and non-statistical *methods to make overall business."* (Pearson, 2001)

"Six Sigma is a highly disciplined process that helps us focus on developing and delivering near-perfect products and services. The central idea behind Six Sigma is that you can measure how many defects you have in a process, you can systematically figure out how to eliminates them and get as close to 'zero defects' as possible. Six Sigma has changed the DNA of GE—it is *the way we work—in everything we do in every product we design"*. (General Electric at www.ge.com)

To that list we want to add our own definition that we believe acknowledges its structures for both innovation, improvement and design (Design for Six Sigma or DFSS) along with its goals and flexibility.

"*Six Sigma is a methodology with accompanying highly structured processes using efficient* statistical approaches for acquiring, assessing, and applying the customer, competitor, enterprise, and market intelligence to produce superior product, process and enterprise *innovations and designs with the goal of creating a sustainable competitive advantage."*

We can see that Six Sigma, as well, is described by many different keywords including strategy, methodology, philosophy, approach and so on, exactly as for TQM. There is, as Goodman & Theuerkauf (2005) say, certainly no common definition of Six Sigma

TOTAL QUALITY THROUGH SIX SIGMA

Some argue that many of the tools Six Sigma uses are not new. However, while Six Sigma uses conventional methods, its application is anything but conventional. Instead it stresses the importance of searching for a new way of thinking and doing. In fact, Six Sigma defines a clear road map to achieve Total Quality:

Leadership Commitment: Top management not only initiates Six Sigma deployment, it also plays an active role in the whole deployment cycle. Six Sigma starts by providing senior leadership with training in the principles and tools it needs to direct the development of a management infrastructure to support Six Sigma. This involves reducing the levels of organizational hierarchy and removing procedural barriers to experimentation and change.

Customer Focus: Systems are developed for establishing close communications with "external customers" (direct customers, end-users, suppliers, regulatory bodies, etc.), and with internal customers (employees). From upstream suppliers to ultimate end-users, Six Sigma eliminates the opportunities for defects.

Strategic Deployment: Six Sigma targets a small number of high-financial leveraged items. It focuses the company's resources: right support, right people, right project, and right tools, on identifying and improving performance metrics that relate to bottom-line success.

Integrated Infrastructure: The Leadership Team defines and reviews project progress. The Champion acts as a political leader and removes the barriers for the project team. The Master Black Belt acts as a technical coach and provides in-depth knowledge of quality tools. The Black Belt controls the project while the Green Belt supports the Black Belt—together they form the Six Sigma Project Teams. In addition, the incentive and recognition systems motivate the project teams to achieve the business goals.

Disciplined Framework: Six Sigma projects are Implemented using the Measure, Analyze, Improve and Control disciplined road map. This MAIC discipline sets-up a clear protocol to facilitate internal communication. In addition, from a business perspective, Six Sigma is also a framework for continuous business improvement.

Education and Training: Six Sigma believes that true commitment is driven by true understanding. As a fact-based methodology, it intensively utilizes quality and statistical tools to transform a practical problem to a practical solution. Thus, a top-to-bottom training is conducted in Six Sigma philosophy and system improvement techniques for all levels.

In conclusion, Six Sigma's approach and deployment makes it distinguishable from other quality initiatives. The Six Sigma approach involves the use of statistical tools within a structured methodology for gaining the knowledge needed to achieve better, faster, and less expensive products and services than the competition. The repeated, disciplined application of the master strategy on project after project, where the projects are selected based on key business objectives, is what drives dollars to the bottom line, resulting in impressive profits. Moreover, fueled by the bottom line improvement, top management will continuously be committed to this approach, the work culture will be constantly nurtured, customers will definitely be satisfied, and Total Quality will ultimately be achieved.

SIX SIGMA *v.* TOTAL QUALITY MANAGEMENT (TQM)

In some aspects of quality improvement, TQM and Six Sigma share the same philosophy of how to assist organizations to accomplish Total Quality. They both emphasize the importance of top-management support and leadership. Both approaches make it clear that continuous quality improvement is critical to long-term business success. However, why has the popularity of TQM waned while Six Sigma's popularity continues to grow in the past decade?

T. Pyzdek (Why Six Sigma is Not TQM, 2001) stated that the primary difference is management. Unlike TQM, Six Sigma was not developed by technicians who only dabbled in management and therefore produced only broad guidelines for management to follow. The Six Sigma way of implementation was created by some of America's most gifted CEOs—people like Motorola's Bob Galvin, Allied Signal's Larry Bossidy, and GE's Jack Welch. These people had a single goal in mind: making their businesses as successful as possible. Once they were convinced that tools and techniques of Six Sigma could help them do this, they developed a framework to make it happen.

The differences between TQM and Six Sigma are summarized in Table 1.

Table 1
TQM *vs.* Six Sigma

TQM	*Six Sigma*
A functional specialty within the organization.	An infrastructure of dedicated change agents. Focuses on cross-functional value delivery streams rather than functional division of labour.
Focuses on quality.	Focuses on strategic goals and applies them to cost, schedule and other key business metrics.
Motivated by quality idealism.	Driven by tangible benefit far a major stockholder group (customers, shareholders, and employees).
Loosely monitors progress toward goals	Ensures that the investment produces the expected return.

People are engaged in routine duties (Planning, improvement, and control).	"Slack" resources are created to change key business processes and the organization itself.
Emphasizes problem-solving.	Emphasizes breakthrough rates of improvement.
Focuses on standard performance, e.g. ISO 9000.	Focuses on world class performance, e.g., 3.4 PPM error rate.
Quality is a permanent, full-time job. Career path is in the quality profession.	Six Sigma job is temporary. Six Sigma is a stepping-stone; career path leads elsewhere.
Provides a vast set of tools and techniques with no clear framework for using them effectively.	Provides a selected subset of tools and techniques and a clearly defined framework for using them to achieve results (DMAIC).
Goals are developed by quality department based on quality criteria and the assumption that what is good for quality is good for the organization.	Goals flow down from customers and senior leadership's strategic objectives. Goals and metrics are reviewed at the enterprise level to assure that local sub-optimization does not occur.
Developed by technical personnel.	Developed by CEOs.
Focuses on long-term results. Expected payoff is not well-defined.	Six Sigma looks for a mix of short-term and long-term results, as dictated by business demands.

TABLE 2

Different Approach for TQM and Six Sigma for better Business Strategy

TQM	*Six Sigma*
Not necessarily part of the Business Strategy	A strategy from the top of the Business Unit
No bottom line accountability	Projects frequently have a profitability hurdle
Improve and uniform processes	3.4 defect per million opportunities
Usually not targeted to a process or business	Targeted areas
Management and employees' involvement	Management takes an active role in all phases of Six Sigma

THE ROLE OF HUMAN RESOURCES (HR) IN SIX SIGMA

Chances are you've heard of Six Sigma, perhaps in connection with General Electric, the company that made it popular in the 1990s. You may even know that Six Sigma uses statistical techniques to improve processes in both manufacturing and service industries. But did you know there is an important role for Human Resources (HR) in this sophisticated process improvement approach? Or that Six Sigma initiatives are unlikely to succeed without HR's help?

HR professionals with the right skills can contribute to a Six Sigma initiative at both strategic and tactical levels. This article describes the areas in which HR should play a role in Six Sigma and discusses how HR professionals can increase their chances of being included in Six Sigma decision-making and implementation.

To appreciate the important role HR has in Six Sigma, it is important to begin this discussion by having an understanding of what Six Sigma is, all the roles played by others in a Six Sigma implementation, and the factors critical to a successful implementation.

Six Sigma Defined

The term "Six Sigma" is widely used to refer to all of the following:

A structured method for improving business processes. This method, called DMAIC (Define, Measure, Analyze, Improve, Control), is supported by an assortment of statistical tools.

A statistical measurement of how well a business process is performing. A process that performs at "Six Sigma" produces only 3.4 defects out of every million opportunities to produce a defect. Processes that perform at lower sigma levels (such as one sigma or four sigma) produce more defects per million opportunities. It is possible for a process to perform at an even higher level (and thus have even fewer defects), but Six Sigma has become popular as the standard for excellent process performance.

An organizational mindset in which people make decisions based on data, look for root causes of problems, define defects based on customer rather than internal requirements, seek to control variation, track leading indicators of problems to prevent them from happening, etc.

Six Sigma Roles

How can Six Sigma be applied to the Human Resources (HR) function?

Listed are some simple examples for Human Resource projects:

1) Employee turnover rate.
2) Job satisfaction issues (surveys).
3) Management satisfaction.
4) Cafeteria food quality.
5) Policy deployment.
6) New hire process quality and cycle time.
7) Health care costs.
(8) Safety and compliance issues.
9) Employee exit analysis.
10) University relations.

Remember, each "issue" is underpinned by at least one critical-to-quality characteristic (CTQ). For example, consider the issue referred to as "university relations." Given this, we might ask: "What must go right during a typical encounter with a university official?" Also: "What could go wrong?" Such an internal examination of your past experience will help to reveal the CTQ's. Without saying, it frequently helps to involve others. In additions, tools such as fault-tree analysis, failure modes effects analysis, fishbone diagrams, and other such methods can greatly assist.

Naturally, this discussion reflects the purpose and intent of the "Define" phase—as related to DMAIC. Following this, it will be necessary to establish a "scale of measure" for each CTQ. For example, let us again look at the issue of university relations. As would be known, it is important for corporations to maintain a good rapport with the university's key staff. Consider the relations that come to play when attempting to recruit new college graduates. Often, executives that have previously cultivated good relations get the "first call" about a really good student. Of course, this constitutes value for the corporation, the university, as well as the student.

A metric that could be used to report on such a phenomenon might be related to "university staff satisfaction." By design, such a scale could assume the numeric values 1 through 5. Of course, these quasi-measurements are really "assessments." Nonetheless, this type of scale seeks to rate the "extent to which you agree (or disagree) with the following statements."

On the surface, such an analysis appears to be nothing more than a simple "smiles test." However, many things can be covertly gleamed from a statistical examination of the data. For example, it might be possible to surface the demographics that are most highly associated with student recruitment rates. Other "process level" factors can be cross-tabulated and subsequently correlated by way of such statistics as chi-square, the phi coefficient, lambda's uncertainty coefficient, and so on. As one might surmise, such a level of investigation constitutes the "Analyze" phase.

The "Improve" phase typically involves the postulation of one or more new ways of doing things and then designing a confirmation study. For example, it might be postulated that "more follow-on by e-mail" will improve relations (on the 1-5 scale). In this case, the study is designed and then implemented. If this factor turns out to be among the "Vital Few" *versus* the "Trivial Many," the Black Belt must then establish a control plan for the given contributory variable. Thus, the "Control" phase of DMAIC is executed. Of course, the ultimate gain in value must be validated over some rational period of time. Once this has been accomplished, the project is "closed out."

SIX SIGMA ON HUMAN RESOURCES PRACTICES?

Six Sigma is a methodology that focuses on understanding and meeting customers' needs by using a variety of tools, especially statistical analyses, to drive performance metrics. Although its roots are in manufacturing, there's no reason you can't adopt Six Sigma for your service environment.

You could use Six Sigma to tackle a variety of strategic human resources projects, such as:

a. Lowering turnover
b. Paring prescription drug costs
c. Reducing injuries at work
d. Improving recruiting time-to-fill

Six Sigma methodologies include a project plan known as DMAIC that is used to improve business processes within human resources. DMAIC is an acronym that describes the basic steps you take:

Define — Identify the problem
Measure — Establish metrics to quantify
Analyze — Figure out what the metrics tell you
Improve — Craft a solution based on your analysis
Control — Find a way to sustain improvements

Let's take an example. Say you want to reverse a trend of high turnover. You would:

Define the problem: reducing unwanted turnover.
Measure: identify key measurements underlying turnover.
Analyze: understand key factors and trends that create turnover.
Improve: identify and execute a plan to address those factors.
Control: implement controls to lower turnover on an ongoing basis.

Historically, human resources professionals have helped with the heavy training requirements when their organizations adopt Six Sigma, either in whole or in part. So expect to play a pivotal role in equipping your workforce. Aside from training, other issues you may need to address include: setting rewards and recognition for project teams; staffing those teams geared toward improving your business processes; and instilling Six Sigma methodology as a staple of your workplace culture. If you're like most human resources professionals, you initially might be uncomfortable with the statistical aspect of Six Sigma. Yet it enables you to get beyond merely measuring HR activities and focus on strategic goals. When integrated with your human resource management practices, Six Sigma should help you improve service levels and efficiency. For your customers, few things are more highly prized.

Six Sigma in Recruitment

Now Six Sigma is applicable to all sectors today, and in recruitment function you should do the following:

- Reduce the time required to hire an employee.
- Reduce the time to process an insurance claim.
- Improve employee on-boarding and orientation processes.
- Reduce expenditures for recruiting firms.
- Improve timeliness and the value of employee performance reviews.
- Reduce absenteeism.
- Improve training efficiency.
- Improve employee satisfaction.
- Identify and correct retention issues.
- Reduce incentive compensation errors.
- Eliminate over payments to terminated salaried employees.
- Improving grievance handling process.
- Consolidation of employee information databases.
- Integration of multiple payroll system for remote location.
- Increase job posting hit rate.
- Increase retention using exit interview information.

The corporate staffing department performs a critical gateway function in a company, bringing people from the outside world into the organization. As such, recruiting has a huge impact on the quality of the assembled workforce. Attaining quality in recruiting and deployment is therefore a natural aim of an organization. How do you pursue quality in hiring and placement?

Measuring the performance of the process is a data-driven exercise, so there must be steps in the process that perform the critical data capture necessary for measurement and reporting. A thorough statistical analysis of all data endeavors to identify those elements of the process that have a direct impact on the quality of its outcome. Once the source of defects has been identified, an improvement program can be defined and implemented to remove these causes of defects.

What is a defect in internal recruiting? The Six Sigma methodology defines a defect in terms of the expectations of the customer, which in the case of an internal recruiting department is the hiring manager. Hiring an unqualified candidate, a below-average performer, or even an employee that demonstrates a lack of fit to the corporate culture could all be considered a defective outcome of the recruiting process. How can you reduce defects in corporate recruiting?

Screening Out Unqualified Candidates

Recruiting can be viewed as a screening process. This is especially true during periods of high unemployment, when the job market is characterized by an oversupply of talent. Under these conditions, the recruiting function in an organization is to eliminate unqualified people as much as to seek out talent. To improve the quality of an overall recruiting process, each step of the process must be designed to maximize the probability that the candidate ultimately selected meets the expectations of the hiring manager. One way to do this is to maximize the chances that an unqualified candidate is screened out at each step. The following are some key areas in which to focus on quality.

Talent Definition

To drive quality into a selection and recruiting process, you must first define what quality is. The selection process must be grounded on the foundation of a proper specification of the requirements of the job. You must articulate the abilities, credentials and experience that will bring about success at the job. Once set, these objective criteria inform all aspects of the recruiting process for the position, from the writing of the job description to the criteria employed by an online pre-screening function.

Employment Branding

The employment brand you project to jobseekers has an important screening role. The corporate Careers website should present a consistent employment brand, and provide visitors with good quality information about the organization, even a realistic portrayal of life working at the company. Cultural fit is as important a factor to the overall quality of hire as the possession of requisite hard and soft skills.

Sourcing Strategy

It is the function of a sourcing strategy to ensure that employment advertising reaches the right audience. The goal is to maximize exposure to qualified candidates while minimizing exposure to unqualified candidates. A job posting appearing in a media vehicle that has too low a proportion of qualified candidates to unqualified candidates will increase the burden on later stages of the selection process to screen unqualified candidates out. A formal sourcing strategy should be informed by actual sourcing yields

Job Description

The job description for a vacancy should provide the candidate ample opportunity to self-screen. It should describe the role, and the activities and responsibilities involved. Moreover, the job description should describe the abilities, credentials and experience possessed by the ideal candidate. Other pieces of information on a job description that give candidates the opportunity to self-screen are salary ranges and details on logistics, such as the location of the vacancy and the amount of business travel involved.

Shortlist

Even an informed sourcing strategy and a carefully crafted job description will not prevent the unqualified from submitting a resume. The selection process must be armed with systems and procedures that ensure these unqualified candidates do not make it to later stages of the internal recruiting process, where costs increase. Historically, the next check for quality in the recruiting process was the resume screen. Screening on the basis of a resume is a highly subjective process, wholly unsuited to bringing consistency and quality to an organization's workforce. Resumes are candidate-driven and generally do not contain information sufficient for a recruiter to assess a candidate's ability to do a job. Furthermore, there are no standards for resume content, meaning that the information common on all resumes received by a recruiter is insufficient to make an accurate ranking of candidates. At best, all a recruiter is able to do is look for an indication that the candidate may move forward to the selection next step, such as a phone screen.

IMPORTANCE OF SIX SIGMA FOR HR PROFESSIONALS

Given today's need for HR professionals to be Strategic Business Partners, to be a 'Voice of Conscience' to the CEOs as well as Champion for the Employees, those with background in proven management methodologies and tools such as Lean, Six Sigma or Kaizen have a great advantage. An HR Professional who can present his business case for HR strategies and interventions with a compelling return on investment will be respected and regarded. Having the knowledge and exposure in cost and time estimates, in analytical thinking processes as well as fact-based strategies and decision making will open doors.

Understanding and using statistics to convey thoughts raises the bar on necessary conversations such as Legal compliance related to Human Resources Management, Developing a Recruiting and Retention Strategy, Performance Management, Job Design, Knowledge Management, Human Resource Information Systems.

HR and Management Methodologies

The role of the HR professional is typically divided into four main categories—Strategic Business Partner, Change Catalyst, Employee Champion and day-to-day Administrative Operator. In today's world an HR professional is expected to act with confidence in all four categories.

Modern Management methodologies such as Six Sigma provide a framework for confidently capturing and presenting information in all these four areas, for acting upon gaps in performance and continuous improvement. HR professionals cannot fall behind in use of modern management methodologies in order to be able to speak the same language as the business, to support them if needed and last but not least for the sake of being accepted as business partners.

Contributing to Metric Design

Today, HR faces demand from the CEOs and senior business managers for metrics that capture the impact of HR activities on business performance. Despite worthy goals, few HR professionals have confidence that their measurement systems provide line managers with the information they need to make critical workforce decisions. Often their metrics are not even linked to the corporate strategy and are unsuitable for contributing to improvement in overall business performance.

Therefore, it is important to distinguish which metrics are truly adding value to the organization. Measuring for measurement's sake is time consuming waste. To determine which metric should be used is imperative to understand both the strategic initiatives of the department as well as the organization's needs. Being familiar with the strategic initiatives, is key to many HR processes such as performance reviews, training, recruitment, succession planning, job descriptions/profiling and employee orientation. Six Sigma provides simple yet valuable tools to help translating the needs of your organization into metrics, identifying and closing gaps hence contributing to business results.

Voice of the Customer (VOC) is a structured multi-step process focusing on capturing the voices of HR's customers—leaders and staff of your organization—and translating it into CTQs (Critical to Quality), metrics and actions.

Kano Diagram is a simple yet powerful tool used to prioritize Customer Needs. Firstly, Musts are expected by your internal customers. By not delivering on Musts, dissatisfaction is inevitable. Since as mentioned earlier, Musts are expected, there is no need for reinforcements on them. Secondly, The-More-The-Better are satisfiers. More providence on these will contribute to satisfaction. Any form of deficiency will definitely create dissatisfaction. Thirdly, Delighters are defined as representatives of a special set of requirements that can contribute vastly to satisfaction if received and diminutive disappointment if they are not present. They are difficult to detain since the customers usually don't even think of them due to the minimal expectancy from them.

VOC and Kano are just an extension of what many organizations do anyway: capturing the employee satisfaction. Unfortunately, not everybody play by the rules. In other words, they rather draw conclusions on high-level data without going to the root causes. The result is often sobering.

Internal benchmarking is a field that numerous HR professionals recognize. Internal benchmarking involves the process of comparing operations/departments within an organization to each other. Metrics drawn from CTQs can assist benchmarking an organization regarding their internal customer satisfaction.

Another popular Six Sigma tool is Process Mapping (SIPOC, Value Added Analysis). SIPOC maps Suppliers, Inputs, Process Steps, Outputs and Customers of any given process. The profit of a SIPOC is in the high-level understanding of the process and the definition of process metrics that lead to CTQ metrics. A straightforward example should show the effect of process mapping:

Mapping a recruitment process was done to identify why recruitment takes so long. After studying the typical processing time each of the steps took it became obvious that the "Short listing Process" consumed a considerable portion of the entire processing time. Why? Digging into the details of this process the team found that one of their HR officers performs batching, i.e. she kept all the recruitment files until end of the week and tried to complete them on each Friday. If the workload was too much, she kept the remaining of the files until the following Friday...

These kinds of findings are everywhere waiting to be discovered. They are easy to embark upon and to resolve once the root cause has been identified. However, resolving the issue is only part of the task. The other—sometimes even more important—part of the task is to promote solutions—without blaming people—and to encourage cross-company learning.

HR professionals can help by establishing and supporting Best Practice Communication linked to R&R systems. To be successful, organizations must implement a process that promotes and rewards the sharing of ideas.

Building Six Sigma Competency Model

Offering to build a Six Sigma competency model, for example, will not only serve to identify candidates with the right mix of technical and leadership skills but also allow the HR professionals to work closely with the Process Excellence team to develop management and leadership competencies of the Six Sigma Green Belts, Black Belts, and Master Black Belts. After all, these Belts are often the best potential personnel in the organisation.The four roles Business Advocate, Change Agent, Process Excellence Expert and Integrator/Enabler together with the competencies shown—to a certain degree—ought to be part of every company's Leadership Profile.

HR professionals also have the opportunity to utilize skills such as change management, and leadership development. Acting as a resource and/or coach for Black Belts who encounter team-related problems will quickly build credibility. Sometimes, the HR professional is positioned better to function as a liaison with the Sponsor and Champion than the project manager.

Managing Change

One of the 4 key roles of HR for an organization is in facilitating and managing change. Introducing Six Sigma into an organization means major changes that will have a profound effect on a broad group of stakeholders. Managers and employees at many levels of the organization will be asked to engage in new behaviours. HR professionals shall be champions in making change happen by owning the change process, customizing the change model and guiding the business through the change process. HR professionals as change agents, helping their businesses both to meet new objectives and to do so quickly, should consider taking the following steps: (a) identify key success factors for building capacity for change; (b) provide the extent to which these key success factors are being managed; (c) identify the improvement activities for each success factor; (d) see the review of the key factors as an iterative process, not an event.

HR professionals with knowledge of Six Sigma tools and other methodologies can deliver better service to their customers—their leaders and colleagues. Identifying requirements and gaps, analyzing and improving processes as well as measuring the performance long-term to sustain the gains applies to all business processes, including HR.

Moreover, HR professionals can support driving and sustaining business initiatives such as Six Sigma that are driving performance and business results. Developing recruitment and retention strategies for Six Sigma personnel, creating job descriptions, and establishing reward and recognition programmes as well as leadership development are only some of many opportunities to become involved.

HR Professionals with Six Sigma knowledge are absolutely an added advantage and a starting point for any organization embarking on achieving a strategic HR role.

Six Sigma has a martial arts convention for naming many of its professional roles. The chart below describes how these roles are typically defined.

Six Sigma Roles and Responsibilities

Sponsor	Senior executive who sponsors the overall Six Sigma Initiative.
Leader	Senior-level executive who is responsible for implementing Six Sigma within the business.
Champion	Middle- or senior-level executive who sponsors a specific Six Sigma project, ensuring that resources are available and cross-functional issues are resolved.
Black Belt	Full-time professional who acts as a team leader on Six Sigma projects. Typically has four to five weeks of classroom training in methods, statistical tools, and (sometimes) team skills.
Master Black Belt	Highly experienced and successful Black Belt who has managed several projects and is an expert in Six Sigma methods/tools. Responsible for coaching/mentoring/training Black Belts and for helping the Six Sigma leader and Champions keep the initiative on track.
Green Belt	Part-time professional who participates on a Black Belt project team or leads smaller projects. Typically has two weeks of classroom training in methods and basic statistical tools.
Team Member	Professional who has general awareness of Six Sigma (through no formal training) and who brings relevant experience or expertise to a particular project.
Process Owner	Professional responsible for the business process that is the target of a Six Sigma project.

Leaders and Champions usually receive high-level training on the technical aspects of Six Sigma and specific training on how to lead an initiative. At the "Belt" level, each candidate is assigned an initial "training project" that he/she will work on during the formal training period. Candidates attend classroom training for a week, work on their projects for three weeks, return to class for another week, and so on until they have acquired all the skills appropriate to their role.

Other HR's Role in Six Sigma

As with any major organizational initiative, many factors contribute to success. Some of these factors will fall within HR's area of responsibility, such as those discussed below.

Black Belt Selection and Retention

Having the right people in the Black Belt role is critical to the success of a Six Sigma initiative. The training investment is substantial for this pivotal role. Further, Black Belts are the visible "face" of Six Sigma. They help shape the organization's impression of Six Sigma, and, consequently, the willingness of many to embrace the initiative. Therefore, you want to pick Black Belts very carefully. (Some organizations only select Black Belts from among those who have already been identified as "high potentials.")

HR professionals can help the Six Sigma Leader find the right people for Black Belt roles and ensure they remain in those positions for the typical two-year rotation. Potential HR contributions in this area include:

Building a competency model that will help identify candidates with the right mix of technical, team, and leadership skills and abilities.

Creating job descriptions that help candidates fully understand the position and expectations prior to signing on.

Developing a retention strategy that will help ensure Black Belts complete their rotation and the organization recoups its investment in training and development.

Rewards and Recognition

Rewarding and recognizing Black Belts and Six Sigma teams is more complex than it may appear. Black Belts join the Six Sigma initiative from various places in the organization where they are likely to have been at different job levels with differing compensation arrangements. Determining whether and how to make appropriate adjustments in level and compensation now that all these individuals are in the same role is both tricky and critical.

Similar complexities are involved at the project team level. Six Sigma projects led by Black Belts typically result in savings in the hundreds of thousands of dollars. Deciding how the team should be rewarded and recognized and who should get credit for what is not easy. Yet ignoring these issues can result in resentment, reluctance to work on Six Sigma projects, and the potential failure of the overall initiative.

HR professionals can help the Six Sigma Leader tackle the challenge of establishing the right rewards/recognition. Potential HR contributions in this area include:

Analyzing existing compensation arrangements to identify the extent to which those arrangements will support the Six Sigma initiative.

Creating a strategic compensation plan that will better support Six Sigma.

Developing a non-monetary reward program for Six Sigma teams.

Project Team Effectiveness

The work of Six Sigma is done mostly at the project team level by a Black Belt leading a small team through the steps of the DMAIC method. If the team itself does not function well or does not interact effectively with others in the organization who ultimately have to support and carry out the process changes, the project probably will not be successful. Given the typical project's potential payback, failure can be expensive.

HR professionals can help the project teams work together more effectively. Potential HR contributions in this area include:

Ensuring team leaders and members get training and/or coaching in teamwork, conflict management, communications, dealing with difficult team members, and other team effectiveness skills.

Providing teams with tools that allow them to diagnose their own performance and identify when and where they need help.

Acting as a resource for Black Belts who encounter team-related challenges they cannot surmount.

Creating a Six Sigma Culture

Many Sponsors, Champions, and Leaders look to Six Sigma as a way to change an organization's culture to one that is more data-driven, proactive, decisive, and customer-oriented. But they often have little idea about how to achieve successful culture change.

HR professionals can help executives approach culture change in a way that addresses the underlying business goals without creating organizational resistance. Potential HR contributions in this area include:

Working with Six Sigma Sponsors, Leaders, and Champions to identify elements of the culture that might hinder the achievement of Six Sigma goals.

Advising on change plans that will target those specific cultural elements.

Identifying how Six Sigma can be rolled out in a way that works with, rather than against, the current culture.

Change Management and Communications

Introducing Six Sigma into an organization is a major change that will have a profound effect on a broad group of stakeholders. Managers and employees at many levels of the organization will be asked to engage in new behaviors. In many cases, those leading other initiatives will see Six Sigma as a source of competition for resources, executive attention, and organizational power. Others may see it as an indictment of their past performance. Many will be confused about how Six Sigma fits with the large number of other ongoing organizational initiatives.

HR professionals can help reduce the uncertainty and anxiety surrounding Six Sigma and increase the levels of acceptance and cooperation in the organization. Potential HR contributions in this area include:

Drafting a change management/communications plan that addresses the people side of the Six Sigma rollout.

Helping create a "case for change" that describes:

The reasons for and benefits of Six Sigma.
How the organization will help employees succeed in new ways of working.
How Six Sigma fits with other ongoing initiatives.

Counseling Six Sigma Leaders and Champions on how their behavior can help or hinder Six Sigma's acceptance throughout the organization.

Being Included in Six Sigma

Just because HR professionals can play a role in the success of Six Sigma, it doesn't automatically follow that they will be asked to participate. Unless you are in an organization that views HR as a partner in all business initiatives, you may have to push to be included in Six Sigma.

HR can greatly increase its chances of being included in the Six Sigma initiative by:

Ensuring HR professionals have the right skills and knowledge.
Marketing its potential contribution early in the initiative.
Gaining the Right Skills and Knowledge.

In addition to HR/organizational development-related areas, HR professionals need a familiarity with Six Sigma itself. Without a basic knowledge of the DMAIC method, supporting tools, roles, jargon, and even simple statistical methods, HR will not have the credibility it needs to be considered a potential contributor to the initiative.

The time to get this knowledge is now. Even if your organization is not rolling out—or even considering—Six Sigma today, there are two reasons why it is worth a HR professional's time to become familiar with the concepts now. If the organization does decide to implement Six Sigma, there won't be enough time to catch up. HR has to be involved at the very beginning of the initiative. In addition, there are many applications of Six Sigma to HR's processes themselves, e.g., the payroll process, benefits administration, selection, and recruiting. HR might even consider setting an example for the rest of the organization by adopting Six Sigma techniques to enhance its own processes.

Marketing HR's Potential Contribution

The marketing challenge is twofold. First, senior executives may not believe that the people issues are just as critical to Six Sigma's success as are its many technical components. In that case, HR will need to sell the importance of the people side. Second, executives must perceive HR as being able to make a significant contribution on the people side of Six Sigma. Besides ensuring that it has both the required skills and knowledge described above, HR can also meet these challenges by:

Gathering data that supports the need for attention to the people side of Six Sigma. Potential sources include Six Sigma publications, case studies, conference sessions, and executives in companies that have already implemented Six Sigma.

Deriving lessons from previous organizational initiatives in which people issues and/or HR actions played an acknowledged role in success or failure.

Meeting with senior executives to discuss their business/Six Sigma goals and then identifying areas where HR could provide very specific and measurable help.

Speaking to Six Sigma Leaders and Champions in the language of Six Sigma, not the language of HR. These executives are typically interested in improving efficiency (i.e., internal cost) and effectiveness (i.e., what the customer sees as "defects"). HR needs to understand what the executives care about and pitch HR's services in relevant terms.

Taking the lead and applying Six Sigma successfully within the HR function.

HR has a substantial role to play in the success of a Six Sigma initiative. But it will have the opportunity to contribute only if its professionals have the right skills and knowledge and are able to show Six Sigma executives the value they can add. Gain those skills now and make sure senior leadership knows how HR can help support the success of the initiative. Only then will they realize they just cannot do it without you!

BENCHMARKING AND TOTAL QUALITY MANAGEMENT

Benchmarking is the process of comparing one's business processes and performance metrics to industry bests or best practices from other industries. Dimensions typically measured are quality, time and cost. In the process of benchmarking, management identifies the best firms in their industry, or in another industry where similar processes exist, and compare the results and processes of those studied (the "targets") to one's own results and processes. In this way, they learn how well the targets perform and, more importantly, the business processes that explain why these firms are successful.

Benchmarking is used to measure performance using a specific indicator (cost per unit of measure, productivity per unit of measure, cycle time of x per unit of measure or defects per unit of measure) resulting in a metric of performance that is then compared to others. Also referred to as "best practice benchmarking" or "process benchmarking", this process is used in management and particularly strategic management, in which organizations evaluate various aspects of their processes in relation to best practice companies' processes, usually within a peer group defined for the purposes of comparison. This then allows organizations to develop plans on how to make improvements or adapt specific best practices, usually with the aim of increasing some aspect of performance. Benchmarking may be a one-off event, but is often treated as a continuous process in which organizations continually seek to improve their practices.

H. Watson outlines the development of benchmarking in five phases (8):

Phase 1	1950-1975	Reverse Engineering
Phase 2	1976-1986	Competitive Benchmarking
Phase 3	1982-1988	Process Benchmarking
Phase 4	1988+	Strategic Benchmarking
Phase 5	1993+	Global Benchmarking

Reverse engineering was tearing things apart, examining them, improving them, and putting them back together. Benchmarking really began in its modern form with the introduction of competitive benchmarking began with Rank Xerox, and its implementation of benchmarking in beginning around 1976. This was followed by process benchmarking which included looking for ideas outside of the direct competition. Strategic benchmarking involves fundamentally changing the business, not just the process (9). Global Benchmarking is the newest and involves comparing your organization on a global scale.

Types

- **Process benchmarking**—the initiating firm focuses its observation and investigation of business processes with a goal of identifying and observing the best practices from one or more benchmark firms. Activity analysis will be required where the objective is to benchmark cost and efficiency; increasingly applied to back-office processes where outsourcing may be a consideration.
- **Financial benchmarking**—performing a financial analysis and comparing the results in an effort to assess your overall competitiveness and productivity.
- **Benchmarking from an investor perspective**—extending the benchmarking universe to also compare to peer companies that can be considered alternative investment opportunities from the perspective of an investor.
- **Performance benchmarking**—allows the initiator firm to assess their competitive position by comparing products and services with those of target firms.
- **Product benchmarking**—the process of designing new products or upgrades to current ones. This process can sometimes involve reverse engineering which is taking apart competitors products to find strengths and weaknesses.
- **Strategic benchmarking**—involves observing how others compete. This type is usually not industry specific, meaning it is best to look at other industries.
- **Functional benchmarking**—a company will focus its benchmarking on a single function to improve the operation of that particular function. Complex functions such as Human Resources, Finance and Accounting and Information and Communication Technology are unlikely to be directly comparable in cost and efficiency terms and may need to be disaggregated into processes to make valid comparison.

- **Best-in-class benchmarking**—involves studying the leading competitor or the company that best carries out a specific function.
- **Operational benchmarking**—embraces everything from staffing and productivity to office flow and analysis of procedures performed.
- **Energy benchmarking**—process of collecting, analysing and relating energy performance data of comparable activities with the purpose of evaluating and comparing performance between or within entities. Entities can include processes, buildings or companies. Benchmarking may be internal between entities within a single organization, or—subject to confidentiality restrictions—external between competing entities.

TQM & Benchmarking

Focus	*TQM* *Internal*	*Benchmarking* *External*
Main Principles	Develop dialogue within a process to improve it through gradual increments	Compare processes with others who do the same and determine best methods

USE OF BENCHMARKING IN ORGANIZATION DEVELOPMENT

Benchmarking can greatly enhance an organization's performance:

- **To forecast industry trends**—Because it requires the study of industry leaders, benchmarking can provide numerous indicators on where a particular business might be headed, which ultimately may pave the way for the organization to take a leadership position
- **To discover emerging technologies**—The benchmarking process can help leaders uncover technologies that are changing rapidly, newly developed, or state-of-the-art.
- **To stimulate strategic planning**—The type of information gathered during a benchmarking effort can assist an organization in clarifying and shaping its vision of the future
- **To enhance goal setting**—Knowing the best practices in your business can dramatically improve your ability to know what goals are realistic and attainable.
- **To maximize award-winning potential**—Many prestigious award programs, such as the Malcolm Baldridge National Quality Award Program, the federal government's President's Quality Award Program, and numerous state and local awards recognize the importance of benchmarking and allocate a significant percentage of points to organizations that practice it.
- **To comply with Executive Order #12862, "Setting Customer Service Standards"**—Benchmarking the customer service performance of federal government agencies against the best in business is one of the eight action areas of this Executive Order.

To identify where in your organization you can start benchmarking:

- Review goals and objectives of your organization's strategic plan.

- Identify your organization's significant processes.
- Identify new customer needs.

BENCHMARKING AND HR PROFESSIONALS

1) It enables a company to calibrate how it is delivering HR practices by examining the way other organizations accomplish tasks and responsibilities
2) Benchmarking enables a company to learn from others successes and mistakes.
3) Benchmarking can create an environment in which active learning is encouraged.
4) It can be used as a tool to motivate people to change.
5) Benchmarking can be used to help set direction and priorities for an HR manager and helps him to focus on critical activities.
6) A well established benchmarking process can help managers set goals and targets designed to make the company the best in its competitive field, and to initiate focused programs that move the company from its current position

By Benchmarking one can find out:

- Who does the business process really well and has processes that are adaptable to my organization ?
- What areas are causing the most trouble ?
- Which employees contribute most to the critical success factors ?
- What are the performance measures to determine the effect of our actions?
- Who is the most compatible for me to benchmark with ?
- Most business processes are common throughout industry.

Benchmarking is a strategic activity aimed at the pursuit of continuous improvement. It is the process of assessing an organization's procedures, product and service Performance against organizations that have achieved a recognized standard of Excellence. Benchmarking is an ongoing, systematic process to search for and Introduce best practice into an organization. Organizations can also use benchmarking techniques to add value to their strategic planning processes. They can be a valuable means of setting appropriate measurable objectives to improve the organization's strategic performance. Benchmarking can also help strategically focus an organization's HRM performance by providing challenging, yet achievable targets or goals across all key areas of the HRM framework.

In the HRM context, benchmarking can provide a useful way to identify and assess the contribution of people management practices to an organization's corporate Performance. By helping organizations learn from other organizations' high Performance standards, benchmarking provides an incentive for organizations to Adapt, where appropriate, that learning to improve the quality of their own people Management practices.

Developing the specific criteria, which define effectiveness for HR activities, is one of the most difficult challenges facing line managers and HR professionals. In this regard, there are two schools of thought.

1) The first school advocates monitoring the costs and benefits of human resource activities, i.e those associated with attraction, selection retention,

development and utilization of people in organizations in economic terms, the assumption being that the ultimate single measures of HR effectiveness is the bottom line. This economic approach of measuring HR performance has the advantage of being simple and understandable, but it fails to provide guidance when implementing effective HR management programs.

2) The second school is to measure the set of HR practices delivered within an organization, and measure the contribution of each practice to the overall competitive advantage of the organization. The attempts are to capture in a single model the variety of HR practices deployed by organizations to augment innovation, improve quality, and be the lowest cost producer of goods and services.

The areas that human resource benchmarking includes are:

- Organization Effectiveness,
- HR Effectiveness,
- Recruitment,
- Training and Development,
- Absence and Turnover, and
- Occupational Health and Safety.

Most of these factors can be then analyzed further into splits such as occupational group or tenure-based. The resulting benchmarking report, prepared on an annual basis, connects a range of people management issues to organizational variables such as revenue, expense and profit, etc., providing benchmarks that allow managers to evaluate, in different areas, This provides managers with essential information to help them in their tasks of maximizing organizational effectiveness.

It is also possible to define key performance indicators, which can help managers, evaluate how their HR practices relate to both the operational and strategic level of enterprise and lay the foundation of comparing the HR practices according to six performance criteria:

1) Quality of delivery (in terms of conforming to some practice ideal or fulfilling the intended purpose)
2) Quantity (expressed in terms such as dollar value, number of units, or number of completed HR cycles)
3) Timeliness (the degree to which an HR practice is completed, or a result produced at the earliest time desirable)
4) Cost effectiveness (in the sense of optimizing the gain or minimizing the loss from each unit or instance of use of human and financial services)
5) Need for supervision (the degree to which a person or unit can carry out a HR practice promotes feelings of self-esteem, goodwill, commitment, satisfaction, co-operation among co-workers and subordinates).
6) Positive impact (the degrees to which an HR practice promotes feelings of self-esteem, goodwill, commitment, satisfaction and co-operation among co-workers and subordinates.

Under the umbrella of strategic human resource management, three sets of HR competencies may be identified : knowledge of the business, quality of service and management of change. Knowledge of the business refers to the extent to which an

HR professional (or a line manager with HR responsibilities) understands the financial, strategic and technological capabilities of the organization. Quality of service refers to the extent to which the HR or the line manager provides high quality HR policies and services (such as training and development) to the other members of the organization. Management of change refers to the extent to which an HR professional or line manager is able to increase the organization's capability for change through creating meeting, problem-solving, relationship influence, innovation, transformation and role influence.

Measures may be established for specific behaviors in each of the three domains of HR competencies. However, these measures and behaviors have not been well established and researched as the performance indicators for HR practices.

Benchmarking HR activities: There is a proposed set of activities for benchmarking the organization's HR department:

1) **Decide the composition of the audit team:** There has to be a representative from the HR function and from among senior line managers if the exercise has to have any credibility. But it is not essential that the head of the senior HR manager lead the team.
2) **Identify the function's main customers:** The key decision is to clarify who makes the final decision to buy the services provided by the function. In a decentralized multi-divisional organization, this is likely to be the general managers of the strategic business units.
3) **Review the HR function's mission statement:** This statement describes the reason for the HR function's existence, it's principal activities and it's most important values.
4) **Review the function's role in formulating and implementing the organization's strategy:** This step is critical to establishing the link between HR policy and practices, on the one hand, and the organization's overall business strategy, on the other.
5) Review the HR function's role in developing relevant HR policies and practices.
6) **Review the delivery of HR policy and practices:** Questions need to be asked here in relation to the HR activities currently being undertaken by HR or personnel staff which could perhaps be done as well or even better by line managers, by computers or by external agencies and consultants. An alternative option is to establish an "internal consultancy or business unit" in which the HR function sells its services both inside and outside the organization. The advantage of this approach is that line managers can go elsewhere if they are not happy with the service they receive from the HR function within the organization.
7) **Make internal comparisons to establish 'best' practice:** The organization need to build and constantly update a unique database of HR practices that gives an overview of developments within the world's largest organizations today.
8) **Review the outcome of analysis:** Performance gaps need to be identified and the policy implications need to be discussed with the customer. The commitment for implementing the necessary improvements should be gained. This implies that those ultimately responsible for implementing the changes,
    a) Acknowledge the need for improving HR policies and practices.

b) Understand the difference between the current HR practice and what is desired.

c) Accept and retain full ownership of the practical steps towards implementation.

9) **Implement the agreed improvements and measure the progress against pre-set targets:** The metrics selected should be the agreed upon true indicators of the HR function's performance and compare the results with industry averages, competitors, 'best' practice firms, and/or with set targets or previous performance ratings. It is usually feasible to produce relevant ratios of the HR performance data. The most likely ratios should cover unit costs and appropriate customer satisfaction measures. If measures are not clear or difficult to obtain, two alternatives are possible. One, the process of determining appropriate HR performance measures becomes a key step in the benchmarking process itself. Or, there are approximate measures available from other functional areas that give an indication on the HR function is performing.

Traditional to Present Focus by Organizations

Traditionally, there has been a focus on remuneration and conditions, staffing practices and human resource planning as the essential components of people management—there has been a tendency to concentrate on the people management system. More recently, the importance of the skills and knowledge of both managers and their staff has been recognized—there has been a move to human resource development. The current trend is to recognize the importance of culture in supporting the people management system and the skills and knowledge of people. This is reflected in the move towards performance management and teamwork as a basis of achieving performance. Managers and their people need to understand the system. They and their people need the skills and knowledge to undertake their responsibilities and a culture is needed to support them. The culture needs to be one that recognizes the value of peoples' performance.

The successful integration of the human resource functions and the effective and efficient performance of those functions are critical to the future success of human resource management within organizations. Only if the functions are performed to a 'Best Practice' level will the productivity gains that are planned be achieved. Ensuring that the total system and each of the individual components are effectively and efficiently performed means that comparisons need to be made to determine the gap between 'Best Practice' and the current level of performance. The vehicle to do this is Human Resource Benchmarking.

ROLE OF HR BENCHMARKING

The role of HR benchmarking in managing the HR function. The question, which is most interesting about the HR function, is the basis on which it determines what it does and does not do. To what extent do we, as a function, systematically assess those initiatives, which will impact most on organizational performance? Or do we become involved in operational issues, which have little lasting value added impact on the success of the organization. The methodology by which we determine what we do and don't do in managing the HR function is called HR strategy. An example is when we become involved in detailed selection activities, but don't have time to understand in detail our level of labor turnover (how it varies by occupational group, organizational unit and tenure, etc.). Consequently, we do not analyze the reasons for labor turnover (poor selection techniques, poor induction, mismatched expectations, lack of career options, quality of management support, etc.) to develop HR initiatives to address the problem. We are so busy on the treadmill of selection that we don't have time to understand what necessitated the selection exercise. We are so busy with urgent work that we don't have time to deal with important issues, which will impact on subsequent activities.

To support the articulation of strategic HR priorities for an organization it is important to determine performance indicators to measure the impact of our HR strategy. The HR strategy is likely to include both people management priorities for the organization (eg. developing a customer responsive culture) as well as generic priorities for the HR function. It is important for the HR strategy to have this dual focus on people and HR function priorities as well as ensuring that the HR/people management priorities are aligned to, and driven by, the business priorities of the organization. This process is becoming more interactive because increasingly, people issues are fundamental inputs into developing the business plan of an organization.

The formulation of HR/People related performance indicators becomes a focus for ensuring the organization is driven by the HR strategy. Without a focus on five to ten key performance indicators we are more likely to regard the HR strategic plan as a general guide to our daily activities, rather than something, which should drive our performance. The existence of HR/people performance indicator categories is only the first step in ensuring that we have a "driven" culture within the HR function. The first requirement is to assess our existing performance in each of the key HR/people performance indicators. This information will typically come from our HRIS with some information likely to come from our finance and production systems. These key performance indicators may consist of both specific © www.hrfolks.com All Rights Reserved indicators—such as the ratio of transfers to promotions, and ratio of internal to external recruits—and broader measures, such as labor turnover rates, absence rates or revenue per employee.

Once an organization knows its performance on the selected performance indicators, it is then essential to set a target performance as part of the HR strategic planning process. It is my belief that it is illogical for an organization to set targets for its strategic HR/people If an organization, say in the Finance Industry, has identified that combining cost reduction with a stronger customer focus culture is core to its business strategy, then it may identify that its absence rate is a key performance indicator. If the organization then determines that its absence rate over the past twelve months for the total organization has been 4.0%, the next stage is to set a target performance for the organization. It is impossible to set a target performance on the strategic Key Performance Indicators without reference to some benchmark norms. The historical performance of the organization is useful, but not sufficient as a basis to establish a target. The benchmarking program is able to provide competitive yet realistic targets for our strategic HR key performance indicators. We may also want to compare the results of other industries to assess the possibility of setting more challenging (but achievable) targets. We may set the Manufacturing 10th percentile of 1.3% as a long-term target (which we can update on a continual basis to ensure a competitive target is maintained). When investigating the desired benchmark standards, we may need to look at international benchmarking standards for our industry. This is particularly critical in international industries if we assess that our performance of 4% absence is a long way from our targeted performance, and then we may wish to investigate best practice initiatives to assist in reaching the desired target. In this case, the best practice investigation will include talking to organizations, which record optimum performance levels within the benchmark area. A key point is that the best practice investigation must be in an area where we have established a KPI to support our HR strategic plan. The best practice investigation may be within our own industry, or preferably, include other industry sectors.

We are not involved in best practice investigations in areas not strategic to us, nor are we investigating best practice unless there is a significant performance gap between our results and the benchmark target. By restricting our investigation to these two criteria, we minimize the prospect of engaging in industrial tourism under the guise of best practice. It is my belief that organizations must know their performance on the HR/people KPIs, which have been identified as supporting their HR strategy. Then they must set targets for these KPIs. Benchmarking plays a critical role in providing achievable but demanding targets for these HR/people key performance indicators.

In addition to setting targets for the key HR/people indicators, HR benchmarking can also play an important role in allowing organizations to monitor their performance on a wider range of benchmark measures. Organizations should continue to monitor their performance on a wide range of organizational and HR indicators. If their performance is outside the desired range, the organization should then assess how critical this is and whether this should be the catalyst to initiate any action, or if it is appropriate/acceptable to have performance out of range with best practice. Whichever decision is made, it is a more informed decision than that which would be make with no HR benchmark reference.

The most common form of HR benchmarking is only restricted to salary surveys principally because of two essential reasons:

1) The difficulty of finding standard and acceptable performance indicators
2) The reluctance of companies to divulge sensitive information about their employees' retention, employees' costs and so on
3) The fundamental belief that a personnel is a mysterious and complex art. As a result, only those who perform it can judge the full value of the work
4) Measuring the effectiveness of Human Resource Management is inappropriate as HRM is devoted to stimulating and supporting human happiness and development

Definition and Principles of Kaizen

Kaizen, Japanese for "improvement", or "change for the better" refers to philosophy or practices that focus upon continuous improvement of processes in manufacturing, engineering, and business management. It has been applied in healthcare, psychotherapy, life-coaching, government, banking, and other industries. When used in the business sense and applied to the workplace, Kaizen refers to activities that continually improve all functions, and involves all employees from the CEO to the assembly line workers. It also applies to processes, such as purchasing and logistics, that cross organizational boundaries into the supply chain]. By improving standardized activities and processes, Kaizen aims to eliminate waste Kaizen was first implemented in several Japanese businesses after the Second World War, influenced in part by American business and quality management teachers who visited the country. It has since spread throughout the world and is now being implemented in many other venues besides just business and productivity.

The Japanese word "kaizen" simply means "improvement," with no inherent meaning of either "continuous" or "philosophy" in Japanese dictionaries or in everyday use. The word refers to any improvement, one-time or continuous, large or small, in the same sense as the mundane English word "improvement". However, given the common practice in Japan of labeling industrial or business improvement techniques with the word "kaizen" (for lack of a specific Japanese word meaning "continuous improvement" or "philosophy of improvement"), especially in the case of oft-emulated practices spearheaded by Toyota, the word Kaizen in English is typically applied to measures for implementing continuous improvement, or even taken to mean a "Japanese philosophy" thereof. The discussion below focuses on such interpretations of the word, as frequently used in the context of modern management discussions.

Kaizen is a daily process, the purpose of which goes beyond simple productivity improvement. It is also a process that, when done correctly, humanizes the workplace, eliminates overly hard work ("*muri*"), and teaches people how to perform experiments on their work using the scientific method and how to learn to spot and eliminate waste in business processes. In all, the process suggests a humanized approach to workers and to increasing productivity: "The idea is to nurture the company's human resources as much as it is to praise and encourage participation in kaizen activities." Successful implementation requires "the participation of workers in the improvement." People at all levels of an organization participate in kaizen, from the CEO down to janitorial staff, as well as external stakeholders when applicable. The format for kaizen can be individual, suggestion system, small group, or large group. At Toyota, it is usually a local improvement within a workstation or local area and involves a small group in improving their own work environment and productivity. This group is often guided through the kaizen process by a line supervisor; sometimes this is the line supervisor's key role. Kaizen on a broad, cross-departmental scale in companies, generates total quality management, and frees human efforts through improving productivity using machines and computing power.

While kaizen (at Toyota) usually delivers small improvements, the culture of continual aligned small improvements and standardization yields large results in the form of compound productivity improvement. This philosophy differs from the "command and control" improvement programs of the mid-twentieth century. Kaizen methodology includes making changes and monitoring results, then adjusting. Large-scale pre-planning and extensive project scheduling are replaced by smaller experiments, which can be rapidly adapted as new improvements are suggested.

In modern usage, it is designed to address a particular issue over the course of a week and is referred to as a "kaizen blitz" or "kaizen event". These are limited in scope, and issues that arise from them are typically used in later blitzes.

History

After World War II, to help restore Japan, American occupation forces brought in American experts to help with the rebuilding of Japanese industry while The Civil Communications Section (CCS) developed a Management Training Program that taught statistical control methods as part of the overall material. This course was developed and taught by Homer Sarasohn and Charles Protzman in 1949-50. Sarasohn recommended W. Edwards Deming for further training in Statistical Methods.

The Economic and Scientific Section (ESS) group was also tasked with improving Japanese management skills and Edgar McVoy was instrumental in bringing Lowell Mellen to Japan to properly install the Training Within Industry (TWI) programs in 1951.

Prior to the arrival of Mellen in 1951, the ESS group had a training film to introduce the three TWI "J" programs (Job Instruction, Job Methods and Job Relations)—the film was titled "Improvement in four Steps" (Kaizen eno Yon Dankai). Thus the original introduction of "Kaizen" to Japan. For the pioneering, introduction, and implementation of Kaizen in Japan, the Emperor of Japan awarded the 2nd Order Medal of the Sacred Treasure to Dr. Deming in 1960. Consequently, the Union of Japanese Science and Engineering (JUSE) instituted the annual Deming Prizes for achievement in quality and dependability of products.

On October 18, 1989, JUSE awarded the Deming Prize to Florida Power & Light Co. (FPL), based in the US, for its exceptional accomplishments in process and quality control management. FPL was the first company outside Japan to win the Deming Prize.

Implementation

The Toyota Production System is known for kaizen, where all line personnel are expected to stop their moving production line in case of any abnormality and, along with their supervisor, suggest an improvement to resolve the abnormality which may initiate a kaizen.

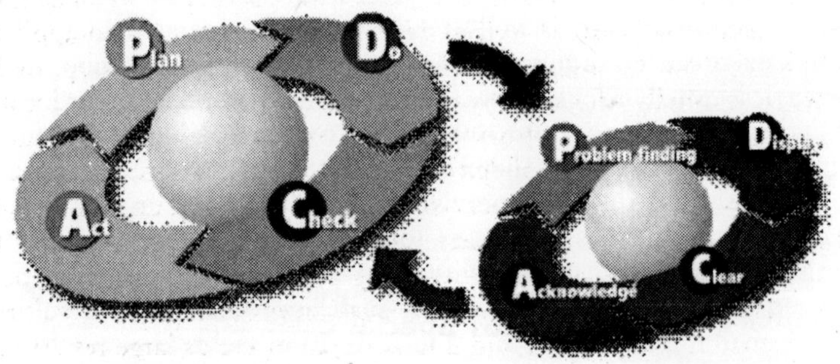

The PDCA Cycles

The cycle of kaizen activity can be defined as:

- Standardize an operation and activities.
- Measure the operation (find cycle time and amount of in-process inventory)
- Gauge measurements against requirements
- Innovate to meet requirements and increase productivity
- Standardize the new, improved operations
- Continue cycle *ad infinitum*

This is also known as the Shewhart cycle, Deming cycle, or PDCA. Other techniques used in conjunction with PDCA include five Whys, which is a form of root cause analysis in which the user asks "why" to a problem and finds an answer five successive times. There are normally a series of root causes stemming from one problem, and they can be visualized using fishbone diagrams or tables.

Masaaki Imai made the term famous in his book *Kaizen: The Key to Japan's Competitive Success*: Apart from business applications of the method, both Anthony Robbins and Robert Maurer have popularized the kaizen principles into personal development principles. In the book *One Small Step Can Change Your life: The Kaizen*

Way, and CD set *The Kaizen Way to Success,* Maurer looks at how individuals can take a kaizen approach in both their personal and professional lives. In the *Toyota Way Fieldbook*, Liker and Meier discuss the kaizen blitz and kaizen burst (or kaizen event) approaches to continuous improvement. A kaizen blitz, or rapid improvement, is a focused activity on a particular process or activity. The basic concept is to identify and quickly remove waste. Another approach is that of the kaizen burst, a specific kaizen activity on a particular process in the value stream

ELEMENTS AND PROCESS OF KAIZEN

- Management teamwork
- Increased labor responsibilities
- Increased management morale
- Quality circles
- Management suggestions for labor improvement

Kaizen is an improvement process that has evolved substantially over the years. As a result, the term Kaizen has developed to have multiple meanings. There are three types of Kaizen:

Teaian Kaizen—Individual Versus Teamed

While almost all Kaizen approaches use a teamed approach, there is the method described as Teian Kaizen or personal. This is the more traditional suggestion system: Teian Kaizen refers to individual employees uncovering improvement opportunities in the course of their day-to-day activities and making suggestions.

It does not include making the change itself, but simply the suggestion for the change. This is the only part of the Kaizen culture to focus on the individual instead of a team. Even so, it does not advocate personal action to improve a process, but suggestions by individuals which will then be assessed by a team.

Quality Circles—Day-to-Day Versus Special Event

An example of a day-to-day Kaizen approach is Quality Circles. Here, a natural work team (people working together in the same area, operating the same work process) uses its observations about the work process to identify opportunities for improvement. During any day or perhaps at the end of the week, the team meets and selects a problem from an earlier shift to correct. They analyze its sources, generate ideas for how to eliminate it, and make the improvement. This continuous improvement of the work process is made in the context of regular worker meetings.

Special events: Kaizen Blitz technique—Large-Scale *v.* Small-Scale Improvement.

Although Kaizen is a Japanese concept, many U.S. firms have adopted it with considerable success by combining the best of traditional Japanese practices with the strengths of Western business practice.

Traditional Kaizen is, by definition, long-term, a gradual incremental change results in small improvements throughout the organisation. A Kaizen Blitz or Kaizen Event (or as it should be called, Kaikaku) is fast and furious: it rapidly implement workcells, improves setups or streamlines processes. These methods plan ahead and then execute a process improvement over a period of days.

The rules:

- Develop a vision of the future. Having defined what is happening now a future state map is created which defines what should be happening if the world was perfect. Realistic but challenging elements are drawn out from this to create a vision for what life will be like by the end of the week. This could be done during or prior to the event.

- Involve everyone. For a blitz to work everyone has to be involved. This may mean shutting down a line or a department for the duration of the event. Planning the event and telling the rest of the organisation is therefore critical. If this proves to be impossible, as many people as possible should be released.
- Prepare the group. It is essential that everyone involved is trained in how to perform a blitz. There will be times during the event when people's paradigms will be seriously tested and, without proper preparation, people will find these times very stressful.
- Plan for success. Choosing the right target for a blitz is also critical. The event must be built for success particularly if it's the first one. Choose something that will have a big impact on the people as well as the organisation. The blitz is not a project tool so selecting something that can be addressed in a week is a challenge. Too big and it will fail, too small and it won't have the impact.
- Keep the kaizen training to what is actually needed for the event. It makes absolutely zero sense to go into the details of a SMED system (Single Minute Exchange of Dies) if your event has no change-overs as an obstacle to improvement.
- Provide the kaizen training at the right time. Many kaizen event training programs spend valuable training time the first day teaching how to complete a report out on Friday. By the time Friday rolls around, they end up teaching this portion of the training all over again because everybody has forgotten the lesson during the week. Mention the report out on Monday morning, leaving the details for Friday morning prior to the report out. When Friday arrives, bring the team together for the quick "How-to-do-a-report-out" session and then the team goes to work without many questions.
- Properly scale the scope of the kaizen event. How many kaizen events bring an elephant to the table for a small team of five people to try to eat in one week? Keep the scope in line with the resources at hand.
- Keep your kaizen goals simple. Many times a kaizen event will put a long list of targets or goals on the team to accomplish, productivity, cycle time, 5-S, floor space, quality, etc. All these goals are noble and beneficial however they may leave a team running in too many directions. Pick one goal to focus your kaizen team.
- Pick the right lean tool for the job and use it well. There are plenty of lean tools to choose for kaizen activities so you must determine the right tool and use it well.
- Buy-in, Buy-in, Buy-in. Without buy-in of the operators in a new process, the improvements of the week will not last past the Friday report-out. It is critical to get the process owners to buy-in to the new process.
- Go to gemba and stay there the entire week. With the exception of your Monday morning training and eating lunch, your kaizen team must remain in the kaizen area the entire week. Its important to have a meeting table, a few chairs and a flip chart placed in your kaizen area sharing information with the area (along with all those that passed by) throughout the kaizen process. Not only did this remove the muda of walking back

and forth to an offsite meeting room, it also limited the team debates on the actual process. Share information on display with your kaizen newspaper for all to see. No secrets, nothing to hide. Even the daily team leader meeting and the final report out were conducted at gemba.
- Speak with data. Hearsay or opinion have no place in a blitz. Decisions to make changes are made based on real hard data gained from the current state.

To support the higher standards Kaizen also involves providing the training, materials and supervision that is needed for employees to achieve the higher standards and maintain their ability to meet those standards on an on-going basis. The cycle of kaizen activity can be defined as:

- Standardize an operation and activities.
- Measure the standardized operation (find cycle time and amount of in-process inventory).
- Gauge measurements against requirements.
- Innovate to meet requirements and increase productivity.
- Standardize the new, improved operations.
- Continue the cycle continuously. Key elements of kaizen are quality, effort, involvement of all employees, willingness to change, and communication.

Kaizen can be applied to the office environment as well as a manufacturing environment. In fact, Kaizen has been applied to the following areas:

- Human Resources
- Sales
- Purchasing
- Materials management
- Product design engineering
- Marketing
- Contracts
- Accounts payable/receivable
- Records/document administration
- Government affairs
- Customer service
- Engineering support
- Research
- Software engineering
- Loan processing
- Order entry
- Quality
- Sales support
- Legal
- Regulatory compliance

KAIZEN PROCESS

Kaizen events are among the most important activities of a Lean enterprise. Successful Kaizens help build a Lean culture and measurably improve company performance. Kaizen success requires effective Planning, Implementation, Follow-up and Evaluation. IMEC's expert Lean implementers will work with your company at each phase of the Kaizen process, helping plan and prepare for events, facilitating Kaizen events, working with your team to ensure effective follow-up and completion of the improvement process, and evaluating the results to continuously improve your Kaizen process.

Plan

The Kaizen Planning phase, within the six Sigma DMAIC framework, seeks to Define, Measure, and Analyze the process that will be the Kaizen focus. There are three levels of Kaizen planning:

- High-Level Planning links the Enterprise Lean Deployment Strategy to the specific processes that need to be improved and the timeline for improvement.
- Mid-Level Planning uses Value Stream Mapping to select specific areas of improvement that will be addressed through Kaizen events *versus* six sigma projects and "just-do-it" activities.
- Event-Level Planning uses checklists and standard documents to ensure that everything is in place so each Kaizen event is conducted successfully. Event planning includes:
  - Kaizen team member selection
  - Kaizen charter approval
  - Location preparation (including equipment, materials, etc.)
  - Data needs identification and preparation

Implement

Kaizen event implementation, within the DMAIC framework, is primarily focused on actual Improvement, although some additional Measurement and Analysis may be required. Kaizen Implementation requires a company to:

- Train members of the Kaizen team on the Lean principles that they will be applying
- Review the VSM and perform additional measurements and analyses, if needed
- Facilitate an ideation/brainstorming process to identify improvement options
- Implement improvements by "breaking apart" the process and putting it back together without the waste
- Prepare an action plan with a list of activities required to complete the Kaizen process
- Verify the alignment of the selected improvements with the future state VSM
- Identify expected measurable improvements
- Obtain participant feedback
- Report Kaizen event results to champions and celebrate success

Follow-up

This phase of the Kaizen process involves the completion of the Improvement and Control DMAIC elements. The success of the Kaizen depends on timely completion of the Improvement process and effective change management. This process involves.

- OVER -
- Following-up to ensure that action items are successfully completed
- Working with the Lean champion to break down obstacles
- Measuring the actual results of the Kaizen to document and quantify benefits
- Establishing process control to ensure the ability to consistently obtained improved performance

Evaluate

This is the last phase of the Kaizen process cycle. A Lean enterprise is a learning organization that recognizes Kaizen as a continuous process of improvement through:

- Identifying improvements to the Kaizen implementation process.
- Encouraging employees to identify further improvement opportunities.
- Establishing a schedule to re-evaluate the VSM and start a new Kaizen improvement cycle.

Kaizen *vs.* Innovation

A table from a 1986 Japanese textbook on Kaizen is interesting. This table shows that how Japanese Kaizen different from innovation.

		Kaizen = Continuous Improvement	*Innovation*
1.	Effect	Long term and long lasting but undramatic	Short-term but dramatic
2.	Pace	Small steps	Big Steps
3.	Timeframe	Continuous and incremental	Intermittent and non-incremental
4.	Change	Gradual and constant	Abrupt and volatile
5.	Involvement	Everybody	Select few "champions"
6.	Approach	Collectivism, group efforts, systems approach	Rugged individualism, individual ideas and efforts
7.	Mode	Maintenance and improvement	Scrap and rebuild
8.	Spark	Conventional know-how and state of the art	Technological breakthrough, new inventions, new theories
9.	Practical requirements	Requires little investment but great effort to maintain it	Requires large investment but little effort to maintain it
10.	Effort orientation	People	Technology
11.	Evaluation criteria	Process and efforts for better results	Results for profit
12.	Advantage	Works well in slow growth economies	Better suited to fast growth economy

Note : Point # 12 and ensure that the differences between the two approaches to improvement are clearly understood.

Performance Appraisal and Total Quality Management

Total Quality Management (TQM) emphasizes the continuous improvement of product and processes to ensure long-term customer satisfaction. Its a problem-solving focus encourages employees empowerment by using the job-related ingenuity and expertise of the workforce. Cross-functional teams develop solutions to complex problems often shortening the time taken to design, develop or produce product and services. Since a team may not include a representative of management, therefore the dividing line between labor and management often becomes blurred. In practice as workers themselves begin to solve organizational problems thus adaptation of TQM generally requires cultural change within the organization as management reexamines its past methods and practices in the light of demands of the new philosophy.

Father of TQM W. Edwards Deming had his way, appraisal system that tie individual performance to salary adjustments would be eliminated. In his view, such system hinders team work, create fear and mistrust and discourage risk taking behavior, thereby stifling innovation. Deming argues, most appraisal system are based on the faulty assumption that individuals have significant control over their own performance, i.e. the most individuals can improve if they chose to do so by putting forth the necessary effort.

In the basis of his arguments everything done in an organization is done within the frame work of one or more systems. The systems provide limit on the activities of machines, processes, employees and even managers. In a well designed system, it is impossible to do a job improperly. Conversely, a poor system can thwart the best effort of the best employee. If the system itself prevents good work, performance appraisal cannot serve its intended purpose of differentiating among individuals for purposes of salary adjustment. Further, since employees have little opportunity to change those systems, they may become frustrated and demoralized.

Organization need not sacrifice their performance appraisal programs on the altar of TQM. Here are three suggestions for harmonizing the two processes.

1. Let customer expectations generate individual or team performance expectations.
2. Include result expectations that identify actions to meet or exceed those expectations.
3. Include behavioral skills that make a real difference in achieving quality performance and total customer satisfaction.

When performance expectations focus on process improvement as well as on the behavioral skills needed to provide a product or service, total quality, excellent customer service, and appraisal of individual or team performance become 'the way we do business'.

People Capability Maturity Model (PCMM)

People Capability Maturity Model (PCMM, People CMM, P-CMM) is a maturity framework that describes the key elements of managing and developing the workforce of an organization. It describes an evolutionary improvement path from an ad hoc approach to managing the work-force, to a mature, disciplined development of the knowledge, skills, and motivation of the people that fuels enhanced business performance.

People CMM is a framework that helps organizations successfully address their critical people issues. Based on the best current practices in fields such as human resources, knowledge management, and organizational development, the People CMM guides organizations in improving their processes for managing and developing their workforces. The People CMM can also be used by any kind of organization as a guide for improving their people-related and work-force practices.

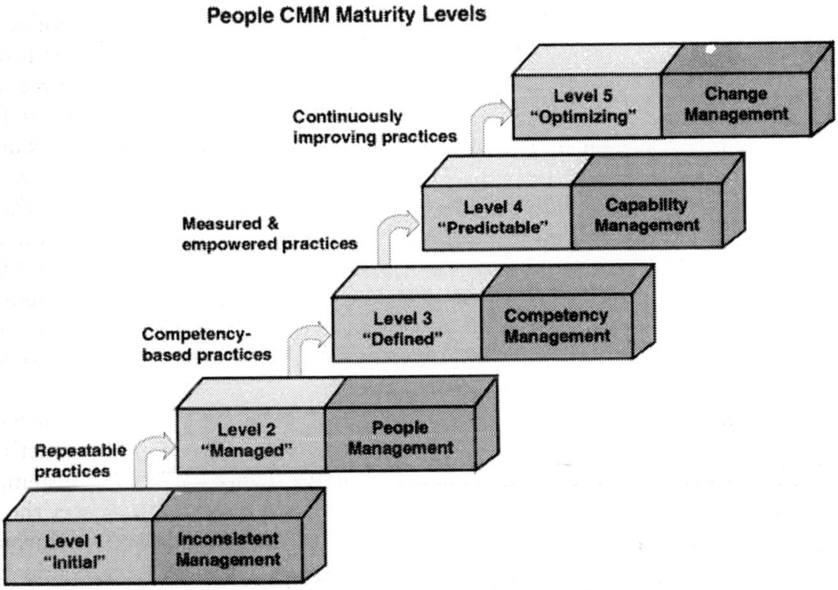

People CMM Maturity Levels

Continuously improving practices
Level 5 "Optimizing" | Change Management
Measured & empowered practices
Level 4 "Predictable" | Capability Management
Competency-based practices
Level 3 "Defined" | Competency Management
Repeatable practices
Level 2 "Managed" | People Management
Level 1 "Initial" | Inconsistent Management

Current Version of the PCMM is Version 2, was released in 2001.

Benefits of Implementing PCMM

Characterize the maturity of their human resource practices
Set priorities for improving the competence of its work-force
Integrate competence growth with process improvement
Establish a culture of workforce excellence
People CMM Maturity Levels

The People Capability Maturity Model adapts the maturity framework of the Capability Maturity Model for Software, to managing and developing an organization's work force.

PCMM has five maturity levels and each maturity level provides a layer in the foundation for continuous improvement and equips the organization with increasingly powerful tools for developing the capability of its workforce.

PCMM Process Area

The maturity level of the PCMM Version 2 is consisting the "22 Process Area". The below depiction shows the name of all the 22 processes areas along with level.

Maturity Level	*Focus*	*Process Areas*
5 Optimizing	Continuously improve and align personal work group and organizational capability	Continuously Workforce Innovation Organizational Performance Alignment Continuous Capability Improvement
4 Predictable	Empower and integrate workforce competencies and manage performance quantitatively	Mentoring Organizational Capability Management Quantitative Performance Management

		Competency-based Assets Empowered Workgroups Competency Integration
3 Defined	Develop workforce competencies and workgroups, and align with business strategy and objectives	Participatory Culture Workgroup Development Competency-Based Practices Career Development Competency Development Workforce Planning Competency Analysis
2 Managed	Managers take responsibility for managing and developing their people	Compensation Training and Development Performance Management Work Environment Communication Coordination Staffing
1 Initial		

The People CMM stages the implementation of increasingly sophisticated workforce practices through these maturity levels. With the exception of the Initial Level, each maturity level is characterized by a set of interrelated practices in critical areas of workforce management.

When institutionalized and performed with appropriate regularity, these workforce practices create new capabilities within the organization for managing and developing its workforce.

Maturity Level I (The Initial Level)

Organizations at the Initial Level of maturity usually have difficulty retaining talented individuals. Even though many low maturity organizations complain about a talent shortage, the inconsistency of their actions belies whether they actually believe it Low maturity organizations are poorly equipped to respond to talent shortages with anything other than slogans and exhortations. Despite the importance of talent, workforce practices in low maturity organizations are often *ad hoc* and inconsistent. In some areas, the organization has not defined workforce practices, and, in other areas, it has not trained responsible individuals to perform the practices that exist.

Organizations at the Initial Level typically exhibit four characteristics:

1. Inconsistency in performing practices,
2. Displacement of responsibility,
3. Ritualistic practices, and
4. An emotionally detached workforce.

Maturity Level 2 (The Managed Level)

The workforce practices implemented at the Managed Level focus on activities at the unit level. The first step toward improving the capability of the workforce is to get managers to take workforce activities as high priority responsibilities of their job. They must accept personal responsibility for the performance and development of those who perform the unit's work. The practices implemented at Maturity Level 2 focus a manager's attention on unit-level issues such as staffing, coordinating commitments, providing resources, managing performance, developing skills, and making compensation decisions. Building a solid foundation of workforce practices within each unit provides the bedrock on which more sophisticated workforce practices can be implemented at higher levels of maturity.

Maturity Level 3 (The Defined Level)

Organizations at the Repeatable Level find that, although they are performing basic workforce practices, there is inconsistency in how these practices are performed across units and little synergy across the organization. The organization misses opportunities to standardize workforce practices because the common knowledge and skills needed for conducting its business activities have not been identified. At Maturity Level 2, units are identifying critical skills to determine qualifications for open positions, evaluate training needs, and provide performance feedback.

However, there is no requirement at Maturity Level 2 for identifying common attributes among these skills across units or for determining the practices that are most effective in developing them. Once a foundation of basic workforce practices has been established in the units, the next step is for the organization to develop an organization-wide infrastructure atop these practices that ties the capability of the workforce to strategic business objectives. The primary objective of the Defined Level is to help an organization gain a competitive advantage from developing the various competencies that must be combined in its workforce to accomplish its business activities. These workforce competencies represent critical pillars supporting the strategic business plan, since their absence poses a severe risk to strategic business objectives. In tying workforce competencies to current and future business objectives, the improved workforce practices implemented at Maturity Level 3 become critical enablers of business strategy.

Maturity Level 4 (The Predictable Level)

An organization at the Defined Level has established an organizational framework for developing its workforce. At the Predictable Level, the organization manages and exploits the capability created by its framework of workforce competencies. The organization is now able to manage its capability and performance quantitatively. The organization is able to predict its capability for performing work because it can quantify the capability of its workforce and of the competency-based processes they use in performing their assignments.

Maturity Level 5 (The Optimizing Level)

At the Optimizing Level, the entire organization is focused on continual improvement. These improvements are made to the capability of individuals and workgroups, to the performance of competency-based processes, and to workforce practices and activities. The organization uses the results of the quantitative management activities established at Maturity Level 4 to guide improvements at Maturity Level 5. Maturity Level 5 organizations treat change management as an ordinary business process to be performed in an orderly way on a regular basis.

The People Capability Maturity Model is a tool that helps you successfully address the critical people issues in your organization. The People CMM employs the process maturity framework of the highly successful Capability Maturity Model for Software (SW-CMM) as a foundation for a model of best practices for managing and developing an organization's workforce. The Software CMM has been used by software organizations around the world for guiding dramatic improvements in their ability to improve productivity and quality, reduce costs and time to market, and increase customer satisfaction. Based on the best current practices in fields such as human resources, knowledge management, and organizational development, the

People CMM guides organizations in improving their processes for managing and developing their workforce. The People CMM helps organizations characterize the maturity of their workforce practices, establish a program of continuous workforce development, set priorities for improvement actions, integrate workforce development with process improvement, and establish a culture of excellence. Since its release in 1995, thousands of copies of the People CMM have been distributed, and it is used world-wide by organizations, small and large, such as IBM, Boeing, BAESystems, Tata Consultancy Services, Ericsson, Lockheed Martin and QAI (India) Ltd.

Why is People Capability Maturity Model Necessary?

The Carnegie Mellon University Software Engineering Institute developed the People Capability Maturity Model (P-CMM) to help businesses manage knowledge workers across global borders, as well as between graying and millennial generations. Similar to CMMI, P-CMM has five maturity levels, but the model is focused on the need to improve the capabilities of a workforce as a differentiating factor from the competition.

In a highly competitive global business, recruiting talents with technical skills is not enough anymore. On top of their technical competencies, workers must have the necessary business skills, particularly in making decisions that are not only technically sound, but also consistent with the visions of their organizations. Moreover, as organizations' internal processes mature, so should workers' decision-making and implementation proficiency. In fact, P-CMM was developed to develop workers' competencies according to the needs of process maturity levels.

Many organizations' practices have matured over time particularly in the area of software engineering. However, practitioners observed that workers must appreciate their roles and responsibilities in the larger organization. This is where P-CMM comes in. Human resources and workforce managers used to hire workers on the strength of technical knowledge alone; but in order to harness the technical knowledge of workers into tangible products (for example: a piece of software), managers have realized that staff development within the company must be compatible with internal process improvements.

In a nutshell, it means helping workers help top managers steer project processes according to current and target capability levels and project directions, as well as providing a framework for optimizing employee competencies for greater measurable value. For human resources and worker development practitioners, P-CMM serves as a framework for developing employees from mere knowledge workers to knowledge managers.

To do so, it is important to always revisit P-CMM's five-level capability architecture. Most organizations with little to no established internal processes, aside perhaps from those related to administrative matters, manage employee development in mostly *ad-hoc* fashion where workers are designated to positions and projects without much consideration for the impact on the long-term vision of the company.

Organizations that have achieved a certain level of maturity assign people development to immediate managers. There is still a certain degree of arbitrariness at this level, but the role that employees play in the smaller organization (for example, a project team or a department) is being reviewed and measured according to agreed-upon standards that managers expect from their subordinates. The focus is mostly on the performance of workers, not on the long-term competency development.

Things change for the better as participation is encouraged among workers. Career path and competency development gain more attention from top management, while collaborative activities are encouraged among staff members. Planning and analysis according to organizational goals are introduced in the people management process.

As people continue to gain further competencies through training and mentoring, it is expected that they become empowered to eventually make professional and organization decisions. The workforce as a whole should develop integrated or complementary competencies and be able to manage their skill sets at organizational level. They must be able to make (or suggest) decisions based on what they know and the processes established within their organizations.

When organizations have developed integrated capability sets among workers, it is then that they can continue to innovate products, services, and processes. Innovation is nearly impossible when the people who should be championing new directions in their business domains have no clear course on how they can get from the basic service delivery level to top-class product development. Moreover, poaching by competing firms and high turn-over can be prevented if employees understand the value of their place and contribution to the organization.

CASE STUDY
SIX SIGMA AT WIPRO TECHNOLOGIES : THRUST ON QUALITY

Wipro Technologies is a global services provider delivering technology-driven business solutions that meet the strategic objectives of clients. Wipro has 40+ 'Centers of Excellence' that create solutions around specific needs of industries. Wipro delivers unmatched business value to customers through a combination of process excellence, quality frameworks and service delivery innovation. Wipro is the World's first CMMi Level 5 certified software services company and the first outside USA to receive the IEEE Software Process Award. Wipro has one of the most mature Six Sigma programs in the industry ensuring that 91% of the projects are completed on schedule, much above the industry average of 55%. Six Sigma provides the tools for continuous improvement on existing processes thereby helping sustain the SEI-CMM Level 5 and CMMi certifications. This case focuses on the initiatives taken by Wipro Technologies to implement the Six Sigma Quality tool to achieve sustained strategic business results. It explores the implementation procedure at Wipro Technologies and the benefits reaped by the company on account of adopting Six Sigma.

The case also throws light on the recent developments in the Six Sigma concept including Wipro's Six Sigma Skill base and consulting experience and explains how the company intends to build its expertise and experience—to bring continuous process improvement to the organization.

Six Sigma at Wipro Technologies: Thrust on Quality

Backdrop

Wipro Limited was established in 1945 and commenced its operations in 1946 as a vegetable oil company. In the early 1980s, Wipro diversified into the Information Technology sector with Liberalization hitting India in the 1980s. This has been a fascinating transformation from a vegetable oil company into a global IT services giant. Today, Wipro Technologies has become a global service provider delivering technology-driven business solutions that meet the strategic objectives of clients. Wipro has 40+ 'Centers of Excellence' that create solutions related to specific needs of Industries. Wipro can boast of delivering unmatched business value to customers through a combination of process excellence quality frameworks and service delivery innovation. A strong emphasis upon building a professional work environment, leaders from within, and having a global outlook for business and growth have led to innovation of people processes on a continued basis. Over the years, Wipro has significantly strengthened its competency based people processes and demonstrated innovative practices in talent acquisition, deployment, and development, based on strategic needs.

A leading provider of communication networks in the US required improvement in the product performance of a telecom application using Six Sigma methodologies. Thus, with the growing importance on aligning business operations with customer needs and driving continuous improvement, Wipro began moving towards focusing on Quality, thereby, creating a learning environment that led to implementation of Six Sigma.

Prepared by Dr. Manisha Sharma, Dr. Kapil Pandla and Prof. Prashant Gupta of Jaipuria Institute of Management, Noida . This case is prepared solely for the basis of class discussion. Cases are not designed to present illustrations of either correct or incorrect handling of administrative problems

Integrating Six Sigma concepts was also intended to bring rigor in effective upstream processes of the software development life cycle. Implementation of Six Sigma methodologies brought in quantitative understanding, cost savings, and performance improvement towards product quality.

Some of the key challenges involved were:

- Reduce the data transfer time
- Reduce the risk
- Avoid interruption due to LAN/WAN downtime.
- Parallel availability of the switch for the other administrative tasks during the same period.

What is Six Sigma?

The word is a statistical term that measures how far a given process deviates from perfection. Six Sigma is named after the process that has six standard deviations on each side of the specification window. It is a disciplined, data-driven approach and methodology for eliminating defects. The central idea behind Six Sigma is that if you can measure how many "defects" you have in a process, you can systematically figure out how to eliminate them and get as close to "zero defects" as possible.

Six Sigma starts with the application of statistical methods for translating information from customers into specifications for products or services being developed or produced. Six Sigma is the business strategy and a philosophy of one working smarter not harder. One sigma gives a precision of 68.27%., two sigma, of 95.45% and three sigma of 99.73%, whereas Six Sigma gives a precision of 99.9997%. Although 99.73% sounds very good, it slowly dawned on companies that there is a tremendous difference between 99.73% and 99.9997%. For example for every million articles of mail, the difference is between 66,738 lost items and 3.4 lost items (Exhibit 1).

To achieve Six Sigma Quality, a process must produce no more that 3.4 defects per million opportunities. An opportunity is defined as a chance for non-conformance, or not meeting the required specifications. This means one needs to be nearly flawless in executing key processes. The process and culture is conditioned for zero defects rather than being one that accepts that it is inevitable, and acceptable, that mistakes will occur.

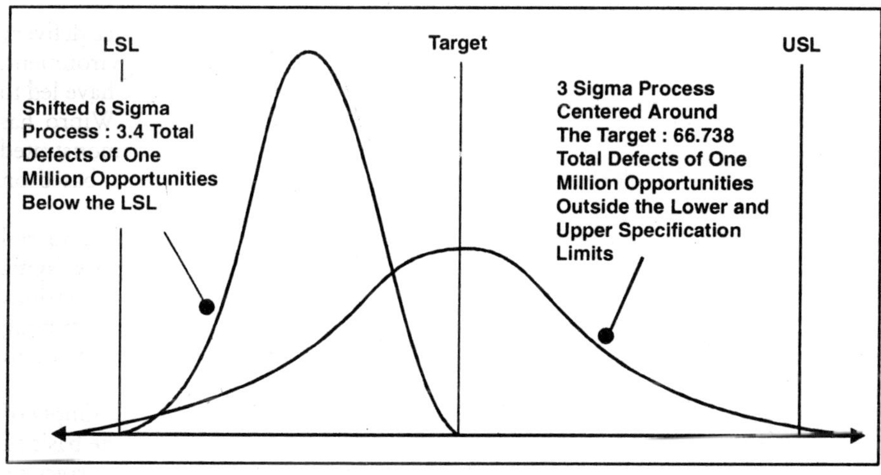

Exhibit 1

Hence Six Sigma delivers substantial cost reductions, enhanced efficiencies, sustainable improvements and increased stakeholder value.

Evolution of Six Sigma at Wipro

Wipro is the first Indian company to adopt Six Sigma. Today, Wipro has one of the most mature Six Sigma programs in the industry ensuring that 91% of the projects are completed on schedule, mush above the industry average of 55%.

As the pioneers of Six Sigma in India, Wipro has already put around ten years into process improvement through Six Sigma. Along the way, it has scaled Six Sigma ladder, while helping to roll out over 1000 projects. The Six Sigma program spreads right across verticals and impacts multiple areas such as project management, market development and resource utilization.

Six Sigma at Wipro simply means a measure of quality that strives for near perfection. It is an umbrella initiative covering all business units and divisions so that it could transform itself in a world class organization. At Wipro, it means:

(i) Have products and services meet global benchmarks
(ii) Ensure robust processes within the organization
(iii) Consistently meet and exceed customer expectations
(iv) Make Quality a culture within.

Difficulties encountered by Wipro and learning from them:

Build the Culture

Implementation of Six Sigma required support from the higher level managers. It meant restructuring of the organization to provide the infrastructure, training and the confidence in the process. Wipro had to build this culture and that took time in implementation.

Project Selection

The first year of deployment was extremely difficult for Six Sigma success. They decided to select the project on the basis of high probability of their success and targeted to complete them in a short period to assess the success. These projects were treated as pilot projects with a focus to learn. For the selection of the right project the field data was collected, process map was developed and the importance of the project was judged from the eyes of customers.

Training: After the set-up, the first step of implementation was to build a team of professionals and train them for various stages of Six sigma. The training was spread in five phases: Defining, measuring, analyzing, improving and controlling the process and lastly increasing customer satisfaction. These phases consisted of statistics, bench-marking and design of experiments. To find the right kind of people and train them was a difficult job. This motivated Wipro to start their own consultancy to train the people.

Resources

It was difficult to identify resources that required for short-term basis and long-term basis as it varied from project to project. Wipro did it on the basis of seriousness and importance of the project.

Project Reviews

As timely reviews play a very crucial role to judge the success of a project. Wipro had to develop a team of experts for this purpose. The task assigned was to see the timeliness, find out gap, week areas and to check the outcome as per the plan.

Implementation of Six Sigma at Wipro

Wipro has adopted the project approach for Six Sigma, where projects are identified on the basis of the problem areas under each of the critical Business Processes that adversely impacts the business significantly.

Wipro has evolved following Six Sigma methodologies (Exhibit 2):

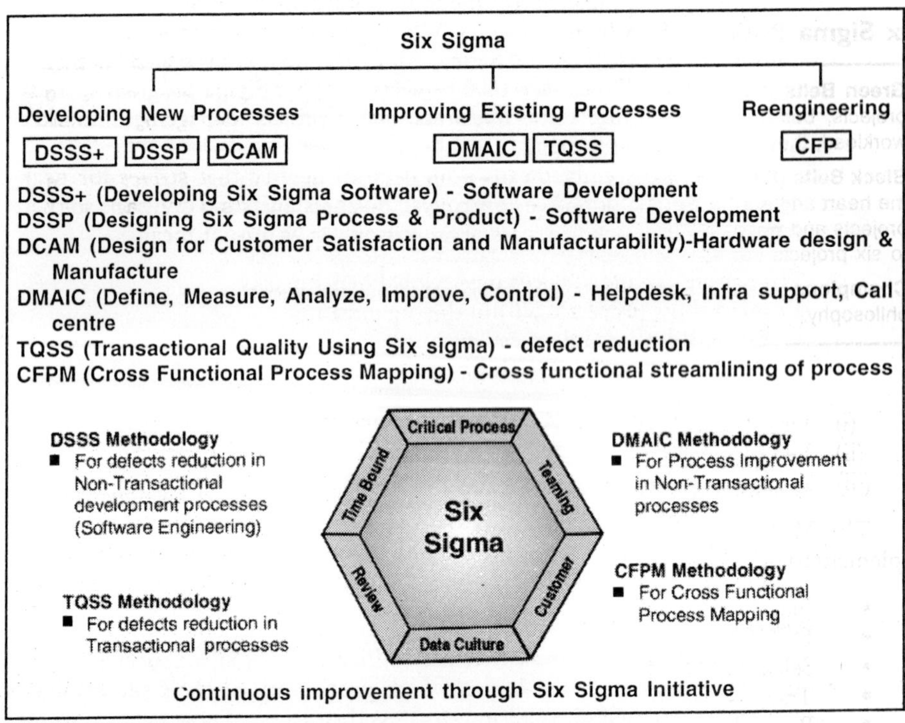

Exhibit 2 : Six Sigma Methodologies

(I) For developing new processes:
 (i) DSSS+ Methodology—Wipro employs DSSS methodology for software development. The methodology uses rigorous in-process metrics and cause analysis throughout the software development lifecycle for defect free deliveries and lower customer cost of application development.
 (ii) DSSP Methodology—used for designing new processes and products.
 (iii) DCAM Methodology—used for designing for customer satisfaction and manufacturability.

(II) For Improving Existing Processes
 (i) TQSS Methodology—used for defect reduction in Transactional processes.
 (ii) DMAIC Methodology—used for process improvement in Non-transactional process

(III) For Reengineering
 CFPM Methodology—used for cross-functional Process mapping.

The list of players at Wipro is as below:

- Executive Management
- Six Sigma Champions and Deployment Leaders
- Financial Executives
- Black Belts
- Green Belts
- Yellow Belts

Six Sigma Projects at Wipro

Green Belts (GB)—Trained in Six Sigma who spend a portion of their time completing projects, but maintain their regular work role and responsibilities. Depending on their workload, they can spend anywhere from 10% to 50% of their time on their project(s).

Black Belts (BB)—The experts in Six Sigma methodologies and its usage. Black Belts are the heart and soul of the Six Sigma quality initiative. Their main purpose is to lead quality projects and work full time until they are complete. Black Belts can typically complete four to six projects per year with savings of approximately $230,000 per year.

Champions—Facilitate the leadership, implementation and deployment of Six Sigma philosophy.

Exhibit 3

(i) Driven by business heads, also called Champions for the projects.
(ii) Led by Green Belts (GB).
(iii) Assisted by Black Belts (BB).

The Management of the project at Wipro follows the following tools for implementation of Six Sigma:

- Ideation
- Definition
- Selection
- Tracking
- Reporting

Currently 15000+ employees are trained in Six Sigma methodologies. Wipro has also built up a Six Sigma skill base of over 180 certified black belts while helping to roll out over a 1000 projects. (Exhibit 4).

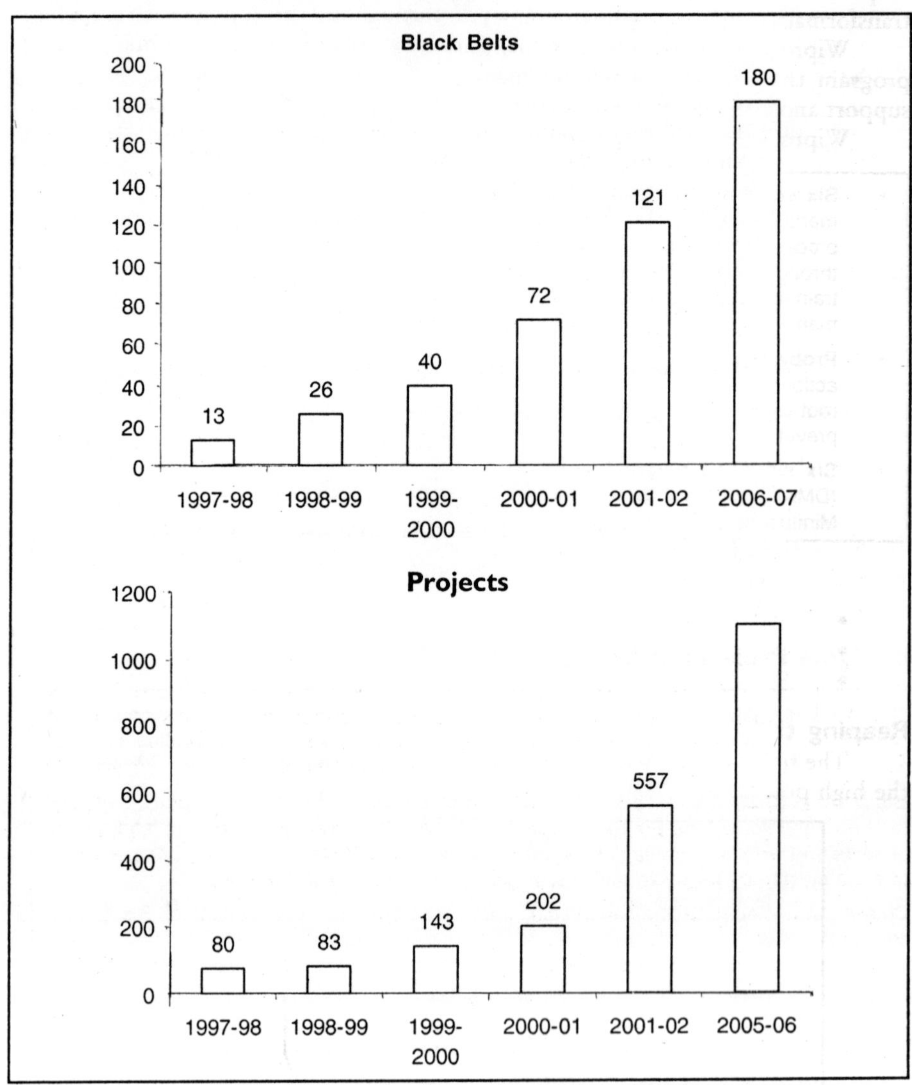

Exhibit 4 : Resources invested in Six Sigma

Six Sigma Consultancy at Wipro

Wipro's Six Sigma consulting experience has peaked with the indigenous development of new methodologies that it takes to its customers. As Wipro continues Six Sigma consulting journey, it builds on its expertise and experience- to provide enterprise-class coverage of topics in business process management and information technology systems integration. The focus is on supporting the project needs and is also integrated with other methods to support process needs. Currently there are over 200 PMI certified consultants at Wipro.

The Wipro quality consulting group trains in achieving the precision of Six Sigma with Wipro's own methodologies, training capabilities and global experience. Wipro also helps in institutionalizing Six Sigma across the organization for transformation.

Wipro provides consulting in institutionalizing an organization wide Six Sigma program that specializes in implementation across IT development, production support and core business operations

Wipro offers the following Six Sigma consulting services (Exhibit 5):

- **Six sigma institutionalization** : Here the Wipro consultants work with the senior management of the client team in identifying pain areas and critical business processes. The Wipro consultants then create a program of implementing six sigma throughout the organization; creates six sigma teams; provides the necessary training to the green belts and black belts; identifies projects to be run; helps manage change; and identifies the benefits.
- **Problem solving using six sigma** : Here Wipro's consultants work with the process action team at the client organization to identify the problem areas, determine the root causes of problems and establish necessary recommendations for corrective/ preventive actions.
- **Six sigma training** : Wipro provides training on various 6 sigma methodologies (DMAIC/DMADV/DSSS+) and statistical tools (Control charts/QFD/etc.), use of Minitab, etc.

Exhibit 5

- Six Sigma institutionalization
- Problem-solving using Six Sigma
- Six Sigma training

Reaping the Benefits

The financial gain that Wipro has achieved by using Six Sigma has been one of the high points. (Exhibit 6)

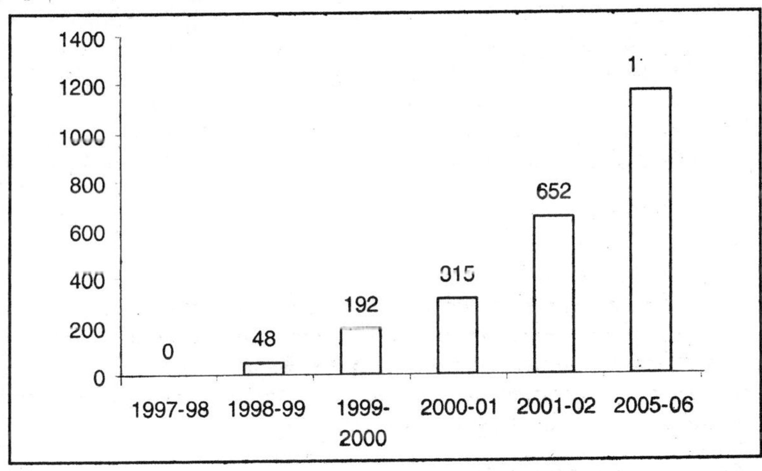

Exhibit 6 : Six Sigma and Financial Gains

Key Words : Zero defects, Nonconformance, Project Management, Resource Utilization, Quality Management.

As the Six Sigma initiative started maturing Wipro identified two major phenomenon:

- The biggest projects had all been completed, and
- The Yellow-belt culture had cured little problems before they became big ones.

At this point, the project-oriented Six Sigma culture began to give way to the sustaining culture.

The Six Sigma process resulted in an achievement of close to 250%, 6 minutes for 1 MB transfer and 18 minutes for average data transfer. The set target was 200%.

Because quality is customer driven, the objective of Six Sigma Implementation at Wipro has continuously been on integrating and implementing approaches through a simultaneous focus on defect reduction, timeliness, and productivity. This has translated to lower maintenance costs, schedule-overrun costs, and development costs for customers. Measurements and progress indicators have been oriented towards what the customer finds important and what the customer pays for. Towards this, Six Sigma concepts have played an important role in:

- Improving performance through a precise quantitative understanding of the customer's requirements thereby bringing in customer focus.
- Improving the effectiveness in upstream processes of the software development life cycle by defect reduction (software defects reduced by 50%) and cycle time reduction (rework in software down from 12% to 5%).
- Waste elimination and increased productivity up to 35%.
- Cost of failure avoidance (installation failures down from 4.5% to 1% in hardware business).
- Tangible cost savings due to lower application development cost for customer.

Analysts remarked that Six Sigma was an indisputable success at Wipro whether in terms of customer satisfaction, improvement in internal performance, or in the improvement of shareowner value.

The results of achieving Six Sigma are rapid and overwhelming at Wipro Its unique methodology provides Six Sigma knowledge and skills to the client, enabling the client to create ownership, generate results and sustain success. The maturity of Wipro's quality processes takes the benefits to another level, ensuring that the customers benefit from:

- 30-40% lower total cost of ownership.
- 20-30% higher productivity.
- On-time deliveries (93% projects completed on time).
- Lower field defect rates (67% lower than industry average). The performance enhancement enabled the client to have an improved product with the overriding benefit that the end customer perception of the quality of the client's product is improved.

Future Focus and Challenges

Six Sigma certainly produces breakthrough improvement. But to achieve this Wipro will have to combine the power of the Six Sigma method and tools with stretch goals, goals that almost seem too aggressive, too optimistic... Also Wipro will have to benchmark itself against the competition on the level of performance achieved by rivals... This focus will lead to the adaptation of newer dimensions of the quality management framework towards embodying a totality of process, people, product, and technology for achieving high process capability.

Six Sigma projects require continuous change. Black Belts and Green belts develop improvements to systems and processes for which they are not accountable. And when these participants are done with their project, they ask the real system or process owner to implement and sustain their solution and hence the challenge before Wipro lies in bringing the commitment towards continuing its process optimization theory.

The Challenge will be to transform Six Sigma from a tool for improving product quality to an overall business improvement methodology. The company's aim will be at having 100% of its management trained in Six Sigma.

To summarize, the quality system will continue to be based on incremental optimization, with rigorous implementation and sustenance of the same. The goal will be to make quality as the No. 1 objective for all employees.

Chapter 5

Business Process Re-Engineering

BASIC CONCEPTS

In 1990, Michael Hammer, a former professor of computer science at the Massachusetts Institute of Technology (MIT), published an article in the Harvard Business Review, in which he claimed that the major challenge for managers is to obliterate forms of work that do not add value, rather Zthan using technology for automating it. This statement implicitly accused managers of having focused on the wrong issues, namely that technology in general, and more specifically information technology, has been used primarily for automating existing processes rather than using it as an enabler for making non-value adding work obsolete.

Hammer's claim was simple: Most of the work being done does not add any value for customers, and this work should be removed, not accelerated through automation. Instead, companies should reconsider their processes in order to maximize customer value, while minimizing the consumption of resources required for delivering their product or service. A similar idea was advocated by Thomas H. Davenport and J. Short in 1990, at that time a member of the Ernst and Young research center, in a paper published in the Sloan Management Review

This idea, to unbiasedly review a company's business processes, was rapidly adopted by a huge number of firms, which were striving for renewed competitiveness, which they had lost due to the market entrance of foreign competitors, their inability to satisfy customer needs, and their insufficient cost structure. Even well established management thinkers, such as Peter Drucker and Tom Peters, were accepting and advocating BPR as a new tool for (re-) achieving success in a dynamic world. During the following years, a fast growing number of publications, books as well as journal articles, were dedicated to BPR, and many consulting firms embarked on this trend and developed BPR methods. However, the critics were fast to claim that BPR was a way to dehumanize the work place, increase managerial control, and to justify downsizing, i.e. major reductions of the work force, and a rebirth of Taylorism under a different label.

Despite this critique, reengineering was adopted at an accelerating pace and by 1993, as many as 60% of the Fortune 500 companies claimed to either have initiated re-engineering efforts, or to have plans to do so. This trend was fueled by the fast adoption of BPR by the consulting industry, bur also by the study made in America conducted by MIT, that showed how companies in many US industries had lagged behind their foreign counterparts in terms of competitiveness, time-to-market and productivity.

Development after 1995

With the publication of critiques in 1995 and 1996 by some of the early BPR proponents, coupled with abuses and misuses of the concept by others, the reengineering fervor in the U.S. began to wane. Since then, considering business processes as a starting point for business analysis and redesign has become a widely accepted approach and is a standard part of the change methodology portfolio, but is typically performed in a less radical way as originally proposed.

More recently, the concept of Business Process Management (BPM) has gained major attention in the corporate world and can be considered as a successor to the BPR wave of the 1990s, as it is evenly driven by a striving for process efficiency supported by information technology. Equivalently to the critique brought forward against BPR, BPM is now accused of focusing on technology and disregarding the people aspects of change.

What is the Business Process Re-engineering

The globalization of the economy and the liberalization of the trade markets have formulated new conditions in the market place which are characterized by instability and intensive competition in the business environment. Competition is continuously increasing with respect to price, quality and selection, service and promptness of delivery. Removal of barriers, international cooperation, technological innovations cause competition to intensify. All these changes impose the need for organizational transformation, where the entire processes, organization climate and organization structure are changed. Hammer and Champy provide the following definitions:

- Reengineering is the fundamental rethinking and radical redesign of business processes to achieve dramatic improvements in critical contemporary measures of performance such as cost, quality, service and speed.
- Process is a structured, measured set of activities designed to produce a specified output for a particular customer or market. It implies a strong emphasis on how work is done within an organization. (Davenport 1993).

Each process is composed of related steps or activities that use people, information, and other resources to create value for customers as it is illustrated in the following example.

Business processes are characterized by three elements: the inputs, (data such customer inquiries or materials), the processing of the data or materials (which usually go through several stages and may necessary stops that turns out to be time and money consuming), and the outcome (the delivery of the expected result). The problematic part of the process is processing. Business process re-engineering mainly intervenes in the processing part, which is reengineered in order to become less time and money consuming.

How can BPR be Applied to an Organization?

When British Telecom had announced their Business Plan, all competitors were eager to find out who would be the new CEO of the organization. To the surprise of all the new CEO it was the customer. The company had decided to transform all the operations of the organization the way customers wanted them to operate. The most important action in applying BPR is the company's strategic goal to provide customer oriented services. BPR is a technique used to implement this type of organizational structure.

Having the management commitment for change, another very important factor for implementing BPR, is the enabling role of Information Technology. The way that businesses are organized around departments is very logical since, for instance, there were physical barriers in the communication of the accounting department with production department. (The warehouse could be in another location in the another part of the city). So it wasn't possible for a cross-functional team to communicate efficiently. In the 90s when telecommunication technologies were becoming abundant and low costing BPR was becoming a world-wide applicable managing technique for business upgrade, enabled by the technology. Employees can easily operate as a team using intranets/extarnets, workflow and groupware applications, eliminating distances. We can work together even though they are located in different places.

Importance of BPRE

Empowering People. Empowerement means giving people the ability to do their work: the right information, the right tools, the right training, the right environment, and the authority they need. Information systems help empower people by providing information, tools and training.

Providing Information. Providing information to help people perform their work is a primary purpose of most information systems although they provide information in many different ways. Some systems provide information that is essential in informing a business process, such as the prices used to create a customer's bill at a restaurant. Other systems provide information that is potentially useful but can be used in a discretionary manner, such as medical history information that different doctors might use in different ways

Providing Tools. In addition to providing the right information, empowering people means giving them the right tools. Consider the way planning analysts produce consolidated corporate plans based on plans of individual divisions and departmants. If the plans are submitted on paper, it is a major task to add up the numbers to determine the projected corporate bottom line. When the plan is changed during a negotiation process, the planning analyst has to recalculate the projected results. With the right tools, the numerical parts of the plans arrive in a consistent, electronic format prmitting consolidation by a computer. This leaves the analyst free to do the more productive work of analysing the quality of the plan.

Providing Training. Since information systems are designed to provide the information needed to support desired work practices, they are often used for training and learning. As shown by an expert system and a decision simulator, they sometimes provide new and unique training methods.

IBM developed an expert system for fixing computer disk drives. The expert system was an organized collection of the best knowledge about fixing these disk drives, and it fostered rapid and efficient training. Before the system was developed, technicians typically took between 1 and 16 months to become certified, but with the expert system, training time dropped 3 to 5 months.

Eliminating Unproductive Uses of Time. Information systems can reduce the amount of time people waste doing unproductive work. A study of how professionals and managers at 15 leading U.S. corporations spent their time concluded that many professionals spent less than half of their work time on activities directly related to their functions. Although the primary function of salespeople is selling, the time breakdown for salespeople averaged 36 percent spent on prospecting and selling, 39 percent spent on prospectin an selling, 3 percent on servicing accouts, 19 percent on doing aministrtative chores, and 6 percent on training. Better use of information systems could save much of their unproductive time performing chores such as collecting product or pricing information, determining order status for a customer, resolving invoice discrepancies, and reporting of time and expenses.

Eliminating Unnecessary Paper. One common way to improve data processing is to eliminate unnecessary paper. Although paper is familiar and convenient for many purposes, it has major disadvantages. It is bulky, difficult to move from place to place, and extremely difficult to use for analysing large amounts of data. Storing data in computerized form takes much less physical space and destroys fewer forests, but that is only the beginning. It makes data easier to analyze, easier to copy or transmit, and easier to display in a flexible format. Compare paper telephone bills with computerized bills for a large company. The paper bills identify calls but are virtually impossible to analyze for patterns of inefficient or excessive usage.

Eliminating Unnecessary Variations in the Procedures and Systems. In many companies, separate departments use different systems and procedures to perform essentially similar repetitive processes, such as paying employees, purchasing supplies, and keeping track of inveítories. Although these procedures may seem adequate from a totally local viewpoint, doing the same work in different ways is often inefficient in a global sense. Whenever the systems must change with new technology, new regulations, or new business issues, each separate system must be analysed separately, often by someone starting from scratch.

Minimizing the Burden of Record Keeping, Data Handling, and General Office Work

Since processing data is included in most jobs, improving the way people process data is an obvious place to look for information system applications. Focus on basic data processing tasks: Reducing the burden of record keeping means being more efficient and effective with the six components of data processing. Those components are capturing, transmitting, storing, retrieving, manipulating, and displaying data. Capture data automatically when generated: Capturing data automatically at the time of data generation is especially important in minimizing the burden of record keeping.

In depth, BPR assumes that the current processes in a business are inapplicable and suggest completely new processes to be implemented by starting over. Such a perspective enables the designers of business processes to disassociate themselves from today's process, and focus on a new process. The BPR characteristics-outcomes include the following:

- Several jobs are combined into one.
- Decision-making becomes part of the job of employees (employee empowerment).
- Steps in the processes are performed in natural order, and several jobs get done simultaneously.
- Processes have multiple versions. This enables the economies of scale that

result from mass production, yet allows customization of products and services.

- Work is performed where it makes the most sense.
- Controls and checks and other non-value-added work are minimized.
- Reconciliation is minimized by cutting back the number of external contact points and by creating business alliances.
- A single point of contact is provided to customers.
- A hybrid centralized/decentralized operation is used.

BPR is achieving dramatic performance improvements through radical change in organizational processes, rearchitecting of business and management processes. It involves the redrawing of organizational boundaries, the reconsideration of jobs, tasks, and skills. This occurs with the creation and the use of models. Whether those be physical models, mathematical, computer or structural models, engineers build and analyze models to predict the performance of designs or to understand the behavior of devices. More specifically, BPR is defined as the use of scientific methods, models and tools to bring about the radical restructuring of an enterprise that result in significant improvements in performance.

Redesign, retooling and reorchestrating form the key components of BPR that are essential for an organization to focus on the outcome that it needs to achieve. The outcome pursued should be an ambitious outcome (as for instance, are a 24 hour delivery to any customer anywhere in the world, approval of mortgage loans within 60 minutes of application, or ability to have on-line access to a patient's medical records no matter where they are in any major city in the world). These types of visionary goals require rethinking the way most organizations do business, careful redesign. They will additionally need very sophisticated supporting information systems and a transformation from a traditional organizational structure to a network type organization.

In resuming, the whole process of BPR in order to achieve the above mentioned expected results is based on key steps-principles which include redesign, retool, and reorchestrate.

Each step-principle embodies the actions and resources as presented in the table below.

The three Rs of Re-engineering

Creating the new enterprise involves considerable change in virtually everything.

REDESIGN	*RETOOL*	*REORCHESTRATE*
• Simplify	• Networks	• Processes
• Standardize	• Intranets	• IT
• Empowering	• Extranets	• Human resource
• Employeeship	• Workflow	
• Groupware		
• Measurements		

Creating the new enterprise involves considerable change in virtually everything to do with people's working lives. Rather than fixing the old, we set out to create the new.

There is a fundamental transformation occurring in business - in terms of its structure, processes, people, and technology. The table following presents the changes in that occur in the business under BPR.

Changes in the World of Work through BPRE

Conventional	To BPR
• Functional Department	• Process Team
• Simple Tasks (Division of Labour)	• Empowered employees
• Controlled people (by Management)	• Multidimensional Work
• Training of employees	• Education of Employees
• Compensation of skill and time spent	• Compensation for Result
• Pay raise based on promotion and seniority	• Low Pay plus high performance-related bonuses
• Advanced based on a ability	• Advancement based on performance
• Protective organizational culture	• Productive organizational structure
• Management supervise and control	• Manager coach and Advise
• Hierarchical organizational structure	• Horizontal (flat) structure
• Executives as a score keepers	• Executives as a leader
• Separation of duties and function	• Cross-functional teams
• Linears and sequential processes	• Parallel process
• Mass production	• Mass customization

In resuming, the whole process of BPR in order to achieve the above mentioned expected result is based on key step-principles which include redesigning, retooling and reorchestrating. Each principle embodies the actions and resources as presented in the table.

Objectives of BPR

When applying the BPR management technique to a business organization the implementation team effort is focused on the following objectives:

Customer focus. Customer service-oriented processes aiming to eliminate customer complaints.

Speed. Dramatic compression of the time it takes to complete a task for key business processes. For instance, if process before BPR had an average cycle time 5 hours, after BPR the average cycle time should be cut down to half an hour.

Compression. Cutting major tasks of cost and capital, throughout the value chain. Organizing the processes a company develops transparency throughout the operational level reducing cost. For instance, the decision to buy a large amount of raw material at 50% discount is connected to eleven cross checkings in the organizational structure from cash flow, inventory, to production planning and marketing. These checkings become easily implemented within the cross-functional teams, optimizing the decision-making and cutting operational cost.

Flexibility. Adaptive processes and structures to changing conditions and competition. Being closer to the customer the company can develop the awareness mechanisms to rapidly spot the weak points and adapt to new requirements of the market.

Quality. Obsession with the superior service and value to the customers. The level of quality is always the same controlled and monitored by the processes, and does not depend mainly on the person, who servicing the customer.

Innovation. Leadership through imaginative change providing to organization competitive advantage.

Productivity. Improve drastically effectiveness and efficiency.

In order to achieve the above mentioned adjectives the following BPR project methodology is proposed.

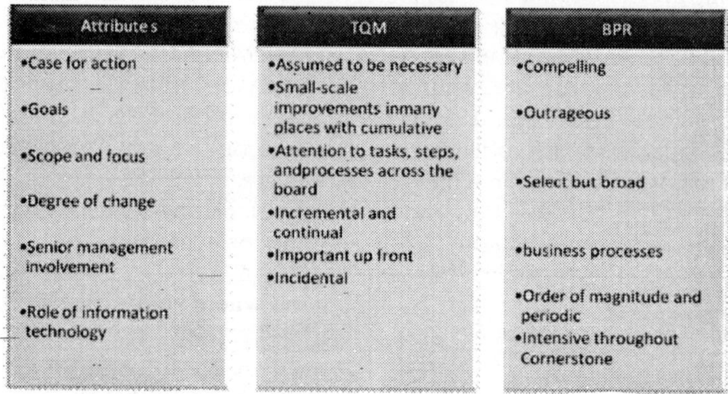

Attributes	TQM	BPR
•Case for action	•Assumed to be necessary	•Compelling
•Goals	•Small-scale improvements inmany places with cumulative	•Outrageous
•Scope and focus	•Attention to tasks, steps, andprocesses across the board	•Select but broad
•Degree of change	•Incremental and continual	•business processes
•Senior management involvement	•Important up front	•Order of magnitude and periodic
•Role of information technology	•Incidental	•Intensive throughout Cornerstone

Source : Gulden and Ewers, 1997.

In opposition with the other existing approaches on business process improvement, which suggest gradual and incremental improvements, as for instance the Total Quality Management approach, BPR does propose dramatic changes.

Elements of Business Engineering

- Reexamination — Rethink existing business processes
- Simplification — Distill business functions into efficient models
- Reorganization — Search for new way to organize work
- Integration — Integrate all critical business processes
- Automation — Use technology to automate redesigned business processes
- Communication — Increase communication to assist new holistic business processes
- Adaptation — Constantly reconsider and improve business process

STEPS IN BUSINESS PROCESS RE-ENGINEERING

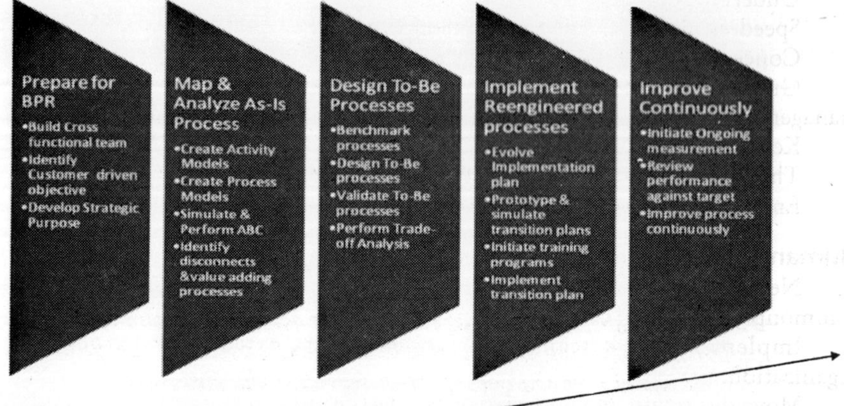

Figure 1 : BPR: The Surest Way to the Top

This activity begins with the development of executive consensus on the importance of reengineering and the link between breakthrough business goals and reengineering projects. A mandate for change is produced and a cross-functional team is established with a game plan for the process of reengineering. While forming the cross functional team, steps should be taken to ensure that the organization continues to function in the absence of several key players. As typical BPR projects involve cross-functional cooperation and significant changes to the *status quo*, the planning for organizational changes is difficult to conduct without strategic direction from the top. The impact of the environmental changes that serve as the impetus for the re-engineering effort must also be considered in establishing guidelines for the re-engineering project. Another important factor to be considered while establishing the strategic goals for the re-engineering effort, is to make it your first priority to understand the expectations of your customers and where your existing process falls short of meeting those requirements. Having identified the customer driven objectives, the mission or vision statement is formulated. The vision is what a company believes it wants to achieve when it is done, and a well-defined vision will sustain a company's resolve through the stress of the re-engineering process. It can act as the flag around which to rally the troops when the morale begins to sag and it provides the yard stick for measuring the company's progress.

The Principles of Business Re-engineering (Coulson-Thomas, 1994)

Process Point of View

Externally, focus on end customers and the generation of greater value for customers.

Give customers and users a single and accessible point of contact through which they can use whatever resources and people are relevant to their needs and interests.

Internally, focus on activities which deliver value to customers.

Encourage learning and development by building creative working environments.

Concentrate on flows and processes (including communication) through the organization.

Remove non-value added activities

Undertake parallel activities

Speed up response and development times

Concentrate on outputs rather than inputs

Give priority to the delivery of value rather than the maintenance of management control.

Keep the number of core processes to a minimum (approx. 12).

They all should be directed to external customers.

Ensure that continuous improvement is built into implemented solutions.

Human and Organizational Point View

Network related people and activities. Virtual corporations are becoming commonplace in some business sectors.

Implement work teams and case managers extensively throughout the organization.

Move discretion and authority closer to the customer.

Re-allocate responsibilities between the organization, its suppliers and customers.

Encourage involvement and participation. This requires error-tolerant leadership.

Ensure people are equipped, motivated and empowered to do what is expected of them.

Whereever possible, people should assume full responsibility for managing and controlling themselves. This requires planning skills.

Work should be broadened without sacrificing depth of expertise in strategic areas.

Avoid over-sophistication. Don't replace creative thinking with software tools.

Build learning, renewal, and short feedback loops into business processes.

USA Business Reengineering Principles

Understand

Simplify

Automate

BPR Flowchart

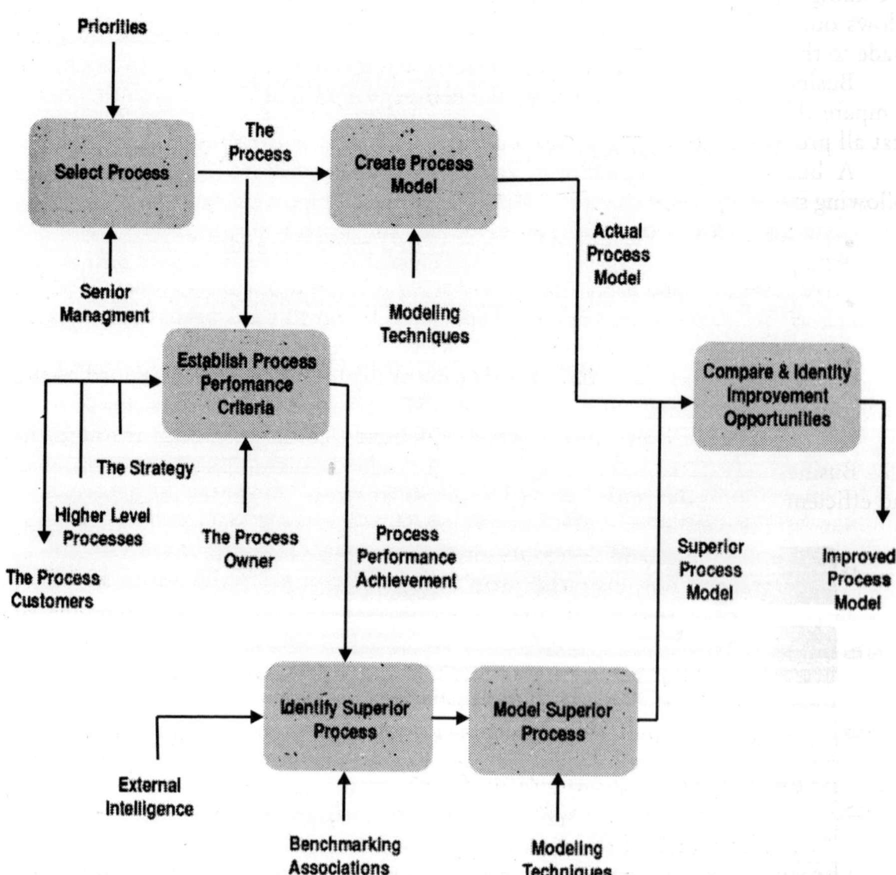

Business process mapping is the procedure of description of exactly what a business entails and the activities carried out by the business. The procedure involves defining who does what, who is responsible for what and the measures of success of the business process.

Business Process Mapping

Business process mapping refers to activities involved in defining exactly what a business entity does, who is responsible, to what standard a process should be completed and how the success of a business process can be determined. Once this is done, there can be no uncertainty as to the requirements of every internal business process. A *business process illustration* is produced. The first step in gaining control over an organization is to know and understand the basic processes (Deming, 1982; Juran, 1988; Taylor, 1911).

ISO 9001 requires a business entity to follow a process approach when managing its business, and to this end creating business process maps*[1]* will assist. The entity can then work towards ensuring its processes are effective (the right process is followed the first time), and efficient (continually improved to ensure processes use the smallest amount of resources).

The main purpose behind business process mapping is to assist organizations in becoming more efficient. A clear and detailed business process map or illustration allows outside firms to come in and look at whether or not improvements can be made to the current process.

Business process mapping takes a specific objective and helps to measure and compare that objective alongside the entire organization's objectives to make sure that all processes are aligned with the company's values and capabilities.

A business process mapping analysis can be structured according to the following steps:

- *Process Identification*: All the steps of a process are identified and defined to all possible extents.
- *Gathering of Information*: The goals of the organization and the potential risks are identified.
- *Mapping*: The different points of view of the individuals involved in the processes are obtained and the process illustrated.
- *Analysis*: Analytical tools are developed in order to optimize the processes.

Business process mapping ensures that the management of a business is effective and efficient.

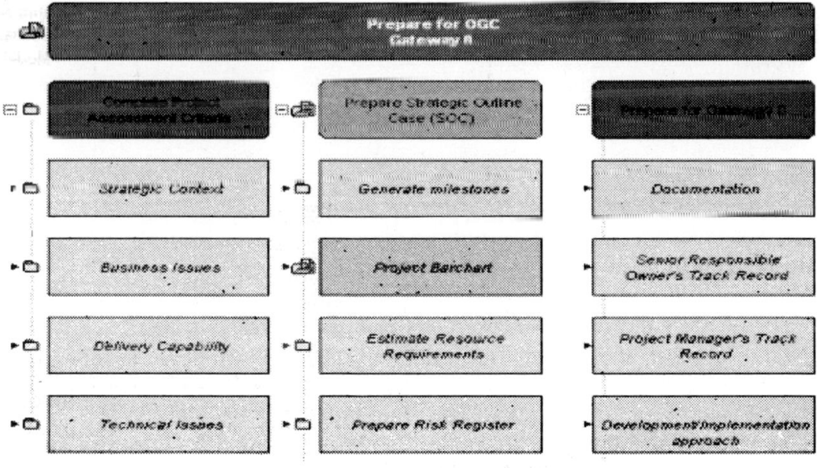

Business Process Mapping

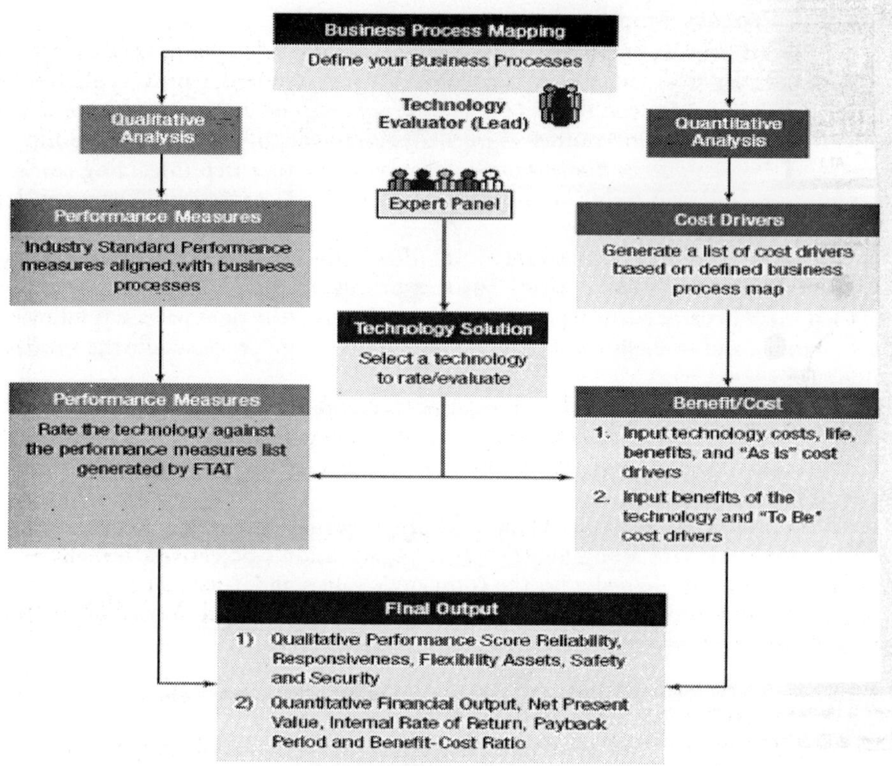

Business Process Mapping

BUSINESS PROCESS MAPPING

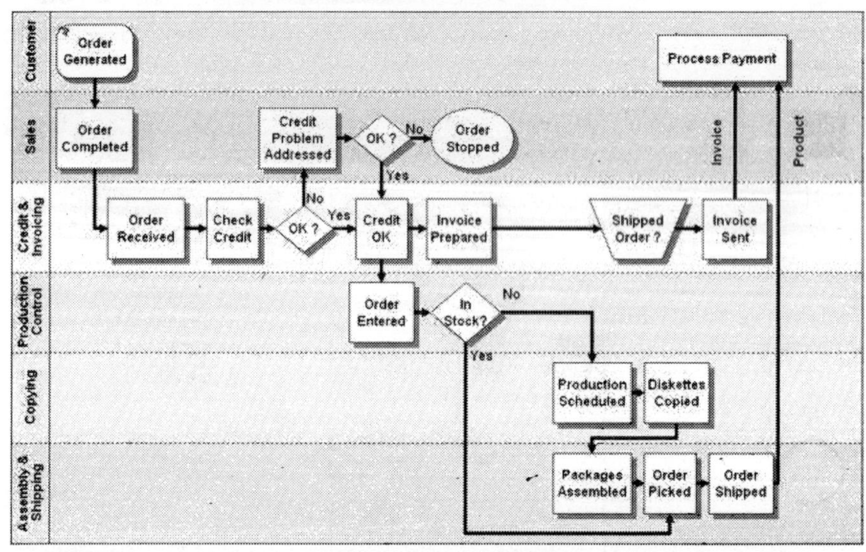

Business Process Mapping

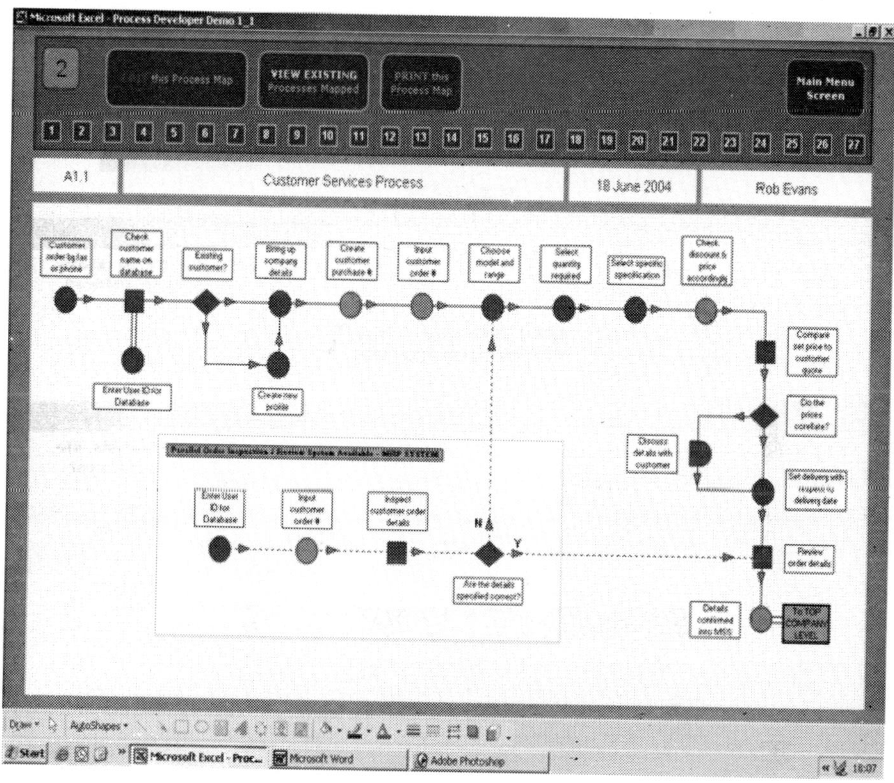

Business Process Mapping

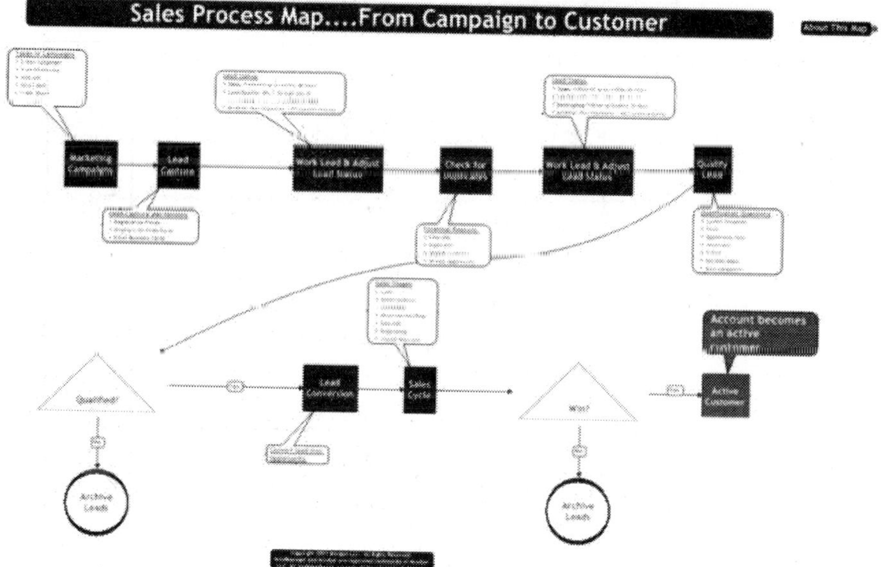

Business Process

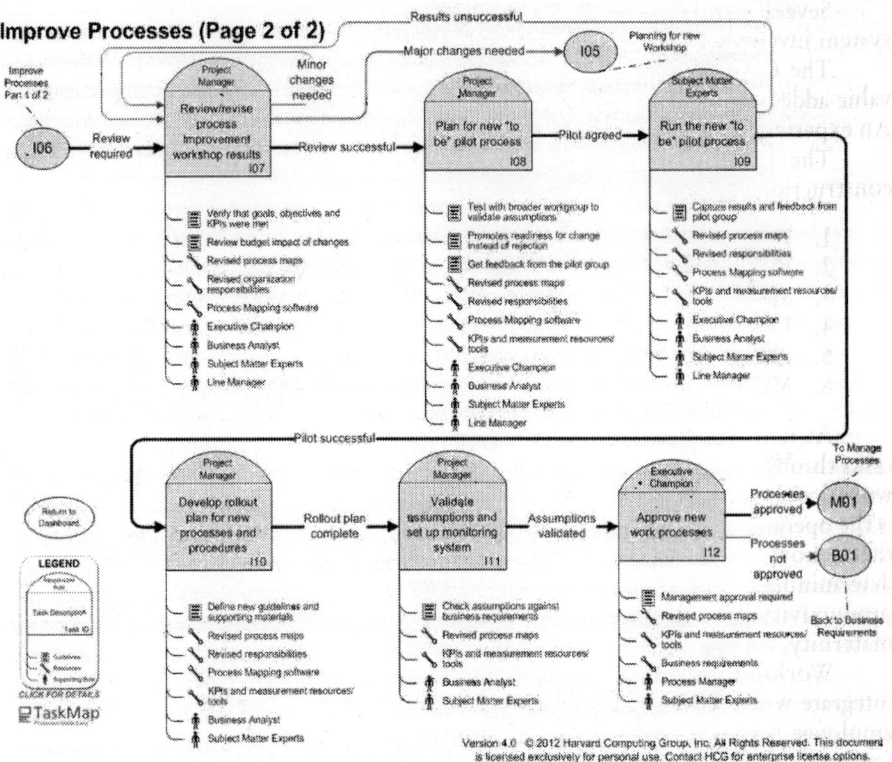

Process Chart Symbols

Sym	Name	Action		Examples
	Operation	Adds Value		Saw, Cut, Paint, Solder, Package
	Transport	Moves Some Distance		Convey, Fork Truck, OTR Truck
	Inspect	Check For Defects		Visual Inspect, Dimension Inspect
	Delay	Temporary Delay/Hold	STOP	WIP Hold, Queue
	Storage	Formal Warehousing		Warehouse or Tracked Storage Location
	Handle	Transfer Or Sort		Re-Package, Transfer To Conveyor
	Decide	Make A Decision		Approve/Deny Purchase

A process map visually depicts the sequence of events to build a product or produce an outcome. It may include additional information such as cycle time, inventory, and equipment information.

Several systems of conventions exist. At Strategies, we find that the original system invented by Frank Gilbreth in the early 1900's is still the most useful.

The Gilbreth approach is highly visual and discriminates between waste and value-added activity. It is also simple, intuitive and easily used by untrained groups. An experienced facilitator, however, is required.

The figure above shows a Process Map example and instructions for its construction. In most situations only the circle symbol (Operation) adds value.

1. Follow one product or a narrow product group.
2. Place the dominant component on the right.
3. Show other components and sub-assemblies on the left.
4. Describe each event concisely.
5. Add additional information as required.
6. Merge items on the chart only when the physical items are merged).

At its simplest definition, workflow is the movement of documents and/or tasks through a work process, and for many people, the idea of Human Resources and workflow in business involves the improvement of processing paperwork. Workflow is the operational aspect of a work procedure: how tasks are structured, who performs them, how they are synchronised, how tasks are tracked; the tasks involved in determining workflow are numerous and can have a serious impact on a business' productivity. The most common HR processes include appraisals, new starters, maternity, absence, holiday booking and leavers.

Workflow involves various components and people and each facet must integrate with the others in order to process and complete a task. For example, an employee wants to book a holiday and fills in a paper form. Details of the holiday from will be delivered to the employee's line manager, who will check to see if there is sufficient cover before authorizing the holiday. The paper form is then delivered to the HR department who then makes a note of details of the employee's holiday and subtracts the time from the employees holiday balance. The employee then receives a form showing that the holiday has been authorized and details of their new holiday balance.

Workflow is critical to driving greater efficiency within HR. It is a process which delivers the right work to the right people at the right time, eradicating the need for highly labour intensive activities and considerably reducing the need for paper to be pushed around the office. In essence Workflow can help to reduce costs, improve productivity, provide faster processing times and of course is a major player in helping to sustain the world's declining tree population. A HR process may require interaction from many departments. Therefore, HR processes are well suited for automation because typically these processes are paper based, manual and prone to error and delay.

With workflow management becoming more and more critical in driving greater efficiency within your business, the ever changing demands on HR and business to become more effective, productive and profitable has led to many software solution companies introducing HR software designed to manage HR workflow; allowing labour-intensive activities to be automated. Operating in tandem with process tracking, businesses can ensure that progress can be monitored effectively. For example, ASR Computers recently launched their .NET HR Workflow module, which is written in .NET technology and compliments the company's existing HR and Payroll software product range.

ASR's .NET HR Workflow module management tool which gives HR professionals the functionality to re-engineer their HR processes and assist with the efficient running of their HR department; allowing for the use of electronic forms instead of paper. Consequently, a range of benefits are achieved—including process visibility, which is a key factor for tracking progress and improvement.

WORKFLOW MANAGEMENT

A key to successful management of flexible work arrangements is the ability to identify the key functions and outputs of the work area as a whole and to organise work to fulfill the required results.

Key questions are:

- What is our purpose? List the major business objectives of the work area. Workplace flexibility should be considered as a means to achieve a more effective outcome for the unit's business objectives.
- What is the essential work that needs to be done? Is the workflow predictable or unpredictable (for example, regular or cyclical reporting deadlines that must be met)?
- Who are our customers (both internal and external)? What are their needs? When do they expect us to be available?
- Is there any work that must be done full-time, five days a week between 9 am and 5 pm? When are our peak workload times? Are they predictable or unpredictable?
- How is the work unit set to manage crises or unforeseen challenges?
- Determine the key results and outputs that the work area must continue to achieve. What are the required results? What are the key tasks to be performed to reach the required results?
- Is it possible to change or vary the pace and methods of working, perhaps through planning for longer-term deadlines, or taking decision-making over longer timeframes?
- Is there clarity around individual roles, as well as expected team outcomes and standards? Do your staff have individual targets that clearly relate to the overall operation of the work unit and the University?
- Do you provide a working environment where employees can freely communicate their ideas and concerns?

Job and Task Management

- How could the tasks be distributed to both ensure that the required work is done and allow the flexibility desired by staff? What impact will staff working reduced hours or taking more leave have on the jobs of others in the team?
- Look at how the individual job could be done in the time available, or how it could be done differently.

  Clarify changes in responsibilities along with the dimension of alterations required.

Focus on use of higher order skills and tasks before routine or lower order tasks which can be reassigned or removed.

- What are the skills required for those tasks which are to be reassigned?

- What are the skills of the staff in this work unit/team?
- What relationships are essential? How significant is the need for people to work together?
- What are the interdependencies between members of the work group? Where do positions intersect?
- Are there tasks, or elements of a larger task, common to two or more people?
- The Professional Staff classification level descriptions are a useful resource, as is the Schedule of Minimum Standards for Academic Staff. For a professional staff position, you could contact Classifications in Human Resources for advice and assistance.
- What other ways are there to reorganise work to produce the expected results? Could work be done as, or more, effectively using job rotation, job sharing, multi-skilling, home-based work, teams, shifts? Ideally, work teams and individuals within a multi skilled team should be able to switch some tasks and projects amongst themselves to meet tight deadlines or other commitments.
- Is there someone in the team able to pick up some of the tasks, perhaps through job redesign or higher duties? Does this present an opportunity for staff development? Or can you use salary savings to buy in support, expertise or to pay staff to work on additional projects?

Resources and Equipment

- Is there technology that could assist with doing the work differently (e.g. student communication via email rather than appointment; forms set-up on the intranet)?
- Does workplace flexibility allow you to make better use of your resources, particularly office space and equipment?

For example, with staff working reduced hours, is their flexible arrangement structured in a way that allows the office space and equipment to be used by someone else in their absence? Similarly, office space may be freed by staff undertaking regular home-based work.

Performance Measures

The perceived difficulty of managing and supervising employees is the most commonly identified barrier to the uptake and implementation of flexible working practices across the board. When questioned, managers in general voice concern about the difficulties of managing a number of staff working flexibly and working from home. This indicates a need to change to performance criteria rather than attendance based evaluation techniques to monitor productivity and quality of work.

There is a widespread perception that performance monitoring is a greater challenge than it actually proves to be once flexible working is implemented.

Changing to outcomes-based systems for performance management rather than using attendance-based criteria is a key ingredient in the successful management of a flexible workplace. In other words, the focus is more on the achievement of results than the time spent working towards them.

- Establish specific performance measures, including individual and team objectives and clearly communicate the standards required for work performance, such as delivery times and quality levels.

- Task identity, that is the allocation of a 'whole piece of work' with clearly defined boundaries and expecations to either an individual or a team, makes it easier to measure performance through outcomes.
- Performance objectives need to be based on clearly defined outcomes; for example, projects completed, number of clients serviced, proportion of work completed, contribution to team goals; availability of staff between certain hours, etc.
- Specific meauress can include:
  Performance Development Review (PDR)
  Performance Appraisal Review (PAR)
  Quality or standard of work
  Quantity of work
  Deadlines met
  Level of service provided
  Personal goals/operational goals/strategic goals achieved
  Feedback from team, clients, staff
  Feedback from students (SPOT, SURF)

Benefits of BPR

Business Process Reengineering (BPR) can be defined as the elemental rethinking and radical redesigning of the business processes in order to achieve remarkable improvements in critical measures of performance like cost, service, quality, and speed. An organization where application of BPR is being done, is process-oriented, where all processes are identified and given specific names. Each individual is aware of the particular process in which he or she is involved and complete process measurement such as monitoring and control is performed. Business Process Re-engineering or BPR is also known by other names like Business Process Redesign, Business Process Change Management or Business Transformation. BPR brings numerous benefits to organizations and companies in which it is implemented. Some of the common benefits of BPR are:

Increase Effectiveness

As all employees are aware of the processes to which they belong , they have a greater sense of responsibility. All processes are completely monitored under the strict control of the management. The net result of this is that employees deliver high quality products to their customers.

Helps to improve efficiency. Proper management and control of all business processes reduces the time lag between different processes, which otherwise is quite high causing delays. This in turn reduces the time to market the product to the target customers and givesquicker response to buyers.

Reduces cost

With the proper management of processes, improved efficiency and quick delivery of products to the buyers ,the overall product costs are reduced resulting in cost saving for the organization in the long-run.

Meaningful job for employees

As the time lag of product processing between different departments gets reduced due to the application of business process reengineering, there are more meaningful tasks to be performed by employees. This leads to increase their levels of motivation and the desire to perform well.

Improvement in Organizational Approach

According to the traditional approach of managing an organization there is no flexibility or adaptability to change. The management formulated strict rules for employees of the organization. Whereas now, when most organizations have implemented business process re-engineering there is an increase in flexibility and adaptability for change. This has created better environment for people to work, thus leading to employee satisfaction.

Growth of business

Implementation of BPR results in the growth of the present business thus enabling the emergence of new businesses within the same organization. Although BPR is very effective in controlling cost and improving efficiency, its implementation is a hard nut to crack. Employees are very resistant to this kind of change thus, it is important to have extensive support from the top management.

BPR and the Organization Transform Connection

After BPR organizes the necessity which transforms The business process merely is the enterprise organizes the system a constituent, specially along with the market competition intense degree increase, the goal which the enterprise managed has had the profound change, from the past emphasized the efficiency, the cost and the control transform for the present is fastidious the innovation and the speed, the service and the quality, but this merely relied on the service flow the improvement is cannot realize, had to change the enterprise entire organizational structure, the rules and regulations and the system. When the work duty passes to another person from a person, passes to another link from a link, passes to another department from a department, the procedure many, the process is long, delays and makes a mistake is inevitable. Therefore the BPR implementation must transform with the organization unifies, thoroughly abandons the establishment in the division of labor principle and Taloy in the scientific management rationale organization system, hits the worn-out function boundary, the structure surmounts the department boundary, take moves as the foundation, take the team as the work way, take the process as the core organization system, thus the enhancement enterprise's flexibility and to the market shift quick reaction capability, the realization enterprise's value increment, enhances the entire enterprise the management achievements.

In BPR Organizes the Function which Transforms

The organization transformed in the BPR process plays the very important safeguard and the promotion role. When an enterprise when carries on BPR, must carry on the corresponding transformation to its organization. Otherwise, this enterprise's BPR is cannot obtain the anticipated effect. The organization transforms in the enterprise BPR process is playing the pivotal role. Carries on enterprise common which BPR but is defeated comes to an end is: While BPR, neglected has carried on the corresponding organization transformation. Therefore, not the corresponding organization transforms makes the safeguard, the enterprise is very difficult to succeed carries on BPR.4.3 efficiency maximization in fact, but non-enterprise overall flow efficiency maximization. BPR will be must the flow which is separated by the function reconnects through in the organization and the management pattern transformation, will cause it to become a continuously flow, through to the flow conformity and the optimization, will realize to the customer serves, the enterprise movement cost and the efficiency global optimization.

Therefore, the BPR effect certainly not merely displays in to the enterprise flow optimization in, urged the enterprise take the flow as the core thought in aspect and so on organizational structure, work content, achievements appraisal to have the whole transformation. Table synthesis had reflected between around BPR organizes the difference. BPR finally initiates the enterprise to organize to transform.

BPR Promoter Action which Transforms to the Organization

Characteristic	*Organization before Re-engineering*	*Organization after Re-engineering*
Organization Structure	The function as the central level structure	The Process as the central flat structure
Movement mechanism	The function as the central Existence function boundary Not continual Processes Operation partial optimization	The Process as the central P to P management to customer Conformity Processes Enterprise overall situation optimization
Staff	According to function arrangement specialized skill individual as the center To customer limited attention	According to process arrangement comprehensive skill group as the center To customer high attention
Technology	Is separated as a result of the function boundary Appraisal by function goal primarily	Is integrated in the processes Appraisal by processes goal primarily
Communication	Vertical direction	Horizontal direction

The BPR process manifests makes the thought again to the organization pattern transformation. Along with BPR in the enterprise interior widespread application, the service flow, the organizational structure, the personnel request which the enterprise organizes and so on the basic pattern can have the change along with it. Again makes after the enterprise to organize to the flow to make the thought the development to be able again to get up the promoter action. The BPR process is a process which the enterprise organizes to make again. Comrade Deng Xiaoping pointed out that, "The science and technology is the first productive forces." The BPR thought obviously subordinates to the productive forces category. The organization flow, the organizational structure have directly manifested the organization interior rank and the authority, had reflected the organization interior person and between person's relations, are the productive relations in microscopic domain manifesting. BPR and between the organization pattern relations have reflected the productive forces and the productive relations contradiction and the unification.

"Das Kapital" as well as between them the relations has made the explicit elaboration to the productive forces and the productive relations. The productive forces is the humanity conquers the nature, the transformation natural ability, the material force and the control natural ability which is refers has the certain production to experience and to work the skill worker, use natural object and when natural forces production matter material forms. The productive relations are the people in the material production process mutually the between social relations. Between the productive forces and the productive relations both is mutually contradictory, and mutually unifies. Relations between BPR and the organization pattern have reflected the productive forces and the productive relations contradiction and the unification. BPR is one kind of new productive forces, it plays the decision role to the organization pattern. The organization pattern is the productive relations in microscopic enterprise domain manifesting. BPR is the productive forces as soon as manifests to the high-level development, the traditional organization pattern is the original industry society's product obviously is unable to adapt the current BPR thought request. The enterprise in realizes in the BPR process inevitably to have to break the original organization pattern, establishes adapts the BPR thought production, the management and the management organization pattern process. This process has manifested the productive forces to the productive relations decision and the transformation, has manifested the productive relations to the productive forces development adaption. Therefore, in the BPR process organization transformation is the productive forces development inevitably request impact of BPR on organizational performance.

The two cornerstones of any organization are the people and the processes. If individuals are motivated and working hard, yet the business processes are cumbersome and non-essential activities remain, organizational performance will be poor. Business Process Reengineering is the key to transforming how people work. What appear to be minor changes in processes can have dramatic effects on cash flow, service delivery and customer satisfaction. Even the act of documenting business processes alone will typically improve organizational efficiency by 10%.

Because it encapsulates the key components of an organisation and because it has Shared Values (or Culture) at its centre, McKinsey's 7S model will be used as a framework to assess the impact of BPR on the organisation.

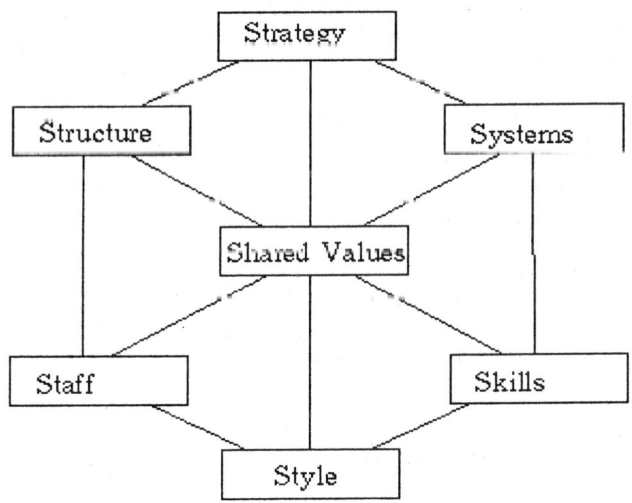

Figure : McKinsey's Seven S Diagram (Henley, 1991, p. 33)

First, each of these elements will be defined.

Systems

"Systems are codified knowledge, organised in a logical sequence." (Henley, 1991, p. 47). They are the processes, methods, procedures, rules, techniques, technology, manuals, etc. that ensure that work is undertaken efficiently and accurately. They are the instructions that guide staff and management in their daily tasks.

All the BPR definitions either explicitly or implicitly refer to these attributes of Systems as the following examples of BPR implementation demonstrate. Rohm, in his review of BPR at the Principal Financial Group Inc., gives an example from its field support transaction. Called Licensing and Contracting, the impact on processes was significant:

"Under the old system, this was a sixteen-step process requiring input from nine people stationed in different areas and on different floors of the home office. The new structure enabled this process to be cut to six steps, requiring the work of only three people". (Rohm, 1992)

As a result, customers were provided with a single contact person who could execute and manage the whole process.

Often, as Davenport highlights, new processes are enabled by new technology. As an example, he mentions Federal Mogul, an auto parts manufacture, who is using technology so that many designers can work on a new prototype design simultaneously (p. 99). Thus, both the new technology and the new multi-function positions demand employees learn new techniques.

Structures

Henley (1991) defines these as "How an organisation breaks down its activities into distinct elements and how these elements are co-ordinated" (p. 34). Henley goes on to identify 6 distinct type of organisation:

"Simple structure (the one man band)
Machine bureaucracy
Professional bureaucracy
Divisionalised form
Adhocracy
Cult organisation"
(Henley, 1991, pp. 35-37)

Having redefine the key processes within an organisation, the next step within BPR is to restructure the organisation along process lines. Process organisations introduce a new form of organisation that aims to break away from many of the above traditional types, particularly the bureaucracies and divisional forms. Hammer & Champy recommend "a move to much flatter structures organised around the processes" (Chap. 4), whereas Davenport recommends "a multidimensional matrix structure, with process responsibility as a key dimension" (p. 160). To achieve this, Johansson *et. al.* (1993) states: "the new organisation must accommodate a balance between functional expertise and process involvement" and goes on to say it is essential to remove functional barriers (p. 191). Andrews & Stalick (1994) emphasise "even the boundaries between your customers and your suppliers and you must be redefined." (p. 219).

In the Principal Financial Group Inc. example given above:

> "Like many other organizations in financial services, the Individual Insurance Department at that time was structured mainly along product lines. ... there were many management layers, ..."

and then, after BPR:

> "From now on, it was agreed, virtually every worker would become part of a multi-functional team, ... To increase responsibility and accountability at the lowest levels, the number of management layers would be reduced to three".
>
> *—(Rohm, 1992)*

Still, whilst a process orientation is a new organisational structure it will incorporate attributes of the adhocracy: "Employees do not need to be supervised; ... They are adults who are willing to take accountability for their work products" (Andrews & Stalick, 1994, p. 220).

Staff

Henley defines Staff as "the quality and quantity of people employed" but also adds the management issues of "motivation, reward systems, the structure of jobs and team work".

—(Henley, 1991, p. 44)

The quality issues will be noted in the Skills section that follows. BPR is often linked to new rewards systems. Davenport (1993) refers to "gain-sharing" (p. 110), "lateral promotion" and a move from "role title to process title" (p. 111), and variety through "work role rotation". "Life time employment", he believes "encourages employees to redesign the processes to eliminate their own job". Pagoda (1993) sees "significant implications for managers and staff":

> "The role of managers is transformed ... and the number middle managers usually reduced. At the same time, staff at all levels have new, more responsive roles, and specialist roles change fundamentally".
>
> *—(Pagoda Associates Ltd., 1993, Flyer, p. 3)*

Team work and the structure of jobs is mentioned by Stevens' account of BPR at Sun Life:

> "In implementing BPR, Sun Life moved from a functional hierarchical approach, via a team-based operation as an intermediate step, to a situation where a single multi-skilled individual took responsibility for an entire process from beginning to end".
>
> *—(Stevens, 1994)*

BPR has certainly made some significant impact on the number of staff. An Economist article states:

> "At least in its initial phase, re-engineering usually means heavy layoffs and substantial job reorganisation. Nynex, an American telephone company, for

example, cut its workforce by almost a quarter, while an American insurance company saw the number of job demarcations reduced from 40 to four."

—*(Anon, 1993a)*

BPR has certainly become associated with down-sizing and right-sizing, and in such circumstances it is difficult to square with Davenport's assertion above, that employees should have the confidence to redesign themselves out of the process.

Skills

Skills is defined as "The competences the organisation needs in its people in order to perform difficult tasks to a high standard".

—*(Henley, 1991, p. 42).*

The word 'empowerment' is invariably associated with BPR. Examples help to illustrate what is meant by this over used word. Bambarger illustrates employee involvement in the decision making. He quotes one of OSRAM Sylvania's BPR team;

"Then we get together with the plant staff to brainstorm potential solutions" and later they are asked: "If this were your candy store, how would you run it?"

—*(Bambarger, 1993)*

The impact at Dominion Insurance was more operational:

"marketing staff were empowered by IT to make quick decisions based on rapid access to meaningful information from the field. Suddenly presenting sales and marketing staff with a lot of information they didn't have before can be as daunting as it is exciting".

—*(Anon, 1993b)*

Hammer & Champy talk about the "New World of Work" where "jobs change from simple tasks to multi-dimensional work". This means "job preparation changes from training to education, from rule following to exercising judgement" and "managers change from supervisors to coaches" and "executives change from scorekeepers to leaders". (Hammer & Champy, 1993, Chap. 4).

Strategy

Johnson & Scholes define Strategy as:

"The direction and scope of an organisation over the long term: ideally, which matches its resources to its changing environment, and in particular its markets, customers or clients so as to meet stakeholder expectations".

—*(Johnson & Scholes, 1993, p. 10)*

Johnson & Scholes go on to characterise strategic decisions as being "complex in nature, ..., involve a high degree of uncertainty, ... involve major changes ... " (p. 10).

Johansson et al definition of the BPR drivers are of a strategic nature: "Customers; Competition; Cost; Technology; Shareholders; Politics; Economics, Legislation, and Regulation [i.e. Environment]" (headings in pp. 37-49). One can see these relate to the Strategy definition given above. Johansson *et al.* first task is to "Discover" the companies strategy and "of what drives competitive advantage in a particular industry; the industry's value chain and the basis for competition, and how a particular company seeks to gain competitive edge" (p. 87). Hammer & Champy talk about the "three Cs: Customers, Competition and Change" (p. 17). Davenport (1993) advocates a "Process Vision" that is driven by "Business Strategy" (p. 127).

BPR decisions, like Strategy decisions, are complex and involves a high degree of uncertainty ("[BPR] is a complex undertaking and carries significant risk". (Carey, 1993), and as noted under Systems and Structures, BPR involves major change.

Style

Style is "the philosophy, values and shared beliefs adopted by managers in their use of power" (Henley, 1991, p. 46).

As noted above, Hammer & Champy's "New World of Work" causes "managers [to] change from supervisors to coaches" and "executives [to] change from scorekeepers to leaders". (Hammer & Champy, 1993, Chap. 4). Davenport also highlights the significant behaviour changes:

> "Change incurred by process innovation is not only broad, but deep, extending from the visions of managers to the attitudes and behaviours of the lowest level workers. ... Its significant behavioural component makes process innovation based change qualitatively different from other forms of large scale restructuring".
>
> *—(Davenport, 1993, pp. 174-5)*

> "Process innovation involves massive change, not only in process flows and the culture surrounding them, but also in organisational power and controls".
>
> *—(Davenport, 1993, p. 13)*

Shared Values (or Super-ordinated Goals)

These are "the basic values and mission of the organisation" (Henley, 1991, p. 49). As Henley puts it: "they rise above profit targets and growth objectives by relating the goals of the firm to deeper human needs and principles".

Andrews & Stalick (1994) assert that in "successful re-engineered business operations, individual belief systems become aligned with the stated beliefs of the organisation" (p. 115). Hammer & Champy, again under his "New World of Work", sees a belief in customers as key:

> Re-engineering entails as great a shift in the culture of an organisation as in its structural configuration. Re engineering demands that employees deeply believe they work for their customers, not for their bosses".
>
> *—(Hammer & Champy, 1993, p. 74)*

Johansson *et al.* see the new process teams "linked by common values" (p. 202) and there is an implication in their writings that individuals must believe in self-management, self-development, and rewards based on skills used (pp. 202-3).

All Elements of the 7S Model

Using the quoted examples from the BPR literature, the descriptions of BPR closely match the definitions of each of the elements of McKinsey's 7S organizational model.

More fully understand this implication, the next chapter will explore the literature on culture and organizational change.

CASE STUDY

M&M's BPR

In the mid-1990s, India's largest multi utility vehicle (MUV) and tractor manufacturer M&M was facing serious problems at its Igatpuri and Kandivili plants in Maharashtra. The plants were suffering from manufacturing inefficiencies, poor productivity, long production cycle, and sub-optimal output.

The reason: highly under-productive, militantly unionized, and bloated workforces. The company had over the years been rather lenient towards running the plants and had frequently crumbled under the pressure of union demands. The work culture was also reportedly very unhealthy and corruption was widespread in various departments.

Alarmed at the plant's dismal condition, Chairman Keshub Mahindra tried to address the problem by sacking people who allegedly indulged in corrupt practices. M&M also tried to implement various voluntary retirement schemes (VRS), but the unions refused to cooperate and the company was unable to reduce the labor force.

During this period, M&M was in the process of considering the implementation of a Business process Reengineering (BPR) Program throughout the organization including the manufacturing units. Because of the problem at the Igatpuri and Kandivila plants, M&M decide to implement the program speedily at its manufacturing units.

The program, developed with the help of the UK based Lucas Engineering systems, was first implement on an experimental basis at the engine plant in Igatpuri. Simultaneously, an exercise was initiated to assess the potential benefit of implementing BPR and its effect on the unions.

M&M's management was not surprised to learn that the unions expressed extreme displeasure at the decision to implement BPR and soon went on a strike. However, this time around, the management made it clear that it would not succumb to union demands. Soon, the workers were surprised to see the company's senior staff come down to the plant and work in their place. With both the parties refusing to work out an agreement, observers began casting doubts on the future of the company's grand plans of reaping the benefits of BPR.

Mahindra & Mahindra Ltd. (M&M) was the flagship company of the Mahindra group, one of the top ten industrial houses in India. The company's history dates back to 1945, when two brothers, J.C. Mahindra and K.C. Mahindra, decided to start a business of general-purpose utility vehicles. The brothers formed a company, Mahindra & Mohammed Ltd., in association with their friend Ghulam Mohammed. In October 1947, the first batch of 75 jeeps was released for the Indian market. In 1948, the company was renamed Mahindra & Mahindra Ltd. Over the next few decades, the group promoted many companies in areas as diverse as hotels, financial services, auto components, information technology, infrastructure development and trading to name a few.

Though M&M had established itself in the markets and was among the leading players in many of the segments it operated in, it realized that some of its businesses were not closely related to its core business. This realization marked the beginning of the biggest change exercise since the company's inception.

In 1994, a major restructuring exercise was initiated as part of a BPR program M&M Introduced a new organizational model in which various division and companies were regrouped into distinct cluster of related businesses, each headed by a president. M&M's core activities automotive and tractors were made autonomous business units. The other activities of the group were organized into infrastructure, trade and financial service, telecommunication and Automotive components. According to company resources, the whole exercise was indented to develop a conceptual map to provide direction for the future growth of various business lines. It was decided that, in future, the group would confine its expansion to the identified thrust sectors.

The two main operating divisions of the company were the automotive division, which manufactured UVs and LCVs, and the farm equipment division, which made tractors and farm implements. The company employed over 17,000 people and had six state-of-the-art manufacturing facilities spread over 500,000 square meters.

The plants were situated at Kandivili (MUVs and Tractors), Nasik (MUVs), Zaheerabad (LCVs, Voyager, three-wheelers), Igatpuri (Engines) and Nagpur (Implements and tractors).

About BPR

The concept of BPR was popularized in the early 1990s by Michael Hammer and James Champy in their best-selling book, 'Re-engineering the Corporation.' The authors said that radical redesign and reorganization of an enterprise was necessary to lower costs and increase the quality of service. According to them, IT was the key enabler for that radical change. Hammer and Champy felt that the design of the workflow in most large corporations was based on assumptions about technology, people and organizational goals that were no longer valid. They recommended seven principles of re-engineering for streamlining work processes and, consequently, achieving significant levels of improvement in quality, time management and cost:

1. Top Management Sponsorship (strong and consistent involvement)
2. Strategic Alignment (with company strategic direction)
3. Compelling Business Case for Change (with measurable objectives)
4. Proven Methodology (that includes a vision process)
5. Effective Change Management (address cultural transformation)
6. Line Ownership (pair ownership with accountability)
7. Re engineering Team Composition (in both breadth and knowledge)

M&M's Experience with BPR

By the mid-1990s, BPR had become a popular tool globally, with many leading organizations implementing it. However, when M&M undertook the exercise, it was still a new concept in India.

M&M's workforce, as mentioned earlier, resisted this attempt to re-engineer the organization soon after the senior staff began working on the shopfloor the first signs of the benefit of BPR become evident. Around a 100 officers produced 35 engines a day as compared to the 1200 employees producing 70 engines in the pre-BPR days.

After five months, the workers ended the strike and began work in exchange for a 30% wage hike. As the situation returned to normalcy, BPR implementation gained momentum. M&M realized that it would have to focus on two issues when implementing the BPR Program : re-engineering the layout and method of working and productivity.

The Future

Summing up the company's BPR experience, Anand Mahindra said, "Let me put it in a simple way. If we have facilities in Kandivili today, which are not just surviving but thriving, it is all due to BPR.

Chapter 6

Management of Change

Change management is an approach to shifting/transitioning individuals, teams, and organizations from a current state to a desired future state. It is an organizational process aimed at helping change stakeholders to accept and embrace changes in their business environment. In some project management contexts, change management refers to a project management process wherein changes to a project are formally introduced and approved. Kotter defines change management as the utilization of basic structures and tools to control any organizational change effort. Change management's goal is to maximize an organization's benefits and minimize the change impacts on workers and avoid distractions.

HISTORY

Linda Ackerman Anderson, co-author of *Beyond Change Management*, described how in the late 1980s and early 1990s top leaders were growing dissatisfied with the failures of creating and implementing changes in a top-down fashion. They created the role of the change leader to take responsibility for the people side of the change. February 1994 is the unofficial beginning of the Change Management Industry, with the publication of the first "State of the Change Management Industry" report in the *Consultants News*. McKinsey consultant Julien Phillips first published a change management model in 1982 in the journal *Human Resource Management*, though it took a decade for his change management peers to catch up with him.

Marshak credits the big six accounting firms and management consulting firms with creating the change management industry when they branded their re-engineering services groups as *change management services* in the late 1980s.

ORGANIZATIONAL CHANGE

Organizational change is a structured approach in an organization for ensuring that changes are smoothly and successfully implemented, and that the lasting benefits of change are achieved. In the modern business environment, organizations face rapid change like never before. Globalization and the constant innovation of technology result in a constantly evolving business environment. Recent phenomenon like social media and mobile adaptability have revolutionized business and the effect of this is an ever increasing need for change, and therefore change management. The growth in technology also has a secondary effect of increasing the availability and therefore accountability from knowledge. Easily accessible information has resulted in unprecedented scrutiny from stockholders and the media. prying eyes and listening ears raise the stakes for failed business endeavors and increase the pressure on struggling executives. With the business environment experiencing so much change, organizations must then learn to become comfortable with change as well. Therefore, the ability to manage and adapt to organizational change is an essential ability required in the work place today.

Due to the growth of technology, modern organizational change is largely motivated by exterior innovations rather than internal moves. And when these developments occur, the organizations that adapt quickest create for themselves a competitive advantage. Meanwhile the companies that refuse to change get left behind and this can result in drastic profit and/or market share losses.

Organizational change directly affects all departments from the entry level employee to the upper management. With recent developments like social media marketing and smart phone applications, the entire company must learn how to handle these new changes to the organization. Whether it's the CMO determining how to incorporate social media, or the secretary representing themselves and their company responsibly online, change occurs rapidly in today's ever developing world.

When determining which latest techniques or innovations to adopt, there are four major components which must be considered:

1. Levels, goals and strategies,
2. Measurement system,
3. Sequence of steps,
4. Implementation and organizational change.

Organizational change can have many faces. But regardless of the type, the critical aspect is a company's ability to win the buy-in of their organization's employees on the change. To effectively implement organizational change there is a four step process. First, recognizing the changes in the broader business environment. Second, developing the necessary adjustments for their company's needs. Third, training their employees on the appropriate changes. And fourth, winning the support of the employees with the persuasiveness of the appropriate adjustments. This four step process is change management in its essence, and organizational change in practice.

Examples of Organizational Change

1. Mission changes,
2. Strategic changes,
3. Operational changes (including Structural changes),
4. Technological changes,
5. Changing the attitudes and behaviors of personnel
6. Organizational change can have many faces.

But regardless of the type, the critical aspect is a company's ability to win the buy-in of their organization's employees on the change. To effectively implement organizational change there is a four step process.

1. Recognizing the changes in the broader business environment,
2. Developing the necessary adjustments for their company's needs,
3. Training their employees on the appropriate changes, and
4. Winning the support of the employees with the success of the adjustments.

This four step process is change management in its essence, and organizational change in practice.

As a multidisciplinary practice that has evolved as a result of scholarly research, Organizational Change Management should begin with a systematic diagnosis of the current situation in order to determine both the need for change and the capability to change. The objectives, content, and process of change should all be specified as part of a Change Management Plan.

Change Management processes may include creative marketing to enable communication between change audiences, as well as deep social understanding about leadership's styles and group dynamics. As a visible track on transformation projects, Organizational Change Management aligns groups' expectations, communicates, integrates teams and manages people training. It makes use of performance metrics, such as financial results, operational efficiency, leadership commitment, communication effectiveness, and the perceived need for change to design appropriate strategies, in order to avoid change failures or resolve troubled change projects.

Successful change management is more likely to occur if the following are included:

1. Benefits management and realization to define measurable stakeholder aims, create a business case for their achievement (which should be continuously updated), and monitor assumptions, risks, dependencies, costs, return on investment, dis-benefits and cultural issues affecting the progress of the associated work.
2. Effective Communications that informs various stakeholders of the reasons for the change (why?), the benefits of successful implementation (what is in it for us, and you) as well as the details of the change (when? where? who is involved? how much will it cost? etc.).
3. Devise an effective education, training and/or skills upgrading scheme for the organization.
4. Counter resistance from the employees of companies and align them to overall strategic direction of the organization.
5. Provide personal counseling (if required) to alleviate any change-related fears.
6. Monitoring of the implementation and fine-tuning as required.

Change happens all around us, all the time. We cannot stop change. So what is change management? In truth, we cannot manage change, we can only *respond* to it. Example, suppose you want to give up cigarettes. Do you tell people you smoke about ten a :

To define **Change**, you could say that it is the process of moving from the current state to a vision of the future. This transition creates a fear of the unknown, which often causes distress for people.

To define **Change Management**, you could say that it is about managing this transition from the old position to the new. You are unfreezing the old state and refreezing the new state so that it becomes established.

In order to manage change, facing the truth of the current situation is really critical. For day, when in reality you smoke twenty? You need to be honest about what it is you need to change and why.

When you get to a new position, you need to reinforce and copper fasten it so that you don't go back. Take a holiday, or buy a new set of golf clubs with the money you have saved through quitting smoking!

The same applies to managing change in the workplace. Typical scenarios would be moving to a new location, or changing to a new performance management system. The more thought and planning you put in to the change project and the stages of change, the more likely it is that the change will happen smoothly.

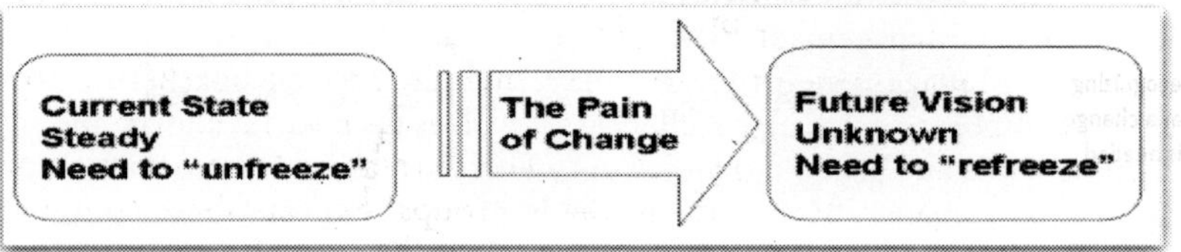

Recognise the Context of Change

When considering what is change management in the workplace, here are some of the factors that influence the need for change:

1. **Demographics**—e.g. an ageing workforce puts a focus on pensions
2. **Competition**—e.g cheap labour elsewhere forces a rethink on payscales
3. **Technology**—e.g. calls for fast turnarounds in some product lines
4. **Legal/Political**—e.g. change may be a legal requirement
5. **Economics**—e.g. increases in indirect taxation change consumer spending levels

Factors can be transient, many and varied and may not always be clearly identifiable. Think about the factors influencing your change project and their significance.

If you want to manage change, you need to ask the following questions:

WHAT is to change? WHERE will this happen? WHEN will this happen? WHO will be affected? HOW will this be done?

Successful change is about communication through questions, at every stage.

Context of Change

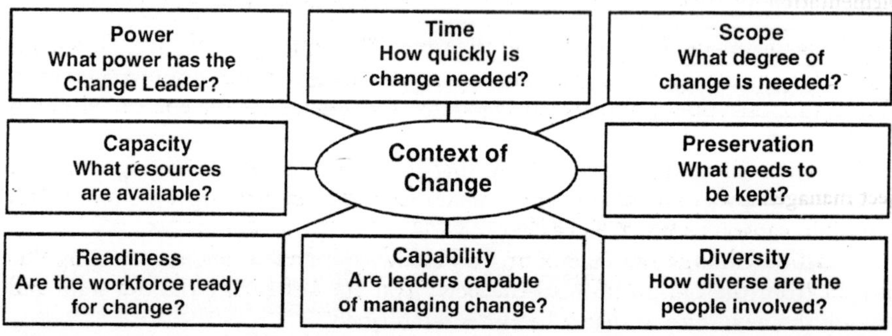

Introducing a Taxonomy

The schematic below presents a taxonomy that can serve as a **discussion framework** for the key **phases** or **elements** of implementing a change within an organization, beginning with the recognition that a change is needed and ending with the realization of the desired benefits sought by the effort.

Prosci's Taxonomy for Scoping Change Management

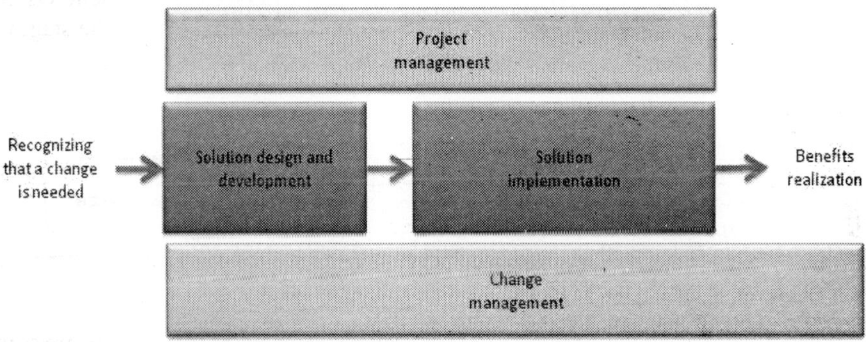

Element	*Objective*	*Examples*
Recognizing that a change is needed	To identify the internal or external stimulus resulting in a need for change	• Internal performance • Customer inputs • Competitive threats • Financial results • New business opportunities • Regulatory changes • Strategic planning
Solution design and development	To create a solution to improve the performance of the organization based on the recognition that a change is needed	• Vision and strategy development • Process design/BPR • New technology • Restructuring • Merger/Acquisition • OD interventions • New product offering • New service offering
Solution implementation	To install a solution that meets technical requirements and is adopted and utilized	• Pilots and trials • Systems and tools deployment • New process implementation • Transition to new organization structure and job roles • Implementation of compensation, appraisal or incentive programs
Project management	To manage the tasks, resources, budget, time and scope of technical design and implementation	• Project planning • Schedule development and tracking • Resource management • Budget development and control • Issue tracking • Project oversight

		• Project reporting
Change management	To encourage employees to rapidly, completely and proficiently make the required changes to their day-to-day work	• Readiness assessments • Change portfolio management • Change saturation analysis • Employee engagement • Change management strategy • Change management planning • Change sponsorship • Communications during change • Training new skills and abilities • Coaching employees through transitions • Resistance management • Performance measurement

Why it is Important to Establish Scope

As with any discipline or methodology—it is important to establish the scope of change management. Boundaries are important to establish what activities fall under the change management umbrella and what work runs **in parallel or conjunction** with change management. Benefits of establishing a clear scope include:

- Dividing work and avoiding overlap between disciplines
- Ensuring that all key elements are addressed
- Showing the relationship between existing techniques and approaches
- Defining the skills and competencies to perform work effectively in a given area

In addition, there is an inherent risk of not clearly establishing scope. It becomes very easy for one group or function to believe that they are responsible for work that falls under the work responsibilities of another group—resulting in **confusion** and **ineffective work steams.** For example, imagine the confusion that would result in developing a new product if there was not a clear distinction between software development, hardware development, physical design and system test. The specific skills and competencies needed to develop software are very different from the skills need to design circuit boards or the physical housing for a product. In the same way, the skills and competencies for project management are specific and very different from change management. Understanding the scope and boundaries enables both functions to work effectively together, and to avoid any overlap of activities that may create conflicts for the project. The boundaries also enable the separation of solution design, development and implementation from the actions required to manage the technical side and people side of that solution's deployment.

THEORIES OF MANAGEMENT OF CHANGE

Models of Change

There are a number of **theoretical** models of change. Each attempts to describe the process through which organizations successfully alter their business practices, their organizational structure, or their organizational climate. The models of change which will be discusses in this section are summarized in Exhibit 1.

Lewin's Three-step Model for Change

In the late 1940s **social psychologist Kurt Lewin** developed a three-step model for implementing change based on the concept of force field analysis. Force field analysis addresses the driving and resisting forces in a change situation. Driving forces must outweigh resisting forces in a situation if change is to occur. Thus, managers must be willing to advocate change strongly in order to overcome resistance from employees.

There are three steps in Lewin's model. The first step is "unfreezing," which involves dismantling those.

A wide variety of forces make organizations resistant to change, and a wide variety of forces push organizations toward change. Researcher Kurt Lewin developed a theory about organizational change. According to his force-field theory, these two sets of forces are always in opposition in an organization.

When the forces are evenly balanced, the organization is in a state of inertia and does not change. To get an organization to change, the managers must find a way to increase the forces for change, reduce **resistance to change**, or do both simultaneously. Any of these strategies will overcome inertia and **cause an organization to change.**

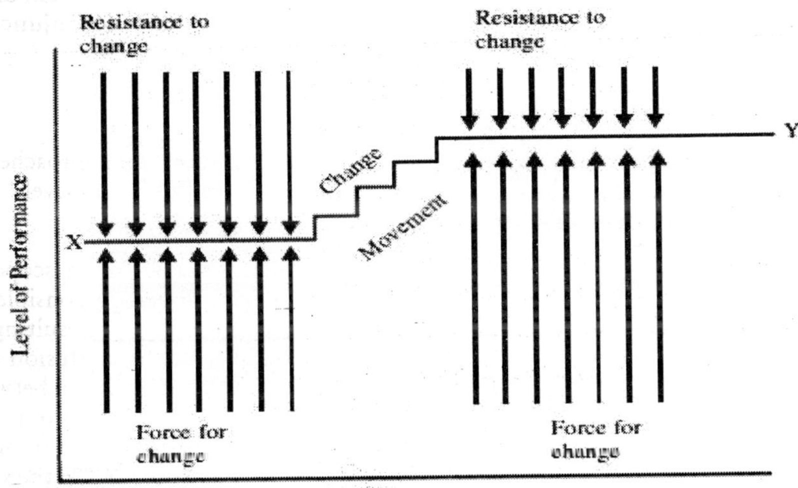

An organization at performance level X is in balance. Forces for change and resistance to change are equal. Management, however, decides that the organization should strive to achieve performance level Y. To get to level Y, the managers must increase the forces for change (the increase is represented by the lengthening of the up arrows), reduce resistance to change (the reduction is represented by the shortening of the down arrows), or do both. If they pursue any of the three strategies successfully, the organization will change and reach performance level Y. Kurt Lewin, whose Force-Field theory argues that organizations are balanced between forces for change and resistance to change, has a related perspective on how managers can bring change to their organization.

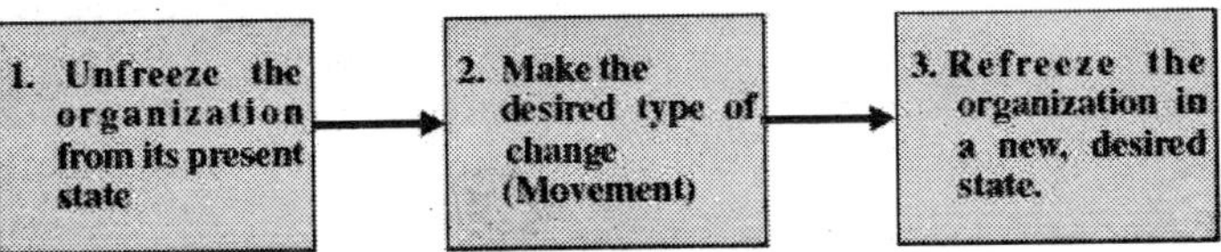

In Lewin's view, implementing change is a three-step process : (1) unfreezing the organization from its present state, (2) making the change, or movement, and (3) refreezing the organization in the new, desired state so that its members do not revert to their previous work attitudes and role behaviors.

Lewin (1951)	Nadler (1998)	Beer et al (1990)	Kotter (1996)
Unfreeze	1. Recognise the change imperative	1. Commitment to change through joint diagnosis of business problems	1. Establishing a Sense of Urgency 2. Creating a Guiding Coalition
Move	2. Develop a shared direction	2. Develop shared vision	3. Developing a Vision and Strategy
		3. Consensus, competence to enact and cohesion around new vision	4. Communicating the Change Vision 5. Empowering Employees for broad-based action
	3. Implement change	4. Spread through all departments without push from the top	6. Generating Short-Term Wins 7. Consolidating Gains and Producing more Change
Refreeze	4. Consolidate change	5. Institutionalise through formal policies etc	8. Anchoring New Approaches in the Culture
	5. Sustain change	6. Monitor & adjust in response to problems	

Kotter's Eight Step Model of Change

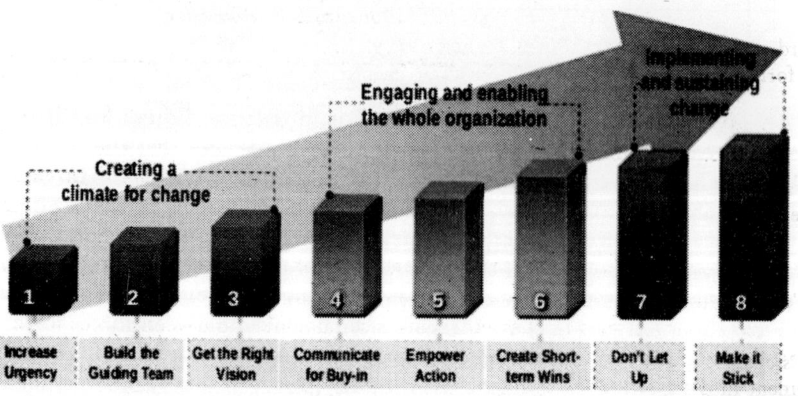

Probably one of the most well known and respected change models is from the Harvard Business School article and later book by **John Kotter—"Leading Change"**. He later followed this with **"The Heart of Change"** and lastly his modern fable **"Our Iceberg is Melting"** which uses a group of penguins to illustrate the change process.

Many have written about the Kotter model, including a very good series of three articles on **Martin Webster's blog.** Another good reference to this model can be found on the **Change Management Blog.**

To summarise the key aspects of Kotter's model:

Creating a Climate for Change—helping the organisation to see the reasons for change, painting the picture of the "burning platform", developing a sense of urgency, gaining commitment from senior leadership and key players, and finally developing a shared vision for the future.

Engaging and Enabling the Whole Organisation—moving the whole organisation towards the new reality, communicating the vision and empowering action. Creating opportunities for short term wins along the way will help the organisation to visualize progress and maintain momentum.

Implementing and Sustaining Change keep pushing the change forward, not letting up and finally anchoring the change into the organisation, including changing HR policies things that support or maintain the previous behavior. In an organization, these elements of the old could be the compensation system or the

Exhibit I

Models of Change

Model/Approach	*Summary*
Lewin's three-step model	Old activities must be unfrozen, a new concept introduced, then new activities must be frozen
Bullock and Batten's planned change	Exploration, planning, action, and integration
Kotter's eight steps	Establish a sense of urgency, form a powerful guiding coalition, create a vision, communicate the vision, empower others to act on the vision, plan for and create short-term wins, consolidate improvements and produce still more change, institutionalize new approaches
Beckhard and Harris's change formula	$C = [ABD] > X$, Where C = change, A = level of dissatisfaction with the status quo, B = Desirability of the proposed change or end state, D = practicality of the change, and X = cost of changing
Nadler and Tushman's congruence model	Organization is a system that draws inputs from internal and external sources and transforms them into outputs through four components: the work itself, the people, the informal organization, and the formal organization
Bridges's managing the transition	Transition, which differs from change, consists of three phases: ending, neutral zone, and new beginning
Carnall's change management model	Change depends on level of management skills in managing transitions effectively, dealing with organizational cultures, and managing organizational politics
Senge et al.'s systematic model	Start small; grow steadily; don't plan everything; expect challenges
Stacey and Shaw's complex responsive process	Change emerges naturally from communication and conflict; and managers are a part of the whole environment

approach to performance management. In the second step, the organization "presents a new alternative." This means introducing a clear and appealing option for a new pattern of behavior. The final step in this model is "freezing" which requires that changed behavior be reinforced both formally and informally in the organization. It is in this step that managers can have a great amount of influence through their use of positive reinforcement.

Lewin's model does not explicitly state the notion that simply introducing change will result in the change being adopted or being sustained over the long run. If an attempt to create change in the organization is unsuccessful, it means that there is a problem in one of the three steps in the model.

Bullock and Batten's Phases of Planned Change

R.J. Bullock and D. Batten derived their ideas from project management and they recommend using **exploration**, planning, action, and integration for planned change. Exploration occurs when managers confirm the need for change and secure resources needed for it. These resources may be physical or they may be mental, such as managers' expertise. The next step, planning, occurs when key decision makers and experts create a change plan that they then review and approve. Next, action occurs with enactment of the plan. There should be opportunities for feedback during the action phase. Finally, integration begins when all actions in the change plan have taken place. Integration occurs when the changes have been aligned with the organization and there is some degree of formalization, such as through policies and procedures in the organization.

Kotter's Eight Steps

John P. Kotter identified eight steps every organization must follow in order to reap long-term benefits from organizational change: establish a sense of urgency; form a powerful guiding coalition; create a vision and strategy; communicate the vision; empower others to act on the vision; generate short-term wins; consolidate improvements and produce still more change; and institutionalize the new approach (i.e., make it a part of the organizational culture).

The first step, establishing a sense of urgency, involves selling the need for change to managers and employees. Kotter recommends creating a "felt-need" for change in others. The second step is for managers to create a powerful group of people who can work together to enact change. Their power will be a driving force in encourages others to adopt change. Third, the organization must have a vision that will guide the entirety of the change effort, and this vision must be communicated repeatedly (step four)—as much as ten times as often as one would expect to.

Steps five through eight occur after the sense of urgency is created, and these steps are easier to delegate or decentralize. In step five, others in the organization are empowered to act on the vision. Managers should assist in this process by eliminating barriers such as old systems or structures. Step six asks managers to plan for and to create short-term wins. This means that small improvements should be recognized and celebrated publicly. In step seven, the current improvements are built upon with new projects and resources. Finally, in step eight, the new approaches should be institutionalized; that is, they should become a routine path to organizational success.

Beckhard and Harris's Change Formula

The change formula is a **mathematical** representation of the change process (see Exhibit 1). The basic notion is that, for change to occur, the costs of change (*X*) must be outweighed by dissatisfaction with the status quo (*A*), the desirability of the proposed change (*B*), and the practicality of the change (*D*). There will be resistance to change if people are not dissatisfied with the current state of the organization (*A*), or if the changes are not seen as an improvement (*B*), if the change cannot be done in a feasible way (*D*), or the cost is far too high (*X*).

This formula can also be conceptualized as $(A \times B \times D) > X$. The multiplicative nature of this formula indicates that if any variable is zero or near zero, resistance to change will not be overcome. In other words, the variables of *A*, *B*, and *D* do not compensate for one another, and when one is very low, the cost of change is likely to be too high.

Nadler and Tushman's Congruence Model

Nadler and Tushman's model presents the dynamics of what occurs in an organization when we try to change it. The foundation of this model is that of the organization as an open system, in which organizational subsystems are influence by the external environment. The organizational system draws inputs from internal and external sources—such as the organization's own strategy, its resources, and its environment—and transforms them into outputs, such as behavior and performance. This transformation from inputs to outputs occurs through four organizational elements: the work, the people, and the formal and informal organization. The work involves the daily activities carried out by individuals in the organization. The skills and capabilities of the people involved in the organization are critical. The formal organization is characterized by its structure, its standard procedures, and its policies. The informal organization encompasses things such as norms, values, and political behavior.

In this model, effective change occurs when all four components (work, people, formal, and informal organization) are managed, because they are all interrelated. A change in the work procedures themselves may not be effective if the people do not have the capabilities to engage in the new practices. A change to the formal organization may not be effective if the beliefs and values of people (i.e., the informal organization) do not support it. If there is a lack of **congruence** among these four elements, then there is resistance to change. Furthermore, there may be control issues in which there is confusion over who regulates the new structures and processes. Finally, power problems may occur as managers and employees feel threatened that their current power may be removed by the change.

William Bridges's Managing the Transition

William Bridges distinguished planned change from transition. He believes that transition is more complex because it requires abandoning old practices and adopting new behaviors or ways of thinking, whereas planned change is about changing physical locations or organizational structures. Bridges believes that transition often lags behind planned change because it is more complex and more difficult to achieve. Because it is psychological, it is harder to manage.

Bridges describes three phases of transition: ending, neutral zone, and new beginning. Ending is similar to Lewin's concept of unfreezing in that you must end a current situation before you can begin something new. So, in this phase, old structures, practices, and behaviors must be stopped. Ideally, this ending can be commemorated or marked in some way. In the second phase, the neutral zone, the old practices have been stopped, but new ones have not yet been adopted. In this phase, many employees will feel disoriented and anxious; nevertheless, it may be a time in which creativity rises. Finally, new beginnings are not planned and predicted, but must evolve as organizational members psychologically adjust to transition. Managers can encourage, support, and reinforce these new beginnings. Bridges recommends that four key elements be communicated to people during a new beginning: the purpose behind the change; a picture of how the organization will be after the change; a step-by-step plan to get to that stage; and the part they can play in that outcome.

Carnall's Change Management Model

Carnall's view of change is focused on managers and the skills they can use to manage change. Carnall describes three skills that must be present at all levels of management: (1) managing transitions effectively; (2) dealing with organizational cultures; and (3) managing organizational politics. Managing transitions involves helping employees learn as they change and supporting a culture of openness and risk-taking. Managing organizational cultures involves creating a "more adaptable culture." This is an organizational culture in which people are more open, there is greater information flow, and perhaps greater autonomy. Finally, to manage organizational politics, the manager should recognize and understand different organizational groups and their political agendas. The manager should be able to build coalitions and control the agenda through his or her political skill.

Senge's Systemic Model

Senge and colleagues encourage managers to think like biologists when approaching organizational change. That is, to better understand how organizations react to change, one should view them as systems bound by many interrelated actions that may affect each other over a long period of time. To enact change, Senge *et al.* recommend that managers start small, grow steadily, do not plan the whole thing, and expect challenges. Furthermore, Senge et al offer a number of issues related to the challenges of first initiating change, then sustaining that change, and finally redesigning and rethinking change.

CHANGE MANAGERS

In both proactive and reactive responses to change and in every model of change, one element remains the same: the need for change managers. There are different types of change managers and their roles encompass a variety of duties. Managers may have responsibility for change that is not ever formally dictated or outlined, or a person or group may be specifically chosen to enact or facilitate change. Described below are two formal ways in which change managers can be identified: transition management teams and change agents. Some responsibilities of change managers are then described.

Transition Management Teams

In some organizations that are experiencing change, a specific group of managers is chosen to coordinate change throughout an organization. This transition management team typically consists of eight to twelve people whose full-time responsibilities are to manage and facilitate the change process in the organization. Transition management teams are responsible not only for the structural and procedural changes that occur, but also for managing emotions and resistance to change. These teams typically report to the chief executive officer of the company on a regular basis.

Transition management teams do the day-to-day work involved in change management, and they are not simply another layer of management between top management and line employees. Furthermore, they are not the planning committee; these teams do not develop the plans for the change, they only facilitate the change that is being enacted. Neither are they responsible for determining when and where change is needed, or how it will be brought about. Instead, they manage changes that have been identified and implemented by upper management. Finally, these teams are not permanent. They exist only while the organization is in flux, and they are dissolved once the company has successfully changed.

Change Agents

A change agent is one person who is formally in charge of guiding a change effort. The change agent is typically a part of organizational development, which is a set of planned change interventions intended to improve a company's long-term performance and survival. A change agent may be appointed from within the ranks of current company managers, or the agent may be an outside consultant who is brought in during the period of change. Unlike the transition management team, which only facilitates a change that has been identified and planned by others, the change agent is involved in all steps of organizational change. The agent helps to clarify problems, gather relevant information, assist managers in creating a plan, evaluate the plan's effectiveness, and implement the plan. After change has been successfully enacted, the change agent either returns to his or her normal duties (if this person is from within the organization), or ends his or her work with the company (if this person is a consultant).

There are advantages and disadvantages to choosing either an organizational member or an outside consultant to be a change agent. Outside consultants can be more costly and there is a greater risk for trade secrets to be leaked. Additionally, the consultant is unlikely to have the knowledge of the organization that an employee has, nor is this person likely to be trusted by others in the organization, as they would trust one of their own organizational members. However, consultants do have a more unbiased view of the organization and its problems. They may also bring more innovative or creative ideas to the company. Finally, they may be used as a scapegoat when change is implemented. That is, the negative emotions of organizational members may be directed towards the outsider rather than at the company's management, which may make for a smoother transition during the change process.

Responsibilities of Change Managers

Change managers are responsible for garnering support for change and overcoming resistance to change. There are ten techniques that change managers can use to accomplish this:

1. **Plan well.** Appropriate time and effort must go into planning change before implementation begins.
2. **Allow for discussion and negotiation.** Employees must have some input into the changes. This two-way communication can help reduce employee concerns.

3. **Allow for participation.** If employees participate in changes that affect them, they are more likely to support those changes.
4. **Emphasize the financial benefits.** If employees can earn higher compensation through organizational change, telling them about this possibility will help to increase support for the change.
5. **Avoid too much change.** Employees can only handle a certain amount of change before there are negative repercussions from stress, so changes should be introduced slowly and over time.
6. **Gain political support.** For change to be successful, certain key employees (those with informal power in the organization) must support it.
7. **Let employees see successful change.** Employees will be more willing to support change if they see that it has worked successfully in other companies or other areas of their company.
8. **Reduce uncertainty.** Uncertainty about the change effort can cause negative emotions and actions, and any information that change managers can give to reduce uncertainty can reduce resistance to change.
9. **Ask questions to involve workers.** Change managers should ask workers questions that move them toward a goal or objective or that reinforce positive accomplishments.
10. **Build strong working relationships.** Better working relationships in general will aid in change management; trust and mutual respect are critical elements of good working relationships.

Managing change can be a reactive or a proactive process, and there are a number of different models of organizational change. Each model emphasizes different approaches to understanding and managing change. In many of these models, the role of the change manager is emphasized. The change manager may be a part of a transitional management team or may be a change agent. This person facilitates the changes to the organization and is often a critical element in the success or failure of the change.

To effectively lead change, you must recognize that the phenomenon of "change" does not need managing as much as do the people involved with it.

There is a lot to learn about the human relationship to change. Just as the nature of change varies, so do the human responses and reactions to it. Some people seem confused and confounded by change and unpredictability, and do their best to avoid it. Others find the prospect of uncertainty invigorating, often seeking out situations that promise opportunities for new adventures and exploration.

You can see this difference in how people experience things in the way two people will describe the same event. What is exciting to one may be a major crisis to another.

The ancient Chinese seem to have understood this paradox of perspective well, as the character for the word *crisis* is a combination of the characters for the words *danger* and *opportunity*. Likewise, people relate to change in unique, varied, and sometimes unpredictable ways.

While people may feel differently about change in general, when it comes to change in the workplace, research shows that most people are open to it—an astounding 78 percent in fact. That's according to research of more than 5,000 mid-to-upper level managers. The bad news is that most of those managers and executives don't know how to effectively lead others through that change.

The good news is, they (and you) can learn. In fact, through increased awareness of your own and others' differing change styles and preferences, you can help your company do more than just handle change — you can create an organization that lives it.

Don't confuse change style with change competency

Often the discussion on change revolves around simplistic ideologies that label some people as "pro-change" and others as "change resistors." Predictably, the pro-change forces are seen as good and the resistors as the evil enemies of progress.

The problem with this thinking is that the people who frame these arguments have their own unique attitudes, beliefs and preferences about change. The fact that the pro-change person may lead his/her organization into a disaster or that the resistor may present very reasonable objections is often overlooked. In other words, personal change styles are often confused with change competency.

Understanding change styles

Research indicates that people have different habits and preferences when faced with change. If you can recognize these differences in yourself and others, and address them when communicating and implementing change, you are much more likely to face fewer misunderstandings, complaints and saboteurs along the way.

In the effort to help organizations recognize these differences, Discovery Learning Inc. has taken the aggregate results from 150,000 change-style assessments performed using the Change Style Indicator and grouped people into three categories according to the way they deal with change: Conservers, Pragmatists and Originators.

On the far left side of the change preference continuum, you'll find the Conservers. Conservers prefer to work within the existing structure to create change incrementally. When facing change, Conservers appear deliberate, disciplined and organized. They prefer change that maintains the current structure. They honor tradition and established practices and usually operate from conventional assumptions. Conservers enjoy predictability so they may appear cautious and inflexible.

In the middle of the continuum you'll find the Pragmatists. Pragmatists deal in outcomes and seek practical, functional solutions to problems. When facing change, Pragmatists appear practical, agreeable and flexible. They often operate as mediators and catalysts for understanding and are open to both sides of an argument. They may take more of a middle-of-the-road approach and often appear more team-oriented.

To the far right are the Originators. (Here is where you'll find most entrepreneurial types.) Originators sometimes favor something that's different just because it's different. When facing change, Originators may appear unorganized, undisciplined, unconventional and spontaneous. They prefer change that challenges current structure and are likely to challenge accepted assumptions. Originators enjoy risk and uncertainty. While they may appear as visionary and systemic in their thinking, they can also be impractical and miss important details and often treat accepted policies and procedures with little regard.

These descriptions make it easy to see how all three change styles are necessary when leading and accomplishing change within an organization. The key to making these styles work best for your organization is to know your own change style preference and understand how that dictates the way you should interact with people with similar and different preferences.

For example, if you are an Originator (many entrepreneurs are) you might be perceived by others as impulsive and unfocused. If your colleague is a Conserver, you may view him as too cautious or as inflexible. If your direct report is a Pragmatist you might view her as indecisive. And while she might understand your point of view, she may feel that you're too risky in certain situations.

And just in case three change styles wasn't enough to consider, there are a couple of other players you also should be aware of: change agents and resisters.

Change agents are often consultants who come in from the outside and without really understanding your company's culture or needs, try to impose the changes they think you need. Change agents can also be overenthusiastic members of your own organization who, just like their external counterparts, run the risk of alienating the very people necessary to make the change work.

Resisters, on the other hand, are often seen as people who don't care about the company's success. It's important to remember however, that often the biggest objections to change come from the people most devoted to the company. Hearing and acting on the concerns voiced by resisters may help you head off problems you hadn't anticipated. Being able to tell the difference between hardcore resisters who will fight any change no matter what and the concerned employees described here is crucial. If you treat every skeptic as a hardcore resister, you risk encouraging alliances between these two groups that could further stall needed changes.

CHANGE PROCESSES

There are two types of change in an organization: planned change and "emergent" change. Planned change refers to initiatives that are driven "top-down" in an organization, while "emergent" change refers to a situation in which change can originate from any level in the organization.

The role of the leader is critical in both types of change. In a planned change initiative, the leader must have a clear vision and a plan that both involves people in the change and ensures there is a support infrastructure for the change. In an "emergent" change, the leader must create and foster a "readiness for change" culture—a culture that encourages and supports change that comes from "within" the organization.

The Role of the Leader in Planned Change

The leadership "hat" in planned change is a critical one to wear that includes two crucial responsibilities:

Communicating the vision for the change.
Establishing the support elements necessary for the change to be successful.
The Vision for Change.

As we've presented in our previous leadership articles, the role of the leader in any organization is to set direction and inspire others to attain the goal. In the case of a change initiative, the leader must first be able to describe what the future will look like after the change. It is important for the leader to find a way to communicate the vision for the change in a way that will inspire people to act. The leader's challenge is to communicate the change in positive terms so that people can rally around the vision for the future.

After the leader has determined a positive vision for the future, the next step is to successfully communicate that vision to all levels of the organization. There is a large difference between crafting a vision for the change, and communicating it effectively. One common problem most organizations face is there is not enough time spent communicating the vision for change. In his book, Leading Change (1996), John Kotter dramatically points out that the average leader under-communicates the vision by a huge factor. This means that any change initiative should have a good, formal communication plan in place before the change initiative begins.

When communicating the vision of the future, be sure to summarize the following points in the vision itself:

- Things that will stay the same
- Things that will be left behind
- New things that we will have that we've never had before

The leader is not only the chief spokesperson for the change vision, but also must ensure that all levels of the organization understand the rationale for the change and how we are going to go about implementing the change. The five critical elements that must be communicated to ensure understanding and awareness include:

- What is the change?
- Why are we doing it?
- How are we going to go about it?
- How long will it take us to do it?
- What will the role be for each department and each individual?

Establishing the Support Elements

The second responsibility for a leader of planned change is to ensure that the support elements that are necessary for the change to be successful have been installed. For most significant change initiatives, those support elements include the following:

A Realistic Project Plan

The leader ensures that a step by step plan, usually entered into a project management software program, as well as a risk analysis and business case analysis have been produced in the planning phase.

An organization structure for managing the change

The leader must ensure the structure for implementing and managing the change is installed. The leader should establish a system that solicits involvement and ownership of key stakeholders. Typically, the organizational structure for doing so consists of a team approach. For large change projects, such as implementing an enterprise-wide software package, it is not unusual to have a cross-functional steering team, a sponsor, a project leader, and sub-teams, as needed.

Internal change agents

The leader identifies and orients a coalition of internal change agents. These agents will act as facilitators and "cheerleaders" of the change.

A formal communication plan

The leader creates a formal communications plan for the life of the change initiative. First, all key stakeholders must be identified. Then, for each stakeholder the leader develops the types of information necessary, the frequency of the information, the method of communication, and the responsible party for carrying out the communication.

A formal training plan

The leader identifies the new skills or training necessary for the change to be successful and establishes a formal training program to fulfill those goals. Often key stakeholders will need new skills in either bringing about the change or in operating in the new environment once the change is completed.

Barrier removal

The leader makes a concerted effort to first identify barriers in the environment that will inhibit or prevent the change, and then develops action steps to systematically remove the barriers. Barriers can include staffing (not enough people or release time to carry out the change), lack of budget, lack of management support, competing initiatives, etc.

A supportive and aligned management group

In many change efforts there is lack of alignment and support among the management group, which hinders the change process. The leader's first responsibility is to ensure that his/her management team presents a united front about the change. Often the leader will insist that successful change performance is tied to the performance management system of the organization.

A system of periodic audits and feedback

In order to map progress against the change goals, as well as to help institutionalize the change, the leader must install an audit process, as she/he would for quality, customer service, or employee satisfaction purposes. Psychologically, it is important to build in a "quick win" or a "quick success" to help build momentum for the change.

Overcoming Resistance to Change

Through our years of working with organizations to implement change, we have found when we ask management groups the question—"Do people resist change?"—we usually get an immediate and resounding "YES." We have found that if the leader paints and effectively communicates a positive vision and establishes the support elements listed above, resistance to change can be minimized.

One quick and easy model we use to help remember how to manage through change is the USEM" model. The USEM" model is actually a generalized performance model that can be applied to several types of organization situations. The following segment shows how this model can be applied to a change initiative.

To maximize a positive response to change you must have the following USEM" parameters in place:

U = people must understand what we're doing and why
S = people must have the knowledge and skills necessary to execute the change
E = we must remove barriers in the environment that will prevent the change from being successful
M = people must have motivation to change, i.e., they must want to help achieve the change

If the organization does a good job of putting in place the U, S, and E parameters, it is our experience that the motivation will follow. In other words, if people have the Understanding, Skills and proper Environment without barriers, then this will go a long way towards solving motivation and resistance issues.

The eight support elements listed above directly correlate with the USEM" model. The first six elements address the U, S, and E factors, while the last two parameters directly influence the Motivation parameter.

Leading change in an organization can be a risk, but when the leader creates and communicates a positive vision and establishes the necessary support elements described in this article, the components of the USEM" model are thus fulfilled, and a change initiative is less likely to experience resistance. Taking on the role of leading change in your organization is a step towards becoming a leader. Stay tuned for the next issue of Impact, where we will explore the Leadership Role of Leading Change in the Organization, Part II: Leading a "Readiness for Change" Culture.

To effectively lead change, you must recognize that the "change" itself does not need managing as much as do the people involved with it. In order to successfully manage and lead people through any size change, it helps to be aware of the different ways people prefer to deal with change; and to realize that your perceptions of the change styles of others are colored by your own.

When everyone in the organization becomes more aware of their own and others preferences when dealing with change, understanding and acceptance of differences overall will increases across the entire organization. This resulting acceptance and valuing of differences is what separates dynamic organizations that "live" change from organizations that simply react to change to try and stay competitive.

*The Change Styles Survey, conducted by Discovery Learning between 1996 and 2001 on over 5,000 mid-to-upper managers, placed respondents on a continuum between "Conserver" and "Originator," with "Pragmatist" in between. Not surprisingly, most individuals are a blend of Conserver-Pragmatist or Pragmatist-Originator. Of the entire population surveyed, 51 percent of managers (57 percent were men and 43 percent were women) scored in the pragmatist range, 26 percent in the originator range and 23 percent in the conserver range.

MANAGING RESISTANCE TO CHANGE

Any new process is bound to meet some degree of resistance. Overcoming it is critical to the successful implementation of lean Six Sigma process improvements. Resistance can cause unnecessary delays, waste and process performance that falls short. As a result, implementation efforts should include strategies to diffuse resistance.

Common Forms of Resistance

Resistance typically arises from fear and a lack of understanding. It can appear in several forms, but the more common tactics include:

Ignoring the new process
Failing to comprehend the process
Challenging the validity of the process' benefits
Criticizing the process tools
Allowing exceptions
Sabotaging or delaying process implementation
Strategies for Dealing with Resistance

Ignoring the new process—There is some truth to this resistance tactic. Lean Six Sigma process improvements cannot succeed if they are not actively adopted. Process improvements must be impossible to ignore. Implementation leaders would do well to base employee reviews and other established processes whose outcome holds value to employees to successful implementation.

Failing to comprehend the process—Effective training is key to the successful adoption of lean Six Sigma process improvements. Training efforts should include clarified communication efforts, one-on-one sessions, and checklists. Methods should offer guidance and simplify adoption of the process as much as possible.

Challenging the validity of the process' benefits—Proven results speak the loudest. Before introducing new processes, research other companies or departments that have had success with their attempts to bring about lean Six Sigma quality improvements.

Criticizing the process tools—The best way to diffuse resistance to using applications or tools in support of a process is to provide a feedback mechanism for enhancements. Allowing employees the opportunity to offer suggestions yields better working applications and less reluctance to use them.

Granting exceptions—The quickest way to develop variation within a process is to allow exceptions. Moreover, once an exception is made, there is a tendency for more to follow, to the point that the process quickly becomes diluted. A policy that makes no exceptions is the best preventative measure.

Sabotaging or delaying process implementation—A common tactic in the face of change is to attempt to delay implementation efforts, claiming the timing is not right. The reality is that internal and external forces will always compete with the improvement process. The sooner implementation occurs, the sooner quality increases, waste is reduced and the benefits of lean Six Sigma operation can be realized.

It is normal to experience resistance whenever there is change. Understanding that there will be **resistance to change** will help you anticipate resistance, identify its sources and reasons, and modify your efforts to manage the issues of change to ensure the success of your **change** efforts.

Resistance is actually healthy. Try not to react against it defensively. It is good for you because it makes you check your assumptions and it forces you to clarify what you are doing. You must always probe the objections to find the real reason for resistance. Many times, it comes down to personal fear.

As the leader, you must take the time to understand resistance and you may have to come at it from several different angles before it is conquered. You must understand what your employees are feeling, as well as thinking.

Ways to Reduce Resistance to Change

Involve interested parties in the planning of change by asking them for suggestions and incorporating their ideas.

Clearly define the need for the change by communicating the strategic decision personally and in written form.

Address the "people needs" of those involved. Disrupt only what needs to be changed. Help people retain friendships, comfortable settings and group norms wherever possible.

Design flexibility into change by phasing it in wherever possible. This will allow people to complete current efforts and assimilate new behaviours along the way. Allow employees to redefine their roles during the course of implementing change.

Consider Methods for Managing Resistance

Method	*How to Use*	*When to Use*	*Advantages*	*Drawbacks*
Education	Communicate the desired changes and reasons for them	Employees lack information about the change's implications	Once persuaded, people often help implement the change	Time consuming if lots of people are involved
Participation	Involve potential resisters in designing and implementing the change	Change initiators lack sufficient information to design the change	People feel more committed to making the change happen	Time consuming, and employees may design inappropriate change
Facilitation	Provide skills training and emotional support	People are resisting because they fear they can't make the needed adjustments	No other approach works as well with adjustment problems	Can be time consuming and expensive; can still fail
Negotiation	Offer incentives for making the change	people will lose out in the change and have considerable power to resist	It's relatively easy way to defuse major resistance	Can be expensive and open managers to the possibility of blackmail
Coercion	Threaten loss of jobs of promotion opportnities; fue or transfer those who can't or won't change	Speed is essential and change initiators posses considerable power	It works quickly and can overcome any kind of resistance	Can spark intense resentment towards change initiators

Be Open and Honest

Do not leave openings for people to return to the *status quo*. If you and your organization are not ready to commit yourselves to the change, don't announce the strategy.

Focus continually on the positive aspects of the change. Be specific where you can.

Deliver training programs that develop basic skills as opposed to processes such as: conducting meetings, communication, team-building, self-esteem, and coaching.

STRATEGIES TO DECREASE RESISTANCE TO CHANGE IN THE WORKPLACE

When it comes to change in the workplace, you might find that even your most loyal and steadfast employees put up resistance. Tried-and-true strategies combat this resistance and ensure employees that while things may be changing, you are just as committed to their overall success as ever before. This kind of reassurance may get them to go along with a new program a bit easier than they have in the past.

Open Conversation

One of the best ways to get your employees to stop resisting change is to simply talk to them about it. Give as much information as you can about the changes and allow them to have an open forum to give feedback. Perhaps you will take some it into account and other feedback will simply be heard so the employees can express themselves, but they may stop resisting as much if they feel as though they've been heard.

Employees' Participating

If you are making major changes in company processes or policies, allow employees to have input on the changes. This is different from simply allowing them to express their thoughts or feelings on changes already taking place; this process is a bit more proactive, allowing employees to actually influence the changes with their own ideas, brainstorms and creative approaches.

Offer Resources

When a change occurs, one of the biggest gripes among employees is that they are unprepared to handle the changes. Provide training classes, equipment and any other resources to not only help them adapt, but also to excel in the changed environment. Help them in any way you can to be more efficient and effective employees before, during and after the changes take place. They may not only stop resisting, but actually feel encouraged and hopeful anytime thereafter that you make changes.

Timing

Timing is everything when it comes to change, and if you try to implement major changes all at once or too quickly, your employees may be more likely to resist. Introduce change in measured doses when possible, to give staff a chance to get used to whatever changes you've made. Not only does this ensure the least amount of interruption to your products or services, but also it makes for a happier — and thereby more productive—staff.

CHANGE PRONENESS : ATTITUDE TOWARDS CHANGE

Changing Employees' Attitudes is Key to Effective Organizations

A landmark study finds that employees' emotions about work can adversely affect organizational success. In its study on work and human emotion, HR consulting giant, Towers Perrin and its research partner, Gang & Gang, found that more than half of the 1,100 North American workers they surveyed had "negative" emotions about their work, while nearly a third had "intensely negative" emotions about their work.

The study, Working Today: Exploring Employees' Emotional Connection to Their Jobs, completed earlier this year, noted that workers' negative emotions adversely affect productivity, profitability, performance, and retention, key factors in organizational success.

In a surprising discovery, researchers cited that among the intensely negative group, a full quarter of the workers planned to remain with their current employer. Their conclusion implies that workers may be just "hanging on" to their present jobs without being engaged in, or by, their work, and that they may be only moderately engaged in their work. The implication is clear: workers who are not fully committed to their work may be hampering organizational success.

Another conclusion that impacts organizations, researchers concluded that disengaged employees may adversely affect co-workers with their negative attitudes. Changing employees' attitudes

With such dour news on the workfront, how can managers change employees' attitudes from negative to positive, and enhance organizational success? What are the factors that influence positive attitudes and increase worker engagement? First, workplace leaders must understand some of the underlying elements that may create emotionally distant workers. Researchers in the study reported that five elements contributed to most of the workers' negativity, including:

- excessive workload;
- concerns about leadership effectiveness;
- anxiety about job and financial security;
- lack of challenging work, boredom, frustration; and
- insufficient recognition.

Negative emotions stemming from these factors spell trouble for employers, especially regarding retention. The study found that among the intensely negative group, nearly 30 percent were actively looking for new jobs, as opposed to only 6 percent of workers, who had positive emotions about work. In the study, workers were asked to describe what their ideal work experience would entail. Their answers focused on the following elements:

- having a sense of self-worth—having confidence, feeling competent and in control of their work and work experience;
- seeing results—the contributions workers make in helping their organizations succeed; and
- being rewarded and recognized—knowing that their contributions are recognized and compensated.

Knowing some of the factors that cause employees to be emotionally distant from their work, as well as some of the elements they value, work leaders can develop plans to dispel negativity, and increase positive emotions among their staff. Some elements managers should include in their plans:

Identify and communicate priorities. Managers can start changing employees' attitudes to a positive mindset by identifying and communicating priorities. Setting priorities with employees helps them to focus on important tasks, and may help to lessen some of the stress they feel when they're overwhelmed by a heavy workload.

Identify work process breakdowns. Determine whether there are better or more productive work methods that staff members can employ. Get the right tools. Frustration often occurs when employees have insufficient or ineffective equipment to work with. Make sure employees have the appropriate tools to do the work. Give them space. Managers should set expectations for the outcome, and provide direction only when needed. Allowing workers a greater sense of autonomy and authority in deciding how to conduct the work breeds trust, and invests employees in the process, as well as the outcome.

Provide training. Training helps employees to feel more competent in their jobs, and prepares them for greater responsibility and more challenging assignments. Confidence is a result of competence; training is the tool.

Talk to workers. Let employees know what is expected of them regarding performance, as well as how and where they "fit" in the organization. Employees need to know that their contributions make a difference. Select specific work examples to demonstrate their contributions. Staff meetings and one-on-one conversations are perfect venues to discuss how employees help the organization to succeed.

Keep employees' informed. Employees want to feel like they are "in the know" about their department, and the organization as a whole. By sharing information, work leaders send the message that they trust and respect their staff. Employees will feel valued and will return their leaders' respect.

Listen. Talk to employees about their workplace concerns. Also, keep abreast of the grapevine for simmering issues—address them quickly and confidently. Dispel rumors with the facts. Be honest about mistakes and problems. Twisting the truth is never advised—employees have long memories and their trust may be lost forever.

Help employees' feel less anxious about job security. Offer feedback about job performance—don't wait until review time to discuss behavioral issues. Talk to workers about their work challenges, and help to find solutions. Also, keep employees informed of departmental functioning; informing employees of events as the year progresses is better than communicating bad news later.

Reward employees' for their efforts. Finally, managers must make sure employees are rewarded for positive behavior and contributions. Studies show that money isn't the motivator of choice for most people. Ask employees what motivates them. Showing genuine appreciation for an employee's work is often enough. Some workers, however, might appreciate having a positive letter placed in their personnel file recognizing a particular contribution. Others might appreciate greater challenges or consideration for high-profile assignments.

VISIONING

Visioning is what it says—creating a very clear about future. It describe the employee visualization towards new Environment . How he calculate length of the change and applied by adopting the organization change. To create the employee Visioning power for accept the organization change following workshop were conducted.

How to Conduct a Employee Visioning Process

Employee visioning can be organized in many different ways utilizing a variety of Employee participation techniques. However, creating a common vision requires several actions to complete the process. While there are no hard and fast "rules" for this process, each employees will need to find its own pace, participants, and techniques that work best. What this guide offers is an example process and a variety of tools that have been used effectively in other communities just like yours.

Here is one example of how employees visioning can be accomplished over the course of several working sessions. It is based upon The Center for Rural Pennsylvania's *Planning for the Future: A Handbook on Employees Visioning.* This example is neither magical nor absolute and it can be modified to meet your own employees 's needs.

REMEMBER: It is always advisable to provide refreshments at your employees' workshops and to videotape all your working sessions.

The three basic elements of the process:

- **Establish a Steering Committee.** This committee should be responsible for oversight and organization of the entire process.
- **Employees Workshops.** Open public meetings that are used to inform citizens about the visioning process, to discuss the progress being made and to discuss issues affecting the employees.
- **Taskforces.** Small groups that gather information on a specific issue affecting the employees and identify possible solutions.

Each of these elements are included in the following example. The timeframe in developing a vision statement can range from 6 to 12 months depending on the level of commitment of the participants. In general, your employees visioning process should proceed as follows:

1. **Getting Started:** Steering Committee forms and begins planning for the first workshop.
2. **First Employees' Workshop:** Steering Committee provides an overview of the visioning process and asks participants to identify issues affecting their employees.
3. **Establishing Taskforces:** Steering Committee tallies results, develops list of taskforces, and plans for second workshop.
4. **Second Employees' Workshop:** Steering Committee reviews activities to date and breaks participants into small taskforces, giving each a specific issue to examine in detail.
5. **Keeping on Track:** Steering Committee ensures that taskforces are meeting regularly and plans for the third workshop.
6. **Third Employees' Workshop:** Taskforces report major findings to the employees. Participants are asked to discuss what they want their employees to look like in the future.
7. **Drafting the Visioning Statement:** Steering Committee ensures that task forces are meeting regularly and drafts a tentative vision statement.
8. **Fourth Employees' Workshop/Celebration:** Public unveiling of vision statement and celebration of the employees and its residents.
9. **Marketing and Making the Vision a Reality:** Steering Committee and taskforces present the vision statement to employees groups, local governments, and other organizations for their formal approval of the statement. Committee and taskforces request these groups to use the statement when making decisions affecting the employees.

10. **Action Plan**: Working with various employees organizations and governments, the Steering Committee develops an action plan by implementing the taskforces' recommendations and other elements of the vision statement.
11. **Annual Progress Report**: The Steering Committee plans a meeting that reviews the activities and accomplishments to date and what activities will be implemented the following year.

Keep in mind in employees visioning there is no absolute formula where step one will automatically lead to steps two, three and four. The steps outlined here have worked in many communities, but not all, so you should feel free to combine, rearrange, or even eliminate steps as needed to expedite the process. The final measure of your vision's success is not how closely you follow this example, but how effective you are in improving your employees's quality of life.

Getting Started

In all communities, there are people and organizations that are respected and active.

Business owners, elected officials, members of non-profit agencies, educators, health care professionals and others who are actively interested in improving their employees should be members of your Steering Committee. Key points to remember in forming a Steering Committee include:

- Open membership up to many organizations;
- Reach out across the employees : public, private, and non-profit;
- Be inclusive, not exclusive;
- Don't avoid differences in opinion; and
- Don't get stuck on the past. Remember this a plan for the future.

Once the list of likely members has been put together, invite them to a meeting. Don't be disappointed if only a few show up. It takes momentum to get going, but once it starts, it is contagious.

At the first meeting, and at others if necessary, do the following:

1. **Identify who is mssing from the group**. Make a concerted effort to identify persons and/or organizations that should be involved. At this point, the list should include those who are considered influential in shaping employees opinions. These individuals should be invited to the next Steering Committee meeting.
2. **Select a Chair or Co-Chair of the Steering Committee**. The Chair's job is to keep the process focused and to give every participant the chance to have a say in the process.
3. **Establish a positive attitude.** Initiate a brief discussion on the employees's strengths to help get a positive tone going.
4. **Develop an action plan.** This plan does not need to very detailed, but it should include the next step in the process, when the public should be involved, what resources are available to see the process through, and who will be available to provide guidance and technical support.
5. **Develop a working definition of your employees.** Meeting participants should leave with an understanding of the geographic boundaries of the

employees and an understanding of the economic, cultural and social bonds that make them a employees.

The outcome is what information is generated during the workshop. Both of these elements are critical for a successful workshop.

Organization

Organizing a employees workshop is not difficult, but it can be challenging. The Steering Committee however needs to be in charge of this process. Below are some of the basic items that should be considered:

1. **Location:** The first step is to select a location. As a general rule, you should choose a facility that people are familiar with and comfortable visiting. There must be good access and available parking.
2. **Date:** Selecting a date can be a tricky matter. Weekday morning workshops can be just as popular as evening workshops. Similarly, Saturday morning can also be very popular. There are two general rules to follow when selecting a workshop date: first, make sure on other employees group has an event scheduled at the same time; second, give the Steering Committee plenty of lead time to adequately promote and organize the workshop.
3. **Agenda:** Developing and following an agenda is essential. An agenda lets participants know what is going on and how long the workshop will last. Some key items to include in the agenda are: (1) welcoming remarks and the purpose of the workshop (Why are we here and what do we want to accomplish?); (2) a large block of time for small group discussions; and (3) concluding remarks and a discussion of the next step (Where do we go from here?).
4. **Speakers:** When selecting speakers, it is important to choose people who have effective communication skills and who are comfortable speaking in front of large groups. The welcoming speaker should be from the Steering Committee. The person giving the overview of the visioning process can also be a Steering Committee member, or someone from outside the employees (such as a government agency, consultant, etc.). Pre-select and train a small group of facilitators for the workshop. Your facilitators can be members of the Steering Committee or local resource people, like your planner, RC&D coordinator, or county extension agent.
5. **Promotion:** To ensure good attendance, promote the workshop throughout the employees . You may consider printed brochures or flyers, which are somewhat expensive and effective tools or you can post signs at visible locations. Contact local media resources: newspapers, radio stations, and public access television stations. Also, consider personally contacting people, municipal officials as well as state and federal legislators.
6. **Food:** Offering food and refreshments, or a meal sponsored by an area organization is always a good idea.

Outcomes

The very first outcome is the responsibility of the speaker. The second is the product of the small group discussions. After the keynote speakers, the large group should be broken down into small discussion groups of no more than 10 people. Participants can be randomly assigned to different groups to help the discussion flow more freely. Each of the small groups should have a facilitator, who must make sure that everyone in the group has a chance to participate and that the group develops a list of issues.

The facilitator's first task is to ask the group members to list the issues in their employees. This can be done as a brainstorm or by asking each group member to write down his or her issues on a piece of paper. Comments should be recorded on flip charts so that the entire group can see. Afterwards, every participant should "vote" for the top five issues by placing a colored sticker next to the most important comments recorded on the flip charts.

Participants should be reminded during this process that they are not here to solve problems, but to identify and take stock of all the issues and to identify the most important issues for the employees' future.

Establishing Taskforces

A week or two after the first workshop, the Steering Committee should meet and assess what went right at the workshop and what needs to be improved. The Committee also needs to take the results of the participants' issues lists and identify similarities and differences among the lists. This lists need to be condensed or combined into four or five broad topics. These topics will serve as the basis for the taskforces.

Each taskforce needs to be assigned a temporary leader, who is usually a Steering Committee member. The leader is responsible for informally recruiting members to the taskforce and collecting the information on that particular topic. In addition to identifying the taskforces, the Steering Committee should begin preparing for the next employees workshop, which should be scheduled within two months after the first workshop.

Second Employees' Workshop

Following the same organizational procedures as the first workshop, the Steering Committee should design the second workshop to get the taskforces up and running. The second workshop should offer employees residents or business owners who could not or would not attend the first public workshop the opportunity to become involved. The workshop should begin with an overview of the activities of the first workshop and the visioning process. Participants should then be directed to meet with their taskforce group. Except for the temporary taskforce leader, try not to pre-assign members to each taskforce group. Participants should be allowed to joint the task force of their choosing.

Within the taskforces, several things should happen:

1. **Select a leader.** The leader may be the temporary leader or someone else.
2. **Identify who is missing from the group.** Are there individuals or organizations that have special expertise that the group needs?
3. **Select the next meeting date.** The taskforces should begin meeting regularly after the workshop.
4. **Complete a SWOT analysis of the taskforce issues** (see SWOT below).
5. **Begin identifying the resources available to address the taskforce issue.** SWOT Analysis—Strengths, Weaknesses, Opportunities and Threats

Borrowed from business management practices, SWOT analysis is a quick way to assess an issue or topic in terms of its strengths–what is good, what are its positive attributes; weaknesses–what is wrong, what are the problems; opportunities–what can be done to improve the situation, both short and long-term; and threats–what are the external/internal threats in the future.

For communities, SWOT analysis is a useful tool to explore an issue. Below is an example of a group that used SWOT analysis to assess their downtown:

Downtown Revitalization

- *Strengths*: Good mix of retail and service; good traffic flow; many historic buildings
- *Weaknesses*: Not enough parking; lots of vacant store fronts; high property taxes
- *Opportunities*: Recruit a downtown manager; coordinate store hours; repave the sidewalks
- *Threats*: Being ignored by municipal government; shopping malls; highway bypass

Key Outcomes

- Establish active taskforces.
- *Time*: 2 to 3 hours
- *Cost*: Promotion, refreshments and supplies.

Marketing and Making the Vision a Reality

After the employees celebration, the Steering Committee should meet and begin developing a marketing strategy for the vision statement and, more importantly, a strategic action plan. Both of these activities can occur at the same time.

The marketing strategy should be designed to get the word out about the vision statement.

More specifically, it should explain what the vision statement is, how it was created, and how it is to be used. The strategy should include features that will help it recruit volunteers for developing the strategic action plan.

HRM AND CULTURE OF CHANGE

Measurement of Organizational Culture

By investigating two disparate organizationsa family-owned business and a global manufacturing companythis article describes ways that management can utilize cultural assessments to increase the likelihood of success in managing change. The Goodwin Company, an organization specializing in contract packaging of household and automotive cleaning products, and Patagonia, a global brand supplying high-quality outdoor clothing and equipment, provide examples of this phenomenon. In both cases, the instrument used to assess culture was the Integrated Cultural Framework (ICF), which was adapted by the authors from the work of Hofsted and Kluckhohn and Strodtbeck. The ICF has been used to analyze culture across a number of companies and industries and stands up to reliability and validity testing. The dimensions of measurement include:

Ability to Influence: The extent to which organization members have an opportunity to influence decision-making.

Comfort with Ambiguity: The extent to which members are comfortable with uncertainty and risk taking.

Achievement Orientation: The extent to which members are assertive, goal-directed, and achievement-oriented.

Individualism versus Collectivism: The extent to which individual *versus* group loyalty exists.

Egalitarianism: The extent to which equal opportunity exists for advancement.

Time Orientation: The extent to which the organizational goal/mission is focused on values from the past, present, or future.

Space Orientation: The extent to which the physical layout of the organization is public, private, or a mix of both.

The **35-item ICF survey** was initially used to collect responses from organization members. Following the collection of survey data, an extensive number of interviews were carried out to provide more substantive information concerning organizational culture.

Goodwin Company

For several years, Goodwin Company, founded in 1922 by Thomas A. Goodwin, manufactured and sold its own line of household cleaning products. However, due to the competitiveness of the retail market, its focus shifted to contract packaging and distribution in the household, industrial, and automotive cleaning markets. Only the original product, Goodwin's Ammonia, maintains the Goodwin label. Still a family enterprise, Goodwin Company currently has approximately 300 employees and manufacturing and distribution facilities in Los Angeles, California, and Atlanta, Georgia.

In response to concerns about increased labor costs and stagnant revenues, an organizational culture study was launched to determine the appropriate change strategy. Forty-three members of the organization, including managerial and clerical staff, completed the ICF survey and 13 one-on-one interviews were conducted.

The results revealed the following key findings:

Ability to Influence: The data indicated that the ability of employees to propose and implement change in the company was low. The interviews suggested that marginal regard for input had caused the staff to become discouraged and had reduced motivation for process improvements.

Individualism/Collectivism: Although Goodwin Company espoused teamwork as a core value, feedback from the management teams in California and Georgia indicated a low level of trust among management, which resulted in a lack of collaboration among the managers.

Time Orientation: The data showed that employees viewed the company as focused on the past and present while lacking a strategic plan for the future.

Proposed Structural Changes

Given the results of the study, three recommendations were presented to the management team:

Establish a strategic management group that meets weekly to address business challenges, coordinate travel between facilities, and find common ground to build trust.

Give employees, customers, and suppliers a voice and increase their ability to influence policy and procedures. Initiate an electronic comment box for employees, and implement surveys on customer service and supplier satisfaction.

Establish a company vision and mission statement to encourage a sense of ownership, and incorporate management teams from Atlanta and Los Angeles to spearhead this effort. Relocate artifacts, such as company photos from the early years and bottles from the product lines of the 1930s and 1940s, to both facilities in order to acknowledge the company's history and longevity and encourage teamwork between members of the two offices.

Outcomes

The establishment of the strategic management team proved to be very beneficial. By having the management team travel between facilities, the group developed a better understanding of the challenges at both locations, and they began to build a baseline of trust. The resulting collaborative effort of the team yielded two new contracts. In addition, Goodwin Company was certified by a major chemical manufacturer as a top facility in the nation, which resulted in requests for manufacturing proposals that would not have been possible without improvements in cooperation among regional managers.

Challenges

Goodwin Company was able to correlate changes that emerged in response to the organizational culture study; however, not all of the recommendations produced the desired results. For example, the customer service surveys did not yield the expected outcomes due to a lack of customer response. Additional customer contact will likely be necessary for future surveys to be effective. And although the recommendation to create a vision, mission, and values statement was originally well received, the management team eventually backed off the project; deciding that the company vision should come from its CEO.

Patagonia

Patagonia's corporate headquarters are located in southern California and the company has overseas offices in Japan and France. Revenues in 2007 totaled $275 million and the firm currently has 1,300 employees worldwide, with 382 located in the corporate office. In 1966, founder Yvon Chouinard was dissatisfied with the conventional equipment used in adventure climbing and so he redesigned and manufactured almost every climbing tool to make each stronger, simpler, more functional, and environmentally friendly. From that operational base, Chouinard Equipment, which later became Patagonia, expanded to include outdoor and casual clothing and a line of underwear. The unique mission and focus of the organization was to make the best products, cause no unnecessary harm, and rely on the business model to inspire and implement solutions to the environmental crisis. Chouinard's management principles were captured in a self-published book, Let My People Go Surfing: The Education of a Reluctant Businessman.

Although the essence of Patagonia's initial philosophy has survived, increased growth and operational complexity have created challenges for the organization in its quest to remain committed to the mission. To better understand the underlying issues and develop a strategic direction, an organizational culture study was initiated. Using the ICF, 27 surveys were completed at the corporate office along with 15 one-on-one interviews with 4 senior managers and 11 mid-level managers from 8 departments.

Key Findings

Ability to influence: The data showed that organization members felt they had a moderately high degree of opportunity to influence, but the inclusion of their input also led to a prolonged decision-making process.

Comfort with ambiguity: Although the climate seemed to foster innovation and encourage risk taking, the lack of a systematic feedback process minimized the flow of ideas. In addition, the dilemma of attending to what appear to be dichotomous goalsattaining a profitable return while maintaining a commitment to environmentally safe productscreated a challenge.

Individualism/Collectivism: Patagonia attempted to build community by establishing an on-site childcare center, comprehensive health insurance, and a family setting. However, the company employs a large number of unique and creative independent-minded people, and in supporting innovation, it created a sense of individualism, as well as a limited incentive for teamwork.

Although Patagonia has been successful, the study indicated that to remain competitive, the organization needed to address the duality of encouraging individual creativity and promoting a collaborative work environment, particularly as this duality related to the corporate mission. In addition, it appeared that information flow and decision-making efficiency needed to be addressed.

Outcomes

The organizational culture study was presented to the Board of Directors, who recognized the need to enhance productivity by reinforcing the organization's mission and emphasizing the importance of a collaborative environment. The following structural changes emerged:

The human resources director was appointed to the senior management steering team to assist in the development of a strategic training initiative. Training courses were developed to provide skills directed toward facilitating performance management feedback, improving communication skills, and enhancing negotiation capability in dealing with suppliers.

A new employee training manual was created to better educate new hires regarding the organizational structure and the flow of product lines from development to sales. The purpose was to build teamwork and collaboration and to emphasize the company's core values related to quality, integrity, environmentalism, and the desire to not be bound by convention. In addition, Yvon Chouinard's book was presented to each hire with the hope of inculcating new members to the principles associated with the organization's mission.

All employees are now encouraged to participate in the Patagonia National Park protection program in Chile and Argentina to reinforce the importance of the mission statement and its meaning in their work. Employees receive a salary and all related expenses are paid by the organization during the three-week program.

The selection process for hiring new members was reviewed with a focus on measuring candidates' knowledge and skills, particularly their ability to work in a team.

Challenges

Shifting a culture that has to some extent moved away from the values established by its founder is always a challenge. A number of Patagonia's high performers have been successful because of their innovative talents. However, unless these individuals are also able to recognize the importance of collaboration, in the long term, the organization may not be able to respond in a timely manner to competitive pressure.

Image : Andrew Johnson

CASE STUDY : HELPING EMPLOYEES ADAPT TO CHANGE AT TEXAS CHILDREN'S HOSPITAL

Introduction

In 2006, Texas Children's began an aggressive $1.5 billion expansion project. The expansion includes the erection of four new buildings, and the addition of new service lines and programs, leading to a large increase in employee resources. By 2010, the organization is expected to grow from 6,600 to 9,000 employees and increase medical staff by 70. Simultaneously, the organization is transitioning from a paper to an electronic medical record system. This expansion initiative is considered to be the largest ever in the United States to be completed within a four-year window.

Project Background

Texas Children's has begun the implementation of an electronic medical record system that will provide immediate access to patient records and information across the organization, thus promoting improved patient care and patient safety while streamlining efficiencies. The electronic medical record will facilitate instant communication between the primary care and specialty services while also allowing on-going access to patient information for research purposes. The first phase of the project was deployed in two major business units in the organization, impacting approximately 6,000 employees or 85% of the workforce.

Change Management Overview

To assist with the "people side" of change associated with the system implementation, a change management team was created. Throughout the project, the change management team partnered with the project implementation team and organizational leaders to facilitate activities designed to reduce employee resistance and build commitment for the implementation. Two notable activities included creating a Change Agent Network and conducting dress rehearsal activities.

Local leaders selected individuals to make up a Change Agent Network. The network was comprised of participants from throughout the organization who served as extensions of the change management team as "on-the-ground" peer champions. The change management team provided Network members with ongoing information, reminders, and tips which they shared with their peers. Periodic meetings and conference calls allowed change agents to connect with each other and exchange ideas about how to build commitment, as well as keep the change management team informed about issues and major areas of resistance that required attention.

In addition to the Change Agent Network, the change management team developed dress rehearsal activities to help prepare end users for the implementation. The activities were set-up as real-life simulations and provided an opportunity for end users to walk-though and practice system and process changes prior to implementation. The dress rehearsals were intended to help end users understand what to expect at Go-live and minimize anxiety. Additionally, the activities helped identify any potential "hiccups" that might not otherwise have been identified until the system went live, including incorrect end user security settings. Being proactive prior to Go-live was important because experiencing problems upon Go-live could have contributed to a mind-set that the system "didn't work" and created unnecessary resistance.

Measurement

To gauge end user commitment throughout the project, the change management team conducted four end user surveys:

- **Baseline:** Sent 6-8 months prior to Go-live
- **Pre Go-live:** Sent 2 weeks prior to Go-live
- **Post Go-live:** Sent 30 days after Go-live
- **90 Day Post Go-live:** Sent 90 days after Go-live

Data from these surveys will be used throughout this case study to indicate where change management practices were effectively utilized and increased the success of the change.

The business units involved in the initiative each had unique characteristics. Business Unit 1 had fairly standardized processes, and was geographically dispersed throughout the region. Business Unit 2 was centralized, but had vastly different processes between the many sub-units. These differences created a variety of implementation challenges. Overall the same basic change management strategy, processes and tools were available for each unit. The degree to which the change management practices were utilized by the unit's leadership team differed greatly. Comparative data gathered from the Post Go-live surveys of both units showed a significant difference in the average increase of favorable responses to key questions about the implementation, as indicated in Figure 1.

This comparative data indicates the benefits of employing effective change management practices. It also suggests potential best practices, including the importance of appropriate end user engagement, leadership sponsorship, and dedicated, on-going support.

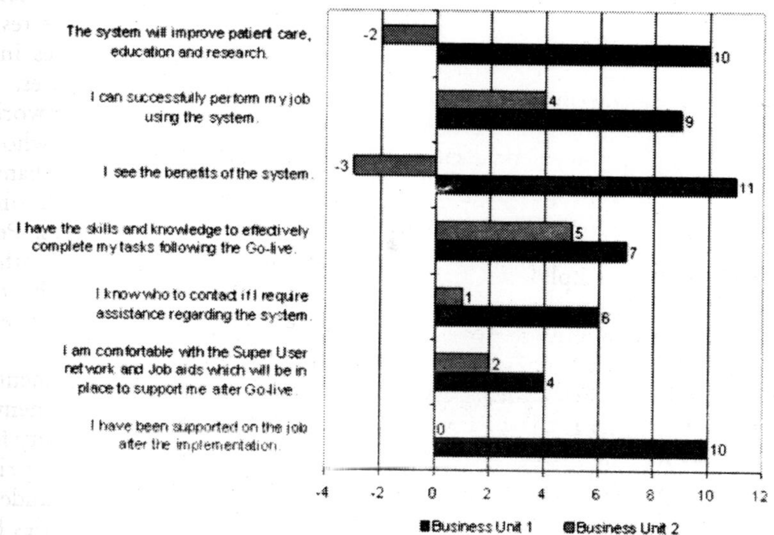

Figure 1 : Average Increase in Favorable Responses by Question

Strong Executive Sponsorship

During the planning phase of the project, Business Unit 1 demonstrated strong executive support and involvement in the project as a whole, and specifically the change management activities. The business unit's executive closely partnered with the change management team, discussing various change management ideas and concepts; tailoring tools and activities to better meet the needs of the business unit; and consistently participating in change management events and activities.

A clear example of her commitment was her sponsorship of the Change Agent Network. She publicly championed the Network to leaders and staff. She appealed to her leadership team to seek volunteers and select individuals to participate in the Network. She and local leaders supported the Network by joining conference calls, participating in activities and personally thanking change agents for their time and commitment. This support proved to be critical to the successful operation of the Change Agent Network. Leadership from Business Unit 1 encouraged and held change agents accountable for fulfilling their responsibilities in the role, which ensured ongoing participation and follow-through.

Another clear example of this executive's support was her willingness to champion dress rehearsal activities. She conducted a careful review of the planned activities to ensure they were appropriate for each area, and required participation for all end users. The simulations depended on various roles working together to complete real-life tasks, and required a significant time investment. Some locations temporarily closed during dress rehearsals to ensure staff had adequate time and attention to devote to practicing and mastering the new skills required for the implementation. Following the dress rehearsals, the executive reviewed the status report from each site.

Feedback from Business Unit 1's leader specified the Change Agent Network and dress rehearsals were keys to the successful Go-live for her business unit. She noted the Change Agent Network increased end user engagement and helped keep end users informed by spreading key project messages. She also indicated the peer-to-peer communication was especially helpful in ensuring important messages were received and understood by end users. The visible sponsorship and participation of the executive sponsor enabled success of the activities by ensuring that leaders and end users understood the importance of managing change as well as their role in it.

Business Unit 2 implemented the new system two months after Business Unit 1. During the planning phase, leaders of Business Unit 2 were involved in the project at a high level, and their degree of sponsorship and support of change management was less visible to end users. Though the leaders agreed to engage in the same change management activities employed with Business Unit 1, they demonstrated less active support of the activities to the end users. The leaders complied with general requests, such as providing lists of users to participate in activities; however, few leaders reached out to the selected end users to show their support and encouragement, or participated in the various end user engagement meetings to demonstrate sponsorship. Throughout the phases of the project, Business Unit 2's end user participation in Change Management activities steadily decreased.

Though leadership from Business Unit 1 publicly advocated the necessity of dress rehearsals, most areas in Business Unit 2 failed to engage in the dress rehearsal process. Many leaders from Business Unit 2 failed to review the dress rehearsal activities or to check for applicability to their specific areas. Few made the activities mandatory or actively encouraged their staff to participate. Most neither held end users accountable for practicing for the Go-live, nor did they provide staff with adequate time to do so. As a result, the percentage of staff who participated in Business Unit 2's dress rehearsals was significantly less than the percentage from Business Unit 1, as seen in Figure below.

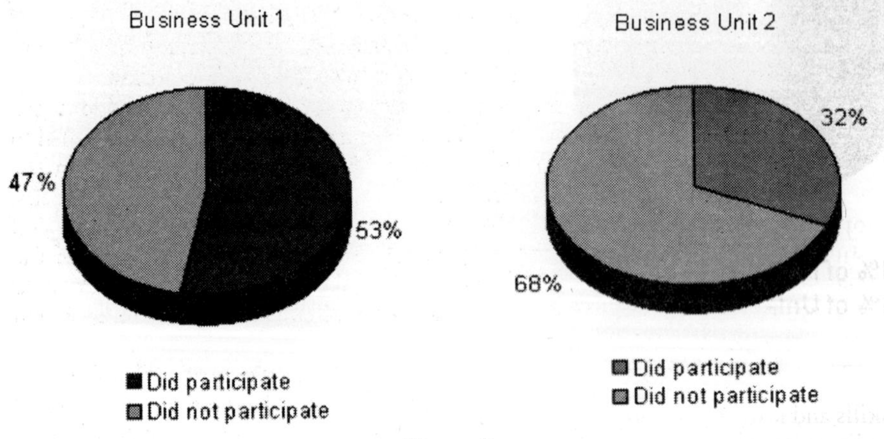

Figure 2

Analysis of the Pre Go-live survey for Business Unit 2 indicated that those employees who did participate in the Dress Rehearsals were more ready for Go-live than those who did not, as indicated by Figure 3.

In addition, a comparison between the Pre Go-live results for both business units showed that Business Unit 1 had significantly more favorable results than Business Unit 2. A greater percentage of end users from Business Unit 1 reported that they understood how the implementation was going to impact them (Figure 4), had

Question: I have the skills and knowledge to effectively complete my tasks following the Go-live.

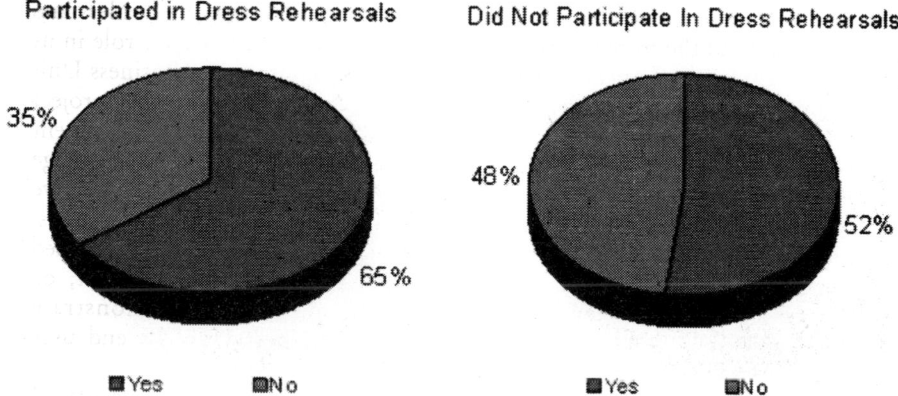

Figure 3

Question: I understand how the new system will impact my daily work.

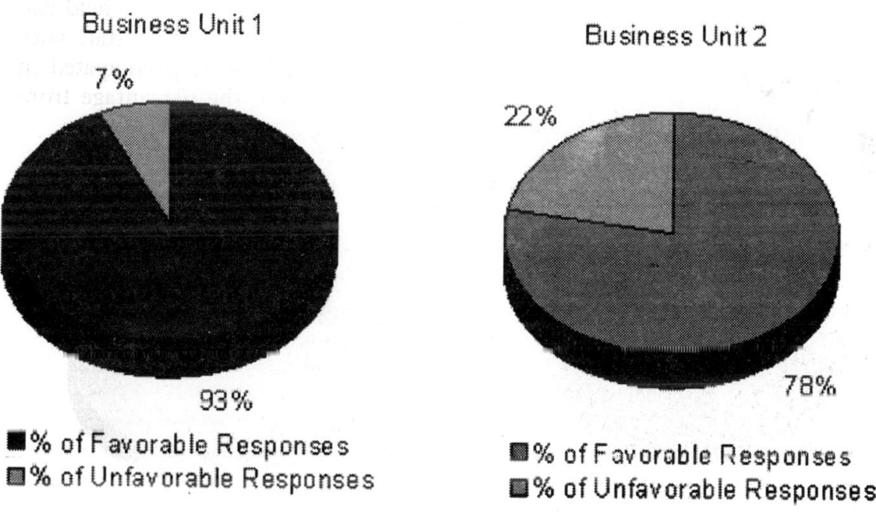

Figure 4

the skills and knowledge to effectively complete their tasks (Figure 5), and were ready to Go live with the new system (Figure 6). Additionally, end users from Business Unit 1 indicated higher levels of commitment to the project, as seen by the 17% difference in favorable responses between the two units to the question: I feel that the new system will work for me (Figure 7).

As demonstrated, data from the Pre Go-live surveys for both units indicate that the effective use of change management practices and leader sponsorship of the change activities in Business Unit 1 made a significant impact to the success of the project. The activities helped raise end user confidence and ability and increase end user commitment.

Question: I have the skills and knowledge to effectively complete my tasks following the Go-live.

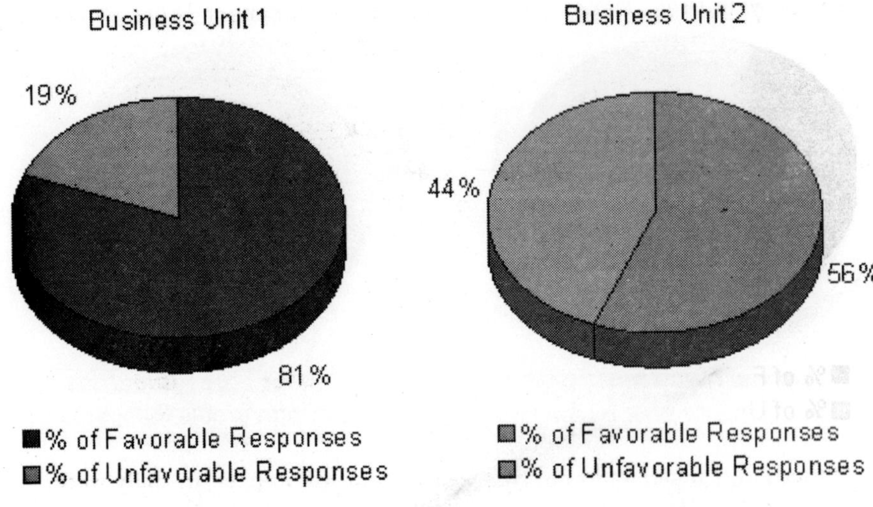

Figure 5

Question: I feel ready to go live with the new system.

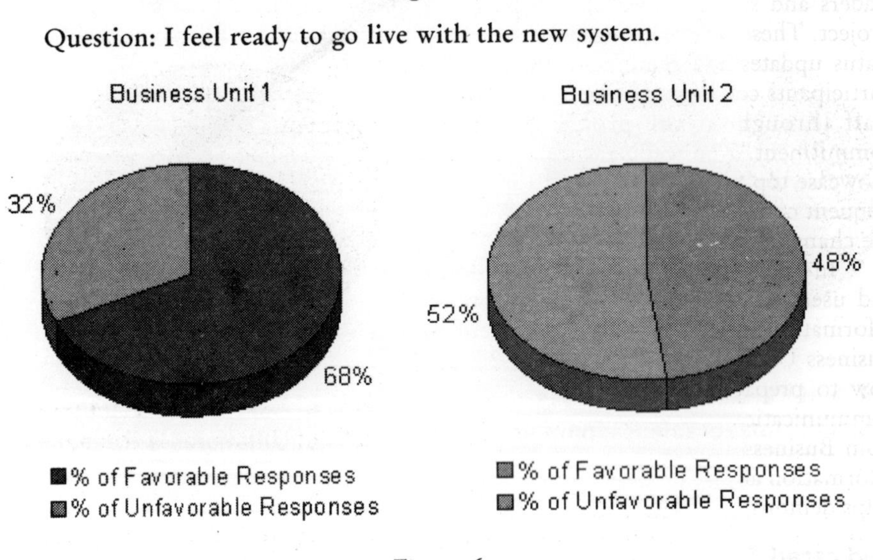

Figure 6

Commitment to End User Engagement

Leadership from Business Unit 1 also demonstrated a commitment to end user engagement activities throughout the project. They set-up project road shows and individual visits by project team members to each impacted area prior to the Go-live. These visits allowed team members to gain understanding about specific site needs and considerations while personally connecting with end users. The visits also helped build excitement for the changes through demonstrations and informative conversations with end users.

Question: I feel that the new system will work for me.

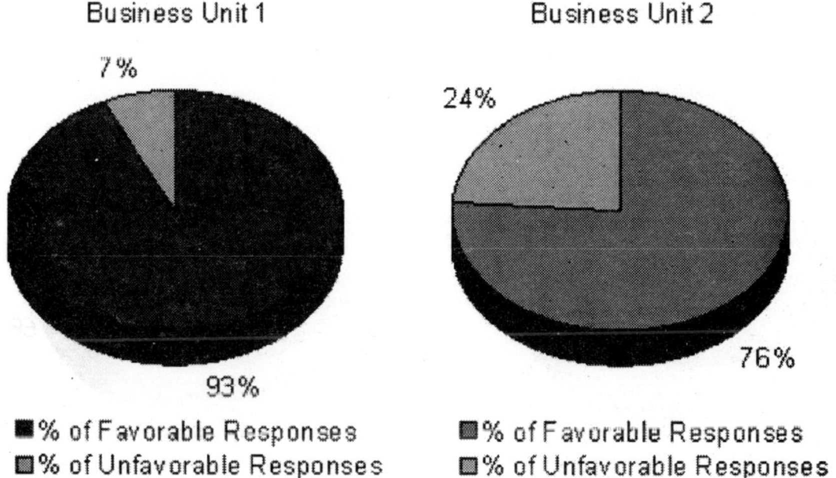

Figure 7

In addition to site visits, the leadership team from Business Unit 1 ensured leaders and staff received on-going and frequent communications throughout the project. These tailored communications from business unit leadership provided key status updates and reminders. Additionally, online meetings were offered so that participants could attend virtually. These webinars were scheduled with leaders and staff throughout the project to ensure engagement and increase end user commitment. The webinars were used to provide on-going updates to end users, showcase top features of the software, and provide *ad-hoc* training as needed. These frequent communications helped end users feel more engaged and less anxious about the changes that were occurring.

In contrast, communications for Business Unit 2 were primarily project driven; end users received general communications from the project team, but minimal information from local leadership. There was less active involvement from leaders of Business Unit 2 to provide updates and communications about what to expect and how to prepare. The importance of leadership commitment to engagement and communications can be clearly demonstrated by the greater percentage of end users from Business Unit 1 who responded favorably to the question: I have sufficient information about the project in the Pre Go-live surveys. (Figure 8) This data further helps demonstrate the importance of active change management.

Dedicated Support Team

Leadership from Business Unit 1 also demonstrated best practices following go-live through proactive end-user support. After the initial implementation period, end user support for Business Unit 1 transitioned from the project team to a dedicated support team. As a result, in the months following go-live, end users reported few concerns over the support process.

To further support end users and build commitment to the change, following the implementation the executive and support team from Business Unit 1 held weekly calls with the sub-units. This allowed them to understand issues, share

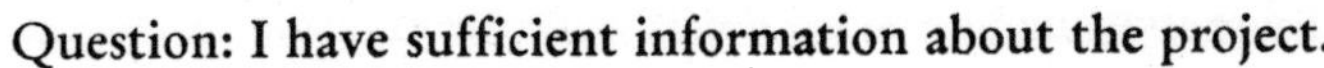

Question: I have sufficient information about the project.

Business Unit 1

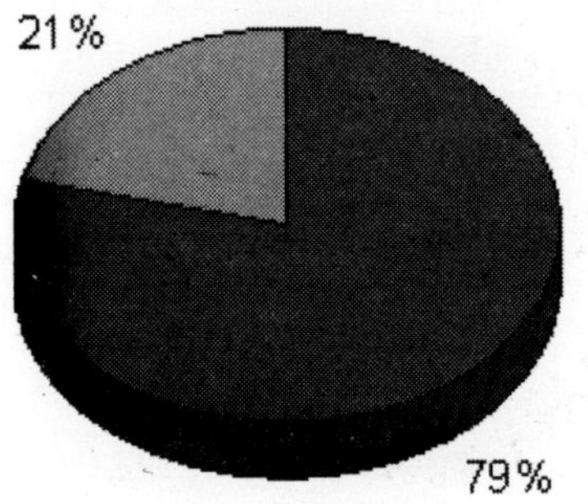

Business Unit 2

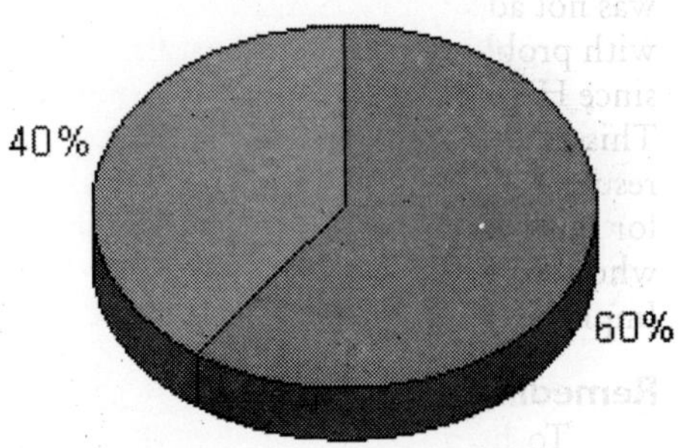

% of Favorable Responses
% of Unfavorable Responses

% of Favorable Responses
% of Unfavorable Responses

Figure 8

information and troubleshoot common problems. The executive actively followed up with sub-units who were not consistently participating in the calls to ensure they had the support they needed. Additionally, the calls coming into the support team each week were analyzed to determine top issues and provide further instructions and training to help reduce issue reoccurrence. An easy access, one-stop portal was designed to ensure end users could easily find instructions, troubleshooting material, and necessary updates. This proactive approach to end user support following Go-live helped reduce end user resistance. The comparative results from the initial 30 day Go-live survey and the 90 day Go-live survey showed an increase in the percentage of end-users from Business Unit 1 who responded favorably to the question: I have been supported on the job after the implementation. (Refer to Figure 9 below)

I have been supported on the job after the IRIS Implementation.

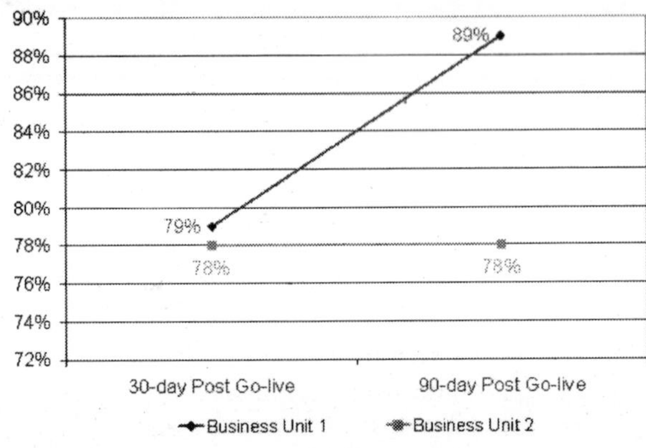

Figure 9

Though Business Unit 2 provided the same degree of initial on-site support for the implementation, post Go-live support calls were transitioned to the organization's general help desk rather than a dedicated support team following the initial implementation period. End users from Business Unit 2 reported that the Help Desk was not adequately trained for the transition and was not always effective in assisting with problems and questions. End-users experienced long wait times and frustration since Help Desk team members often had to contact the project team to get answers. This resulted in delays in getting questions answered and problems resolved. The results from the initial 30 Day Post Go-live survey and the 90 Day Post Go-live survey for Business Unit 2 showed no improvement over time in the percentage of end users who responded favorably to the question: I have been supported on the job after the Implementation. (Refer to Figure 9)

Remedial Training

To help ensure that end-users were adequately supported in Business Unit 1, remedial training was offered on an ad-hoc basis following the implementation. Members of the dedicated support team visited various areas to ensure end-users were performing activities correctly and provided coaching as needed. While end-users still reported a desire for additional training, a greater percentage of end-users responded favorably to the question: I can successfully perform my job using the new system than with Business Unit 2, where there was no dedicated support team to offer remedial training (see Figure 10.)

I can successfully perform my job using IRIS.

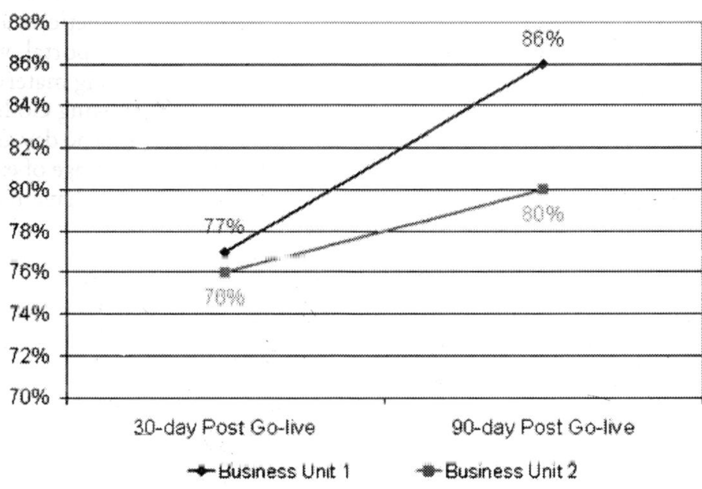

Figure 10

CONCLUSION

Comparisons of data between the business units for the 90 Day Post Go-Live Surveys show that while favorable results for Business Unit 1 increased an average of 8%, results for Business Unit 2 only increased an average of 1% overall (see Figure 1 above.) Through there are many possible reasons for the significant differences in improvement, the survey data for each business unit underlines the importance of effective change management practices on the overall success of the project. Specifically, a commitment to strong executive sponsorship, end-user engagement, a dedicated support team, and remedial training were shown to be key components for ensuring a successful change.

Chapter 7

Knowledge Management and Learning Organization

KNOWLEDGE MANAGEMENT

There are several different, and sometimes quite confusing statements that claim to be a definition of 'Knowledge Management' and there are different perspectives on what Knowledge Management is. For example:

- KM is about systems and technologies
- KM is about people and learning organizations
- KM is about processes, methods and techniques
- KM is about managing knowledge assets
- KM is a holistic initiative across the entire organization
- KM is not a discipline, as such, and should be an integral part of every knowledge workers' daily responsibilities

What is most important, is for you to have your own definition of Knowledge Management; what KM is to you and your organization. What is even more important is that you and your colleagues have a 'common shared understanding' of what KM means for you all.

To help you get started, we have included immediately below a few definitions of what KM means to some organizations. We suggest you consider them, together with any other definitions you may have, and see if there are any words or phrases that particularly 'resonate' with what you are trying to do. This will help you formulate your own definition of knowledge management.

At the end of this page, we invite you to share with us all, any definitions you have discovered and/or formulated. We can then all comment and rate the usefulness of each definition as we wish. This then provides us, at the bottom of this page, with a list of KM Definitions, listed in highest rated/ranked order, to help us even further. So please share your definitions and/or any comments or rating to definitions.

Some well-known KM Definitions

"If only HP knew what it knows it would make three times more profit tomorrow".

Lew Platt, ex CEO Hewlett Packard

"Knowledge Management is the discipline of enabling individuals, teams and entire organizations to collectively and systematically create, share and apply knowledge, to better achieve their objectives"

Ron Young, CEO/CKO Knowledge Associates International

"Most activities or tasks are not one-time events. Whether its drilling a well or conducting a transaction at a service station, we do the same things repeatedly. Our philosophy is fairly simple: every time we do something again, we should do it better than the last time".

Sir John Steely Browne, BP, Harvard Business Review, 1997

"The capabilities by which communities within an organization capture the knowledge that is critical to them, constantly improve it and make it available in the most effective manner to those who need it, so that they can exploit it creatively to add value as a normal part of their work".

GlaxoSmithKline

"Knowledge management will deliver outstanding collaboration and partnership working. It will ensure the region maximizes the value of its information and knowledge assets and it will help its citizens to use their creativity and skills better, leading to improved effectiveness and greater innovation".

West Midlands Regional Observatory, UK

"We recognize that our most important asset is people and their knowledge. We understand Knowledge Management (KM) as the cultivation of an environment within which people are willing to share, learn and collaborate together leading to improvement".

Care Services Improvement Partnership (CSIP)

"Knowledge Management ('KM') comprises a range of practices used by organisations to identify, create, represent, and distribute knowledge. It has been an established discipline since 1995 with a body of university courses and both professional and academic journals dedicated to it. Many large companies have resources dedicated to Knowledge Management, often as a part of 'Information Technology' or 'Human Resource Management' departments. Knowledge Management is a multi-billion dollar worldwide market.

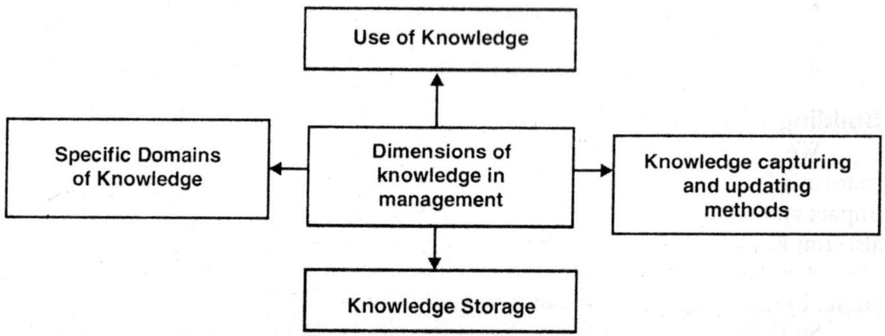

Figure 1 : The dimensions of knowledge in management institutions

Knowledge Management programs are typically tied to organizational objectives such as improved performance, competitive advantage innovation, lessons learnt transfer (for example between projects) and the general development of collaborative practices. Knowledge Management is frequently linked to the idea of the learning organization although neither practice encompasses the other. Knowledge Management may be distinguished from Organizational Learning by a greater focus on specific knowledge assets and the development and cultivation of the channels through which knowledge flows.

KNOWLEDGE MANAGEMENT AND LEARNING ORGANIZATION

What is Learning?

Personally, I like simple definitions that are easy to understand. The best definition of learning for me came from KM specialist Hubert Saint-Onge who, at a KM conference in London in the mid-1990s, simply, but profoundly, said that "learning is the process of turning information into knowledge".

There we have it:

> Effective information management, together with embedding the best learning processes and culture throughout the organization, will inevitably lead to the much better creation of organizational knowledge.

But is it Really that Simple?

Whilst consulting with General Motors (GM) in 1993, I was struck by the company's approach to transforming its culture into a more collaborative and knowledge-sharing one. Executives at GM asked themselves the question, "Is it possible to bring about a more 'naturally' flourishing knowledge-sharing culture?"

In other words, are there any natural principles that we can apply to learning and knowledge driven organizations? We concluded that:

- Trust is the lifeblood of any organization, and when sufficient trust is developed, people will "naturally" want to communicate.
- Open and frequent, two-way communication will develop even more trust and people will "naturally" want to collaborate and work better together.
- More open and more frequent communication of information "naturally" brings about more rapid, more accelerated learning.
- Increased and continual learning will "naturally" increase peoples' levels of confidence and competence.
- Confident and competent people "naturally" want to share their knowledge.
- Sharing knowledge, naturally, is enjoyable.

Building a Virtuous KM Cycle

We also concluded that these principles all build on one another and interrelate to form a "virtuous circle" . That is to say that, if you improve in any one area, it will impact and improve all the others. Conversely, if any one principle is neglected, it will also impact all the others, to create a vicious circle of doubt, fear and distrust.

A virtuous circle, will lead to much better "knowing what we know". A vicious circle, by contrast, leads to "not knowing what we know".

So GM tried to implement the principles to naturally bring about more trust, improved communications, faster learning and natural knowledge sharing. They sent me and members of their senior management team, to outdoor experiential learning camps in Europe, Asia and the USA where we set about learning how to trust one another more through exercises such as "trust falls" and team activities.

Although we were all blood brothers and sisters in the bar each evening on these trips, that bonding didn't last in all cases. After returning to work for just one month, it was "business as usual".

Trust must be earned, not just learned. It develops over a long period, but can be destroyed in seconds.

The next principle was to improve communications by implementing the best communications and information technologies.

But if there is not sufficient trust, this won't work either. People must want to learn and share knowledge. They cannot be forced to do this.

What worked best, and remarkably well, at GM were the initiatives undertaken to help people learn faster and develop their own personal competencies. And why did these work best? Ithink it's because this approach answers the key question that most people involved in a KM project ask:

"What's in it for me?"

Everybody, or certainly most people, want to improve themselves, to develop and grow and to become more marketable and successful. Capturing new learning and ideas as they occur (through both direct work experience and formal training) transforms an organization from an environment of 'episodic learning and innovation' to one of 'continual learning and innovation'.

People are also far more likely to naturally share their knowledge in that environment. As a result, making the principle of improved learning the primary focus was the most successful approach at GM.

Without doubt, learning organization initiatives can work extremely well and can reward individuals, teams and organizations handsomely.

So where does KM fit in?

I claimed earlier that the key contributor to organizational success is the acquisition of the best knowledge and its wise application. The two key words here are "acquisition" and "application".

Learning is about the acquisition of knowledge, turning information into knowledge. KM should be about having access to, and applying, that knowledge.

So I see learning and KM as two sides of the same coin.

If we look at the roots of the learning organization, it is predominantly about enabling individuals and teams to learn. It began as a bottom-up approach and is primarily a people-centric one.

If we look at the roots of KM, it is predominantly about categorizing, storing, sharing and applying organizational knowledge in a collective and systematic way. It started as a top-down approach and was, initially, more technology centric.

Both complement one another. In fact, they're highly synergistic. So much so that, over the years, the learning organization has made significant and natural inroads into KM, and *vice versa*.

Today, I look at mature and highly successful learning organizations, such as Standard Chartered Bank, and see the principles and characteristics of KM embedded throughout the organization.

There's no doubt in my mind that organizations with strong learning-organization roots will wish to continue their initiatives and efforts in that direction, perhaps under the direction of a Chief Learning Officer (CLO). And organizations that have strong KM roots will similarly wish to continue their initiatives and efforts in their chosen direction, perhaps led by a Chief Knowledge Officer (CKO).

Some organizations may wish to continue initiatives and efforts that embrace both disciplines. It doesn't matter at all. These are simply useful labels, and maybe one day, someone will invent a new label that embraces both.

What does matter is that we constantly remind ourselves of the evergreen business principles that will naturally lead to organizational success and then apply the best strategies, processes, methods, tools and techniques available at any given time to bring those principles fully to life.

Learning and Knowledge Management

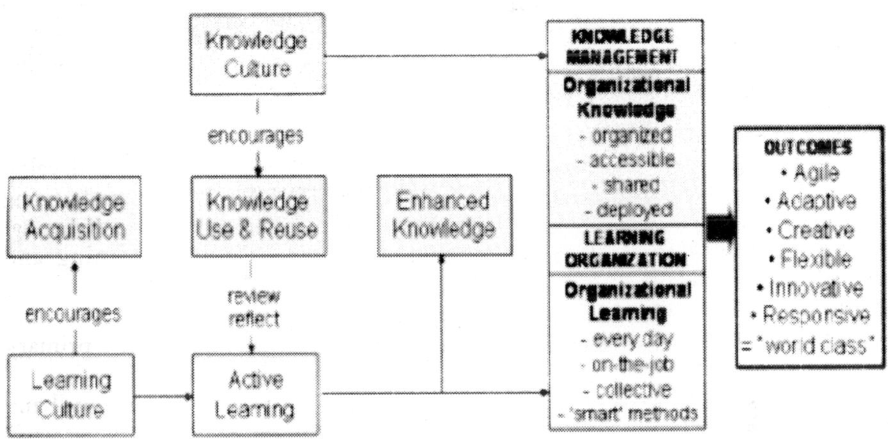

It is a sad reflection on 'silo' mentalities that often Learning Organization and Knowledge Management are viewed as separate initiatives. After all, they often originate in different parts of the organization (typically HR/training for the former and IT/marketing/strategy etc. for the latter). However, in *Creating the Knowledge-Based Business*, knowledge management and organizational learning are described as being "two sides of the same coin":

> "Learning comes through creating and applying knowledge, whilst learning increases an individual's and organization's knowledge asset".

KM and LO are inter-dependent. The above diagram shows some of these linkages. For example, a disposition to learning encourages the acquisition and development both of personal and organizational knowledge, while KM provides the infrastructure and techniques to assimilate learning and enhance the quality of organizational knowledge. Today, learning is a key feature in many KM practices, such as After Action Reviews and sharing best practice. On the other hand KM can support learning activities, such as through the better classification, organization and management of e-learning modules on a corporate portal.

Knowledge Culture and Learning Organization

An organization is a group of individuals. A group has evolved a culture, with the strength of that knowledge culture dependent on the length of group's existence, the stability of the memberships of individuals in the group, and the emotional intensity of the actual historical experiences they have shared. Consequently, it takes time to foster a new Knowledgeable culture, e.g. a learning one. A Learning

Organization has a culture that supports learning and innovations both by individuals and by the organization itself The environment promotes a culture of learning, a community of learners, and it ensures that individual learning enriches and enhances the organization as a whole The process of learning must ultimately be made part of the culture, not just be a solution to a given problem.

Learning organizations demand a new view of leadership, leader as designer. Culture begins with leadership, but because culture is the result of a group's accumulated learning the culture itself will later define the wanted leadership. The first step in building a learning organization requires a leader who inspires the vision of the learning organization.

To be a LO has no value in itself, it must always serve the broader aims of the organization. Shared visions emerge from personal visions. A Learning Organization has a design and a culture which takes into account the needs of the individuals in the organization, and in a LO members know why. In other organizations they know how A LO is organized in such a way that it scans for information in its environment, creates information by itself, and encourages individuals to transfer know-ledge between the individuals in team. This must be guided by the structure and by the vision that is guided by the strategic leadership of the organization Employees must have time for learning and management must regard learning as real work. In a learning organization work processes must integrate attention to every aspect of knowledge. The processes must enable knowledge dissemination and the culture must encourage knowledge sharing.

Learning is when changes in knowledge happen inside an individual, and learning and accumulation of (new) knowledge always starts with the individual. Individual learning does not necessarily imply changes in organizational knowledge. Organizational knowledge is knowledge independent of specific members in the organization, e.g. knowledge in knowledge repositories, and knowledge embedded in policies, and routines. Organizational Learning (OL) is considered to depend on the collective cognitive processes of individuals. Individuals can be regarded as sub-systems in the organization. The concept of LO regards the organization as an entity and focuses what are the characteristics such that encourages its members may learn. OL, on the other hand, focuses on how learning is developed in an organization. Learning that changes the strategies, but leaving the values unchanged, is often referred as Single loop learning, and learning that results in changes in the values as Double loop learning. According to Kezar there are differences in these two areas of study:

- LO tends to focus more on external threats as the reason for fostering learning.
- OL tends to focus more on internal concerns for performance and learning as part of condition of human beings within settings.

A LO must be able to meet demands of both its internal and external environments. Some argue that LO is a vision. OL is a continuous learning cycle and an organization can never come to a point in time when it can declare itself a LO. On the other hand, no organization can be in a constant state of learning and declare itself to be practicing OL

According to Senge the core of learning organization work is based upon five "learning disciplines", each providing a true dimension in building an organization that can truly learn:

- Personal mastery
- Mental models
- Team learning
- Shared vision
- System's thinking

Senge's five disciplines are integral components in a learning organization, providing tools and methods that are applicable and useful in the process of OL. Each of the five disciplines can be thought of on three levels: practices, principles, essences. These levels are on accordance with the three levels of Van Gigch.

TABLE I
Keywords in LO and KM

Keyword	*LO—"an entity", which requires KM*	*KM—"a process", which assumes a LO*
Culture	A LO has a learning culture. (e.g. Personal Mastery, Team Learning, Mental Models)	Culture constraints the efficient use, because KM is carried out by individuals
Leadership/ management	Leadership fosters the culture	Management has a central role, but acts within a culture
Vision	A shared vision is necessary	KM must have a vision
Work processes	A LO integrates attention to every aspect of knowledge	KM must be integrated
Organizational Learning	A LO is good at OL, OL is a collective cognitive process	Knowledge is the result of OL
External factors	Must meet these demands	—
Internal factors	Must meet these demands	Constraints the efficient use, e.g. culture and IT
System's thinking	How a LO thinks about the world	—
Organizational Memory	—	E.g. data repository
Technical	—	Is a prerequisite

Factors of Knowledge LO/KM

- Factors only in LO:
  - o External factors
  - o System's thinking
- Factors only in KM:
  - o Organizational Memory
  - o Technical

This phenomenon indicates that LO and KM are on different levels of abstraction with different focus and purpose. We first discuss why we assume this in the perspective of External factors and System's thinking, and then in the perspective of Organizational memory and Technical.

A LO is about the whole organization which in turn is a part of the world. As a sub-system in the world the organization must interact with other sub-systems in the world and also manage external factors outside the organization, e.g. competitors, and customers. This is necessary for survival. KM is performed in the organization, is a sub-system in the organization. KM is therefore more focused on internal factors inside the organization. When KM literature mentioned external factors they do it in an implicit way and talk about it as factors that the organization must manage. How efficient KM is depends on internal factors. KM discusses internal factors in terms of constraints. When LO discusses internal factors it is mostly in the view of meeting internal demands. An organization consists of individuals, and meeting internal demands is therefore about meeting demands from members in the organization. Each member has its own image of itself in relation to the organization. The organization's practice stems from these images, which the members remake when conditions change. Each individual is a sub-system in KM, and in that perspective it is strange that system's thinking to our knowledge not explicit is discussed in this domain. On the other hand, to have system's thinking when discussing LO, implies this approach also to KM.

The organizational memory refers to stored know-ledge and aims to enable knowledge sharing and knowledge reuse. It corresponds to that type of KM which accumulates knowledge outside people In the perspective of knowledge storage, dissemination and sharing, IT is a prerequisite for effective KM, and we can therefore see that Organizational Memory and Technical are tightly coupled. Both re-gard knowledge as a product, which is in line with KM. Knowledge is an input to and/or a result from OL. KM regards OL as a process that transforms knowledge. A LO is good at organizational learning, and views OL more as a collective cognitive process. LO literature does not explicit discuss organizational memory; it discusses organizational knowledge, where organizational memory is a part. The Learning Organization is so much more than KM, and has its focus on a higher level. A LO is more about fostering a learning culture, and developing structures that support learning. Of course efficient use of IT in turn will support learning structures, but a LO focuses on learning structures in general, where IT is only one part. Therefore, it is natural that LO does not have a technical focus. As we see it a LO more or less takes IT for granted in the same way as with mail, telephone, documents, etc.

Our analysis based on the four keywords that did not appear in both domains strengthens the indication that LO and KM are at different levels of abstraction. This is also supported in those cases where the same keyword appears in both domains. A LO has a learning Culture, "is" the culture, but KM is limited by the culture. The same type of relation results in the fact that LO literature mainly discusses Leadership, and KM literature Management. Leadership creates and changes culture, and management or administration acts within a culture. Both KM and LO must have a Vision, but in LO literature the importance of a shared vision is stressed. KM as an isolated event could be successful even if the vision is not shared, but an organization must have a shared vision to be able to develop a learning culture. On the other hand, KM aims to support the organization to be a LO, and in that perspective KM also needs a shared vision. The keyword work processes is the only one that appears in the same way in both domains. Both LO and KM literature discusses the importance of integrating aspects of knowledge in these processes. The remaining keywords identified in both domains, Internal factors and Organizational Learning, were discussed when analyzing the four keywords which only appear in one domain.

Our comparative analysis has clearly shown relationships, differences and similarities between LO and KM. In a simplistic way we can say that LO and KM is about the same thing, but with different aims and on different levels. In the view of Van Gigch's three levels of inquiry, LO can be compared with the Reflecting level—"Why"—level, and KM with the Diagnostic level—"What to do"—level. A LO aims to support learning. Learning implies changes in knowledge. A LO therefore requires to manage knowledge effective, and effective KM is what to do in order to fulfill this requirement. KM aims to support distribution of knowledge, of course in turn aiming to support learning. LO requires KM, and KM assumes a LO. A LO is on a higher level and includes so much more than KM. Work processes must enable learning and integrate every aspect of knowledge. As we see it, this indicates that work processes in a LO can be regarded as an important connection between LO and KM.

A LO can be regarded as the system, which in-cludes the subsystem KM. This is in accordance with Senge's idea that system's thinking must be the conceptual cornerstone. Consequently, a change in KM affects the organization, and a change in the organization, e.g. the culture, affects KM. As a result, the process to become a Learning Organization must take place on both levels. Enabling organizations to become learning organizations therefore requires introducing LO as well as KM. A LO has a climate.

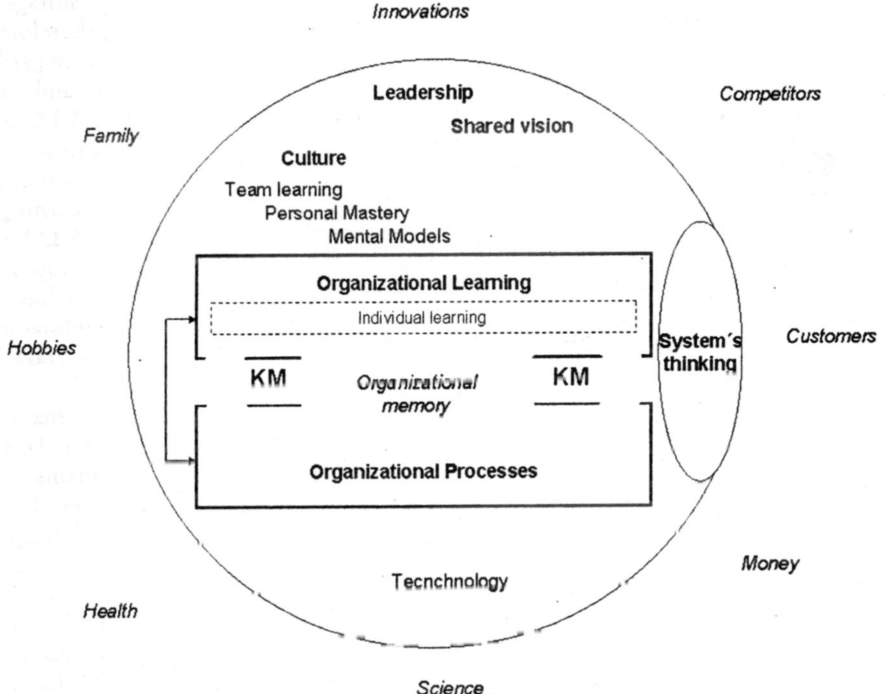

A Conceptual Model of LO and KM

It is a cornerstone of how learning organizations think about the world, and how they look at the world. Thus the conceptual model is shaped as an eye which regards the world from a system's perspective. Personal mastery, Mental models, and Team learning are as we see it different perspectives on the organizational culture.

Culture is the result of the organization's accumulated learning about values, assumptions etc. It evolves with the strength of that culture; in turn dependent on the length of its existence, the stability of the individuals' membership, and the emotional intensity of the actual historical experiences they have shared. It is the leader who initiates this process by imposing his or her beliefs, values, and assumptions, but culture only arises when individuals′ assumptions lead to shared experiences. The importance of a Shared vision is well stated in the literature. There cannot be a learning organization without a shared vision. A shared vision is a part of the organizational culture. The importance of the vision is well stated in literature.

HR and Knowledge Management

There are several roles that can be played by HR in developing knowledge management system. First, HR should help the organization articulate the purpose of the knowledge management system. Investing in a knowledge management initiative without a clear sense of purpose is like investing in an expensive camera that has far more capabilities than you need to take good pictures of family and friends. Too often, organizations embrace technologies to solve problems before they've even identified the problems they are trying to solve. Then, once they realize the error, they find it difficult to abandon the original solution and difficult to gather the resources needed to invest in a solution to the real problem. Effectively framing the knowledge management issue, before deciding on a course of action, is a crucial prerequisite for success.

Second, as a knowledge facilitator, HRM must ensure alignment among an organization's mission, statement of ethics, and policies: These should all be directed toward creating an environment of sharing and using knowledge with full understanding of the competitive consequences. Furthermore, HRM must nourish a culture that embraces getting the right information to the right people at the right time.

Third, HRM should also create the "ultimate employee experience." That is, by transforming tacit knowledge into explicit knowledge through education, organizations must build employee skills, competencies, and careers, creating "bench strength." This combines the traditional training and development responsibilities of HRM with the new responsibilities of human capital steward: using all of the organization's resources to create strategic capability. Disney's new staff orientation, which emphasizes the firm's mission, values, and history within a context of the "magic kingdom" experience, is an example of this process of making tacit knowledge more visible.

Fourth, HRM must integrate effective knowledge sharing and usage into daily life. That is, knowledge sharing must be expected, recognized, and rewarded. For many individuals and organizations, this reverses the conventional relationship between knowledge and power. Often, the common pattern was to hoard knowledge because it made the individual more valuable and more difficult to replace. Effective knowledge management requires this trend to be overturned and requires those with information to become teachers and mentors who ensure that others in the firm know what they know. Teaching must become part of everyone's job. Clearly, for such a cultural shift to take place, HRM must overhaul selection, appraisal, and compensation practices. Human resource management has the capabilities for creating, measuring, and reinforcing a knowledge-sharing expectation.

Fifth, HRM must relax controls and allow (even encourage) behaviors that, in the clockwork world of industrial efficiency, never would have been tolerated. For example, conversations at the water cooler were viewed in the past as unproductive uses of employee time—after all, employees were not at their desks completing specified tasks detailed in their job descriptions. In the knowledge economy, conversations inside and outside the company are the chief mechanism for making change and renewal an ongoing part of the company's culture.

As another example, consider individuals in organizations described as "gossips," who would rather talk than work. Frederick Taylor's industrial engineers would have eliminated these gossips from workplaces in the early twentieth century, since they did nothing that was perceptibly valuable. However, in the knowledge economy, if the conversations are relevant to the firm's strategic intent, these same people may be described as "knowledge brokers": those individuals who like to move around the company to hear what is going on, sparking new knowledge creation by carrying ideas between groups of people who do not communicate directly. If the topics serve organizational needs, these individuals play a role similar to bees that cross-pollinate flowers and sustain a larger ecosystem.

Organizations should selectively recognize and reward, rather than universally discourage and punish, these types of behaviors. Clearly, not all conversation is productive and constructive. Human resource management still must play a role in discouraging gossip that undermines, rather than promotes, a learning community. Human resource management will need to adjust both its own perspective (from rule-enforcer) as well as that of managers and others who hold outdated notions of what is "real work."

Sixth, HRM must take a strategic approach to helping firms manage email, instant messenger, internet surfing, and similar uses of technology. Clearly, the Internet has a role in generating and disseminating knowledge, and therefore is an integral part of knowledge management. But what are the unintended effects of monitoring email, tracking employees' web searches, and similar issues related to privacy? Certainly some control is needed, but the larger question for HRM is determining appropriate boundaries. When does control become counter-productive? When does excessive monitoring become an inappropriate invasion of privacy?

A related issue is HRM's role in helping firms manage the distancing consequences of electronic communication. As employees increasingly rely on technology to communicate, they lose opportunities to develop the rich, multifaceted relationships that encourage the communication of tacit knowledge. Human resource management can contribute to developing social capital by sensitizing employees to the negative consequences of excessive reliance on electronic media and by creating opportunities for face-to-face contact.

Seventh, HRM must champion the low-tech solutions to knowledge management. Although it should not ignore the high-tech knowledge management tools, HRM contains the expertise to develop low-tech knowledge management strategies. For example, when the team that developed the Dustbuster vacuum tool was created, they were given a "war room" in which they could spread out their materials and leave sketches, models, notes, and so on plastered on walls and throughout the workspace. These visible outputs of their thinking processes helped create a shared context for their efforts and turned the room into a truly collaborative workspace.

Some Asian firms, such as Dai-Ichi, create special rooms (with green tea and comfortable places to sit), where researchers are expected to spend a half-hour daily, telling whomever they meet about their current work. Neither of the two preceding examples requires large financial investments in technology that will rapidly become

TABLE 2

KM Applications Mapped to the Six Elements of the KM Spectrum

Transactional	*Analytical*	*Asset Management*	*Process*	*Developmental*	*Innovation and Creation*
• Case Based Reasoning (CBR) • Help Desk Applications • Customer Service Applications • Order Entry Applications • Service Agent Support Applications	Service Agent Support Applications • Data Warehousing • Data Mining • Business Intelligence • Management Information Systems • Decision Support System • Customer Relationship Management (CRM) • Competitive Intelligence	Intellectual Property • Document Management • Knowledge Valuation • Knowledge Repositories • Content Management	Total Quality Management (TQM) • Benchmarking • Best Practices • Quality Management • Business Process (Re)Engineering • Process Improvement • Process Automation • Lessons Learned • Methodology	Skills Development • Staff Competencies • Learning • Teaching • Training	• Communities of Practice/ Interest • Collaboration • Discussion Forums • Networking • Multi-Disciplined Teams • Virtual Teams • Research and Development (R&D)

Source : (Binney, 2001: 35).

obsolete. Yet both examples demonstrate how HRM could help a firm orchestrate and facilitate knowledge sharing.

The first three elements (comprising transactional, analytical and asset management KM applications) are mostly used by 'technologists' seeking to collect and systematize existing information. The last three elements (comprising process, developmental and innovation/creation KM applications) are mostly used by those KM consultants focused on organizational Management and processes. It is concludes by urging organizations to use the KM spectrum as a tool to choose KM applications from a wider range than they might normally tend to use.

In simple terms, it is one that is able to effectively tap into peoples' commitment and capacity to learn, at every level in its hierarchy.

At the recent Bali study meeting, Arnold Chan, chief learning officer for Standard Chartered Bank in Singapore, told me that his company's learning agenda involved:

- Aligning learning and development strategies/initiatives to business strategies through the Bank's "strategic people agenda";
- Implementing a strong engagement model to solicit commitment from stakeholders;
- Integrating high-impact learning processes into the Bank's people-development program;
- Creating a seamless learning portal to offer a wide range of learning opportunities, catering to different learning styles; and
- Transforming to sustain the Bank's competitive advantage in the marketplace.

And Praba Nair, director of consultancy company KDI Asia, and my colleague and fellow keynote speaker at the event, defines some key characteristics of a learning and knowledge organization as one that is committed to:

- Lifelong learning;
- Creating a learning environment;
- Fostering a climate of openness and trust;
- Encouraging free exchange and flow of information;
- Learning and personal development.

The Five Learning Disciplines

The five learning disciplines outlined by are:

1. **Personal mastery**–Learning to expand our personal capacity to create the results we most desire and creating an organizational environment that encourages all its members to develop themselves toward the goal and purposes that they choose.
2. **Mental models**–Reflecting upon, continually clarifying and improving our internal pictures of the world, and seeing how they shape our actions and decisions.
3. **Shared vision**–Building a sense of commitment in a group, by developing shared images of the future we seek and the principles and guiding practices by which we hope to get there.
4. *Team learning*–Transforming conversational and collective thinking skills, so that groups of people can reliably develop intelligence and ability greater than the sum of individual members' talents.

5. **Systems thinking**–A way of thinking about the forces and interrelationships that shape the behavior of systems. This discipline helps us see how to change systems more effectively and to act more in tune with the larger processes of the natural and economic world.

Role of Chief Knowledge Officers in Learning Organization

In many organizations, a new position has emerged in recent years that will significantly affect the knowledge management activities in the firm. The title of this position is the Chief Knowledge Officer (CKO). Many of the Fortune 500 companies already have a Chief Knowledge Officer or knowledge management teams in place. The CKO has also been referred to as the Director of Competitive Learning, Chief Learning Officer, VP of Learning, Director of Organizational Learning, Knowledge Management Director, Knowledge Strategies Director, Director of Intangible Assets, Corporate Director of Intellectual Capital, and Head of Knowledge Management Development.

The CKO, according to TFPL, Inc. (an international consulting firm that conducts CKO Summits), acts in four ways [TFPL, 2002]: first, as a "cartographer" in mapping expertise and making connections; second, as a "geologist" in drilling into specific areas and applying tools; third, as a "spark plug" in igniting an awareness of the need to change; and last, as an "architect" in designing the physical and cultural environment. The typical CKO finds a means to utilize corporate knowledge to help corporate growth, understands the skills and competencies of knowledge teams, creates powerful corporate cultures that recognize common values, enables the effective flow of information, and communicates the meaning of information and knowledge.

A chief knowledge officer (CKO) is an organizational leader, responsible for ensuring that the organization maximizes the value it achieves through "knowledge". The CKO is responsible for managing intellectual capital and the custodian of Knowledge Management practices in an organization CKO is not just a relabeling of the title "chief information officer"—the CKO role is much broader. CKOs can help an organization maximize the returns on investment in knowledge (people, processes and intellectual capital), exploit their intangible assets (know-how, patents, customer relationships), repeat successes, share best practices, improve innovation, and avoid knowledge loss after organizational restructuring.

CKO responsibilities include such things as:

Collecting relevant data that is useful for the organization as knowledge
Developing an overall framework that guides knowledge management
Actively promoting the knowledge agenda within and beyond the company
Overseeing the development of the knowledge infrastructure
Facilitating connections, coordination and communications.

CKOs must have skills across a wide variety of areas. They must be good at developing/understanding the big picture, advocacy (articulation, promotion and justification of the knowledge agenda, sometimes against cynicism or even open hostility), project and people management (oversight of a variety of activities, attention to detail, ability to motivate), communications (communicating clearly the knowledge agenda, have good listening skills and be sensitive to organizational opportunities and obstacles), leadership, team working, influencing, and interpersonal skills. The CKO who successfully combines these skills is well equipped as an excellent agent of change for their organization.

Other terms for CKO include knowledge manager, director intellectual capital (e.g. Scandia), director knowledge transfer (e.g. Buckman Laboratories), and knowledge asset manager (e.g. Dow Chemical).

The CKO has to win cooperation and "buy-in" from all levels of the organization; must identify and utilise a diverse set of skills and expertise; and demonstrate the value of knowledge management (KM) to the business. In many organizations, like The World Bank in Washington, D.C., the Chairman of The World Bank has made knowledge management part of its strategic mission. As such, knowledge management activities like capturing and putting knowledge on-line as global help desks, and developing and nurturing online communities of practice (called thematic groups at The World Bank) are being conducted.

According to Tom Davenport, of Accenture and Babson College, the CKO [Davenport and Prusak, 1998]:

- Must be an advocate or evangelist for knowledge and learning;
- Is the designer, implementer, and overseer of an organization's knowledge infrastructure, including its libraries, knowledge bases, human resources, computer knowledge networks, research centers, and academic relationships;
- Is the primary liaison between external providers of information and knowledge;
- Provides critical input into the creation of knowledge and uses processes that already exist within the company, such as product development;
- Plays a leading role in the design and implementation of a company's knowledge architectures;
- Has deep experience in some aspect of knowledge management, including its creation, dissemination, or application;
- Has familiarity with knowledge-oriented companies and technologies, such as libraries and groupware;
- Has the ability to set a good example by displaying a high level of "knowledge ability" and success.

The CKO assumes responsibility for knowledge and unstructured information and is in charge of managing those assets. These assets are often referred to as "intellectual capital", "knowledge assets", or "intangible assets".

Robert Neilson, from the National Defense University who chairs the Role of the CKO Working Group for the US Federal CIO Council's Sub-committee on Knowledge Management [http:www.krn.gov] believes that the following competencies make a successful CKO—communications (storyteller—avid communicator), strategic thinking, tools and technology, personal behaviour, personal knowledge and cognitive capability, and leadership and management. Specifically, he feels that a CKO must have passion, patience, persistence, sensitivity, organizational savvy, intelligence, wisdom, life long learning capabilities, depth and breadth of knowledge, and be thick skinned and an integrator. The CKO typically measures outcomes, promotes best practices and processes, creates a knowledge-sharing culture, champions communities of practice, uses incentives and rewards, provides tools and technology, champions education, creates and uses taxonomy (common language), secures resources, and provides leadership and strategy.

Michael Earl (1999) of the London Business School performed a study to examine what is a CKO. Some of his findings indicated that those CKOs who emphasized explicit knowledge tended to promote the use of technology to enable knowledge distribution and sharing. Those CKOs who emphasized tacit or implicit knowledge spent a great deal of their time enabling, facilitating, and promoting informal dialogues. Richard Herschel and Hamid Nemati (1999) at the University of North Carolina-Greensboro concurred with these findings.

Bob Guns of Probe Consulting and Price Waterhouse Coopers, studied 52 of the top CKOs in the US (Daffy, 1998) and found that CKO's generally had a broad base of experience within a business, and most had experience in a wide range of functions. The ability to withstand a myriad of pressures was generally acknowledged as an important trait among the CKOs. This study had similar results to Earl's work and showed that the CKOs have strong nurturing qualities and are "influencers". David Skyrme Associates (1997) that CKOs are good at conceptual thinking, advocacy, project and people management, communications, leadership, team working, influencing, and interpersonal skills.

- Knowledge strategies influence future business strategy direction;
- Knowledge initiatives need to be integrated into business processes and embedded into workflows;
- The central knowledge team is increasingly seen as the catalyst and facilitator;
- Core competencies required throughout the company need to be changed to reflect a knowledge sharing activity among their core areas;
- A shift from employment to employability and portfolio careers has resulted and knowledge initiatives need to support this trend;
- New drivers and justifications are emerging for knowledge strategies (e.g., to support other corporate initiatives like e-business);
- A clear recognition exists for the need to identify tools and techniques that enable people to navigate through vast repositories (i.e., content management is a significant issue);
- Synergies should exist between knowledge and learning initiatives and the two areas should benefit from each other;
- Measurement is still a major issue to further convince senior management of the benefits of knowledge management;
- Knowledge management is more about flows of knowledge rather than stocks of knowledge;
- Culture realignment is the key challenge; and
- Functional silos (such as IT, HR) present barriers to implementing KM—they need to be more integrated together.

Where should the CKO position be placed in the organization? Some organizations have placed the CKO within the information systems or human resources departments. Others have positioned the CKO comparable to a VP position or a staff position reporting directly to the CEO. In order for knowledge management to succeed, the CKO should be placed in a position that commands authority and responsibility in the upper echelon of management. Since knowledge management is typically a "strategic" function. Of course, the overriding consideration is that the knowledge management activities put into place should blend in well with the organization's corporate culture.

Why is a CKO needed in an organization? In the same manner that the University of California at Berkeley has established a Professorship of Knowledge, organizations should also realize the strategic importance of knowledge as the competitive edge for their organization. This is happening by means of creation of CKO positions and company resources being expended towards developing knowledge management systems in the organization. Knowledge management involves creating, securing, combining, distributing, and retrieving knowledge. Being able to develop and maintain the knowledge repositories in the organization, as part of these knowledge management systems is a critical element, which needs to be coordinated (and possibly managed) by the CKO and his/her staff. The CKO also needs to work closely with the human resources managers to ensure that incentives and other forms of encouragement are provided to employees to stimulate their knowledge sharing.

The CKO Job Description

To help understand the role of a CKO a knowledge profile or job description for the CKO may be illuminating. Appendix 1 at the end of the paper illustrates the duties and responsibilities of CKOs in the General Services Administration and the US Navy [http://www.km.gov].

According to TFPL Inc. [2000, 2002], the CKO should lead in the development of corporate culture, processes, infrastructure and information resources to facilitate the creation and utilization of corporate knowledge, expertise, and information to create competitive advantage and support creativity.

CHIEF INFORMATION OFFICERS AND CHIEF KNOWLEDGE OFFICER

The CKO and the CIO: Should they be the Same?

A number of organizations feel that their Chief Information Officer (CIO) can handle the duties of a Chief Knowledge Officer (CKO). This belief is probably the wrong approach for a number of reasons. First, the CIO typically has a technology-oriented focus and may develop a knowledge management strategy that concentrates mostly on technology, rather than on the people and culture aspects of knowledge management. Second, the CKO needs to possess a different skill set than the typical CIO. Michael Earl's (1999) study of twenty CKOs in North America and Europe, found that CKOs have distinct functions that are different from those of CIOs. The CIO is typically involved with IT strategy, IT operations, and managing the IT function, and has not taken on the full range of knowledge management activities. Earl's study of CKOs found that the CKO typically has a breadth of career experience and familiarity with the organization, is a good influencer, highly motivated, even tempered, deals with stress well, is extroverted, and can vary his/her behaviors to meet the demands of a situation, is social, goal-oriented and interested in change. Last, the CIO typically has a large staff whereas the CKO normally has small staff of 3-12 people working mainly as specialist consultants.

The CIO's role, however, has been changing somewhat over the years. In a survey of 340 CIOs in the U.S., England, Germany, and France conducted by Korn/Ferry, *The Financial Times*, and the CIO Executive Research Centre, the following key trends were uncovered:

- The role of the CIO is moving from technical planning and implementation to strategic planning.
- The CIO's ideal resume will include both technical/engineering qualifications, plus a background in finance, marketing, and strategic planning.

- The CIO will become increasingly involved with external as well as internal customer support.
- There needs improvement in communication between the CIO and senior policy makers in the organization.

In some organizations, like the General Services Administration (GSA) in the US government, some CIOs have successfully transitioned into the role of CKOs. Dr. Shereen Remez, GSA's CIO, was selected to be the agency's first CKO. She now serves as the CKO at the American Association for Retired Persons. According to Federal Computer Week (June 14, 1999), Dr. Remez as CKO is responsible for leading the agency's use of knowledge management practices. However, Dr. Remez had a unique set of skills that vary from the typical CIO, a Ph.D. in the human resources/ education area, which made her a perfect fit for a CKO.

Davenport (1996) believes that CKOs have three critical responsibilities—creating a knowledge management infrastructure, building a knowledge culture, and making it all pay off economically. A good CKO should combine an orientation to structured, explicit knowledge with an intuitive feel for the influence of cultural and behavioural factors on the leveraging of knowledge in an enterprise.

John Sviokla (2001) of Diamond Cluster International suggested that CIOs must redefine knowledge management in terms that focus on what is most valuable to a business. He stated the CIO needs to focus the knowledge management people on the goal of lowering asset intensity and improving the cash collection cycle. In the same issue of CIO Magazine, the CIO for Warner Music Group, Jim Noble, suggested that a CIO needs to connect with everyone and adds that the CIO has to engage the "hearts and minds" of the executive team. Mony Group's CIO, E.P. Rogers, indicates that his role as ClO has changed over the years. He used to spend 90 percent of his time on IT, but today he probably spends 80 percent of his time on corporate business projects. He adds that with new technologies, new skills, and a more collaborative style, IS has evolved into an organisation much more attuned to the business. EDS' CIO, Terry Milholland, says that there are higher expectations from business leaders—they have to react in days not months!

Tom Koulopoulos, President of The Delphi Group, feels that the primary purpose of having someone in charge of leveraging knowledge inside an organization is to search for opportunities (Brown, 1999). Koulopoulos indicates that the best CKOs, no matter what they're called, are "nomads" or "bounty hunters", browsing the entire company searching for opportunities. A knowledge leader, like the CKO, must also be adept at traversing the information technology communities, which are part of the corporation, and must understand the basic principles behind intellectual capital. Koulopoulos points out that the critical success factor for a CKO is being incredibly competent and serving as a conduit or "super facilitator" for creating knowledge, not merely acting as "knowledge czars".

Ogden Forbes, who has served as Chief Knowledge and Research Officer at shopping.com, indicates that "CIOs are charged with implementing technology; I assist them as the eyes and ears of what strategies to follow while they also remind me of what can be done" (Carrillo, 1997). According to Wayne Toms of the Delphi Consulting Group, the CKO's role is expected to grow, because companies are focusing more on employees than on technology. David Jones of Xerox says that the CKO's role is mostly concerned with cultural change.

Weinstein (1998), a Knowledge Officer of an online retail store, described his job as increasing the knowledge base of the company's workers so that better decisions are made and assisting the CIO in implementing technology. Additionally, the CKO may also be in charge of managing intellectual property. Typically the CKO should have a broad mix of personal, corporate, and technical skills. Sue Gilly, the Chief Knowledge Officer at Cavanaugh Leahy & Company, feels that the core of her work as CKO is how people collaborate and learn.

So the question remains—can a CIO be the CKO in most organisations? In the view of this author, these two positions should be separate unless the organisation has an exceptional individual with the necessary skill sets for serving as both CIO and CKO. The two positions should be closely aligned; however, if knowledge management is to fruly succeed, and a CKO should be appointed in the organisation to develop and implement a knowledge management strategy in the organisation and to spearhead these knowledge management initiatives.

Developing Knowledge Sharing Proficiencies

One of the basic tenets of knowledge management is to build a supportive culture for knowledge sharing The adage "knowledge is power" needs to be replaced by the motto "**sharing** knowledge is power" for organizations to truly maximize their intellectual capital (Neches *et al.*, 1991). Very little research in the knowledge management field has focused on determining how effective knowledge sharing is occurring in organizations. As organizations start to incorporate learning and knowledge sharing proficiencies as part of their annual job performance evaluations (The World Bank, Gemini Consulting, and Accenture), it becomes necessary to establish criteria for such proficiencies or competencies and then to measure how well people are doing with respect to these knowledge sharing factors.

Companies are already realizing that knowledge sharing gives them their competitive edge by leading to accelerated learning and innovation (Hickins, 1999). Xerox's reputation as a leading knowledge company has been built on a strong knowledge sharing culture (Hickins, 1999). Xerox claims that knowledge sharing is going to become part of a fabric inside the company for all employees. Similarly, Dow Corning has expressed its commitment to team-building and knowledge sharing. At Dow Corning Europe there are various professional clubs that share common aims such as to improve the understanding of fundamental concepts, raise awareness of techniques available in Dow Corning and elsewhere; to learn by example how to interpret the results of measurements and relate them to applications, to identify gaps in Dow's overall understanding and to formulate ways to fill those gaps, share experiences, problems, failures, successes, provide a forum for the peer review of ideas, theories, and the interpretation of test data (Easton & Parbhoo, 1998). Lockheed-Martin's, key to knowledge sharing is matching the type of knowledge with the right transfer method (Dixon, 2000). Three factors—whether the task is routine or non-routine; whether the knowledge related to it is tacit or explicit; and the similarity between the originator and the receiver of the information—determine the method through which the knowledge can be most effectively transferred (Dixon, 2000).

To help build a knowledge sharing culture, various knowledge sharing proficiencies should be developed and integrated into the performance system of the organization. A number of organizations like Capital Works in Williamstown (Massachusetts) have developed learning effectiveness inventories, since learning is at the core of human capital performance and knowledge creation in the new economy. Capital Works, for example, has a Learning Value Analysis where learning is assessed across multiple dimensions by the indicators:

- Operating performance (economics, productivity, human capital)
- Knowledge performance (applied knowledge, knowledge creation, social capital)
- Learning performance (portfolio composition, organisational dynamics, individual dynamics)
- Organizational performance (social practice, workplace dynamics, critical behaviors, job dimensions)
- Strategic performance (alignment objectives, economic objectives, and human capital objectives).

Other organizations like Human Synergistic and the Centre for Applied Research Inc. have developed an Organizational Effectiveness Inventory to provide information about itself, its effectiveness, and its impact on members.

In order to create knowledge sharing roles and a nurturing knowledge management culture, the American Society for Interior Designers under the Chief Knowledge Leader, Dr. Michael Berens, has worked on various knowledge competencies with Jay Liebowitz as applied to ASID. The following table indicates such competencies:

Knowledge Competencies for Asid HQ

Knowledge Competencies	*Directors*	*Professional*	*Administrative*
Knowledge Identification & Capture			
Identity and conceptualize complementary knowledge processes and knowledge assets across departments and other silos	XXXX	XXXX	
Oversee creation of integrated comprehensive knowledge capture and transfer programme (e.g., key SME Jknow-how, proven practices)	XXXX	XXXX	
Establish knowledge requirements for quality work and capture lessons learned from each major project (make them available on the intranet)	XXXX	XXXX	XXXX
Establish poticies on how to manage knowledge, arid build infrastructures to support management of knowledge	XXXX	XXXX	
Knowledge Sharing			
Create knowledge-related capabilities shared across enterprise	XXXX		
Support enterprise strategy end direction by facilitating effective communication to all	XXXX	XXXX	XXXX
Institute incentives to motivate personal knowledge sharing, creation, end-use		XXXX	
Manage (and facilitate) corporate memory, web site, intranet, threadeddiscussions, and communities of prsctioel chat rooms	XXXX	XXXX	XXXX
Knowledge Application			
Align knowledge strategies and tactics with enterprise direction	XXXX	XXXX	

Facilitate and monitor knowledge management-related activities and programmes	XXXX	XXXX	
Encourage cross-functicnal team collaboration	XXXX	XXXX	XXXX
Develop and maintain an expertise locator directory on the intranet and website		XXXX	XXXX
Knowledge Creation			
Build and maintain content knowledge		XXXX	XXXX
Develop new intellectual capital	XXXX	XXXX	XXXX
Generate new products or services for the ID professiort' community	XXXX	XXXX	XXXX

Other possible knowledge sharing proficiencies could include:

- The number of new colleague-to-colleague and member relationships spawned;
- The reuse rate of "frequently accessed/reused" knowledge;
- The number of key concepts that are converted from tacit to explicit knowledge in the knowledge repositories;
- Used by staff and members;
- The dissemination of knowledge sharing (i.e., distribution of knowledge) to appropriate individuals; the number of new ideas generating innovative products or services; and
- The number and quality of lessons learned and proven practices applied to create value-added; the number of "apprentices" that one mentors, and the success of those apprentices as they mature in the organisation.

HIGH PERFORMANCE ORGANIZATION AND KNOWLEDGE MANAGEMENT

Building High Performance Organizations Through Knowledge Management

Organizations are engaging in knowledge management for a number of key reasons: to increase innovation and creativity, to better leverage knowledge internally and externally for improved worker productivity and customer relations; to capture and preserve knowledge for building the institutional memory of the organization; and to improve efficiency and effectiveness of decision making. If an organization is to be high performance organization, knowledge management plays a critical role in transforming it into a well oiled, thriving business.

What does it mean to be high performance mean? Many analysts feel that an organization needs to be quickly adaptable to changes in the marketplace, and knowledge management offers a way to do this. According to Lawton (2001), knowledge management's key underpinning technologies enable content and workflow management which categorize knowledge and direct it to workers who can benefit from it; search functionality, to let users look for relevant knowledge; and collaboration, to help workers share knowledge. Through the use of "intelligent" agents, knowledge management systems should be able to push relevant lessons learned to appropriate individuals in the organisation who can best benefit from them in order to build the organisational intelligence of the firm. "Data and text mining" can also be used to develop user profiles to push relevant information and knowledge from repositories to employees and customers.

High-performance organisations generally have a high organisational intelligence. Liebowitz (1999, 2000) views organisational intelligence as the collection of all intelligence that contributes toward building a shared vision, a renewal process, and a direction for the entity. Organisational intelligence involves the following knowledge functions—transforming information into knowledge; identifying and verifying knowledge; capturing and securing knowledge; organizing knowledge; retrieving and applying knowledge; combining knowledge; creating knowledge; learning knowledge; and distributing/selling knowledge.

In order to promote and build a high performance organisation, knowledge exchange a basic tenet of knowledge management is a critical element. In some interesting work on electronic communities of practice McClure-Wasko and Faraj (2000), found that for increasing knowledge exchange, organisations should consider using knowledge management systems that connect members to open-membership electronic communities of practice, and that organisations should establish a cultural norm that encourages people to participate and share knowledge by acknowledging the reputation and status of organisational members actively engaged in their electronic community. They found that extrinsic (versus intrinsic) reward systems may not be the best approach to use for increasing knowledge exchange but rather that, successful communities have members that act out of community interest (intrinsic value) rather than self-interest (extrinsic rewards promote self-interest). Increased knowledge exchanges hopefully leads to increased knowledge flows and innovation within the community and the organisation.

Ryder System Inc., the transportation and logistics firm based in Miami, has developed a knowledge centre using Lotus Notes, Quick Place, Same-time, and Prevail Solutions Suite. According to Knowledge Management (2000), the Ryder executives and others in the organisation have embraced knowledge management and the knowledge centre supports various internal communities and provides a way to produce better and quicker business proposals. This type of knowledge management activity helps in having Ryder as a high performance organisation.

If organisations are to be adaptable, flexible, and innovative, knowledge management needs to be an essential part of the organisation's strategy. In today's rapidly changing and competitive environment, those organisations that are high performance are most likely the ones that will survive. Creating knowledge through knowledge management initiatives will help to produce high performance organisations, and the "double-loop" learning effect should increase an organisation's innovation and adaptability.

What's Beyond Knowledge Management?

Authors such as Davenport and Beck (2001) have indicated that "attention management" will compliment knowledge management, involving the application of intelligent agents and other software programming techniques to browse and prioritise the CEO's daily email, news, voice mail, and digitised documentation and to determine what should attract their attention. Others indicate that E-CRM (Electronic-Customer Relations Management), E-Business, and specialised niche markets will continue to grow in emphasis and usage by businesses, and will be the prevailing trend after knowledge management. Others predict that wireless communications and mobile computing will dominate applications in the business world beyond knowledge management. Still others predict that hard coding 'knowledge on chips' will be commonplace in the years ahead. Certainly, improved user interfaces to knowledge management systems, such as through speech and natural language understanding, will be developed in the near term to enhance the collection, access, and usage of these systems.

If these predictions come true, how should businesses better position themselves to compete in the marketplace beyond knowledge management? First, in the same vein as using knowledge management to better leverage knowledge internally and externally, companies will probably need to merge and acquire other companies in related businesses to leverage their know how and create new products and services. Synergy will ensure that the whole is greater than the sum of the parts. Namely, taking the best from complementary businesses will hopefully produce more competitive products or services, and should also stimulate creativity and innovation.

Second, companies should take advantage of developing, selling, or buying "knowledge full" products. These types of products will capture the expertise and experience of a company's knowledgeable employees and encode this knowledge in the forms of web-based and intranet based expert systems, hard coded "knowledge" chips, or in wireless knowledge repositories. In this manner, the institutional memory of the organisation can be built as critical, core competency knowledge and expertise are preserved.

Third, developing niche markets in the Internet and e-business age will offer new opportunities, especially for dot.com companies. Whether developing intelligent agents to profile customers and to push relevant information to them or to create online "community" software or the like, businesses in the coming years will continue to find new ways of improving existing processes.

Last, companies will need to get the products to market even faster via the internet age. Product development times and entry-to-market times will be greatly reduced in order for companies to maintain their competitive edge. In all these areas, knowledge management and the CKO can greatly move the organisation towards being a "high performance, knowledge organisation."

Getting Started

As with many 'interventions', there are many good places to start, depending on the specific context. Some ones often recommended are:

- **Start at the top**—helpful to give an impetus
- **Start with a chronic problem**—always a good place to get the thinking caps on
- **Initiate a task force**—a common response, but they will need drive and vision
- **Start with an organizational diagnosis**—HR and management consultants favour this one—guess why!
- **Link to an existing process or initiative**—go where there is existing energy and 'pull' (see comments on knowledge management below)
- **Review existing systems and processes**—a skills and/or training needs analysis to identify a 'capability' gap
- **New Product Development**—offers a focussed project, often with new teams and an open outlook, in which to introduce some of the proven techniques

We particularly favour the latter. It is tangible, is an opportunity to be innovative, and needs a lot of 'boundary crossing' to succeed. It draws on many of the processes, tools and techniques to become effective at learning.

The Role of HR Systems in Learning Organization

It is our belief that many learning organization initiatives are high-jacked by the HR function or outside specialists. This should not be the case. Developing a learning organization is about **doing it from within** and taking a **holistic systems perspective.** MIS departments and IS professionals have a major contribution to make.

- they have a systems approach and mind-set: a strong background in logical methods and process and are generally capable of developing creative solutions and holistic views.
- they often provide some of the best project managers within an organisation, capable of co-ordinating multiple activities across several functions and involving significant change in work processes.
- an information infrastructure that enables information flows, including networked connections between internal systems and access to external networks and databases
- likely to be "early adopters" of important learning enabling technologies, such as groupware, computer conferencing, videoconferencing, Internet exploration, multimedia
- have systems integration knowledge, essential aspect of making efficient connections between information, and more importantly knowledge

In conjunction with an information management/services function (of the library tradition rather than IT tradition) they play a key part in the management of information and knowledge resources. Providing the systems and processes for the management of knowledge and flow of information is, we believe, a crucial and underrated aspect of the learning organisation.

Inhibitors to becoming a Learning Organization

These are some of the most common obstacles to becoming a learning organization:

- operational/fire fighting preoccupation—not creating time to sit back and think strategically
- too focused on systems and process (e.g. ISO 9000) to exclusion of other factors (bureaucratic *vs.* thinking)
- reluctance to train (or invest in training), other than for obvious immediate needs
- too many hidden personal agendas
- too top-down driven, overtight supervision = lack of real empowerment

Examples

Here are a few examples of how different organizations have embraced the Learning Organization approach in practice over the last couple of decades:

- **Motorola University**—this is the learning division of Motorola and was responsible for developing the Six Sigma methodology for quality management. In the 1980s, the then CEO Bob Galvin recognized the importance of Motorola's employees "gaining timely mastery" in "mental processes". The emphasis of the universty—still going strong today—is to distil knowledge and learning that is essential to day-to-day operations.

- **US Army**—The US Army is renowned as the organization that developed After Action Reviews a key plank of its work. This "learning after doing" approach started around 1985 and is now a formal regulation (Army Regulation (AR) 11-33), backed up by guidance. Knowledge is extracted and codified from AARs by CALL (Center for Army Lessons Learned) and is turned into practice through military doctrine and ongoing training.
- **Glaxo Wellcome (now Glaxo SmithKline)**—following the merger of Glaxo and Wellcome in 1995, a strategy reviewed identified the need for the company to become an effective learning organization. Its then CEO, Sir Richard Sykes, addressed a workshop of senior managers, with the remit to articulate what the concpet meant in practice. As a result a number of learning and KM initiatives emerged including customer intimacy, a revised IT strategy (to give more focus to the needs of knowledge workers) and a revised reward and recongition system.
- **Dow Chemical**—Learn@Dow is Dow's online elearning system. Under the guiding principle that "training and knowledge should be available to every employee", a wide range of course modules is available online. Part of the stimulus was the need for culture change to transform a geographically spread and diverse company into an integrated global player. Early courses were on workplace responsibility and business ethics. Dow reports considerable savings over classroom tuition, but the main benefits are flexibility, control and convenience for the employee and a consistent quality of training output across the company.
- **BAe Systems**—The Virtual University (VU) at BAe Systems was developed as an intranet portal to help knowledge sharing across this global organization. It provides a focus for elearning and for sharing best engineering practice quickly. Making the interface intuitive and easy-to-use, as well as a rapid launch were crucial aspects of the project. But the key aspect of the project is that it brings together KM and LO in a cohesvie way. The VU is the umbrella for many activities including links with academia, and access to a wide range of information databases and personal expertise (not just elearning modules) through a standard interface that is customisable for different people and different work teams.

High Level Steps to Build a Knowledge-based Learning Organization

1. Build out the push/pull information infrastructure.
2. Make participation part of the goals/review/bonus structure.
3. Pilot this inside the IT organization.
4. Roll out to the entire IT organization.
5. Scale up and modify push/pull infrastructure.
6. Pilot within a BU or business organization (i.e. begin to converge IT and the business).
7. Capture lessons learned and adjust then roll out to the broader business community.
8. Repeat the steps to roll out to the customer base.
9. Repeat the steps to roll out to broader (possibly targeted) market segments.

CASE STUDY
Knowledge Management @ Xerox Corp

Chester F. Carlson invented the photocopy machine in 1938. He tried to sell his invention to companies like IBM and GE, but failed in his efforts as the companies did not believe that there was a significant market for photocopiers. It was left to a small New York based company called Haloid to finally market a product that later became indispensable for making multiple copies of documents. Xerox Corp officially came into existence in 1961 after Haloid changed its name to reflect its core business. Over the decades, Xerox diversified into a number of other businesses, some of which added value to its business model and others which had to be liquidated.

In the mid-1990s, the company repositioned itself as the 'Document Company', to better reflect its core business. The knowledge management movement of the 1990s prompted the company to focus on knowledge sharing initiatives. It started "Eureka" which captured the tips shared informally by the company's service reps and created a database of tips that could be accessed by reps all over the world. Other initiatives, both internal and commercial, also followed and Xerox was recognized as one of the Most Admired Knowledge Enterprises in the world.

Issues

To study how the knowledge present within a system can be harnessed to yield major benefits to the organization as well as to the people within it.

To understand the importance of matching new initiatives with the behavioral and working motivations of people to obtain better acceptance of these initiatives and greater benefits.

Keywords

Chester F. Carlson, photocopy machine, 1938, IBM, GE, photocopiers, New York-based, Haloid, documents. Xerox Corp, 1961, liquidated, mid-1990s, repositioned, Document Company, core business, knowledge management, 1990, sharing initiatives, Eureka, informally, company's service, database, tips, reps, Most Admired Knowledge Enterprises.

Chapter 8

Six Sigma—A Case Study

Six Sigma Application to Decrease Utility Costs and Improve Engineering System Reliability in a Healthcare Setting

Dr. L.H. Hiranandani Hospital, Mumbai is a 130 bed multi speciality tertiary and quaternary care hospital. It is the first hospital in the city of Mumbai and the western region of India to have received the prestigious National Accreditation for Hospitals and Healthcare Providers (NABH). Among other specialties, the hospital has energy efficient structure design to achieve day light harvesting and to reduce HVAC load, rain water harvesting system and integrated building management system (IBMS).

THE NEED

The hospital is in the process of expanding from current 130 beds to additional 71 beds to cater to its growing patient base by constructing and adding additional six floors of 90,000 sq feet space. The senior management of the hospital felt that it would be crucial to control and reduce its utility costs with the current expansion plan to meet its strategic objectives that included providing ultimate patient services. Therefore, it was decided to implement the Six Sigma methodology in its engineering operations and maintenance services to control and contain the operations and maintenance budget.

Project Objectives	*Metrics*	*Units*	*KPI*
Utility Consumption	Water and Power Consumption	KL and KWH	FWS/PO, DWS/PO, KWH/PO
Engineering System Reliability	Engineering complaints	No. of complaints	No. of complaints/ day
FWS = Flushing water supply	DWS = Drinking water supply	KWH = Kilo-watt-hour	PO = Patient Occupancy

APPROACH

The six sigma DMAIC methodology was used for achieving the desired improvement in engineering system reliability and utility costs.

Phase I : Defining the Opportunity for Improvement

The first phase of Six Sigma methodology started with deciding and defining the metrics to be improved. The engineering team of the hospital decided to improve the power consumption and water consumption (both flushing and drinking). In terms of engineering system reliability, the team decided to reduce the number of engineering complaints received per day.

Metrics and Key Performance Indicators

The table shows the various metrics and their associated key performance indicators that were targeted for improvement. Traditionally, utility consumption has been reported in terms of per square feet of consumption. However, the team felt that it would be more appropriate to measure and monitor the metrics in terms of per patient consumption.

Opportunity Statement for Improvement

Benchmarks for each of the metrics were established based on historical data. Table 1 shows the benchmarks established for power, water (flushing and water) and gas consumption. The data shown in the table are reflective of average consumption per patient per month. The table also shows the average number of engineering complaints received per day.

Table 1 shows Benchmarks for utility consumption and engineering system reliability based on twelve months data (March 2008-Feb. 2009)

TABLE I

KPI	*Monthly Average*	*STDEV*
KWH/PO	104	12.1
FWS/PO	1.12	0.3
DWS/PO	0.93	0.2
No. of engineering complaints	19	5

Phase-II: Measure: Monitoring and Measuring Day-to-Day Performance

The second phase of Six Sigma involved mapping out the processes and then monitoring and measuring the performance indicators in a predefined and planned manner. Each of the above key performance indicators were tracked by the Six Sigma engineering project team on a daily basis.

Utility Consumption Monitoring

The Key Performance Indicators for utility consumption were monitored for stability using statistical process control (SPC) charts. Individual control charts (Average and Moving Range) were used on a daily basis.

The control limits for the charts were established using historical process data. The team monitored the process performance using these charts on a daily basis.

Monitoring of Engineering System Reliability

Monitoring and measurement of engineering system reliability was done by monitoring the number of complaints received on a daily basis. Further the number of complaints receive on a monthly basis were stratified into various types of system complaints.

The Table 2 shows the stratification of total number of engineering complaints in the month of March 2009 into various types of complaints.

TABLE 2

Tradewise	*Total*
Electrical	263
HVAC	52
Plumbing	96
Carpentry	35
Gas Operation	34
Painting	47
Phone	40

A Pareto chart for the above data is shown in Figure 3.

It can be seen from the above Pareto chart that about 65 per cent of the engineering complaints in March 2009 were of plumbing and electrical type. The total number of plumbing and electrical problems was further stratified (second level of stratification) into problems or complaints received from each floor. The Table 3 shows the stratification of plumbing and electrical problems per floor.

A Pareto chart for the data is shown in Table 3. The Pareto chart above shows that about 65 of the complaints came from four floors, viz. 2nd floor, ground floor, 4th floor and 1st floor. In other words, almost 65 per cent of the complaints can be reduced by focusing improvement efforts on these four floors only. Maximum complaints i.e. almost 20 per cent of the electrical and plumbing complaints were received from second floor itself.

TABLE 3

Trade-wise	*Basement*	*Ground*	*1st Fl.*	*2nd Fl.*	*3rd Fl.*	*4th Fl.*	*5th Fl.*	*6th Fl.*
Electrical	40	58	43	68	28	33	30	18
Plumbing	8	13	10	12	13	26	9	5

Phase-III: Analyse

The purpose of this phase of Six Sigma methodology is to analyze the root causes of process deficiencies in an effort to completely eliminate them or at least reduce the effect of the root causes on process parameters.

Utility Metrics

In the initial phases of the project, the team focused on understanding and investigating the reasons for day-day-variations observed in the performance of the utility metrics as shown by the control charts. The intent was to understand and eliminate all sources that caused unusual variation in day-do- day performance of the key performance indicators showing utility consumption, i.e. power, gas and water.

A close watch was kept on the Moving Range chart to observe the variation in performance between two consecutive days of operation.

System Reliability

The Six Sigma team also investigated and brainstormed various factors and root

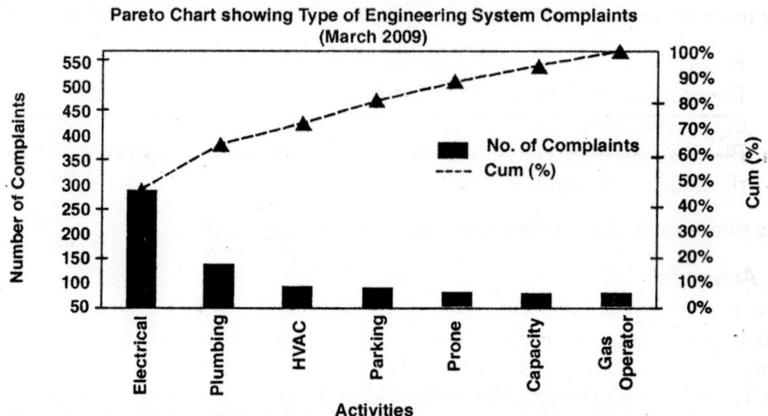

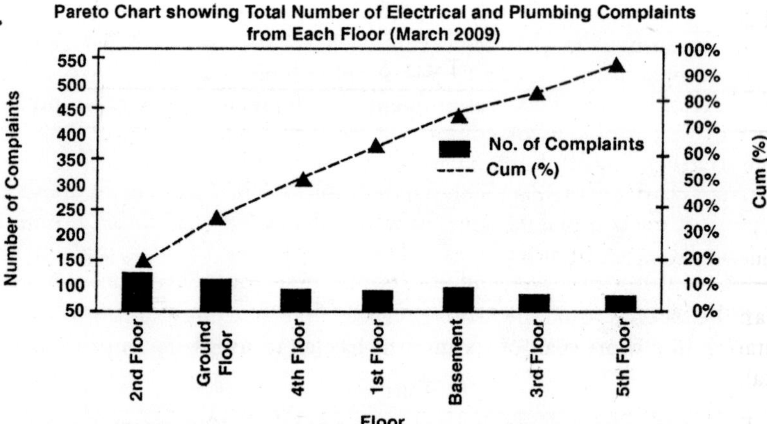

cause(s) resulting in higher plumbing and electrical complaints coming from ground, first, second and fourth floor.

Table 4 shows the various electrical complaints and their root causes identified by the Six Sigma team.

TABLE 4

Electrical Problems	*Common complaints*	*Root Cause (s)*
	Central Monitor Problem	Biomedical work
	Tube light problem	Reuse of Blast
	Call Bell Problem	Misuse by user
	Power supply trip	Overloading
Plumbing Complaints	Flush leakage	Algae/SIPON
	Geyser problem	Incorrect thermostat setting

Phase-IV: Improve

Once the root causes were identified, then team moved on to the next phase of Six Sigma i.e. improvement phase. The purpose of this phase is to plan and implement various measures to eliminate various root causes of problems identified in the analyse phase.

The team successfully achieved the following tasks in this phase of the project:

(a) Brainstorm various countermeasures to eliminate the root causes.
(b) Develop an implementation as well as contingency plan to implement the countermeasures.
(c) Plan and measure the improvement resulting from the implementation of the countermeasures.

This phase took almost two months, i.e. May-June 2009.

Benefits Achieved

As a result of the implementation in May and June, the team recorded significant improvement in almost all of the utility metrics consumption as well as engineering system reliability in the third quarter of 2009.

The Table 5 shows the results for third quarter performance of 2009 compared to that in 2009. The last column in the table shows the % improvement in third quarter of 2009 performance.

TABLE 5

KPI	*Q3-08*	*Q3-09*	*% Improvement*
KWH/PO	89.5	82.7	7.60%
FWS/PO	0.82	0.8	2.40%
DWS/PO	0.78	0.58	25.60%
No. of engineering complaints per day	21	13	38%

It can be seen from the above table that Six Sigma methodology implementation in a short span of six months has led to following improvement at the hospital:

(a) Engineering complaints has reduced as much as 40 per cent per day.
(b) Drinking water consumption per patient has decreased as much as 26 per cent.
(c) Power consumption has decreased by almost 8 per cent per patient per day.
(d) Flushing water shows a marginal improvement only. The consumption has reduced by about 3 per cent per patient per day.

It must be noted that the above improvements, i.e. reduction in utility consumption were achieved without any compromise on patient care services and patient satisfaction. As a matter of fact, in October 2009 the hospital has won the Malcolm Baldrige Quality Award (Asia Pacific) for its outstanding quality services to patients. This is the only hospital in India to have won this prestigious award.

Phase-V: Control

Quality is dynamic and not static and hence Six Sigma pursuit is a journey and not an end result in itself. The hospital management realises that the benefits achieved so far must be sustained by maintaining strict vigilance on the underlying systems and processes. Therefore, the team has successfully implemented several process control checks on the day to engineering operations and maintenance tasks. These checks includes detailed procedures, audits, training of operators, training of end-users and last but not the least the measurement and monitoring of all the KPI's on process control charts on a daily basis.

—With inputs from Anil Dhamdhere, Manager, Engineering—Hiranandani Hospital

TOTAL QUALITY MANAGEMENT—ANALYSIS, TAJ HOTEL MODEL

I. Introduction

Taj hotels are an international chain of hotel which is based in India. Taj hotels are the under the group The Indian Hotels Company Limited. Taj hotels are a part of India's leading business enterprise, TATA. Taj hotels have 76 hotels, twelve resorts and spas, seven palaces which are spread over in five continents. Apart from Taj hotels operating in India, they are having their properties operating in USA, Australia and Srilanka.

Founder of TATA group is Jamshetji Nusserwanji Tata; on December 1903 he opened TATA's first Hotel in Mumbai, Taj mahal Palace and tower. Behind of starting Taj Mahal and tower was because of the racial discrimination which was there at the Watson's hotel, Mumbai. He got refused to enter that hotel, because that hotel does not permit any Indians to enter. Hotels like this, in which, except European citizens they do not permit any others to enter were common in British occupied India. He imported the finest products and materials from the European countries to start his first luxurious hotel in Mumbai. Taj Mahal and tower soon gained the status of India's iconic hotel, because of its architecture and location.

Taj Hotels now became a leading chain hotels in India, and they have won several awards for its contribution to the Indian tourism, they have got around 1,70,000 employees working for Taj hotels and palaces around the globe.

II. Services which they provide to their customers:

- Different types of rooms for accommodation.
- 24 hours help desk
- Airport Pick up and drop on customer request.
- 24 hour business Centre
- Rental of cars
- Provision for car parking
- Care taking
- Car wash
- 24 hours concierge services
- Foreign exchange
- Doctor on call
- Telephone services (in house and outgoing)
- 24 hour express checkout and check in
- Delivery of grocery
- Gymnasium and spa
- Free of cost housekeeping facilities
- Internet access
- 24 hours laundry services
- Library
- Banquet halls and lounge
- Courier and mail services

- 24 hours maintenance services.
- Personal Locker
- Television with satellite channels
- Site seeing
- Swimming Pools
- Complete power back up
- Well maintained gardens

Source: www.tajhotels.com

III. Review of Literature

In 1980's when Hewlett-Packard criticised their chip manufacturers for their poor quality compared to their competitors from Japan. It's apparently contradictory when Total Quality Management introduced by W. Edward Deming, While USA Rejected the philosophies of TQM, when Japanese adopted philosophies of TQM. The Japanese became successful in their following years after adopting the principles of Total Quality Management by Deming with his colleagues Josep M. Juran, Genichi Taguchi, and others. After ten years also when Hewlett-Packard introduced suddenly the principles of TQM in USA, small organisations find it as difficult. But introduction of TQM to their organisations wasn't unsuccessful, surveys shows that the organisations which adopted the principles of TQM to their operations made them much stronger than their competitors.

Total Quality Management (TQM) defines broad set of control and management process developed to focus an organisation completely and maximum customer satisfaction by the employees of that organisation while they provide products or services to their customers. According to Sashkin and Kiser (1993), Total Quality Management means the achievement of constant customer satisfaction with the help of training, techniques and tools of an integrated system. This includes continuous progress in organisational process which will result in the high quality of services and products.

Quality—A competitive tool.

Source: (Mohammad Talha, 2004)

Quality is defined by the American Society for quality control is as follows, the complete characteristics and features of a service or product which is delivered depending on a satisfied customer during the use or purchasing. There are many companies in the world choose quality as one of the main strategic tool for organisational development. It is because focusing on quality reduces the cost and increase the level of customer satisfaction.

Design Quality

Design quality refers to how closely the features and characteristics of a service or product meet the customer's expectation. For example, if a customer of a bank can access account of another customer, then we can say that the design of that is failed.

Quality of Conformance

Quality of conformance means that the performance of a service or a product's relation towards its specification and design. As an example if a bank deposits a customer's cheque in to a wrong account we can say that the bank has failed in the quality of conformance.

Companies should design the product to satisfy their customers through the design quality. Afterwards they must meet the specifications of design by the quality of conformance. Figure 1 demonstrates As a result of design quality failure due to the failure of quality of conformance the real performance can fall short of the customer satisfaction.

Improvement of Quality v. Assurance of Quality

It is important to avoid considering improvement of quality with assurance of quality. Quality assurance is the system which is developed to ensure pre-established are met with the production. Customers will get quality guarantee by conformance measurement with performance and process specifications. Improvement of quality refers to the steps put forward to increase efficiency and effectiveness. This process is continuous, to have a better understanding of the market; process and products innovation; Distribution and managing of products and materials; and to deliver service to the customers. The achievement in achieving improvement of quality is depending on the employees awareness of their customers' needs (external and internal). To maintain this there should be a proper conversation with the customers regarding their expectations and measuring their standard with the customers' expectation (Schlenker, 1998).

Total Quality Management Strategy Development

The overall strategic plan of TQM adopts the values and vision of the organisation's philosophy and makes these in to their long-term goals to achieve. Identification of particular goals which an organisation wants to achieve can be identified in a successful TQM strategy. How these strategies which they adopted to achieve their goal will depends on the each department's strategy to outline their strategy. This process must have the involvement of the each and everyone in the organisation, empowering each and every one to contribute for improving the quality continuously. The authority should be there within the employees to implement new ideas and for problem-solving. An effective strategy for improving the quality will help people of an organisation to initiate improving their own department and other departments. Every person in an organisation is responsible for producing targeted results. Customers' idea should also be checked on improving their current services and products.

Few techniques using for the quality process are the following, flowcharts, brain storming, trend charts, etc. improvement opportunities can identified with the help of these techniques. To achieving the objectives and goals employees should have the knowledge on TQM, to ensure this is the key role of a TQM committee. Selection and recruitment also required to include in the quality factors as part of the process. Incentives should be given by the organisations to the employees in achieving the results.

Tools in Total Quality Management

Here follows a brief description of the basic set of Total Quality Management tools. They are:

- Check Lists
- Scatter Plots
- Effect and cause, Ishikawa, Fish Diagram
- Check Sheets
- Pareto Principle
- Flow Charts
- Histogram or Bar Graph
- Control Charts

Source : (Burr, 1997).

Check Lists

The lists of items are relevant or important to a particular situation or issue. It is used under the operational conditions to make sure that each important tasks are done in time. Check lists main importance is not for data collecting, but for operation guidance. It is generally used to check that all aspects of a particular situation have been taken in consideration before making or action.

Scatter Plots

A line graph without lines is the Scatter plotsthere is physical line where the data are joining together, but it is marked in the graph.

Effect and cause, Ishikawa, Fish Diagram

Process dispersion can be analysed in this effect and cause diagram. The main purpose of this diagram is to relate effects and cause.

Check Sheets

It is the recording of data form which has been developed for the interpretation of results in the form itself. Qualitative repetitive and quantitative data's are collected in this method.

Pareto Principle

In this principle it suggests that from relatively few courses only most effects are emerging. Eighty percentages of problems are emerging from the twenty percentages of the causes; for example, 20% of people own 80% of the wealth. So we can solve the 80% of problems by aiming the rite 20%. This chart is helpful to compare after and before situations.

Flow Charts

Text, pictures or symbols connected with lines, direction is showed with help of arrows. Help to demonstrate a particular process with the help of Flow charts.

Histogram or Bar Graph

Variation in set of data's are demonstrated in a histogram. Patterns which we cannot see in a simple table of numbers can be analysed in Histogram. Set of data's conclusion can be analysed with the help of histogram.

Control Charts

It is the method of statistical process control (SPC). Rather than controlling each individual variation it controls variation distribution.

IV. Total Quality Management in Taj Hotels and Palaces

Service Excellence

From the last few years Indian Hotel Company Limited (IHCL) has taken several steps to enhance the service standards of their hotels. They regularly benchmarked international luxurious chain hotels and they try to increase their service standards constantly. Philosophy of the service of IHCL is the core.They had taken several steps to enhance their personalised services to their Customers, butler services in IHCL's in their Premium properties. They had improved their concierge services to take care the entire stay of their customer. They provide proper training to their employees to achieve the service standard of a five start hotel. In order to increasing their service standards Tata Business Excellence Model (TBEM) plays a major role.

Tata Business Excellence Model (TBEM)

This is to enhance their service standards to the international service standards they conduct proper assessment regularly. For the external assessment also luxury division has applied, this is processed by the Tata Quality Management Services. With the help of external and internal assessment report, they plan their actions to constantly increase their bar of service standards. The key things they focus will be on the following, improving their level in terms of service and product quality: To raise the service standards to the international level of service standard they conduct external audits.

International Standards Introduction

In order raise their service standards to the international level, they take the services and advices from the hands of international expertise. They have introduced concierge service, butler services, and valet services to improve their customers' satisfaction while staying in Taj hotel and palaces.

Customer Feedback System

They introduce Customer Feedback System back in 2003, and they have implemented this in their various hotels. CFS is the main customer feedback system of IHCL group. Each feedback is recorded and aggregated then it is evaluated properly in order to raise their service standards, also it will help to point out where they are lacking in terms of customer services and their products. It is not only consisting of guests' complaints, they also try to get the guests suggestions to improve the standard of services, which is a vital. Based on the customer feedbacks they can plan and design the products more customer oriental. They reinforce the Balanced Score Board (BSC) to maintain the equal standard throughout their properties. It is used as the key deployment strategy. The objectives of key strategy are taken in the Balanced Score Board (BSC) and across the departments and units they implement this.

Restructuring of corporates:

To make the Indian Hotel company limited carry their standards to all their hotels and to make them leaner international division is collaborating with leisure divisions and luxury divisions. They constantly look for the underperforming or assets which do not earn any income for the business and then they restructure it. Last year they earned around 30 crores of Indian Rupees by selling one of their underperforming hotel in India. They will continue to evaluate their assets to find out the underperforming assets and then they will re-structure it to, make them generate income to their business.

V. Conclusion

After the world war Total Quality Management helped to resurrect the economy of Japan. The concept of Total Quality Management is originated in the manufacturing industry, so its terms are concepts are more related to manufacturing industry. Adaptations of ideas are required to implement the concepts of Total Quality Management in the Service Industry.

Product is the main distinction of service industry and Manufacturing industry.

Service industry Products

- Are ephemeral and intangible.
- Are Perishable.
- Involvement of customers in the delivery of the service and products
- Is not considered as a product.

Intangible: placing quantifiable terms are difficult. Measuring the quality of product in service industry then become hard.

Perishable: they have to produce on demand, it can't stockpile.

Involvement of customers: it can produce unpredictable or unknown influences on the product delivered. There will be also a chance of uncertainty as no one can understand what a customer accurately need and what can they assume as nonstandard.

The uncertainty remains in terms of measuring service as it cannot be stored, then the service standard should be measured at the same time. Lastly service is delivered when on demand of the customer, so measurement taken will too late to avoid the decrease in service standard

TROCÁIRE CASE STUDY

Teambuilding.ie was commissioned to deliver a half day team development intervention for Trócaire Ireland, as an important component in building a more cohesive team.

Trócaire is the official overseas development agency of the Catholic Church in Ireland. It was set-up by the Irish Catholic Bishops in 1973 to express the concern of the Irish Church for the suffering of the world's poorest and most oppressed people. Trócaire's partnership approach makes it different. It works through global Catholic networks and with local partners on the ground. This approach helps people and works with them, so that they drive the entire process themselves. Solutions are not imposed on the people Trócaire help. Instead, they become the authors of their own destiny.

The Need

The teambuilding.ie response was designed to meet the following requirement, as outlined by the senior team:

> "As Trócaire was going through significant change, the main aim of working with teambuilding.ie was to improve communication across the different departments within the organisation, to improve the team environment and help forge better cross departmental linkages In response to teambuilding.ie suggestions, an active workshop-based activity on communication was organised."

Before, during and after the activities participants were encouraged to reflect on a number of important questions:

> "How can active listening and communication help us to interact effectively with our colleagues and management in our own departments and across the different departments in Trócaire? How can active listening and communication help us to be better at what we do and to deliver on our organisational objectives more successfully?"

The Outcome

The day was designed as the Trócaire World Challenge, with the 6 different activities linked to the 6 different regions where Trócaire works. Teams comprised of staff members from different departments who would not usually work closely together. The organised activities highlighted the importance of good communication, delegation, listening and active participation in achieving the team goals.

Feedback

The teambuilding.ie event was extremely successful and all staff really enjoyed it. The staff evaluation conducted after the event showed that 100% of the staff who completed the evaluation felt that they had improved relationships with colleagues that they didn't know so well beforehand. What staff enjoyed the most was:

"getting to know other staff members better"
"working with people I usually don't work with"
"operating as a team"

Staff also found the 'hands on' and 'activity-based' approach of team-building i.e. very enjoyable and a great way to get to know other staff in a fun environment. One comment made was: "It reinforced the importance of positive relationships in working effectively."

All of the activities designed by team-building, i.e. were well organised and very successful. Teams had to work together to accomplish the activities and win points for their team. The favourite activities mentioned were the bridge building and archery.

All teams came together at the end for the grand finale—the Leap of Faith. Most staff felt that their team performed well together and everyone had the opportunity to participate.

96% of staff felt that there was an improved atmosphere in the office following the event and most staff felt that they could incorporate what they had learnt about working in a team in their every day work in Trócaire. Other responses in the evaluation indicated that:

new staff feel more comfortable talking to different departments and being able to ask for help
a feeling that previously unknown staff are more approachable
an acceptance that good communication is vital
people need to listen to each other more
working together can achieve better results
it is good to know and use peoples different strengths

The programme with team-building, i.e. was a very positive experience for Trócaire copy to the Risk Management department. However, no one conducted any investigation or revised her care plan.

TQM CASE STUDY: NEWSPAPER FOCUSES ON CUSTOMER SERVICE

Quality in the total quality management (TQM) method is defined as customer delight. Customers are delighted when their needs are met or exceeded. The needs of the customer are:

- Product quality
- Delivery quality
- Service quality
- Cost value

Improving customer service was the focus of two projects within the deployment of TQM in a mid-sized newspaper in India. This is the second piece in a three-part series of articles featuring case studies from that deployment; Part 1 of the series featured projects leading to improvements in product quality. Part 3 looks at supply-chain improvements.

Reducing Advertisement Processing Time

The newspaper closed its window for booking advertisements at 4 p.m. every day. However, many of the newspaper's advertisers expressed that they would be delighted if this limit could be extended to 5 p.m., as they were not able to send ad materials on time for the 4 p.m. deadline.

The TQM leaders formed a team consisting of representatives from each link in the ad-processing chain of work. The team attended a two-day quality-mindset program to expose them to the concepts of TQM and also to open their minds about experimenting with change.

Defining the Problem

In TQM, *problems* are defined as *Problem = Desire – Current status*. Therefore, in this case:

Problem = Desired closing time – Current closing time = 5 p.m. – 4 p.m. = 60 minutes.

The 4 p.m. deadline had been instituted because:

- Deadline for sending the ad pages to the press was 6:30 p.m.
- Standard cycle time for processing ads into pages was 2.5 hours

Achieving a 5 p.m. ad closure deadline meant reducing the standard ad processing time by 40 percent, or one hour. To define the current state, the actual time spent preparing pages to go to press was collected over several days.

Defining the metric: If T = *(page processing time – page-to-press deadline)*, then for 99.7 percent on-time delivery, or 3 sigma performance, the average T + 3 standard deviations of T should be less than 0.

Measure the current state: The ad closing deadline could not be delayed by an hour without delaying the dispatch of the newspaper to press by an equivalent amount. Therefore, the current state was calculated by measuring the delay compared to a notional 5.30 p.m. dispatch time rather than the actual deadline of 6:30 p.m. Calculations showed that:

- Average T = 72 minutes
- Average T + 3 sigma of T = 267 minutes

The problem was defined: reduce 267 minutes to less than 0 minutes.

Analyzing the Problem

The team monitored the time spent on each activity of the ad process (Table 6).

TABLE 6
Time Spent on Ad Process

Activity	*Deadline*
Ad receiving	4 p.m.
Dummy "dump"	4:30 p.m.
Pagination complete	6:30 p.m.

During the 4 to 4:30 p.m. period, ads received at the last minute were still being processed. At 4:30 p.m., the material was dumped into the layout for *pagination*, meaning arrangement on the newspaper pages using software and manual corrections. To achieve the objective of a 5 p.m. ad content deadline, the pagination time had to be reduced.

Brainstorming why pagination took two hours produced three possible major reasons:

- Error correction
- Delayed receipt of ad material for a booked ad
- Last-minute updates from advertiser

All this work was carried out after the last ad was submitted. Team members suggested that if ads were released for pagination earlier, removing errors could begin simultaneously with the processing of the last ads in order to reduce cycle time. They agreed to give two early outputs at 3:30 and 4 p.m., before the final dump at 4:30 p.m.

Testing the Ideas

TABLE 7
Problems with New Process

Problem	*Effect*	*Root Cause*	*Solution*
Missing material removal	15 to 30 min.	Material delayed or not received	Only feed ads once all materials received
Error file found after last release	10 min.	Not checking pre-dump	Check for errors pre-dump
Special placement instructions not followed	10 min.	Processing team not aware of special instructions	Give instructions as received
Distorted ads in PDF	15 min.	Ads not corrected before feeding	Correct before feeding, include in SOP
Ads inserted post-pagination completion	20 min.	Ads accepted after deadline	Enforce deadline
Total time savings possible	70 to 85 min.		

The process was repeated four times (Table 8).

TABLE 8
Further Process Observations

Problem	*Effect*	*Root Cause*	*Solution*
Observation 2			
Repeating old practices			Reiterate SOPs
Scanning of materials delayed	45 min.		Agree on scan turnaround time
PDF conversion problem	15 min.	Programming problem	IT to resolve
Zip error file not scanned			Zip not required
Observation 3			
System failure at peak time	75 min.		Use back-up system
Observation 4			
Add-on section integration delayed	25 min.	Start integration in pre-dumps	Add to SOP

Checking the Results

Nine weeks of continuous implementation yielded dramatic improvement. Average processing time was reduced by an hour, from 72 minutes to 12 minutes. However, the level of variability, although 50 percent lower, was still unacceptable. Analysis of the variability showed that it was largely due to slip-ups in implementing the SOPs.

Standardizing Controls

The team used an x-bar control chart (Chart below) to monitor and improve performance regularly.

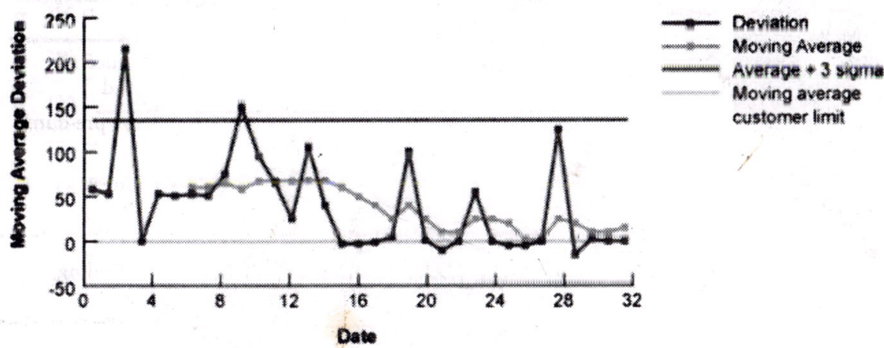

Control Chart of Ad Processing Time

Gradually the performance improved. Two months after implementation, delivery time had progressed from 267 minutes late to 12 minutes early. The deadline for receiving ads could now be relaxed to 5 p.m., delighting the advertisers.

Reducing Customer Complaints

Management indicated that the number of credit notes given to advertisers was too high. Credit notes, issued to rectify errors made in sales invoices, were used to fend off considerable customer annoyance. But this system caused trouble for the paper. Besides increasing non-value-added work, credit notes sometimes resulted in financial loss because customers could use the credit toward ads that had already been booked as sales.

During the previous 12 months, the newspaper had received 80 credit notes per week. The team agreed to try to reduce that number by 50 percent in Phase 1.

Finding the Root Causes

About 200 credit notes were examined to determine why they had been issued. Categorization of the causes was charted in a Pareto (Chart below).

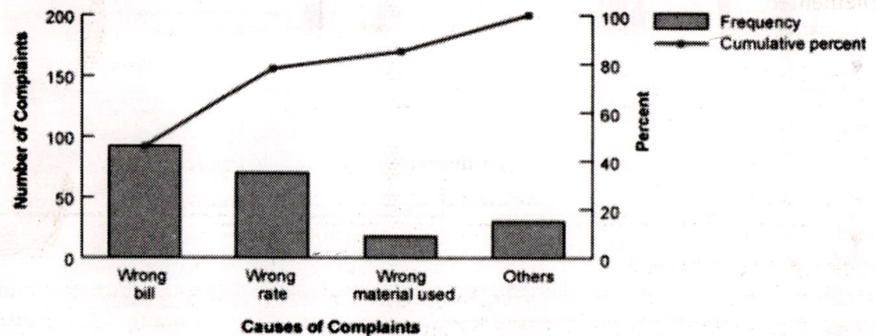

Pareto Chart of Complaints Resulting in Credit

Three causes constituted 84 percent of the problem:

1. Wrong billing – 46 percent

TABLE 9

Explanation of Credit Causes and Countermeasures

1st Why?	*2nd Why?*	*3rd Why?*	*Countermeasure*
Wrong billing	Unbilled charge picked up; Discount applied incorrectly to all ads in series	System bug	Removed
Wrong rate	Sales scheme not in sales card; Old scheme continues after updating of sales rate card; Scheme in rate card but not picked up by system	Sales cards not updated; Bill system does not pick up entry	SOP
Free ads billed	System does not pick up operator entry		Modify system to pick up operator's entry when prompted, rather than automatically taking billing information from the rate table.

2. Wrong rate - 24 percent
3. Wrong material used - 14 percent

Table 9 shows the root causes of a majority of the credits issued, determined using the 5 Whys method, and their corresponding countermeasures.

The team tested the ideas, which resulted in an 80 percent reduction in credit notes, from 80 per week to 14 per week. The process was adopted in regular operation, and the results were documented and presented to senior management.

Change in Thinking

TQM often leads to radical changes in employee mindsets. The improvements resulting from the two customer service-related projects helped to create a team environment in which any change idea is easily accepted, tested and—if it works—implemented.

APPENDIX

LIST OF BAIDRIGE AWARD RECIPIENTS

Baldrige Award Recipients

Year	*Award Recipient*	*Sector*
2011	Concordia Publishing House, St. Louis, MO	non-profit
	Henry Ford Health System, Detroit, MI	health care
	Schneck Medical Center, Seymour, IN	health care
	Southcentral Foundation, Anchorage, AK	health care
2010	MEDRAD, Warrendale, PA	manufacturing
	Nestlé Purina PetCare Co. St. Louis, MO	manufacturing
	Freese and Nichols Inc., Fort Worth, TX	small business
	K&N Management, Austin, TX	small business
	Studer Group, Gulf Breeze, FL	small business
	Advocate Good Samaritan Hospital, Downers Grove, IL	health care
	Montgomery County Public Schools, Rockville, MD	education
2009	Honeywell Federal Manufacturing & Technologies, Kansas City, MO	manufacturing
	MidwayUSA, Columbia, MO	small business
	AtlantiCare, Egg Harbor Township, NJ	health care
	Heartland Health, St. Joseph, MO	health care
	VA Cooperative Studies Program Clinical Research Pharmacy Coordinating Center, Albuquerque, NM	non-profit
2008	Cargill Corn Milling North America, Wayzata, MN	manufacturing
	Poudre Valley Health System, Fort Collins, CO	health care
	Iredell-Statesville Schools, Statesville, NC	education
2007	PRO-TEC Coating Co. Leipsic, OH	small business
	Mercy Health System, Janesville, WI	health care
	Sharp Healthcare, San Diego, CA	health care
	City of Coral Springs, Coral Springs, FL	non-profit
	U.S. Army Armament Research, Development and Engineering Center (ARDEC), Picatinny Arsenal, NJ	non-profit
2006	MESA Products, Inc., Tulsa, OK	small business
	Premier Inc., San Diego, CA	service
	North Mississippi Medical Center, Tupelo, MS	health care

2005	Sunny Fresh Foods, Inc., Monticello, MN	manufacturing
	DynMcDermott Petroleum Operations, New Orleans, LA	service
	Park Place Lexus, Plano, TX	small business
	Richland College, Dallas, TX	education
	Jenks Public Schools, Jenks, OK	education
	Bronson Methodist Hospital, Kalamazoo, MI	health care
2004	The Bama Companies, Tulsa, OK	manufacturing
	Texas Nameplate Company, Inc., Dallas, TX	small business
	Kenneth W. Monfort College of Business, Greeley, CO	education
	Robert Wood Johnson University Hospital Hamilton, Hamilton, NJ	health care
2003	Medrad, Inc., Indianola, PA	manufacturing
	Boeing Aerospace Support, St. Louis, MO	service
	Caterpillar Financial Services Corp., Nashville, TN	service
	Stoner Inc., Quarryville, PA	small business
	Community Consolidated School District 15, Palatine, IL	education
	Baptist Hospital, Inc., Pensacola, FL	health care
	Saint Luke's Hospital of Kansas City, Kansas City, MO	health care
2002	Motorola Inc. Commercial, Government and Industrial Solutions Sector, Schaumburg, IL	manufacturing
	Branch-Smith Printing Division, Fort Worth, TX	small business
	SSM Health Care, St. Louis, MO	health care
2001	Clarke American Checks, Incorporated, San Antonio, TX	manufacturing
	Pal's Sudden Service, Kingsport, TN	small business
	Chugach School District, Anchorage, AK	education
	Pearl River School District, Pearl River, NY	education
	University of Wisconsin–Stout, Menomonie, WI	education
2000	Dana Corp.-Spicer Driveshaft Division, Toledo, OH	manufacturing
	KARLEE Company, Inc., Garland, TX	manufacturing
	Operations Management International, Inc., Greenwood Village, CO	service
	Los Alamos National Bank, Los Alamos, NM	small business
1999	ST Microelectronics, Inc.-Region Americas, Carrollton, TX	manufacturing
	BI Performance Services, Minneapolis, MN	service
	The Ritz-Carlton Hotel Company, L.L.C., Atlanta, GA	service
	Sunny Fresh Foods, Monticello, MN	small business
1998	Boeing Airlift and Tanker Programs, Long Beach, CA	manufacturing
	Solar Turbines Inc., San Diego, CA	manufacturing
	Texas Nameplate Company, Inc., Dallas, TX	small business
1997	3M Dental Products Division, St. Paul, MN	manufacturing
	Solectron Corp., Milpitas, CA	manufacturing

	Merrill Lynch Credit Corp., Jacksonville, FL	service
	Xerox Business Services, Rochester, NY	service
1996	ADAC Laboratories, Milpitas, CA	manufacturing
	Dana Commercial Credit Corp., Toledo, OH	service
	Custom Research Inc., Minneapolis, MN	small business
	Trident Precision Manufacturing Inc., Webster, NY	small business
1995	Armstrong World Industries' Building Products Operation, Lancaster, PA	manufacturing
	Corning Telecommunications Products Division, Corning, NY	manufacturing
1994	AT&T Consumer Communications Services, Basking Ridge, NJ	service
	GTE Directories Corp., Dallas/Ft. Worth, TX	service
	Wainwright Industries Inc., St. Peters, MO	small business
1993	Eastman Chemical Co. Kingsport, TN	manufacturing
	Ames Rubber Corp., Hamburg, NJ	small business
1992	AT&T Network Systems Group/Transmission Systems Business Unit, Morristown, NJ	manufacturing
	Texas Instruments Inc. Defense Systems & Electronics Group, Dallas, TX	manufacturing
	AT&T Universal Card Services, Jacksonville, FL	service
	The Ritz-Carlton Hotel Co. Atlanta, GA	service
	Granite Rock Co. Watsonville, CA	small business
1991	Solectron Corp., Milpitas, CA	manufacturing
	Zytec Corp., Eden Prairie, MN	manufacturing
	Marlow Industries, Dallas, TX	small business
1990	Cadillac Motor Car Division, Detroit, MI	manufacturing
	IBM Rochester, Rochester, MN	manufacturing
	Federal Express Corp., Memphis, TN	service
	Wallace Co. Inc., Houston, TX	small business
1989	Milliken & Co. Spartanburg, SC	manufacturing
	Xerox Corp. Business Products and Systems, Rochester, NY	manufacturing
1988	Motorola Inc., Schaumburg, IL	manufacturing
	Commercial Nuclear Fuel Division of Westinghouse Electric Corp., Pittsburgh, PA	manufacturing
	Globe Metallurgical Inc., Beverly, OH	small business

1989	Milliken & Co. Spartanburg, SC	manufacturing
	Xerox Corp. Business Products and Systems, Rochester, NY	manufacturing
1988	Motorola Inc., Schaumburg, IL	manufacturing
	Commercial Nuclear Fuel Division of Westinghouse Electric Corp., Pittsburgh, PA	manufacturing
	Globe Metallurgical Inc., Beverly, OH	small business

DEMING PRIZE FOR INDIVIDUALS

(* - Deceased)

1951	Motosaburo MASUYAMA*
1952	Tetsuichi ASAKA
	Kaoru ISHIKAWA*
	Masao KOGURE*
	Masao GOTO*
	Hidehiko HIGASHI
	Shin MIURA*
	Shigeru MIZUNO*
	Eizo WATANABE
1953	Toshio KITAGAWA*
1954	Eizaburo NISHIBORI*
1955	Shigeiti MORIGUTI*
1956	Yasushi ISHIDA*
1957	Ziro YAMAUTI*
1958	Takeshi KAYANO*
1959-60	Kenichi KOYANAGI*
	Genichi TAGUCHI
1961	Takeo KATOU*
1962	Ikuro KUSABA
1963	Noboru YAMAGUCHI*
1964	Sadakichi SHIMIZU*
1965	Masumasa IMAIZUMI*
1966	Masashi ASAO
	Kiyomi KADOKAWA*
	Kazufumi SEKI*
	Tadasu FUJITA*
1967	Jiro KONDO
1968	Shinobu TOSHIMA*
1969	Tadakazu OKUNO*
1970	Tatsuo SUGIMOTO*
1971	Teiichi ANDO*
	Yoshio KONDO
	Shoichi SHIMIZU
1972	Kotaro ITOH*
1973	Koichi OHBA*
1974	Koji KOBAYASHI*
1975	Taro YAMAMOTO
	Yoshitsugu OHMAE
1976	Katsuyoshi ISHIHARA*
1977	Osamu FURUKAWA*
1978	Yoji AKAO
1979	Hajime MAKABE
1980	Shoichiro TOYODA

1981	Hajime KARATSU
1982	Hiroshi SHIOMI
1983	Minoru TOYODA*
1984	Tatsuo IKEZAWA
1985	Yoshinobu NAYATANI
1986	Ryoichi KAWAI*
1987	Ryuichi KOBAYASHI
1988	Ren-ichi TAKENAKA*
1989	Hitoshi KUME
1990	Shoichiro KOBAYASHI
1991	Kenji KUROGANE
1992	Masao NEMOTO*
1993	Yasutoshi WASHIO
1994	Takanori YONEYAMA
1995	Ayatomo KANNO
1996	Kenzo SASAOKA
1997	Noriaki KANO
1998	Katsuya HOSOTANI
1999	Yotaro KOBAYASHI
2000	Matabee MAEDA
2001	Shiro FUJITA
2002	Shoji SHIBA
2003	Tadashi YOSHIZAWA
2004	Akira TAKAHASHI*
2005	Hajime SASAKI
2006	Yoshinori IIZUKA
2007	Masayoshi USHIKUBO
2008	Masahiro SAKANE
2009	Hiroshi OSADA

DEMING APPLICATION PRIZE

Notes : Before 1994
<D> Deming Application Prize for Divisions
<S> Deming Application Prize for Small Companies
<O> Deming Application Prize for Overseas Companies
After 1995, there are no categories for Deming Application Prize

1951 Fuji Iron & Steel Co. Ltd.
Showa Denko K.K.
Tanabe Seiyaku Co. Ltd.
Yawata Iron & Steel Co. Ltd.

1952 Asahi Chemical Co. Ltd.
Furukawa Electric Co. Ltd.
Nippon Electric Co. Ltd.
Shionogi & Co. Ltd.
Takeda Chemical Industries, Ltd.

	Toyo Spinning Co. Ltd.
	Kyushu Cloth Industry Co. Ltd.
1953	Kawasaki Steel Corp.
	Shinetsu Chemical Industry Co. Ltd.
	Sumitomo Metal Mining Co. Ltd.
	Tokyo Shibaura Electric Co. Ltd.
1954	Nippon Soda Co. Ltd.
	Toyo Bearing Manufacturing Co. Ltd.
	Toyo Rayon Co. Ltd.
1955	Asahi Glass Co. Ltd.
	Hitachi Ltd.
	Honshu Paper Manufacturing Co. Ltd.
1956	Fuji Photo Film Co. Ltd.
	Konishiroku Photo Industry Co. Ltd.
	Mitsubishi Electric Corp.
	Tohoku Industry, Co. Ltd.
1957	(None)
1958	Kanegafuchi Chemical Industry Co. Ltd.
	Kureha Chemical Industry Co. Ltd.
	Matsushita Electronics Corp.
	Nippon Kokan K.K.
	<S>Nakayo Communication Equipment Co. Ltd.
1959-60	Asahi Special Glass Co. Ltd.
	Kurake Spinning Co. Ltd.
	Nissan Motor Co. Ltd.
	<S>Towa Industry Co. Ltd.
1961	Nippondenso Co. Ltd.
	Teijin Ltd.
	<S>Nihon Radiator Co. Ltd.
1962	Sumitomo Electric Industries, Ltd.
1963	Nippon Kayaku Co. Ltd.
1964	Komatsu Manufacturing Co. Ltd.
1965	Toyota Motor Co. Ltd.
1966	Kanto Auto Works, Ltd.
	<D>Matsushita Electric Industrial Co. Ltd., Electric Components Division
1967	Shinko Wire Co. Ltd.
	<S>Kojima Press Industry Co. Ltd.
1968	Bridgestone Tire Co. Ltd.
	Yanmer Diesel Engine Co. Ltd.
	<S>Chugoku Kayaku Co. Ltd.
1969	<S>Shimpo Industry Co. Ltd.
1970	Toyota Auto Body Co. Ltd.
1971	Hino Motors, Ltd.
1972	Aisin Seiki Co. Ltd.
	<S>Saitama Chuzo Kogyo K.K.
1973	<S>Sanwa Seiki Manufacturing, Co. Ltd.

<S>Saitama Kiki Manufacturing, Co. Ltd.
1974 <S>Horikiri Spring Manufacturing Co. Ltd.
<S>Kyodosokuryosha Co. Ltd.
1975 Ricoh Co. Ltd.
<S>K.K. Takebe Tekkosho
<S>Tokai Chemical Industries, Ltd.
<S>Riken Forge Co. Ltd.
1976 Sankyo Seiki Manufacturing Co. Ltd.
Pentel Co. Ltd.
<S>Komatu Zoki Ltd.
<D>Ishikawajima-Harima Heavy Industries Co. Ltd., Aero-Engine & Space Operations
1977 Aisin-Warner Ltd.
1978 Tokai Rika Co. Ltd.
<S>Chuetsu Metal Works Co. Ltd.
1979 Nippon Electric Kyusyu, Ltd.
Sekisui Chemical Co. Ltd.
Takenaka Komuten Co. Ltd.
Tohoku Ricoh Co. Ltd.
<S>Hamanakodenso Co. Ltd.
1980 Kayaba Industry Co. Ltd.
Komatsu Forklift Co. Ltd.
Fuji Xerox Co. Ltd.
The Takaoka Industrial Co. Ltd.
<S>Kyowa Industrial Co. Ltd.
1981 <S>Aiphone Co. Ltd.
<S>Kyosan Denki Co. Ltd.
<D>Tokyo Juki Industrial Co. Ltd., Industrial Sewing Machine Division
1982 Kajima Corp.
Nippon Electric Yamagata Ltd.
Rhythm Watch Co. Ltd.
Yokogawa Hewlett-Packard
<S>Aisin Chemical Co. Ltd.
<S>Shinwa Industrial Co. Ltd.
1983 Shimizu Construction Ltd.
The Japan Steel Works, Ltd.
<S>Aisin Keikinzoku Co. Ltd.
1984 Komatsu Zenoah Co.
The Kansai Electric Power Co. Inc.
Yasukawa Electric Manufacturing Co. Ltd.
<S>Anjo Denki Co. Ltd.
<S>Hokuriku Kogyo Co. Ltd.
1985 Nippon Carbon Co. Ltd.
Nippon Zeon Co. Ltd.
Toyoda Gosei Co. Ltd.
Toyoda Machine Works, Ltd.
<S>Comany Inc.

	<S>Hoyo Seiki Co. Ltd.
	<S>Uchino Komuten Co. Ltd.
	<D>Texas Instruments Japan Limited, Bipolar Department
1986	Hazama-Gumi, Ltd.
	Toyoda Automatic Loom Works, Ltd.
	<S>Nitto Construction Co. Ltd.
	<S>Sanyo Electric Works Ltd.
1987	Aichi Steel Works, Ltd.
	Aisin Chemical Co. Ltd.
	Daihen Corporation Co. Ltd.
	NEC IC Microcomputer Systems, Ltd.
1988	Aisin Keikinzoku, Co. Ltd.
	Asmo Co. Ltd.
	Fuji Tekko Co. Ltd.
	<D>Joban Kosan Co. Ltd., Joban Hawaiian Center
1989	Aisin Sinwa Co. Ltd.
	Itoki Kosakusyo Co. Ltd.
	Maeda Corporation
	NEC Tohoku, Ltd.
	TOTO Ltd.
	<O>Florida Power & Light Company
	<S>Ahresty Corporation
	<S>Toyooki Kogyo Co. Ltd.
[illegible]	Aisin Hoyo Co. Ltd.
	Amada Wasino Co. Ltd.
	NEC Shizuoka, Ltd.
1991	NEC Kansai Ltd.
	Nachi-Fujikoshi Corp.
	Hokushin Industries Inc.
	<S>Sinei Industries Co. Ltd.
	<S>Niigata Toppan Printing Co. Ltd.
	<O>Philips Taiwan, Ltd.
1992	Aisan Industry Co. Ltd.
	JATCO Corporation
1993	NTT Data Communications Systems Co.
1994	Maeda Seisakusho Co. Ltd.
	<O>AT & T Power Systems
	<S>AW Industries Co. Ltd.
	<S>NT Techno Corp.
	<S>Kouritsu Sangyosha Ltd., Partnership
	<S>Diamond Electric Mfg. Co. Ltd.
1995	Ishikawajima-Harima Heavy Industries Co. Ltd., Nuclear Power Division
	Mtex Matsumura Corporation
	Kikuchi Metal Stamping Co. Ltd.
	Toyoseiki Co. Ltd.
1996	Aisin-Shinei Co. Ltd.
	Ando Electric Co.
	Konica Corporation, Hino Production Division

	NEC Musen-Denshi Co. Ltd.
	Fuji Photo Optical Co. Ltd.
1997	Aisin Kiko Co. Ltd.
	Kojima Press Co. Ltd.
	Toyo Glass Co. Ltd.
1998	Aisin AW Seimitsu Co. Ltd.
	Ando Electric Engineering Service Co. Ltd.
	Itoki All Steel Co. Ltd.
	Okinawa Sekiyu Seisei Co. Ltd.
	Sanden Corporation
	Sundaram-Clayton Limited, Brakes Division
	Fujimi Koken Co. Ltd.
1999	Miyama Kogyo Co. Ltd.
2000	Kanehide Aluminum Co. Ltd.
	Sanden Transportation Co.Ltd.
	Sanwa Tech Co. Ltd.
	GC Corporation
2001	Sanden System Engineering Co. Ltd.
	Sundaram Brake Linings Ltd. (India)
	Thai Acrylic Fibre Co. Ltd. (Thailand)
	Thai Carbon Black Public Co. Ltd. (Thailand)
2002	The Siam Cement (Thung Song) Co. Ltd. (Thailand)
	TVS Motor Company Ltd. (India)
2003	GC Dental Products Corp.
	Brakes India Ltd., Foundry Division (India)
	Mahindra and Mahindra Ltd., Farm Equipment Sector (India)
	Rane Brake Linings Ltd. (India)
	Siam Refractory Industry Co. Ltd., The (Thailand)
	Sona Koyo Steering Systems Ltd. (India)
	Thai Paper Company Ltd. (Thailand)
2004	CCC Polyolefins Company Limited (Thailand)
	Indo Gulf Fertilisers Limited (India)
	Lucas-TVS Limited (India)
	Siam Mitsui PTA Company Limited (Thailand)
	SRF Limited, Industrial Synthetics Business (India)
	Thai Ceramic Company Ltd. (Thailand)
2005	Hosei Brake Industry Co. Limited (Japan)
	Krishna Maruti Limited, Seat Division (India)
	Rane Engine Valves Limited (India)
	Rane TRW Steering Systems Limited, Steering Gear Division (India)
2006	Nishizawa Electric Meters Manufacturing Co. Limited (Japan)
	Sanden International (Singapore) PTE Limited (Singapore)
	Sanden International (U.S.A.), Inc. (U.S.A.)
2007	Asahi India Glass Limited, Auto Glass Division (India)
	Rane (Madras) Limited (India)
2008	Tata Steel Limited (India)
2009	Niigata Diamond Electric Co. Ltd. (Japan)
	The Siam White Cement Company Limited (Thailand)

WINNERS OF THE QUALITY CONTROL AWARD FOR OPERATIONS BUSINESS UNITS

Given to operations business units of a company that have achieved distinctive performance improvement through the application of quality control/management in the pursuit of TQM in a designated year.

Quality Control Award for Operation Business Units

(Quality Control Award for Factories before)

1973 Mitsubishi Heavy Industries Co. Ltd., Kobe Shipyard
1975 Sekisui Chemical Co. Ltd., Tokyo Plant
1976 Kubota Iron & Machinery Works, Ltd., Engine Tech-Research Department Kubota Iron & Machinery Works, Ltd., Sakai Works
1977 Japan Aircraft Manufacturing Co. Ltd., Atsugi Works
1979 The Japan Steel Works, Ltd., Hiroshima Plant
1980 Kobayashi Kose Co. Ltd., Manufacturing Division
1981 Matsushita Electric Works, Ltd., Hikone Factory
1983 Fuji Electric Co. Ltd., Matsumoto Plant
1988 Suntory Ltd., Musashino Brewery
1989 Kobe Steel, Ltd., Chofu-Kita Plant
Maeta Concrete Industry, Ltd., Honsha Plant
1990 Suntory Ltd., Yamanashi Winery
1992 Nissan Motor Company Ltd., Oppama Plant
Toppan Printing Company Ltd., Electronics Division, Kumamoto Plant
1995 Nissan Motor Co. Ltd., Murayama Plant
1996 Nissan Motor Co. Ltd. Tochigi Plant
2002 Hi-Tech Carbon GMPD (India)
2003 Birla Cellousic, Kharach—A Unit of Grasim Industries Ltd. (India)
2007 Reliance Industries Limited, Hazira Manufacturing Division (India)

Winners of The Japan Quality Medal

The Japan Quality Medal was established to encourage Deming winners to continue practicing and upgrading TQM. The Medal is only awarded to those companies that demonstrate continuous improvement efforts toward quality and dependability of products according to guidelines established by the year.

1970 Toyota Motor Co. Ltd.
1973 Nippon Electric Co. Ltd.
1975 Nippon Steel Corporation
1977 Aisin Seiki Co. Ltd.
1980 Toyota Auto Body Co. Ltd.
1981 Komatsu Ltd.
1982 Aisin-Warner Ltd.
1985 The Takaoka Industrial Co. Ltd.
1990 Aisin Seiki Co. Ltd.

1991	Aisin AW Co. Ltd.
1992	Aisin Chemical Co. Ltd.
	Takenaka Corporation
1994	Aisin Keikinzoku Co. Ltd.
1995	Maeda Corporation
1997	Philips Taiwan Ltd.
2002	Sanden Corporation
	Sundaram-Clayton Ltd., Brakes Division (India)
2004	GC Corporation (Japan)
2005	Thai Acrylic Fibre Co. Limited (Thailand)
2006	GC Dental Products Corp. (Japan)
2007	Mahindra & Mahindra Limited, Farm Equipment Sector (India)

Bibliography

Benchmarking Work book-bent Kaliof, John Wiley and Sons, Sigapore.

Value Engineering Theory By Donald E Parker, Soundaram Publishers W-62, Kovalpudur, Coimbatore.

The compeorganization by Gordon Pearson, Mc Graw Hill book company

Reengineering Human Resources, Lylem Spencer, Jr. John Wiley and Sons Inc, New York.

The Human Dimensions of Quality by Brain Thomas, Mcgraw Hill Book Company.

The Innovative HR Leader By Scott D. Anthony, Tara Young.

Creativity: Flow and the Psychology of Discovery and Invention by Mihaly Csikszentmihalyi.

Sternberg, R.J. (1995). The Nature of Creativity: Contemporary Psychological Perspectives.

Worley, C.G., Hitchins, D.E., and Ross, W.L. (1996). Integrated Strategic Change: How OD builds Competitive Advantage. Reading, MA: Addison-Wesley.

Watkins, J.M. and Mohr, B.J. (2001). Appreciative Inquiry: Change at the Speed of Imagination. San Francisco: Wiley.

Weisbord, M. and Janoff, S. (2000). Future Search: An Action guide to Finding Common Ground in Organizations and Communities. (2nd ed.). San Francisco: Berrett-Koehler.

Daft, R.L. and Weick, K.E., "Toward a Model of Organizations as Interpretation Systems", *Academy of Management Review*, 9, pp. 284-95.

Davenport, T.H. "Coming Soon: The CKO", Information, Week, September 5, 1994a.

Davenport, T.H. "Saving IT's Soul: Human-Centered Information Management", *Harvard Business Review*, Mar.-Apr. 1994b, pp. 119-31.

Davenport, T.H. "Think Tank: The Future of Knowledge Management", CIO, December 15, 1995a.

Davenport, T.H. "Think Tank: The Virtual and the Physical", CIO, November 15, 1995b.

Davidow, W.H. and Malone, M.S., The Virtual Corporation, Harper Collins, New York, 1992.

Dragoon, A. "Knowledge Management: Rx for Success", CIO, 8(18), July 1995, pp. 48-56.

Hackman, J.R. (2002). Leading Teams: Setting the Stage for Great Performances. Boston, MA: Harvard Business School Press.

Hartzler, M. and Henry, J.E. (1994). Team Fitness: A how-to Manual for Building a Winning Work Team. Milwaukee, WI: ASQ Quality Press.

Katzenbach, J.R. and Smith, D.K. (1999). The Wisdom of Teams. New York: Harper Business.

Osborn, A.F. (1963). Applied Imagination (3rd ed.). New York: Scribner's.

Parker, G. (2007). Team Workout: A Trainer's Source Book of 50 Team-building Games and Activities. New York: AMACOM.

Parker, G.M. and Kropp, R.P. (1992). 50 Activities for Self-directed Team-building, Vol. 1. Amherst, MA: HRD Press.

Parker, G.M. (1998). 25 Instruments for Team-building. Amherst, MA: HRD Press.

Priest, S. and Rohnke, K.E. (1999). 101 of the Best Corporate Team-building Activities we know. Dubuque, IA: Kendall/Hunt.

Scholtes, P.R., Joiner, B.L., and Streibel, B.J. (2003). The Team Handbook (3rd ed.). Salem, NH: GOAL/QPC.

Sinclair, A. (1992). The Tyranny of a Team Ideology. *Organizational Studies*. 13(4), 611-26.

Torrance, E.P. (1962). Guiding Creative Talent. Englewood Cliffs, NJ: Prentice-Hall.

Six Sigma in Human Resources—Human Resources Departments Benefit from the Methodology. by Praveen Gupta, Quality Digest.

Index